EXAM CRAM™

The Series 7 Securities Licensing Cram Sheet

1. Withholding: Broker/dealers illegally holding back shares of a new issue from the public for gain.
2. Stabilizing bid: Allows the broker/dealer to prop up the price of a new issue that has dropped below the offering price.
3. Shelf registration: Allows a broker/dealer to maintain a registration of a new issue with the SEC for up to two years.
4. Common stock: Equity issue gives investor voting rights in the issuing company.
5. Statutory voting: Investor has one vote for each share owned.
6. Cumulative voting: One vote per share owned for each board member up for election; 1000 shares x two new board members = 2000 votes.
7. Right of transfer: Investor's right to sell his equity securities to another investor.
8. Par value: Bonds issued and mature at $1000 value.
9. Yield: Coupon, nominal rate, face value, or interest rate of a bond issue.
10. Current yield: Existing rate on the value of a bond, adjusting for price changes.
11. Yield to maturity: Rate of return on a bond issue, adjusting for a premium paid or discount earned on the bond.
12. Bond rating: Financial or credit rating on a bond issue given by rating agency, from the highest AAA to the lowest D.
13. Zero coupon bonds: Bonds that are sold at a deep discount and mature at par.
14. Accrued interest: Amount of interest a new bond owner owes to the existing bond holder.
15. Commercial paper: Short-term corporate issues under 270 days to maturity; not required to register with SEC.
16. Repurchase agreement: FRB injects money into supply by buying eligible securities from member banks.
17. Reverse repurchase agreement: FRB sells eligible securities to member banks, tightening money supply.
18. Federal funds: Excess reserves lent among Federal Reserve member banks; called overnight borrowing.
19. GNMA: Government National Mortgage Association; sells government-backed securities to raise funds for VA and FHA residential mortgages; explicitly backed.
20. FNMA: Federal National Mortgage Association; Issues securities to purchase VA, FHA, and conventional mortgages in the markets, implicitly backed.
21. Pre-payment risk: Risk that homeowners pay off mortgages early, causing the funds used for bond issues to be redeemed earlier than expected.
22. CMO: Collateralized Mortgage Obligations; mortgages made into a derivative product which derives its value from the performance of another investment.
23. Fiscal agent: Brokerage house acting as a representative of a government agency to market and sell new issues to the public.
24. Round lot: Municipal security is 5 bonds for individual and 100 bonds for broker/dealers.
25. Redemption: Bond retired by the issuer either at maturity or at an earlier date.
26. Mandatory redemption: Municipal bond retired in yearly increments according to a call schedule.
27. Refunding: Replacing existing municipal debt with a new issue when the old issue matures.
28. Defeasance: Purchase of U.S. government securities from the trustee; used to effectively retire existing debt for a municipality.
29. Overlapping debt: Municipal debt owed by multiple municipalities such as school districts.
30. General obligation bonds: Bonds backed by taxation of the issuing municipality.
31. Revenue bonds: Bonds issued for new project funding such as new roads that with usage fees.
32. Gross revenue pledge: Revenue bonds funds to pay bondholders before operation and maintenance costs.

137. Accretion: The internal expansion or asset growth of an investment taking into account the discount earned by an investor; added to yearly income.

138. Amortization: Prorating of assets for a period of time, taking into consideration the excess or premium paid; deducted from yearly income.

139. Married put: Purchasing shares of a stock and a put option contract on the same stock on the same day; the IRS allows the cost of the put option to be added to the cost basis of the underlying security.

140. Short sale: Borrowing a security from a broker and selling it with the understanding that it must be bought later and returned to the broker.

141. Macroeconomics: Study of the economy using such as price levels, unemployment, inflation, industrial production, and consumer products.

142. Business cycle: Expansion > peak > recession > trough.

143. Reserve requirements: Amount of money that member banks must keep on deposit with the Federal Reserve Bank.

144. Gross national product: Sum of all goods and services produced in a given year within a country.

145. Gross national income: Sum of all income earned in relation to the gross national product of a country.

146. Inflation: A measurable increase in the cost of goods and services when demand is greater than supply.

147. Consumer price index: Measures the rate of inflation or change in the cost of products and services.

148. Reserve requirements: Amount of money that member banks must keep on deposit with the FRB.

149. Reserve requirements: Amount of money that member banks must keep on deposit with the FRB.

150. Discount rate: Rate at which the Federal Reserve lends money to Federal Reserve member banks.

151. Broker loan rate: Interest rate that the Federal Reserve charges brokers to finance margin loans to investors.

152. Fed funds rate: Interest rate that Fed member banks charge each other for overnight loans to meet reserve requirements.

153. Fundamental analysis: Study of financial data of a company, such as the balance sheet and income statement, to determine a company's value.

154. Asset: Any item on a balance sheet that a company deems of value.

155. Liability: Any claim on the assets of a company balance sheet, such as wages owed, interest owed, and accounts payable.

156. Ratio analysis: Comparison of certain assets and liabilities using ratios to determine a company's value.

157. Ratio analysis: Comparison of certain assets and liabilities using ratios to determine company's value.

158. Retained earnings: Profits of a company that are used to operate the business.

159. Capitalization: Raising capital to fund expansion and development through stocks and bonds.

160. Book value: Value of the assets of a company after all liabilities are paid.

161. Market value: Theoretical worth of a company determined by the number of shares issued times the price per share.

162. Earnings per share: Portion of company profits that are allocated to the common shares of the company.

163. Technical analysis: Use of historical data and price movement of a security to predict future price.

164. Moving average: Technical look at the price of a security over a time, such as a 90 or 120 days.

165. Support level: Lowest price at which a stock price does not drop lower.

166. Bullish: Belief that prices will increase.

167. Bearish: Belief that prices will decrease.

168. Risk-free rate of return: Interest rate of a risk-free security, such as a 3-month Treasury bill.

169. Junk bonds: High-yield, speculative bonds that have a high risk of possible default.

170. Interest rate risk: Risk of changing interest rates thereby affecting security prices.

171. Fiscal policy: Government policy on taxation of individuals and the investments they make.

172. Monetary policy: Government's control of the money supply.

173. Credit risk: Risk to a creditor that interest and principal will be repaid to the lien holder.

174. T-bills: Short-term government debt with maturities of 13, 26, or 52 weeks; issued each Monday in increments of $1000; sold at discount; mature at par.

175. T-notes: 1- to 10-year maturity issued by the U.S. government in increments of $1000.

176. T-bonds: Long-term bonds offered by the U.S. government with maturity of 10 to 30 years.

177. 32nds: Quote of government securities; 16/32 represents 1/2 of a point or $5 on the value of a government issue with 1 point representing $10 (so 100 points is $1000).

178. Monetary policy: Government's control of the money supply.

91. Interest rate options: Based on changes in interest rates for government issues such as T-bills.
92. Long-term interest options: Based on longer-term government issues such as T-notes.
93. Fiduciary account: Investment account managed by another for a person who is unable to do so.
94. Regulation T: FRB requirement amount that an investor can risk when buying stock on margin; currently 50%.
95. Debit balance: Amount customer owes in a margin account.
96. Equity: Amount customer owns in a margin account after paying off her borrowed amount.
97. Broker loan rate: Rate that a broker can borrow from a bank to extend to a customer in a margin account.
98. Minimum maintenance: Cash and/or securities deposited in a brokerage account to fulfill the margin requirements of the brokerage and NASD.
99. Restricted account: Margin account that has fallen below the 50% requirement.
100. SMA: Special Memorandum Account or Special Miscellaneous Account; amount in a margin account above the original 50% Regulation T rate.
101. Long margin account: Securities that are purchased on credit in a margin account.
102. Short margin: Selling securities not owned, anticipating a future decline in market value.
103. Stock loan: Lending securities between brokers.
104. Unit investment trust: Fixed portfolio of income-producing securities.
105. Nonqualified plan: Grows tax-deferred but cannot be deducted from the investor's income.
106. Qualified plan: Allows an investor to invest pretax dollars in an IRA, Keogh, 401K, or 403B.
107. Open ended fund: Mutual fund that continually issues and redeems shares in the marketplace.
108. Closed end fund: Mutual fund that offers a one-time offering of shares in the market.
109. Public offering price: Current offering price of a mutual fund (POP = net asset value + sales fee).
110. Net asset value: Value of mutual fund shares divided by the number of outstanding shares in the market.
111. Load fund: Mutual fund that charges a sales fee to investors when buying or selling.
112. No-load fund: Mutual fund with no charges or sales fee on fund transactions.
113. Diversified fund: Mutual fund with at least 75% of assets invested in securities and no more than 5% of total assets invested in any one security.
114. Breakpoints: Discounted sales fee when an investor purchases a certain number of shares.
115. 12b-1 mutual fund: Fund that passes charges of advertising fees on to investors to solicit new business into the fund.
116. Annuity: Insurance contract between an investor and an insurance company that guarantees a fixed or variable rate of return to the holder.
117. Fixed annuity: Insurance contract that pays annuitant fixed rate of return.
118. Variable annuity: Insurance contract that does not guarantee fixed rate of return.
119. Accumulation units: Determined value of the annuitant's holdings in the separate account.
120. Life annuity: Pay-out option on an annuity that pays annuitant for life and ceases at death.
121. Life with period certain: Pay-out option that pays annuitant for life but continues to pay a beneficiary if the annuitant dies before the end of the period.
122. Joint and last survivor: Pay-out option that pays the annuitants listed until both are deceased.
123. Unit refund annuity: Pay-out option that continues to pay the beneficiary if the annuitant dies before the full value of the annuity is reached.
124. ERISA: Employee Retirement Income Security Act of 1973 protects the rights of workers to have qualified retirement plans.
125. IRA: Individual Retirement Account; $3000 maximum tax-deductible individual contribution; $3500 over age 50.
126. IRA rollover: Moving funds from one IRA to another; must be completed within 60 days to avoid taxes and penalties.
127. Keogh plan: Retirement account for self-employed individuals. Maximum contribution is the lesser of 25% of earned income or $40,000.
128. Defined contribution: Contributions to a qualified plan paid by a percentage or formula.
129. Defined benefit plan: Qualified pension plan in which the employer is required to fund a specific retirement benefit to employees.
130. Money purchase plan: Based on a percentage of salary applied toward a pension.
131. Tax-deferred plan: Taxes are paid only on distributions, such as a 401K or 403B.
132. 403B plan: Tax-deferred plan for nonprofit organizations such as a hospitals and schools.
133. Passive income: Income derived from real estate ventures and limited partnerships that passes on to personal taxes.
134. Progressive tax: An increasing tax for varied income levels, such as the IRS income tax.
135. Regressive tax: Flat tax rate such as sales tax.
136. Capital gain: Money earned on the sale of a security above the original cost basis.

33. Net revenue pledge: Revenue bonds funds to pay operation and maintenance costs before bondholders.
34. Scale: Rate of interest at which dealers determine investors will buy a new municipal bond.
35. Munifacts: Wire system of new offerings in the municipal marketplace.
36. Blue list: Daily list of nearly all current municipal bonds. Officially, the *Blue List of Current Municipal Offerings*.
37. MSRB: Municipal Securities Rule-Making Board; establishes rules for securities industry.
38. Regulators: Agencies that enforce MSRB rules, such as the FRB, FDIC, SEC and NASD.
39. Bona fide quote: Fair market price.
40. Nominal quote: An estimated quote.
41. Subject quote: Conditional quotes verified before acceptance.
42. Group net order: Filled presale orders.
44. Designated net order: Filled third after bid is won.
45. Member orders: Syndicate member takedown orders that are filled last.
46. Big Board: New York Stock Exchange.
47. Seat: Membership on a stock exchange.
48. Specialist: Entity that is ready, willing, and able to buy or sell a listed security and maintain an inventory.
49. DOT system: Designated order turnaround, electronic trade system.
50. Day order: Good only for-the-day trade.
51. GTC Order: Good-till-cancelled order remains open until executed or cancelled by client.
52. Odd lot: Trades of 1 to 99 shares handled by specialist.
53. SLD: Stock reported out of sequence.
54. Block trade: Trade over 10,000 shares.
56. OTC: Over-the-counter negotiated marketplace with no physical trading floor; all transactions are conducted via telephone and computer systems.
57. Market maker: An OTC specialist.
58. NASDAQ: National Association of Securities Dealers Automated Quotation System.
59. Level I: NASDAQ system - summary of a stock's price.
60. Level II: NASDAQ system - lists all market makers, their bids, and ask quotes.
61. Level III: NASDAQ system - allows market maker to change an existing bid or ask quote on stock.
62. Arbitrage: Simultaneous buying and selling of a security to profit from an existing price discrepancy.
63. SOES: Small Order Execution System; OTC electronic system for executing orders.
64. Call provision: The right of a company to call back its bond issue after a certain period of time.
65. Inverse effect: Interest rates and bond prices move in opposite directions.
66. Call protection: Period of time in which bonds may not be called; usually two to three years.
67. Put provision: Allows the holder to redeem a bond at par value on specific dates prior to maturity.
68. Call option: Right to buy a security at a specific price for a prescribed period of time.
69. Put option: Right to sell a security at a specific price for a prescribed period of time.
70. Option contract: Equals 100 shares of a security.
71. Underlying security: Stock on which an option is issued.
72. Strike price: Price at which the buyer of an option can either buy the security (for a call) or sell the security (for a put).
73. Premium: Amount paid for the purchase of an option contract; sellers receive the premium paid.
74. Expiration: Date an option contract expires.
75. Intrinsic value: In-the-money amount of the option contract equates to the intrinsic value.
76. Time value: Premium less any intrinsic value equals the time value for the option contract.
77. Open interest: Number of existing option contracts for a security.
78. Options Clearing Corp: Issuer and guarantor of all option contracts.
79. CBOE: Chicago Board of Options Exchange.
80. Long call strategy: Buying a call option on an upward trend to buy at the lower strike price.
81. Short call strategy: Selling or writing a call option to receive the premium income.
82. Covered writer: Selling an option while holding the security long in an existing account.
83. Uncovered writer: Selling an option while not having the security long in an existing account.
84. Long put strategy: Buying a put option at a higher strike price hoping the value falls below the strike price.
85. Short put strategy: The sale of a put option to receive the premium on the contract.
86. Bullish strategy: Belief that the price of a security will rise in value.
87. Bearish strategy: The belief that the price of a security will fall in value.
88. Index options: Option contract on stocks that are part of a defined index such as the S&P 500.
89. Broad-based index: Index that derives its value from a variety of stocks such as the S&P 500.
90. Narrow-based index: Index that derives its value from a particular industry or economic sector.

EXAM CRAM™

Series 7 Securities Licensing Review Questions

Richard Majka

Series 7 Securities Licensing Review Questions Exam Cram

International Standard Book Number: 0-7897-3286-6

Library of Congress Catalog Card Number: 2004112112

Printed in the United States of America

First Printing: December 2004

07 06 4 3 2

Trademarks

All terms mentioned in this book that are known to be trademarks or service marks have been appropriately capitalized. Que Publishing cannot attest to the accuracy of this information. Use of a term in this book should not be regarded as affecting the validity of any trademark or service mark.

Warning and Disclaimer

Every effort has been made to make this book as complete and as accurate as possible, but no warranty or fitness is implied. The information provided is on an "as is" basis. The author and the publisher shall have neither liability nor responsibility to any person or entity with respect to any loss or damages arising from the information contained in this book or from the use of the CD or programs accompanying it.

Bulk Sales

Que Publishing offers excellent discounts on this book when ordered in quantity for bulk purchases or special sales. For more information, please contact

U.S. Corporate and Government Sales

1-800-382-3419

corpsales@pearsontechgroup.com

For sales outside the U.S., please contact

International Sales

international@pearsoned.com

Publisher
Paul Boger

Executive Editor
Jeff Riley

Acquisitions Editor
Carol Ackerman

Development Editor
Ginny Bess

Managing Editor
Charlotte Clapp

Project Editor
Andy Beaster

Copy Editor
Kris Simmons

Proofreader
Linda Seifert

Technical Editor
Richard V. Hall

Publishing Coordinator
Pamalee Nelson

Multimedia Developer
Dan Scherf

Interior Designer
Gary Adair

Cover Designer
Anne Jones

Page Layout
Bronkella Publishing

About the Author

Richard P. Majka has served the financial community for the past 23 years as a financial trainer. He was employed by Credit Suisse–First Boston, as the Director of its International Bankers School for Investment Advisors and Private Bankers. After leaving Wall Street in 1997, he was commissioned to author four financial textbooks for various New York, Boston, and international publishing firms. He has taught for many of the major financial institutions in the country. His clients include Citigroup; Paine Webber; Lloyds Bank; HSBC; and numerous banks, broker/dealers, and insurers. He is well versed in the field of derivative products, debt and equity securities, and insurance products. He is licensed by New York State as a life and health agent as well as by the NASD as a registered representative. Rich has also authored numerous case studies on ethics in the securities industry, which are used as training tools by many broker/dealers throughout the United States.

As a financial services representative, Rich has combined his financial background and strong desire to help people in his practice. He offers his clients clear, concise, and honest advice in meeting their financial and investment needs. Rich's philosophy is that each of his clients is a valued partner with whom he will work together to build a long-term relationship. With careful evaluation combined with educating his clients, he strives to meet their financial goals.

A lifelong resident of Long Island, Rich; his son, Garrett; and his daughter, Sabrina, live in Suffolk County. He is active in coaching Little League, as well as being a manager and player in the Men's Senior Baseball League. Rich also actively serves on the board of directors for both the Men's Senior Baseball League and the Suffolk Stan Musial Baseball League. In 1998, he became the first original inductee into the MSBL Long Island Baseball Hall of Fame.

About the Technical Editor

Richard V. Hall has more than nine years of experience in the banking industry as a portfolio manager. He became a certified financial planner in 2002. He has a B.S. in investment finance and an M.B.A. from Wayne State University, a Series 7 License and a Series 63, and he is working toward a masters in economics from Indiana University.

He currently works for Wealth Management, which includes Sterling, PCG, and NatCity Investments, a single-source solution for managing personal and family wealth. Through dedicated relationship managers, clients benefit from a team-based approach to customized investment management, financial advice, private banking, brokerage services, estate administration, and other fiduciary services.

Contents at a Glance

Table of Contents

We Want to Hear from You!

As the reader of this book, *you* are our most important critic and commentator. We value your opinion and want to know what we're doing right, what we could do better, what areas you'd like to see us publish in, and any other words of wisdom you're willing to pass our way.

As an executive editor for Que Publishing, I welcome your comments. You can email or write me directly to let me know what you did or didn't like about this book--as well as what we can do to make our books better.

Please note that I cannot help you with technical problems related to the topic of this book. We do have a User Services group, however, where I will forward specific technical questions related to the book.

When you write, please be sure to include this book's title and author as well as your name, email address, and phone number. I will carefully review your comments and share them with the author and editors who worked on the book.

Email: feedback@quepublishing.com

Mail: Jeff Riley
Executive Editor
Que Publishing
800 East 96th Street
Indianapolis, IN 46240 USA

For more information about this book or another Que Certification title, visit our website at www.examcram2.com. Type the ISBN (excluding hyphens) or the title of a book in the Search field to find the page you're looking for.

Foreword

The Series 7 examination was designed by the Educational Testing Service and developed by an Advisory Committee created by the NYSE in 1972. The NYSE assembled a task force of security individuals to develop multiple-choice questions that would be evaluated by the Advisory Committee. These questions were developed based on a study outline that would cover the critical functions performed by registered representatives:

- Advertising, Qualifying Customers Industry regulations
- Securities Instruments
- Handling Customer Accounts, Taxation and Margins
- Securities Markets, Order Handling, Confirmations
- Economics, Securities Analysis, Sources of Financial Information
- Portfolio Analysis, Investment Strategies, Retirement Plans

The Series 7 exam is a qualification examination, intended to safeguard the investing public by helping to ensure that registered representatives are competent to perform their jobs. The exam is a six-hour test containing 250 four-option multiple-choice questions. To achieve a passing score, a candidate must answer correctly 70% of the 250 questions on the exam.

The first exam was administered as a paper and pencil test, September 1974. The NYSE maintains the exam and the NASD administers the exam at test sites across the country. The exam is administered each workday on a computer through the NASD PROCTOR system at either PROCTOR Centers or Sylvan Learning Centers.

This educational program has been carefully designed to cover all items that are tested on the examination. The first book covers questions and explanations. It is therefore, important that you understand the concepts that are being tested.

The author, Richard P. Majka has served the financial community for over 20 years. He was Program Manager of Credit Suisse International Bankers School and was instrumental in creating and implementing the first International Bankers Training Program. Mr. Majka previously was associated with Dean Reynolds, Inc. and has extensive experience teaching programs in management development, selling skills and finance courses. He was a member of the management team and instructor with Global Training & Development Group, Inc. for over 5 years until he joined MetLife as a Financial Consultant. During his tenure with Global Training & Development, he successfully prepared individuals for the Securities Qualification exams and has written numerous Securities Industry educational materials.

Mr. Majka has been associated with Mr. James J. O'Donnell for many years. Mr. O'Donnell is currently the President of Global Training & Development Group, Inc. He was previously Vice President with White Weld and Co. and Vice President and Sales Training Manager with Merrill Lynch. Mr. O'Donnell was a member of the NYSE Advisory and NASD Qualification Committees and a Co-founder of the Series 7 Examination. He is currently an Arbitrator with the NYSE and the NASD and serves on the NYSE/NASD Supervisory Continuing Educational Committee.

Introduction

So you want to be a stockbroker? With all the volatility and unpredictability of the stock market, many individuals want to be part of this fast-paced, cutting-edge environment. The road to becoming a stockbroker is a challenging one, but for the right individual, it can also be a rewarding highway to success.

What Is This Book About?

Welcome to the *Series 7 Securities License Review Questions Exam Cram 2*! The sole aim of this book is to provide you with review questions and explanations of the answers that will help you learn, drill, and review for the Series 7 exam.

Who Is This Book for?

This book is for anyone studying for the Series 7 exam who is ready to test his or her knowledge before taking the real exam. If you have been preparing but you want to test yourself before taking the exam, this book is for you! Maybe you have taken other practice exams, reviewed other material, or unsuccessfully taken the real exam, and you want to try more review questions before taking the exam again: then this book is for you, too!

What Will You Find in This Book?

This book is about review questions; that's it! There is no study guide, there are no review notes, just tons of review questions. Each chapter represents a topic on the exam, and in each chapter, you will find the following elements:

- *Review Questions*—The questions that will help you drill and review.
- *Quick Check Answer Key*—The section where you can quickly check your answers. Only correct answers are given here; no explanations are offered.

- *Answers and Explanations*—The correct answers plus explanations about the content posed in the questions. Use this information to learn why an answer is correct and reinforce the content in your mind.

You will also find a Cram Sheet at the beginning of the book specifically written for this exam. This popular element also appears in the *Series 7 Securities Licensing Review Exam Cram* (Que Publishing, 0-7897-3287-4). The Cram Sheet condenses all the necessary facts in this exam onto one easy-to-handle tear card. The Cram Sheet is something you can carry with you to the exam location and use as a last-second study aid. Be aware that you cannot take it into the exam room, though!

Hints for Using This Book

Because this book is a paper practice product, you might want to complete the practice exams on a separate sheet of paper so that you can reuse the questions over and over without seeing the answers. Also, a general rule of thumb across all review-question products is that you should make sure you score in the 80% to 90% range in all topics before attempting the real exam. The higher percentages you score on review question products, the better your chances for passing the real exam. Of course, we can't guarantee a passing score on the real exam, but we can offer you plenty of opportunities to practice and assess your knowledge level before entering the real exam.

The Road to Becoming a Stockbroker

To become a registered representative, the qualified applicant is required to meet some demanding requirements:

- The applicant must be a minimum of 18 years old or, at some of the larger firms, a minimum of 21 years old.
- The applicant is required to possess a clean personal record, with no criminal convictions in the past.
- The applicant is required to be employed by a broker/dealer before she can actually apply to become a registered representative. The broker/dealer can be either a NYSE member firm or an NASD member firm.

- The applicant is not required to have a college degree, but many larger firms do not hire an individual without a degree.
- After employed by a broker/dealer, the applicant has a 30-day waiting period before he can apply to become licensed.
- The applicant must complete a NASD form called the U-4 application for General Securities Registration and submit the completed form to the Central Registration Depository (CRD) for investigation.
- The applicant must receive a CRD approval for her application to be qualified to sit for the Series 7 qualifying examination. Applicants with any previous criminal convictions are denied approval from the CRD. Additionally, any applicant who has previously been barred from the securities industry for past violations is also denied approval.

As the applicant prepares for the exam, the registration or compliance personnel of the firm open a "window" for the applicant to schedule her exam with a certified testing site. This window typically lasts 90 days because the applicant must sit for the examination within that time frame.

The Series 7 is a 250 multiple-choice question examination that the applicant must pass with a minimum attained grade of 70%. The applicant must answer a minimum of 175 questions correctly to attain the 70% passing grade. Then the successful applicant is licensed by the NASD to buy and sell securities. Most firms have a probationary period for new brokers.

After successfully passing the Series 7 examination, all candidates must also pass the Series 63–Uniform State Law Examination to buy and sell securities for their clients. An individual can fail the Series 7 exam and still sit for the Series 63 exam.

If an applicant fails the examination, he must wait another 30 days before he can schedule another testing date. Any applicant who has failed the Series 7 Exam three times is required to wait six months before he can refile his application to take the exam.

Many new stockbrokers are required by their firms to "build a book" of new clients. This building includes cold calling qualified leads. As the new stockbroker builds her business and a list of clients, she can expect to earn a "draw" from her employer over a period of time. This draw is considered a salary until the new stockbroker can sufficiently sustain herself from the commission business she generates.

In this age of Internet trading, it is becoming more difficult for stockbrokers to earn commission income from clients. The most successful stockbrokers must be more than just an order taker for their clients. They must know their customers and their investment profiles to make a living in this business. The better versed a broker is in the markets and products that are available to investors, the more successful he will become.

Need Further Study?

Are you having a hard time correctly answering these questions? If so, you probably need further review. Consult the sister product to this book, *Series 7 Securities Licensing Review Exam Cram* (Que Publishing, 0-7897-3287-4) for further review.

The Primary Market: Getting Ready to Sell

Quick Check

1. The maximum number of shares that a company can issue in the primary market is equal to the total of which of the following?
   - ❍ A. Issued shares
   - ❍ B. Authorized shares
   - ❍ C. Outstanding shares
   - ❍ D. Treasury shares

Quick Answer: **7**
Detailed Answer: **8**

2. Preemptive right gives the shareholder the ability to do the following:
   - ❍ A. Sell his or her shares without a 144 filing.
   - ❍ B. Retain his or her percentage ownership in a company.
   - ❍ C. Purchase one share for each share that he or she already owns.
   - ❍ D. Purchase shares in the company for an unlimited time period.

Quick Answer: **7**
Detailed Answer: **8**

3. A security that sells in the primary market and has no further authorized shares to sell moves on to which of the following?
   - ❍ A. The NYSE
   - ❍ B. The OTC market
   - ❍ C. The AMEX
   - ❍ D. The exchange where the company will be listed

Quick Answer: **7**
Detailed Answer: **8**

4. The proceeds of a sale in the primary market is initially received by which of the following?
   - ❍ A. The underwriter
   - ❍ B. The issuing company
   - ❍ C. The managing syndicate
   - ❍ D. The client who has sold the shares

Quick Answer: **7**
Detailed Answer: **8**

Quick Check

5. The managing underwriter of a syndicate handles all the following responsibilities except for which one?
   - ❍ A. Making all investment decisions for the offering
   - ❍ B. Settling the account with all syndicate members
   - ❍ C. Choosing the members of the syndicate
   - ❍ D. Registering the security offering with the SEC

Quick Answer: **7**
Detailed Answer: **8**

6. The lead underwriter in a security offering earns which of the following for each share sold by the syndicate team?
   - ❍ A. A markup
   - ❍ B. A management fee
   - ❍ C. The entire spread
   - ❍ D. A commission

Quick Answer: **7**
Detailed Answer: **8**

7. An investment banking firm handles which of the following functions?

   I. A merger between two companies

   II. A tender offer for a company wanting to take over another

   III. An underwriting of a new security issue

   IV. Representing the SEC in a corporate audit

   - ❍ A. III only
   - ❍ B. I and III
   - ❍ C. I, II, and III
   - ❍ D. I, II, III, and IV

Quick Answer: **7**
Detailed Answer: **8**

8. Under the SEC Act of 1933, all of the following are true except which one?
   - ❍ A. The issuing corporation must file a registration statement with the SEC.
   - ❍ B. The cooling-off period after registration lasts for 30 days.
   - ❍ C. The underwriter can take indication of interest from potential clients.
   - ❍ D. The issuer must also register its offering with state regulators.

Quick Answer: **7**
Detailed Answer: **8**

9. The Securities and Exchange Commission was officially created by an act of Congress through which of the following?
   - ❍ A. The Securities Act of 1933
   - ❍ B. The Securities Act of 1934
   - ❍ C. The Trust Act of 1940
   - ❍ D. The Congressional Act of 1929

Quick Answer: **7**
Detailed Answer: **9**

Quick Check

10. A registration filing with the SEC for a new issue includes all of the following except which one?
    - ❍ A. A listing of the directors of the firm
    - ❍ B. A listing of all 10% shareholders
    - ❍ C. A declaration of where the proceeds of the offering, or "Flow of Funds," go
    - ❍ D. The price of the underlying securities

Quick Answer: 7
Detailed Answer: 9

11. Blue sky laws for new security offerings can be met by which of the following methods?

    I. Registration by coordination

    II. Registration by qualification

    III. Registration by notification filing

    IV. Registration by offering circular

    - ❍ A. I and II only
    - ❍ B. I and III only
    - ❍ C. I, II, and III
    - ❍ D. I, II, III, and IV

Quick Answer: 7
Detailed Answer: 9

12. The date on which a corporation files a registration statement with the SEC for a new offering is known as the what?
    - ❍ A. Effective date
    - ❍ B. Filing date
    - ❍ C. Offer date
    - ❍ D. Application date

Quick Answer: 7
Detailed Answer: 9

13. A letter of intent is best described by which of the following explanations?
    - ❍ A. The agreement between the underwriter and the issuing company
    - ❍ B. The agreement between the underwriter and the syndicate
    - ❍ C. The agreement between the SEC and the issuer
    - ❍ D. The agreement between the underwriter and the SEC

Quick Answer: 7
Detailed Answer: 9

14. Which of the following underwriting commitments best serves the interests of the issuing company?
    - ❍ A. A best effort underwriting
    - ❍ B. An all or none offering
    - ❍ C. A firm commitment
    - ❍ D. A standby agreement

Quick Answer: 7
Detailed Answer: 9

Quick Check

15. If an issuer wants to raise $500,000,000 in a debt offering but could accept a lesser amount of $400,000,000 and still go through with the offering, this situation is an example of what type of commitment?
   - ❍ A. Firm commitment
   - ❍ B. Minimum/maximum offering
   - ❍ C. Best effort offering
   - ❍ D. A standby agreement

Quick Answer: **7**
Detailed Answer: **9**

16. Any unsold shares of an underwriting that are retained by the underwriter are common to what type of offering?
   - ❍ A. A minimum/maximum
   - ❍ B. A best effort
   - ❍ C. A firm commitment
   - ❍ D. An all or none offering

Quick Answer: **7**
Detailed Answer: **9**

17. What type of offering has the proceeds of the sale held in escrow until final disposition is determined?
   - ❍ A. All or none
   - ❍ B. Firm commitment
   - ❍ C. Best effort
   - ❍ D. Standby agreement

Quick Answer: **7**
Detailed Answer: **10**

18. When an investment banking firm attempts to secure the underwriting business of an issuer, it commonly offers which of the following to win the issuer's confidence?
   - ❍ A. A tentative agreement
   - ❍ B. A road show
   - ❍ C. A feasibility study
   - ❍ D. A phantom stock plan

Quick Answer: **7**
Detailed Answer: **10**

19. A tombstone ad has all the characteristics except which of the following?
   - ❍ A. The price the security will sell at
   - ❍ B. A list of the syndicate members
   - ❍ C. A list of the selling group members
   - ❍ D. It is not considered a legal requirement of a new issue

Quick Answer: **7**
Detailed Answer: **10**

20. Which of the following is a responsibility of the issuer when taking a new security to the public in an offering?
   - ❍ A. The actual printing of the securities
   - ❍ B. The filing of the registration statement with the SEC
   - ❍ C. The management fee to be paid to the lead underwriter
   - ❍ D. The notification to the state regulators of blue sky registration

Quick Answer: **7**
Detailed Answer: **10**

Quick Check

21. Which of the following entities is represented at a due diligence meeting?

    I. The lead underwriter

    II. The Issuer

    III. The General Public

    IV. The SEC

    ❍ A. I and II only
    ❍ B. I, II, and III
    ❍ C. II and III only
    ❍ D. I, II, III and IV

Quick Answer: 7
Detailed Answer: 10

22. The portion of the underwriting spread that a Selling Group member would receive is known as what?

    ❍ A. Management Fee
    ❍ B. Syndicate fee
    ❍ C. Reallowance fee
    ❍ D. Concession fee

Quick Answer: 7
Detailed Answer: 10

23. If the SEC has determined that the registration statement for a new issue has not provided all of the necessary information required, they can do which of the following?

    ❍ A. Make the issue effective
    ❍ B. Issue a deficiency letter
    ❍ C. Indict the issuer for fraud
    ❍ D. Indict the underwriter for conspiracy to commit fraud

Quick Answer: 7
Detailed Answer: 10

24. Once a Broker Dealer has been invited to be a member of the syndicate for a new offering, and he has determined that the issue does not meet the sales projections, he can do which of the following?

    ❍ A. The syndicate member cannot back out of the deal they have agreed to
    ❍ B. He can enact their market out clause
    ❍ C. He can enact the penalty bid clause
    ❍ D. He can petition the SEC for a deficiency letter

Quick Answer: 7
Detailed Answer: 10

Quick Check

25. After the SEC has approved an offering for sale by the issuance of the Effective date the SEC in effect has done what?

    I. Endorsed the issue

    II. Vouched for the accuracy of all information regarding the shares

    III. Permitted the sale of the shares with notice of neither approval or disapproval of the securities

    IV. Stated the issue has met Due Diligence

❍ A. I and II only
❍ B. I, II, and III
❍ C. III only
❍ D. III and IV

Quick Answer: **7**
Detailed Answer: **10**

Quick Check Answer Key

1. B
2. B
3. D
4. B
5. D
6. B
7. C
8. B
9. B
10. D
11. C
12. A
13. A
14. C
15. B
16. C
17. D
18. B
19. C
20. B
21. D
22. D
23. B
24. B
25. D

Answers and Explanations

1. **Answer B is correct.** Authorized shares are the total number of shares the company can issue according to its corporate charter. Issued shares are the number it has issued, treasury shares are the number of shares that have been bought back by the company, and outstanding shares are the number held by shareholders.

2. **Answer B is correct.** Preemptive right allows the shareholder to maintain a proportionate interest in the total number of shares owned. This right prevents a corporation from diluting the ownership percentage of a shareholder. Rights typically last for 30 to 90 days before expiring.

3. **Answer D is correct.** After the shares are sold out of the primary market, they move on to sell in the respective market where the new offering is registered to trade. This market can be any one of the three exchanges listed.

4. **Answer B is correct.** In a primary offering, the proceeds of the sale are received by the issuing company. Secondary market trades are from client to client.

5. **Answer D is correct.** The lead underwriter makes all the investment decisions of the offering. They settle the account at the end of the offering with all syndicate members, selling group members and outside brokers who have sold shares in the offering. Only the lead underwriter can invite a broker to be part of the syndicate. The issuing company is required to take on the task of registering with the SEC.

6. **Answer B is correct.** The lead underwriter receives a management fee on every share of stock sold in the primary offering. A markup is charged by a broker dealer in an Over-the-Counter (OTC) trade, and a commission is charged by a broker when executing a client's trade. The entire spread is broken down among the syndicate members, selling group members, and outside broker/dealers with the management fee as part of the spread.

7. **Answer C is correct.** An investment banking firm handles mergers, acquisitions, tender offers, and the underwriting responsibilities of new issues for corporate clients. They never represent the SEC in an audit.

8. **Answer B is correct.** The cooling-off period typically lasts for 20 days and not 30 days. During this time, indications of interest can be taken by syndicate members, and the issuer must register with the SEC and blue-sky the issue with state regulators.

9. **Answer B is correct**. Although the SEC Act of 1933 alludes to the SEC filing and registration, the actual creation of the SEC occurred through an act of Congress as stated in the SEC Act of 1934. The Trust Indenture Act covered bondholders, and the Congressional Act of 1929 does not exist.

10. **Answer D is correct**. When filing with the SEC, the issuer provides all the necessary information required, such as the names of directors, insiders, 10% shareholders, and what the proceeds of the sale are used for. The price of the underlying stock has not been ascertained as of this filing.

11. **Answer C is correct**. Blue sky laws can be met in three ways: registration by coordination where the SEC assists in registering the offering with state regulators; registration by qualification, which is a comprehensive application that is required; or registration by filing, which is a renewal of an earlier application for a firm that has previously sold stock in a state. An offering circular is a prospectus-like statement for Regulation D private placements.

12. **Answer A is correct**. The effective date is the day that the SEC approves the application for sale to the public. The filing date is when the issuer applies to the SEC for registration, and offer and application dates hold no tangible meanings in this process.

13. **Answer A is correct**. The letter of intent is the agreement that the underwriter has negotiated with the issuer in respect to the new issue offering. Terms are described in the letter of intent.

14. **Answer C is correct**. A firm commitment underwriting is best for the issuer because the underwriter agrees up front to take all the shares in the offering for resale. A best effort returns any unsold shares to the issuer. An all or none offering can possibly be cancelled if all the shares are not sold, and a standby agreement is typically used in rights offerings.

15. **Answer B is correct**. A minimum/maximum offering states that after a minimum amount the offering is sold on a best-effort basis, the deal is considered good. The underwriter continues to sell the remaining shares up to the maximum on a continued best-effort basis. A firm commitment has the underwriter taking the entire offering up front, and a best effort has no minimum contingency. Again, a standby agreement is used for rights offerings.

16. **Answer C is correct**. When unsold shares are retained by the underwriter, it is a firm commitment. Minimum/maximum, all or none, and best effort have unsold shares being returned to the issuer, not the underwriter.

17. **Answer D is correct.** Escrowed funds are typical of an all or none offering. If the underwriter does not sell out the entire offering, then the issuer cancels the deal and proceeds are returned to customers from the escrow account. Firm commitment, best effort, and standby agreements do not require escrowed funds because the deal is not going to be cancelled.
18. **Answer B is correct.** A road show is when the underwriter makes a comprehensive presentation to the issuer highlighting the offering to win confidence. A tentative agreement is not applicable to this process, whereas a feasibility study is the hiring of an outside engineering firm to study the merits of a municipal revenue bond offering. A phantom stock plan is used for executive incentives and does not apply to underwritings.
19. **Answer C is correct.** A tombstone ad does not list the selling group members. It only lists the syndicate members and the price of the offering. Although common on new offerings, it is not a legal requirement of the underwriting.
20. **Answer B is correct.** The following choices are the responsibilities of the issuer. The issuer must register the offering with the SEC and blue sky state regulators. It prints the stock certificates and must agree on the spread but not the management fee that is a portion of the spread. The management fee is agreed upon by the syndicate members with the lead underwriter as part of the underwriting syndicate agreement. Thus, choice III is not part of the responsibilities of the issuer.
21. **Answer D is correct.** All of the listed entities would be at the due diligence meeting to go over the pertinent points of the offering.
22. **Answer D is correct.** The selling group member receives a portion of the spread known as the concession. The lead underwriter receives a management fee, syndicate members receive a takedown from the spread, while outside broker dealers receive a reallowance.
23. **Answer B is correct.** If the SEC has not received sufficient information from the issuer, they can issue a deficiency letter, requiring additional information. Fraud would only be charged if the SEC uncovered blatant lies or deception in the registration statement that was intended to defraud investors.
24. **Answer B is correct.** A syndicate member who feels that the issue is too risky for their firm, based on indications of interest they have received from potential clients, can back out of the syndicate agreement through a market out clause, typically done after the 20 day cooling off period.
25. **Answer D is correct.** SEC granting an Effective date will allow the shares to begin selling, but with a disclaimer of neither approval or disapproval of the offering by the SEC. The SEC has determined the issuer has met Due Diligence. In no way does the SEC endorse or vouch the accuracy of the issuer provided information.

The Primary Market: Selling

Quick Check

1. With a hot issue, the underwriter is restricted in selling shares to all the following purchasers except for which one?
   - ❍ A. An employed officer of the brokerage that is part of the syndicate team
   - ❍ B. The brother of the financial accountant who assisted in drafting the preliminary and final prospectus
   - ❍ C. The father of an employee who works for a large commercial bank
   - ❍ D. The trading account for the lead underwriter

Quick Answer: **18**
Detailed Answer: **19**

2. When an underwriter allows shares of a hot issue to be purchased by individuals who are considered insiders in the offering, this is known as what?
   - ❍ A. Withholding
   - ❍ B. Free riding
   - ❍ C. Fire sale
   - ❍ D. Turnaround trading

Quick Answer: **18**
Detailed Answer: **19**

3. When a broker dealer fails to make a bona fide offer on shares that are still available for a hot issue to an interested client, this is known as what?
   - ❍ A. Free riding
   - ❍ B. Withholding
   - ❍ C. A market out clause
   - ❍ D. A DK (don't know) trade

Quick Answer: **18**
Detailed Answer: **19**

4. When an underwriter requests additional shares from the issuer on a hot new issue, this is known as which of the following?
   - ❍ A. Market out clause
   - ❍ B. Penalty bid clause
   - ❍ C. Green shoe clause
   - ❍ D. Greenmail clause

Quick Answer: **18**
Detailed Answer: **19**

Quick Check

5. An underwriter is permitted to request up to an additional number of shares for a hot issue through the green shoe clause. The number of shares can total up to what amount?

❍ A. 10% additional shares of the entire offering
❍ B. 20% additional shares of the entire offering
❍ C. 50% additional shares of the entire offering
❍ D. 100% additional shares of the entire offering

Quick Answer: 18
Detailed Answer: 19

6. When a new issue is having difficulties selling in the primary market because of low demand or too high of a price, this is known as which of the following?

❍ A. A do-not-reduce offering
❍ B. A sticky issue
❍ C. A destabilized offer
❍ D. A fire sale

Quick Answer: 18
Detailed Answer: 19

7. An underwriter is permitted to buy back shares of a sticky issue in the market at which of the following?

❍ A. At a price higher than the public offering price
❍ B. At any price they desire
❍ C. At a price at the public offering price or just below
❍ D. Only at the public offering price

Quick Answer: 18
Detailed Answer: 19

8. All the following statements regarding stabilizing bids entered by an underwriter are true except for which of the following?

❍ A. The stabilizing bid is permitted under the SEC Act of 1934.
❍ B. The stabilizing bid must be at the public offering price or lower.
❍ C. Stabilizing bids can only happen in the primary market offering.
❍ D. Stabilizing bids are price manipulation and are therefore illegal.

Quick Answer: 18
Detailed Answer: 19

9. A stabilizing bid on a new issue is most commonly found in what type of underwriting commitment?

❍ A. Firm commitment
❍ B. Best effort
❍ C. All or none
❍ D. Minimum/maximum offering

Quick Answer: 18
Detailed Answer: 20

Quick Check

10. All the following underwriting commitments have sales proceeds held in an escrow account while still trading in the primary market except for which of the following?

   ❍ A. All or none
   ❍ B. Best effort
   ❍ C. Firm commitment
   ❍ D. Standby offering

Quick Answer: 18
Detailed Answer: 20

11. When speculative investors enter the primary market looking for a quick profit and then dump their shares when they do not realize it, it forces the stock to drop in price. Then, the lead underwriter can enact which of the following?

   ❍ A. Penalty bid clause
   ❍ B. Market out clause
   ❍ C. Green shoe clause
   ❍ D. Reallowance clause

Quick Answer: 18
Detailed Answer: 20

12. The Securities Act of 1933 was designed to protect investors by requiring which of the following?

   I. All securities must register with the SEC when being offered to the public.

   II. All securities must issue a final prospectus.

   III. All securities must have SEC approval to begin trading.

   IV. None of the above.

   ❍ A. I only
   ❍ B. I and II only
   ❍ C. I, II, and III
   ❍ D. IV

Quick Answer: 18
Detailed Answer: 20

Quick Check

13. Which of the following securities are not exempt from the Securities Act of 1933?

    I. Common stock

    II. Preferred stock

    III. Warrants

    IV. Rights

    ❍ A. I only
    ❍ B. I and II
    ❍ C. I, II, and III
    ❍ D. I, II, III, and IV

Quick Answer: 18
Detailed Answer: 20

14. All the following securities are exempt from the Securities Act of 1933 except for which of the following?

    ❍ A. FNMA
    ❍ B. GNMA
    ❍ C. Commercial paper with a maturity of less than 270 days or under $5,000,000
    ❍ D. Warrants

Quick Answer: 18
Detailed Answer: 20

15. Which of the following statements are true regarding direct government obligations such as t-bills, t-notes, and t-bonds?

    I. All government issues must issue a prospectus.

    II. All government issues are exempt from registering with the SEC.

    III. Government issues with a maturity of one year or less must register with the SEC.

    IV. Government issues with a maturity of one year or more must register with the SEC.

    ❍ A. I and II only
    ❍ B. I and IV only
    ❍ C. III only
    ❍ D. II only

Quick Answer: 18
Detailed Answer: 20

16. Which of the following securities are exempt from SEC registration requirements under the Securities Act of 1933?

Quick Answer: 18
Detailed Answer: 20

I. Nonprofit organizations

II. Municipal bonds

III. Commercial paper under 270 days in length

IV. Agency debt

❍ A. I only
❍ B. I, II, and III
❍ C. I, II, and IV
❍ D. I, II, III, and IV

17. REM Incorporated issues the following securities in the market. Which of these securities are exempt from registering with the SEC when offered?

Quick Answer: 18
Detailed Answer: 21

❍ A. Common stock
❍ B. Preferred stock
❍ C. Commercial paper under 270 days in maturity
❍ D. Debenture bonds

18. ARC Incorporated is an advisory business established under the Small Business Administration. All the following statements are true regarding ARC except for which one?

Quick Answer: 18
Detailed Answer: 21

❍ A. They can provide counseling and small loans to small businesses owned by minorities and the disabled.
❍ B. They are encouraged and funded by the Small Business Administration.
❍ C. They are exempt from registering with the SEC.
❍ D. They are considered an agency of the U.S. Government.

Quick Check

19. An accredited investor is considered someone who meets the following requirements:

    I. Has a net worth of $1,000,000

    II. Has made $200,000 per year for the past two years or has a net worth of $1,0000,000

    III. Is an officer or director of the issuing company

    IV. Is a bank or an insurance company with assets greater than $3,000,000

    ❍ A. I only
    ❍ B. I, II, and III
    ❍ C. I, III, and IV
    ❍ D. IV only

Quick Answer: **18**
Detailed Answer: **21**

20. Another distinction for a private placement is commonly known as a what?

    ❍ A. Regulation T offering
    ❍ B. Regulation D offering
    ❍ C. Regulation U offering
    ❍ D. Regulation G offering

Quick Answer: **18**
Detailed Answer: **21**

21. Which of the following are true statements regarding a private placement?

    I. It is exempt from registering with the SEC.

    II. It can be sold to the general public.

    III. It must issue an offering memorandum.

    IV. The purchaser agrees to hold the private placement as an investment, rather than for quick resale.

    ❍ A. I only
    ❍ B. I, II, and III
    ❍ C. I, II, and IV
    ❍ D. I, III, and IV

Quick Answer: **18**
Detailed Answer: **21**

Quick Check

22. Private placements that are sold to qualified accredited investors must meet which of the following conditions?

    I. They can only be sold to a maximum of 35 accredited investors.

    II. They can be sold to any number of accredited investors.

    III. They must issue a prospectus.

    IV. They must issue an offering memorandum.

    - ❍ A. I only
    - ❍ B. I and III
    - ❍ C. II only
    - ❍ D. II and IV

Quick Answer: 18
Detailed Answer: 21

23. Regulation D private placements may be sold to which of the following investors?
    - ❍ A. A minimum of 10 nonaccredited investors
    - ❍ B. A maximum of 35 nonaccredited investors
    - ❍ C. A maximum of 90 accredited investors
    - ❍ D. A maximum of 35 accredited investors

Quick Answer: 18
Detailed Answer: 21

24. Restricted stock is best defined by which of the following statements?
    - ❍ A. Stock that has been purchased on margin and that has fallen below 50% in equity
    - ❍ B. Stock that does not meet the SEC filing requirements
    - ❍ C. Stock that has been purchased in a Regulation D offering that is not required to be registered
    - ❍ D. Stock that can only be purchased by institutions

Quick Answer: 18
Detailed Answer: 21

25. Control stock is best defined by which of the following statements?
    - ❍ A. Stock that is owned by an officer, director, or 10% shareholder
    - ❍ B. Any group of 35 shareholders that represents controlling interest in a company
    - ❍ C. Preferred stock that has special voting rights for the holder
    - ❍ D. Stock that has been issued at a par value of $100

Quick Answer: 18
Detailed Answer: 21

Quick Check Answer Key

1. C
2. B
3. B
4. C
5. A
6. B
7. C
8. D
9. A
10. C
11. A
12. C
13. D
14. D
15. D
16. D
17. C
18. D
19. B
20. B
21. D
22. D
23. B
24. C
25. A

Answers and Explanations

1. **Answer C is correct.** Hot issues are closely watched by the SEC to ensure that a fair market is created. Hot issues cannot be sold to financial employees that are part of the syndicate team or to any immediate family member who worked on the underwriting. The lead underwriter is prohibited from withholding hot issue shares in its own trading account for resale. The father of an employee who works for a large commercial bank would be able to purchase the shares.

2. **Answer B is correct.** Free riding is an SEC-prohibited practice in the underwriting of a new issue. It is when the underwriter allows insiders to buy the shares to resell at a quick profit.

3. **Answer B is correct.** If a broker has received an inquiry for hot issue shares and it tells the customer that it does not have any available when indeed it does, this is known as the prohibited practice of withholding.

4. **Answer C is correct.** To compensate for a hot issue, an underwriter can request up to 10% additional shares from the issuer under the green shoe clause to sell. A market out clause is when a syndicate member drops out of an underwriting syndicate. The penalty bid clause is when an underwriter penalizes a member for bringing a speculator into the offering that has driven the price of the shares down. Greenmail is the paying off of corporate raiders by a board of directors by buying back shares at an inflated price.

5. **Answer A is correct.** Under the green shoe clause, an underwriter is permitted to request up to an additional 10% of the new issue shares from the issuer, to compensate for a hot issue.

6. **Answer B is correct.** New issues that are having difficulty selling in the market and that run the risk of dropping in price are known as a sticky issue. A do-not-reduce offering is placing an order to buy a dividend on a stock. The other answers have no real defined meanings in the industry.

7. **Answer C is correct.** When an underwriter experiences a sticky issue that has seen the price of the shares drop in value, it is permitted to purchase the shares in the market to stabilize the stock at the public offering price or below. Stabilizing bids can never be higher than the public offering price.

8. **Answer D is correct.** Under the Act of 1934, stabilizing bids are allowed as long as they are at the public offering price or below and the stock issue has not yet moved into the secondary market. This is the only time market manipulation is allowed under SEC rules.

9. **Answer A is correct.** A firm commitment is the type of underwriting that most often sees a stabilizing bid because the underwriter agrees to take the entire issue from the issuer for resale in the primary market. To secure its price, the lead underwriter uses a stabilizing bid if it sees the shares dropping in the market.

10. **Answer C is correct.** All or none and best effort underwritings have escrowed amounts held until the offering is determined to have gone through for the issuer. If the issue are cancelled, then the proceeds are returned out of the escrow account to the buyers. A firm commitment is agreed upon in principle that the underwriter is taking the entire issue from the issuer. A standby agreement is used primarily for rights offerings.

11. **Answer A is correct.** A penalty bid clause is enacted when a lead underwriter is forced to buy back shares from speculators that have been brought into the offering by syndicate team members. The clause allows the lead underwriter to penalize the broker who brought the client into the offering by taking away its portion of the spread that it would have earned.

12. **Answer C is correct.** The Act of 1933 made it a requirement that all nonexempt new issues must register with the SEC, issue a final prospectus, and receive SEC approval to trade by the receipt of an effective date, before they are permitted to be sold.

13. **Answer D is correct.** Most corporate securities are considered nonexempt offerings that must follow the registration rules of the SEC. Common and preferred stock, warrants, and rights are all corporate securities that must meet the requirements of the Act of 1933.

14. **Answer D is correct.** In this question, all the securities listed are exempt from filing with the SEC except for corporate warrants. FNMA and GNMA are government agencies that are exempt from filing with the SEC, and commercial paper, even though a corporate debt instrument, is not required to file a registration with the SEC, as long as the paper has a maturity of less than 270 days and under $5,000,000.

15. **Answer D is correct.** The only true statement is that government issues are exempt securities that are not required to file with the SEC under the Act of 1933. No time limits on these issues would change this fact, nor are they required to issue a prospectus to investors.

16. **Answer D is correct.** All the securities listed in this question are considered exempt securities under the Act of 1933. Nonprofit organizations and commercial paper (under 270 days in length) are exempt. Municipal bonds and government agency debt are not required to register either. One note: municipal bonds are required to follow the antifraud provisions of the Act of 1933.

17. **Answer C is correct.** Corporate securities are required to register with the SEC when being brought to the market. Commercial paper that is a money market instrument with a maturity under 270 days is exempt from filing a registration statement with the SEC.

18. **Answer D is correct.** Companies that are set up with financing from the Small Business Administration are considered small issue exempt, or Regulation A. They are not required to register with the SEC, and they can make loans and give advice to minority groups. They are not, however, considered government agencies.

19. **Answer B is correct.** An accredited investor is an individual who has a net worth of $1 million, has an income for the past two years of $200,000, or is an insider of the issuing company. A bank or investment company must have assets greater than $5,000,000 and not $3,000,000 million to qualify as an accredited investor.

20. **Answer B is correct.** A Regulation D offering is also known as a private placement of securities. Regulation T covers margin accounts, Regulation U covers the amount of money a bank may loan to a margin customer, and Regulation G is the Federal Reserve Board rule that regulates lenders.

21. **Answer D is correct.** Private placements are exempt from SEC registration requirements. They need to produce an offering memorandum for potential investors, and accredited investors are expected to hold the securities as a long-term investment. They are not permitted to be sold directly to the general public.

22. **Answer D is correct.** Private placements can be sold to an unlimited number of accredited investors and a maximum of 35 nonaccredited investors. They are not required to issue a prospectus, but rather issue an offering memorandum to interested investors.

23. **Answer B is correct.** Regulation D private placements can be sold to an unlimited number of accredited investors and up to 35 nonaccredited investors.

24. **Answer C is correct.** Restricted stocks are those shares purchased in a private placement that are not required to issue a registration statement with the SEC. Stock that has fallen below 50% of equity to market value in a margin account is known as a restricted account, whereas stock that does not meet SEC requirements receives a deficiency letter on its filing status.

25. **Answer A is correct.** Control stocks are those shares in the hands of insiders such as officers, directors, and 10% shareholders of the company.

Quick Check

The Secondary Market

1. The American Stock Exchange is most commonly noted for which of the following securities that trade there?

   I. Oil and gas companies

   II. Foreign stocks

   III. Options

   IV. Dually listed NYSE stocks

   ❍ A. I and III
   ❍ B. I, II, and III
   ❍ C. I, III, and IV
   ❍ D. IV only

Quick Answer: **30**
Detailed Answer: **31**

2. Which of the following situations constitutes a dual listing for an underlying security?

   ❍ A. A stock listed on the NYSE and the AMEX.
   ❍ B. A stock listed on the NYSE and the OTC.
   ❍ C. A stock listed on the NYSE and a regional exchange.
   ❍ D. All the above choices represent a dual listing.

Quick Answer: **30**
Detailed Answer: **31**

Quick Check

3. Which of the following exchanges is representative of a major exchange in the United States?

   I. NYSE

   II. AMEX

   III. OTC

   IV. Regional exchanges

   ❍ A. I only
   ❍ B. I and II
   ❍ C. I, II, and III
   ❍ D. All of the above

Quick Answer: **30**
Detailed Answer: **31**

4. The National Association of Securities Dealers (NASD) enforces the rules and regulations for which of the following exchanges?

   I. The NYSE

   II. The AMEX

   III. The OTC

   IV. The CBOE

   ❍ A. I only
   ❍ B. I, II, and III
   ❍ C. III only
   ❍ D. III and IV

Quick Answer: **30**
Detailed Answer: **31**

5. The Over-the-Counter market is set up as which of the following types of markets?

   ❍ A. An auction market
   ❍ B. A negotiated market
   ❍ C. A specialist market
   ❍ D. A regional market

Quick Answer: **30**
Detailed Answer: **31**

6. If a broker/dealer in Tokyo, Japan, wants to buy 1000 shares of General Motors when the NYSE is closed, where can he get his order filled?

   ❍ A. He would have to wait for the NYSE to open for business to get his order filled.
   ❍ B. He could go to the first market of the secondary market.
   ❍ C. He could go to the second market of the secondary market.
   ❍ D. He could go to the third market of the secondary market.

Quick Answer: **30**
Detailed Answer: **31**

Quick Check

7. An NYSE member firm receives an order from a trader in London at 7:00 p.m. New York time to purchase 500 shares of IBM at the best possible price immediately. Which of the following scenarios best describes what the NYSE member could do in handling the trade?

   ❍ A. He would sell the stock out of the inventory account of the firm to the London trader.

   ❍ B. He would not be able to execute the order for the London trader.

   ❍ C. He would go to the specialist who handles IBM for execution.

   ❍ D. He would forward the trade to the Instinet Market.

Quick Answer: 30
Detailed Answer: 31

8. Which of the following statements regarding the Instinet Market are true?

   I. It provides trading between large institutional investors.

   II. It is registered with the SEC as a stock exchange.

   III. It was created to save on brokerage commissions.

   IV. It is part of the fourth market of the secondary market.

   ❍ A. I only

   ❍ B. I and III

   ❍ C. I, II, and III

   ❍ D. I, II, III, and IV

Quick Answer: 30
Detailed Answer: 31

9. A broker/dealer that sells a security out of its own inventory to a customer in the OTC market is acting as a what?

   ❍ A. Broker

   ❍ B. Account executive

   ❍ C. Dealer

   ❍ D. Trader

Quick Answer: 30
Detailed Answer: 31

Quick Check

10. Which of the following statements are true regarding Over-the-Counter broker/dealers?

Quick Answer: **30**
Detailed Answer: **32**

I. All broker/dealers maintain an inventory of every Over-the-Counter security.

II. A majority of initial public offerings are brought to the market by OTC brokers.

III. All broker/dealers must be a member of the NASD.

IV. They can only sell securities for which they are a market maker to their customers.

❍ A. I and IV
❍ B. II and III
❍ C. I, III, and IV
❍ D. I, II, III, and IV

11. The Maloney Act of 1938 was designed to regulate which of the following exchanges?

Quick Answer: **30**
Detailed Answer: **32**

❍ A. NYSE
❍ B. AMEX
❍ C. CBOE
❍ D. OTC

12. The NASD was created by the approval of which of the following entities?

Quick Answer: **30**
Detailed Answer: **32**

❍ A. NYSE
❍ B. Securities and Exchange Commission
❍ C. Federal Reserve Board
❍ D. U.S. Treasury

13. Securities that do not meet the listing requirements of the NASDAQ system have their quoted prices printed in what?

Quick Answer: **30**
Detailed Answer: **32**

❍ A. Yellow sheets
❍ B. Pink sheets
❍ C. Blue sheets
❍ D. The *Wall Street Journal*

Quick Check

14. When an Over-the-Counter broker/dealer executes an order for its client, which of the following information is required on the confirmation that is sent to the client?

    I. The price of the security

    II. The role the broker/dealer acted as

    III. The commission, if any, that was charged

    IV. The name of the security that was bought or sold

    ❍ A. I and II
    ❍ B. I, II, and III
    ❍ C. I, III, and IV
    ❍ D. I, II, III, and IV

Quick Answer: **30**
Detailed Answer: **32**

15. The highest price that an individual is willing to pay for an OTC stock is known as what?

    ❍ A. Bid
    ❍ B. Ask
    ❍ C. Spread
    ❍ D. Markup

Quick Answer: **30**
Detailed Answer: **32**

16. The lowest price at which an individual is willing to sell a security in the OTC market is known as what?

    ❍ A. Bid
    ❍ B. Ask
    ❍ C. Spread
    ❍ D. Markdown

Quick Answer: **30**
Detailed Answer: **32**

17. Stocks that have a wide spread in the market are considered securities that have which of the following characteristics?

    ❍ A. High volume and widely traded
    ❍ B. Low volume and thinly traded
    ❍ C. High volume and thinly traded
    ❍ D. Low volume and widely traded

Quick Answer: **30**
Detailed Answer: **32**

18. The Security Act of 1934 was established to regulate all the following actions except what?

    ❍ A. Requires all nonexempt securities to be registered with the SEC
    ❍ B. Prohibits the manipulation of a stock's price
    ❍ C. Requires that all exchanges and members register with the SEC
    ❍ D. Establishes regulations that govern margin accounts

Quick Answer: **30**
Detailed Answer: **32**

Quick Check

19. The Securities and Exchange Commission was created to regulate the securities industry under which of the following acts of government legislation?

Quick Answer: **30**
Detailed Answer: **32**

- ❍ A. Securities Act of 1933
- ❍ B. Securities Act of 1934
- ❍ C. Trust Indenture Act of 1939
- ❍ D. Maloney Act of 1938

20. Which of the following statements are true regarding the regulation of margin accounts in the brokerage industry?

Quick Answer: **30**
Detailed Answer: **33**

I. Margin is the amount that a customer must deposit with his or her broker when purchasing securities in a margin account.

II. Margin is the amount that a customer can borrow in his or her margin account when purchasing securities.

III. Regulation T covers the extension of credit to customers by brokers, dealers, and members.

IV. Regulation U covers the limit on the amount of credit that a bank may extend a customer to purchase margined securities.

- ❍ A. I only
- ❍ B. II and III
- ❍ C. I, III, and IV
- ❍ D. I, II, III, and IV

21. The short sale rule under the Act of 1934 states that all the following are true except what?

Quick Answer: **30**
Detailed Answer: **33**

- ❍ A. The Regulation T requirement on a short sale is 50%.
- ❍ B. A short sale can only happen on a minus tick.
- ❍ C. A short sale can happen on a plus tick or a zero plus tick.
- ❍ D. The customer must borrow stock when selling short.

22. Tom Gordon enters an order with his broker to sell short 100 shares of QVC. Which of the following trades will trigger his short sale of QVC stock?

Quick Answer: **30**
Detailed Answer: **33**

33 1/8…33…33 1/4 …33 1/4 …33 1/2 sld…33 5/8…33 3/8…

- ❍ A. 33 1/8
- ❍ B. 33
- ❍ C. 33 1/4
- ❍ D. 33 1/2 sld

Quick Check

23. Which of the following entities is not required to register with the SEC?
    - ❍ A. The AMEX
    - ❍ B. An NYSE member firm
    - ❍ C. GNMA
    - ❍ D. A stockbroker

Quick Answer: **30**
Detailed Answer: **33**

24. The authority to establish margin requirements was given to which of the following entities under the Securities Act of 1934?
    - ❍ A. NYSE
    - ❍ B. NASD
    - ❍ C. FRB
    - ❍ D. SEC

Quick Answer: **30**
Detailed Answer: **33**

25. Rule 10-B-5 under the Insider Trading and Enforcement Act of 1988 states which of the following to be true?
    - ❍ A. Mutual funds can charge shareholders for advertising costs incurred.
    - ❍ B. It limits the definition of insiders to officers and directors only.
    - ❍ C. It is considered a catch-all fraud rule.
    - ❍ D. If convicted of fraud, an individual could receive a maximum of 10 years and a minimum of 5 years in jail.

Quick Answer: **30**
Detailed Answer: **33**

Quick Check Answer Key

1. B
2. C
3. B
4. C
5. B
6. D
7. B
8. D
9. C
10. B
11. D
12. B
13. B
14. D
15. A
16. B
17. B
18. A
19. B
20. C
21. B
22. C
23. C
24. C
25. C

Answers and Explanations

1. **Answer B is correct.** The AMEX is most noted for its listing of oil and gas companies, foreign stocks, and options. A dually listed NYSE security cannot be listed on the NYSE and AMEX, but rather would be on the NYSE and a regional exchange.

2. **Answer C is correct.** Dually listed securities can only be listed on a major exchange such as the NYSE and one of the numerous regional exchanges across the country. A dual listing cannot occur on two major exchanges such as the NYSE and AMEX or the NYSE and the OTC market.

3. **Answer B is correct.** There are only two major exchanges in the United States, the NYSE and AMEX. Both of these exchanges are located in New York and are considered auction markets.

4. **Answer C is correct.** The National Association of Security Dealers (NASD) was created by the SEC specifically to oversee the OTC market.

5. **Answer B is correct.** The OTC is a negotiated market that uses the market maker system with bid and ask prices quoted. The NYSE and AMEX are both known as auction markets that use the specialist system in trading all securities.

6. **Answer D is correct.** Traders around the world who want to purchase NYSE-listed securities when the NYSE is closed have to go to an off-the-floor broker in the third market to get their orders filled. Around 30 million shares per day get filled in the third market.

7. **Answer B is correct.** An order coming from a foreign trader to a NYSE member firm cannot be filled due to the NYSE rules that limit their members to conducting business only during trading hours. They could not sell the stock out of their inventory, nor would they be able to go to the specialist during hours the exchange is not open, to accommodate the foreign trader.

8. **Answer D is correct.** All the statements are true regarding the Instinet Market. It was designed by institutional investors to trade between themselves and to save on commissions that brokers charge, and it is registered as an exchange with the SEC. It is the fourth market of the secondary market.

9. **Answer C is correct.** When a broker/dealer sells stock out of its own inventory, it is acting as a dealer. If it goes to another broker to get the security, it is acting as an agent or broker for the customer. An account executive is another term for a stockbroker, and a trader works on a trading desk.

10. **Answer B is correct.** OTC broker/dealers typically make a market in only a few securities. Most IPOs are brought to the market in the OTC marketplace, due to easier listing requirements. All broker/dealers must be members of the NASD and provide their customers with the security they want to buy or sell regardless of whether they are market makers.

11. **Answer D is correct.** The Maloney Act was created in 1938 as an amendment to the Act of 1934, which was scripted to regulate the Over-the-Counter marketplace.

12. **Answer B is correct.** The NASD was created to regulate the OTC market by the approval of the Securities and Exchange Commission under the Maloney Act of 1938.

13. **Answer B is correct.** OTC stocks that are considered too small to meet NASDAQ listing requirements are printed each day in the pink sheets. The blue sheets list municipal bonds, and the yellow sheets list corporate bonds.

14. **Answer D is correct.** A customer confirm includes the name and price of the security bought or sold, the commission that was charged on the transaction, and the role in which the broker acted.

15. **Answer A is correct.** The highest price that a customer is willing to pay is known as the bid in the negotiated OTC marketplace.

16. **Answer B is correct.** The lowest price at which a seller is willing to sell the security is known as the ask price. The difference between the bid and ask is the spread on the stock.

17. **Answer B is correct.** A stock in the OTC market that has a wide spread is indicative of a security that has little interest and minimal volume. Conversely, the smaller the spread, the more active the security trades in the market.

18. **Answer A is correct.** The Act of 1934 made stock manipulation illegal, required exchanges and members to register with the SEC, and set the rules on margin. Nonexempt securities are required to register with the SEC but under the Security Act of 1933 and not the Act of 1934, as this question suggests.

19. **Answer B is correct.** The Securities and Exchange Commission was officially created under government legislation that was part of the Securities Act of 1934. Many students assume that because the Act of 1933 states that all nonexempt issues must register with the SEC, the SEC was already in existence by the Act of 1933. In fact, it took several years for the new legislation of the Acts of 1933 and 1934 to be fully enforced.

20. **Answer C is correct.** Again, this is a tricky question. Margin is the amount that a customer must deposit when purchasing securities in a margin account. By definition, it is not the amount that the customer borrows, even though the amounts are the same. Regulation T covers the extension of credit to a customer from a broker, and Regulation U covers the extension of credit from a bank, through what might be considered a secured loan by the pledged securities in a margin account to secure the loan.

21. **Answer B is correct.** The short sale rule states that a short sale can only happen on a plus tick or a zero plus tick (upward price movement). The customer must borrow the security sold short, and the Regulation T requirement is set at 50%.

22. **Answer C is correct.** A short sale can only happen on a plus tick or a zero plus tick; thus, the first 33 1/4 represents an increase in the security price, where QVC stock could be shorted at. The 33 1/2 sld is not a denotation of a short sale but rather for a priced trade that is now being reported out of time sequence for QVC stock.

23. **Answer C is correct.** Government securities are considered exempt from SEC registration. All exchanges such as the NYSE and AMEX must register with the SEC, as well as individuals giving advice to clients such as stockbrokers.

24. **Answer C is correct.** The establishment of margin was given to the Federal Reserve Bank by the SEC under the Act of 1934. NYSE rules only apply to minimum maintenance in a margin account.

25. **Answer C is correct.** The 10-b-5 rule was a way for the SEC to create a catch-all definition of what constitutes insider trading and to whom the law applies. Mutual funds that are considered 12-b-1 funds can charge shareholders for advertising, but this point is not applicable to this question. The definition of an insider is an officer, director, or 10% shareholder. The 10-b-5 rule does not suggest that if an individual is convicted of insider trading, he or she receives a set prison sentence.

Equity in the Secondary Market

Quick Check

1. All the following statements are true about common stock except for which one?

   Quick Answer: 42
   Detailed Answer: 43

   ❍ A. Common stock represents equity ownership in a company.
   ❍ B. Common shareholders must receive the right to vote.
   ❍ C. Common stocks pay a fixed dividend each year.
   ❍ D. Common stockholders have the right to transfer ownership.

2. Which of the following statements is true regarding dividends that are paid to common shareholders of a corporation?

   Quick Answer: 42
   Detailed Answer: 43

   ❍ A. Shareholders vote on the declaration of a dividend.
   ❍ B. Dividends are paid semi-annually to shareholders.
   ❍ C. Dividends must be paid if the company has made a profit.
   ❍ D. Dividends can be paid in either cash or stock to shareholders.

3. Which of the following statements are true regarding shareholder rights as they apply to the ownership of common stock?

   Quick Answer: 42
   Detailed Answer: 43

   I. They have the right to receive dividends.

   II. They have the right to receive physical delivery of the stock.

   III. They are second in line for a claim on assets in the event of a liquidation.

   IV. They have the right to maintain their proportionate ownership in a company.

   ❍ A. I and II
   ❍ B. I, II and III
   ❍ C. I, II, and IV
   ❍ D. I, II, III, and IV

Quick Check

4. If a company has shares in the market that are selling at $60 per share and the same company declares a 10% stock dividend, which of the following statements is true regarding a customer with 100 shares?

   ❍ A. The company pays a dividend of $6.00.
   ❍ B. The price of the stock is adjusted to $54.
   ❍ C. The price of the stock is adjusted to $66.
   ❍ D. The number of shares is adjusted downward.

Quick Answer: **42**
Detailed Answer: **43**

5. The entity responsible for making sure that a company does not issue more shares in the market than its company charter allows is which of the following?

   ❍ A. Transfer agent
   ❍ B. Registrar
   ❍ C. Purchase and sales department
   ❍ D. Article of incorporation

Quick Answer: **42**
Detailed Answer: **43**

6. Which of the following matters do common shareholders the right to vote on?

   I. Who sits on the board of directors

   II. A stock split

   III. The issuance of a convertible bond

   IV. The issuance of a rights offering

   ❍ A. I only
   ❍ B. I and II
   ❍ C. I, II, and III
   ❍ D. I, II, III, and IV

Quick Answer: **42**
Detailed Answer: **43**

7. If Helen Kearns owns 500 shares of TNT stock and the company uses statutory voting rights for 5 open board positions, what is the maximum number of votes that Helen could give to any one candidate?

   ❍ A. 500
   ❍ B. 1000
   ❍ C. 1500
   ❍ D. 2500

Quick Answer: **42**
Detailed Answer: **43**

Quick Check

8. Garrett Smith owns 500 shares of HTH stock with a current market price of $60 per share. HTH received shareholder approval to split its stock under a 3-for-2 stock split. How many shares does Garrett now have in his account and at what price?
   - ❍ A. 750 shares at $60 per share
   - ❍ B. 1500 shares at $30 per share
   - ❍ C. 750 shares at $40 per share
   - ❍ D. 1500 shares at $20 per share

Quick Answer: **42**
Detailed Answer: **43**

9. Jordan King owns 800 shares of IOU Stock in his account at a current market price of $12 per share. IOU received approval to conduct a 1-for-4 reverse stock split on its shares. How many shares does Jordan now own and at what price?
   - ❍ A. 3200 shares at $12 per share
   - ❍ B. 200 shares at $48 per share
   - ❍ C. 3200 shares at $3 per share
   - ❍ D. 200 shares at $32 per share

Quick Answer: **42**
Detailed Answer: **44**

10. Investors who decide not to use their rights to buy additional shares of a company stock perform which of the following actions?
   - ❍ A. Allow their rights to expire worthless
   - ❍ B. Sell their rights in the open market
   - ❍ C. Sell their stock cum rights
   - ❍ D. Sell their stock ex-rights

Quick Answer: **42**
Detailed Answer: **44**

11. PDQ Corporation declares a dividend of $1.00 to all shareholders of record on Friday, June 15. Kevin Conroy owns 500 shares of PDQ stock at a price of $44 and decided to sell his shares the regular way on Wednesday, June 13. His shares of PDQ stock will sell how?
   - ❍ A. Cum dividend
   - ❍ B. Ex dividend
   - ❍ C. Cash settlement
   - ❍ D. At $43 per share

Quick Answer: **42**
Detailed Answer: **44**

12. Who makes an adjustment for a stock that has paid a dividend to shareholders?
   - ❍ A. The board of directors
   - ❍ B. The exchange where the stock trades
   - ❍ C. The transfer agent
   - ❍ D. The clearing house

Quick Answer: **42**
Detailed Answer: **44**

Quick Check

13. GHI Inc. issued 10,000,000 shares of 8% $100 par value preferred stock in the market. HTH Corporation owns 3,000,000 shares of the GHI preferred stock. Assuming that GHI makes all dividend payments, what amount must HTH claim as dividend income for yearly tax purposes on its holdings?
   - ❍ A. $2,400,000
   - ❍ B. $1,920,000
   - ❍ C. $480,000
   - ❍ D. $720,000

Quick Answer: **42**
Detailed Answer: **44**

14. CDC Corporation issued 1,000,000 shares of 7% $100 par value preferred stock in the market. JDT Corporation owns 100,000 shares of the CDC preferred stock. Assuming CDC makes all dividend payments, what amount must JDT Corporation claim as dividend income for yearly tax purposes on its holdings?
   - ❍ A. $70,000
   - ❍ B. $700,000
   - ❍ C. $210,000
   - ❍ D. $280,000

Quick Answer: **42**
Detailed Answer: **44**

15. LTV Corporation owns 25% of the outstanding preferred shares of CCC Corporation. For corporate tax purposes, what percentage of the dividend income earned from the preferred shares is exempt from having to pay corporate taxes for CCC Corporation?
   - ❍ A. 20%
   - ❍ B. 30%
   - ❍ C. 70%
   - ❍ D. 80%

Quick Answer: **42**
Detailed Answer: **44**

16. Assume that a company issued a $100 preferred stock with a 7% dividend payment in the market. A year later, interest rates in the market rise to 9%. How does this affect the 7% preferred stock?
   - ❍ A. The price of the preferred stock would remain the same.
   - ❍ B. The price of the preferred stock would drop in value.
   - ❍ C. The price of the preferred stock would increase in value.
   - ❍ D. The preferred stock would now pay a 9% dividend.

Quick Answer: **42**
Detailed Answer: **44**

Quick Check

17. A company issues participating preferred stock in the market at a $100 par value paying a 6% dividend. The company also has common shares in the market that pay a $.25 quarterly dividend. The company does exceptionally well for this year and declares an additional $.50 dividend in the last quarter of the fiscal year for common shareholders. What will the preferred shareholders receive as dividend income for the year?

    ❍ A. $6.00
    ❍ B. $6.25
    ❍ C. $6.50
    ❍ D. $6.125

Quick Answer: 42
Detailed Answer: 45

18. A company issued 1,000,000 shares of $100 par value 6% cumulative preferred stock in the market. The company missed its last two preferred dividends. The board of directors wants to now pay a $1.00 dividend to the 5,000,000 shares of common stock, payable for the next quarter. How much money must the board come up with to pay the common dividend to shareholders?

    ❍ A. $5,000,000
    ❍ B. $8,000,000
    ❍ C. $9,500,000
    ❍ D. $1,250,000

Quick Answer: 42
Detailed Answer: 45

19. ARK Incorporated has 1,000,000 shares of convertible preferred shares in the market. With a conversion ratio of 4 to 1, what must the preferred shares sell at to trade at a parity price of $23?

    ❍ A. $92
    ❍ B. $96
    ❍ C. $100
    ❍ D. $106

Quick Answer: 42
Detailed Answer: 45

20. TNT Corporation has convertible preferred stock in the market with a conversion ratio of 4 to 1. At what price would the common shares have to trade to trade at parity if the preferred shares are trading at 94?

    ❍ A. $23
    ❍ B. $23.50
    ❍ C. $24
    ❍ D. $24.50

Quick Answer: 42
Detailed Answer: 45

Quick Check

21. Warrants issued by a company always have a subscription price in the market at a price that would be which of the following?
    - ❍ A. Above the stock's market price
    - ❍ B. Below the stock's market price
    - ❍ C. At the stock's market price
    - ❍ D. Changing as the stock's market price changes

Quick Answer: **42**
Detailed Answer: **45**

22. Jordan owns 1000 shares of CDF common stock. Each share of stock has one warrant attached that gives the right to purchase the stock at $65. The shares of CDF have now risen in value to $68 in the market. What is the total value of the warrants that Jordan is holding?
    - ❍ A. $65,000
    - ❍ B. $68,000
    - ❍ C. $3,000
    - ❍ D. $1,000

Quick Answer: **42**
Detailed Answer: **45**

23. Which of the following securities has the longest life expectancy when trading in the market?
    - ❍ A. LEAPS
    - ❍ B. Caps
    - ❍ C. Warrants
    - ❍ D. Rights

Quick Answer: **42**
Detailed Answer: **45**

24. Which of the following statements are true in respect to the issuance of a dividend by a company?

    I. They can be paid in cash.

    II. They can be paid in stock.

    III. They can be paid in rights.

    IV. They can be paid in warrants.

    - ❍ A. I only
    - ❍ B. I and II
    - ❍ C. I, II, and III
    - ❍ D. I, II, III, and IV

Quick Answer: **42**
Detailed Answer: **45**

Quick Check

25. Which of the following types of preferred stock are least affected by a price movement if interest rates suddenly rise in the market?

❍ A. Callable preferred

❍ B. Adjustable preferred

❍ C. Convertible preferred

❍ D. Participating preferred

Quick Answer: **42**

Detailed Answer: **46**

Quick Check Answer Key

1. C
2. D
3. C
4. B
5. B
6. C
7. A
8. C
9. B
10. B
11. B
12. B
13. C
14. C
15. D
16. B
17. C
18. C
19. A
20. B
21. A
22. C
23. C
24. B
25. B

Answers and Explanations

1. **Answer C is correct.** Common stock represents ownership in a corporation, giving the shareholders the right to vote and the ability to trade their stock at the owner's discretion. Common stock does not pay a fixed dividend. Preferred stock pays a fixed dividend, but common pays at the discretion of the board of directors.

2. **Answer D is correct.** Dividends are paid to shareholders on a quarterly basis at the discretion of the board of directors—not the shareholders. The profitability of a company does not dictate the fact that they must pay a dividend. The only true answer is that a dividend can be paid in either cash or additional stock.

3. **Answer C is correct.** Shareholders of common stock have the right to receive dividends and to take physical delivery from the transfer agent of the stock they own. They also have the right to maintain their pre-emptive right of proportionate ownership. They are last in line to receive assets in the event of a bankruptcy or liquidation of company assets.

4. **Answer B is correct.** When a company pays a stock dividend to its shareholders, it is issuing additional shares to the shareholders. The market price of the stock is adjusted downward accordingly. Thus, a 10% stock dividend on a stock selling for $60 would be adjusted to approximately $54 per share.

5. **Answer B is correct.** The registrar is responsible as the watchdog agency over the transfer agent, to ensure that it does not issue more shares of the stock than the company is authorized to issue. A purchase and sales department handles the back-office settlement of trades for a brokerage, and articles of incorporation are drawn up by the company.

6. **Answer C is correct.** Shareholders have the right to vote on the members of the board and to determine whether the company can do a stock split. The issuance of convertible feature securities also requires shareholder approval because it can dilute the earnings of the company if a debt for equity swap is conducted. For this reason, shareholders must approve a convertible security. A rights offering does not need shareholder approval but rather is decided by the board of directors.

7. **Answer A is correct.** Statutory voting gives the shareholder one vote for each share owned. For example, a shareholder with 500 shares is allowed 500 votes maximum.

8. **Answer C is correct.** A 3-for-2 stock split gives the shareholder 3 shares for every 2 that he owns, for a total of 750 shares. The new price after the stock split is two-thirds of the original price, or $40 ($60 × 2/3 = $40).

9. **Answer B is correct.** On a reverse split, the number of shares owned decreases, but the value per share increases. The shareholder would now have 800 × 1/4 = 200 shares with an adjusted price of 12 × 4 = $48.

10. **Answer B is correct.** Shareholders who decide not to use their rights to purchase additional shares could still offer their rights for sale in the open market for whatever value that they have. The sale of their stock cum rights or ex-rights is not as profitable to the investor as directly selling them in the market. Allowing the rights to go unused and expire worthless is the least profitable action for an investor to take.

11. **Answer B is correct.** An investor who sells his shares two days prior to the record date in a regular-way trade still receives the dividend that will be paid as of a record date two days later. This trade will settle on Monday, June 18, so Kevin receives the dividend as shareholder of record on Friday, June 15, with the stock selling ex-dividend, or without dividend, to the new owner.

12. **Answer B is correct.** A stock that has gone ex-dividend is adjusted downward accordingly for the amount of the dividend by the exchange where the security trades. This is done to reflect the payment of the dividend.

13. **Answer C is correct.** Corporations that own more than 20% of another company's preferred stock are able to claim an 80% exemption on the dividend income earned. HTH owns 30% of GHI preferred stock, so it is entitled to the 80% exemption. The 3,000,000 shares owned pay a fixed dividend of 8%, or $24,000,000 each year. Eighty percent of the $24,000,000 is exempt from taxes, which leaves $4,800,000 as taxable income for HTH.

14. **Answer C is correct.** Corporations that own less than 20% of another company's preferred stock are entitled to a 70% corporate tax exclusion on the dividend income earned. JDT owns 10% of the CDC preferred stock. The 100,000 shares owned by JDT receive a yearly preferred dividend of $700,000, of which 70% is excluded from having to pay taxes. Dividend income that is taxable is $700,000 × 30% = $210,000.

15. **Answer D is correct.** A company that owns more than 20% of the total of outstanding preferred shares of another company is entitled to an 80% corporate tax exclusion on the dividends received. Ownership of less than 20% of the outstanding shares gives a company a 70% tax exclusion on the dividend income earned.

16. **Answer B is correct.** Preferred stock is considered a fixed income security and is subject to price changes due to the fluctuation of interest rates in the market. With rates increasing to 9% in the market, the preferred stock that pays only 7% drops in value accordingly, due to the inverse effect of interest rates on fixed-income security prices.

17. **Answer C is correct.** Participating preferred shareholders are entitled to the fixed dividend that the preferred stock pays, as well as any extraordinary dividends that are paid to common shareholders. In this question, the participating shareholders are entitled to 6% plus the extra $.50 dividend, totaling $6.50 in dividend income for the year.

18. **Answer C is correct.** Cumulative preferred stock is entitled to receive any missed dividends before any common dividend can be paid to shareholders. In this case, the preferred stock pays a 6% dividend, or $1.50 per quarter. The company wants to pay a $1.00 common dividend to the 5,000,000 shares of common stock, which requires $5,000,000. For the company to be able to pay the common dividend, it needs to pay the two missed preferred dividends of $1,500,000, for a total of $3,000,000, plus the current preferred dividend of $1,500,000, for a total preferred dividend of $4,500,000. Therefore, the total required funds needed is $9,500,000.

19. **Answer A is correct.** Convertible preferred shares with a conversion ratio of 4 to 1 require a selling price of $92 to trade at parity in the market with the common stock price of $23. The result is $23 × 4 shares = $92.

20. **Answer B is correct.** Convertible preferred stock that is selling at $94 in the market with a conversion ratio of 4 to 1 must have the common shares selling at $23.50 to be selling at parity. The result is 94 ÷ 4 = $23.50.

21. **Answer A is correct.** Warrants that are issued by a company have a subscription price that is always much higher than the current market price of the underlying security. Warrants are used as sweeteners or incentives to induce investors to purchase the security that the warrants are attached to.

22. **Answer C is correct.** Warrants that give the right to purchase the security at a price lower than the current market price mean that the stock has increased in value above the warrant subscription price. These warrants to buy the stock at $65 are worth $3.00 each when the shares are trading in the market at $68. The 1000 shares that Jordan owns are worth $3,000.

23. **Answer C is correct.** The only listed securities in this question that has a life expectancy of an unlimited nature are warrants. Long-term equity anticipation options (LEAPS) typically have a life expectancy of 3 years maximum. Rights expire in 30 to 60 days, and caps expire when the index reaches a certain amount in the money points.

24. **Answer B is correct.** Dividends that are paid to shareholders can be issued either in the form of cash or as additional stock by the company (stock dividend). Rights and warrants cannot be used as a form of dividend payment to shareholders.

25. **Answer B is correct.** Of the choices listed as possible answers, adjustable preferred stock is the least affected by the movement of interest rates in the market. The reason is that adjustable preferred stock is reset every six months in response to interest-rate movements. If rates go up, the adjustable preferred dividend goes up. If rates go down, the adjustable preferred goes down. Because the adjustable preferred stock is reset every six months, it tends to trade at or close to par value.

Corporate Debt: Bonds and Yields

Quick Check

1. All the following are true regarding the benefits of issuing debt securities except which one?
   - ❍ A. There is a tax advantage to the corporation by being able to deduct interest payments.
   - ❍ B. The issuer does not give up ownership in the company.
   - ❍ C. The company can establish a credit history.
   - ❍ D. The company's common stock will increase in value.

Quick Answer: **53**
Detailed Answer: **54**

2. Which of the following security acts affects the issuance of corporate debt the most?
   - ❍ A. Security Act of 1934
   - ❍ B. Trust Indenture Act of 1939
   - ❍ C. Investment Company Act of 1940
   - ❍ D. Maloney Act of 1938

Quick Answer: **53**
Detailed Answer: **54**

3. A bond indenture is required on all corporate debt issues that have an aggregate value in excess of which amount?
   - ❍ A. $1,000,000
   - ❍ B. $5,000,000
   - ❍ C. $10,000,000
   - ❍ D. All debt issues require a bond indenture.

Quick Answer: **53**
Detailed Answer: **54**

4. Which of the following entities are appointed to oversee a bond indenture of a corporate issue?
   - ❍ A. Registrar
   - ❍ B. NASD
   - ❍ C. Trustee
   - ❍ D. Executor

Quick Answer: **53**
Detailed Answer: **54**

Quick Check

5. Which of the following features are required to be included in a bond indenture of a corporate bond issue?

    I. The interest rate of the bonds

    II. The total amount borrowed

    III. The maturity date

    IV. The amount of equity securities the company has issued

- ❍ A. I and II
- ❍ B. I and III
- ❍ C. I, II, and III
- ❍ D. I, II, III, and IV

Quick Answer: 53
Detailed Answer: 54

6. On the maturity date of a corporate bond issue, which of the following statements is true?

- ❍ A. The bond continues to earn interest until it is redeemed.
- ❍ B. The bondholder receives the price the bonds are selling at in the market place.
- ❍ C. The principal amount must be repaid to the holder.
- ❍ D. The bonds are called back by the issuer.

Quick Answer: 53
Detailed Answer: 54

7. A call provision on a debt security that has been issued allows the issuer to carry out which of the following actions?

- ❍ A. Lower the interest rate that the bonds pay
- ❍ B. Pay back the bondholders at a call discount
- ❍ C. Pay back the bondholders at a call premium
- ❍ D. Reissue the bonds at a higher interest rate

Quick Answer: 53
Detailed Answer: 54

8. A call premium that is written into the indenture of a bond issue requires which of the following?

- ❍ A. Allows the issuer to charge the bondholders a premium to redeem the bonds
- ❍ B. Forces the issuer to pay the bondholders back at par value
- ❍ C. Forces the issuer to pay the bondholders back at a price above par
- ❍ D. Allows the bondholders to deduct a premium on their interest earnings

Quick Answer: 53
Detailed Answer: 55

Quick Check

9. In 1985, UTC Corporation issued $200,000,000 worth of 9% 20-year debenture bonds in the market with a 10-year call feature attached. In 1998, interest rates dropped to 7% in the market. How much could UTC Corporation save on its interest charges over the remaining life of the bond if it calls the bonds in 1998?
   - ❍ A. $4,000,000
   - ❍ B. $8,000,000
   - ❍ C. $14,000,000
   - ❍ D. $28,000,000

Quick Answer: 53
Detailed Answer: 55

10. When a company is required in the bond indenture to put a certain amount of money away each year to be used to retire its debt issue, this is known as what?
    - ❍ A. Indenture call
    - ❍ B. Dual purpose fund
    - ❍ C. Sinking fund
    - ❍ D. Call protection fund

Quick Answer: 53
Detailed Answer: 55

11. A company purchases government securities that pay a higher coupon rate than their bond issue and then deposits these securities with a trustee to be used to pay off its current outstanding bond issue. Which of the following has it performed?
    - ❍ A. A sinking fund call
    - ❍ B. Defeasance
    - ❍ C. Subscription privilege
    - ❍ D. A principal reevaluation

Quick Answer: 53
Detailed Answer: 55

12. When a bondholder has the right to place bonds back to the issuer due to an increase in interest rates, this is known as a what?
    - ❍ A. Defeasance
    - ❍ B. Put provision
    - ❍ C. Call provision
    - ❍ D. Break in the spread

Quick Answer: 53
Detailed Answer: 55

13. Which of the following yields on a bond issue never changes over the life of the bond?
    - ❍ A. Nominal yield
    - ❍ B. Current yield
    - ❍ C. Yield to maturity
    - ❍ D. Yield to put

Quick Answer: 53
Detailed Answer: 55

Quick Check

14. If interest rates go up in the market to 8%, which of the following statements is true regarding a 7% 20-year bond?

Quick Answer: 53
Detailed Answer: 55

I. The bond will sell at a discount.

II. The bond will sell at a premium.

III. The nominal yield remains the same.

IV. The current yield is higher than the coupon rate.

❍ A. I only
❍ B. II only
❍ C. II and III
❍ D. I, III, and IV

15. What price would a 20-year 9% debenture bond that has been quoted in the market at 102 1/4 be selling at?

Quick Answer: 53
Detailed Answer: 55

❍ A. $102.25
❍ B. $1002.25
❍ C. $1020.25
❍ D. $1022.50

16. A corporate bond that was issued at $1000 par with a 7% coupon and a selling price of 93 has a current yield of which of the following?

Quick Answer: 53
Detailed Answer: 56

❍ A. 13.28%
❍ B. 7.53%
❍ C. 10.75%
❍ D. 7%

17. A bond that was issued with a nominal yield of 8.25% and now has a current yield of 7.50% would be selling in the market at which price?

Quick Answer: 53
Detailed Answer: 56

❍ A. $1000
❍ B. $1100
❍ C. $910
❍ D. $1200

18. Which of the following yields would be the highest on a bond that is currently selling in the market at a premium?

Quick Answer: 53
Detailed Answer: 56

❍ A. Nominal yield
❍ B. Current yield
❍ C. Yield to maturity
❍ D. Yield to call

Quick Check

19. Which of the following yields would be the lowest on a bond that was issued at a par but is now selling in the market at a price of 94?
    - ❍ A. Nominal yield
    - ❍ B. Current Yield
    - ❍ C. Yield to maturity
    - ❍ D. Yield to put

Quick Answer: 53
Detailed Answer: 56

20. An investor purchases the following bond in the market: 1 TNT 6% debenture with 15 years to maturity at a price of 90. What is the amount the investor could accrete on this bond each year if held to maturity?
    - ❍ A. $6.00 per year
    - ❍ B. $6.67 per year
    - ❍ C. $66.00 per year
    - ❍ D. $66.67 per year

Quick Answer: 53
Detailed Answer: 56

21. What is the highest credit rating that Standard & Poor's gives to investment grade securities?
    - ❍ A. AAA
    - ❍ B. Aaa
    - ❍ C. A+
    - ❍ D. AAA+

Quick Answer: 53
Detailed Answer: 56

22. What is the lowest rating that Moody's places on investment grade securities?
    - ❍ A. BB
    - ❍ B. Ba
    - ❍ C. Baa
    - ❍ D. BBB

Quick Answer: 53
Detailed Answer: 56

23. What is the highest speculative rating that both S&P and Fitch give to junk bonds?
    - ❍ A. B
    - ❍ B. C
    - ❍ C. BB
    - ❍ D. Ba

Quick Answer: 53
Detailed Answer: 56

24. Which of the following ratings is considered consistent with a speculative security or junk bond?
    - ❍ A. BBB
    - ❍ B. Baa
    - ❍ C. Ba
    - ❍ D. A

Quick Answer: 53
Detailed Answer: 56

Quick Check

25. How does a company rated AA that issues a bond with a 30-year maturity compare to a company rated AA that issues a bond with a 20-year maturity?
    - ❍ A. It pays the same interest costs.
    - ❍ B. It pays a higher interest cost.
    - ❍ C. It pays a lower interest cost.
    - ❍ D. None of the above

Quick Answer: **53**
Detailed Answer: **56**

Quick Check Answer Key

1. D
2. B
3. B
4. C
5. C
6. C
7. C
8. C
9. D
10. C
11. B
12. B
13. A
14. D
15. D
16. B
17. B
18. A
19. A
20. B
21. A
22. C
23. C
24. C
25. B

Answers and Explanations

1. **Answer D is correct.** When a company issues debt, it is not giving up ownership of the company to bondholders. In addition, the interest charges on servicing the debt can be written off as a tax deduction. Just like an individual who builds a credit history, a company also aims to establish a credit history for future borrowing. Issuance of debt securities does not increase the value of common stock.

2. **Answer B is correct.** The Trust Indenture Act of 1939 represents the government legislation that oversees the issuance of corporate debt. It covers bond indentures and the protective covenants in the indenture. The Act of 1934 covers the rules of the stock market, and the Investment Company Act of 1940 covers investment companies and mutual funds. The Maloney Act governs the OTC markets.

3. **Answer B is correct.** The Trust Indenture Act of 1939 requires that all debt issues in excess of $5,000,000 have a trust indenture for the issuance of a bond.

4. **Answer C is correct.** The trust indenture of a bond is required to have a trustee appointed to make sure that the issuer abides by the covenants written into the indenture. The trustee also holds title on any property pledged as collateral to secure the bond. Upon the repayment of principal, the lien on any properties pledged is released by the trustee. A trustee typically is a commercial bank. A registrar is the watchdog agency that makes sure the issuer does not issue more bonds than allowed, and the NASD governs OTC firms. An executor is appointed by a court to oversee the handling of an estate.

5. **Answer C is correct.** A bond indenture includes the total amount of debt that the issuer is incurring, the rate of interest that will be paid on the debt, and the date the issue will mature. It does not include the amount of equity securities the company has in the market.

6. **Answer C is correct.** On the maturity date for a debt security, the company is required to pay the bondholders back their original principal invested. The bond ceases paying interest, and the investors receive par value at maturity, not the price in the market. A bond maturing is not considered a call because the issue has completed its maturity term.

7. **Answer C is correct.** A call provision allows the issuer to pay back the bondholders early, typically at a call premium. The bonds are retired, and the company would most likely reissue debt at the current lower interest rate. A call provision does not allow the issuer to lower the interest paid on the current outstanding bonds.

8. **Answer C is correct.** A call premium that is written into a bond indenture forces a company to pay a premium above par value for bonds that it is calling back from bondholders. The call premium is added to the indenture to entice investors to purchase bonds with a call feature.

9. **Answer D is correct.** UTC Corporation issued $200,000,000 worth of bonds that pay 9% in the market. The bonds would mature in the year 2005. If UTC calls back the bonds in 1998, it happens seven years prior to maturity. The company can refinance at 7%, which would save it interest charges of $4,000,000 per year × 7 years to maturity = $28,000,000.

10. **Answer C is correct.** A sinking fund provision that is written into a bond indenture requires a company to put aside a predetermined amount of funds each year to retire its outstanding debt issue. An indenture call and call protection fund do not exist. A dual purpose fund is a type of mutual fund that has two classes of shares issued.

11. **Answer B is correct.** A company that purchases high quality government securities to replace its current outstanding debt would be defeasing the issue. The government obligations are deposited with a trustee and take on the liability of the outstanding debt for the issuer. A sinking fund is the setting aside of funds each year to retire an outstanding issue, and a subscription privilege is associated with a rights offering. A principal reevaluation is the analysis of an issuer's total outstanding debt.

12. **Answer B is correct.** A put provision allows a bondholder to place the bonds back to the issuer in the case of rising interest rates. Defeasance is the use of government securities to be placed with a trustee to retire debt. A call provision allows a company to call back bonds from bondholders, and a break in the spread is not a commonly used expression.

13. **Answer A is correct.** The nominal yield on a bond is also known as the coupon rate, or interest rate the bond pays. This amount does not change over the life of the bond. Current yield, yield to maturity, and yield to put are all measures that are computed using the changing current price of the bonds in the market.

14. **Answer D is correct.** A bond issued at 7% that experiences rising interest rates in the market would be sold at a discount in the market to remain competitive. The current yield increases accordingly to bring the bond in line with the new higher interest rates of the market. The nominal yield remains at 7%.

15. **Answer D is correct.** Corporate bonds trade in 1/8ths, so a bond price of 102 1/4 represents a selling price of $1022.50 in the market. The 102 equals $1020, and the 1/4 represents $2.50.

16. **Answer B is correct.** The formula for computing current yield is the coupon rate divided by the current market price. In this example, the current yield is 7% divided by the current market price of 93, which equals 7.53%.

17. **Answer B is correct.** A bond with a nominal yield or coupon rate of 8.25% would sell at a premium if interest rates were to decline in the market to 7.50%. The bond selling at $1100 would bring the yield in line with the current yield of 7.50%. The equation is 8.25% ÷ 1100 = 7.50%.

18. **Answer A is correct.** A bond selling in the market at a premium has a nominal yield as the highest yield on the bond. Remember, interest rates have an inverse effect on bond prices. Thus, if interest rates go down, the price of the bond increases in value, to bring the bond in line with the lower current interest rates.

19. **Answer A is correct.** A bond selling at a discount means that interest rates have gone up in the market. The nominal yield is the lowest yield of a discounted bond. The current yield is higher than nominal, and the yield to maturity is the highest yield.

20. **Answer B is correct.** An investor purchasing a bond at a discount of $100 ($900 purchase price) and holding the bond to maturity (15 years) is able to accrete the discounted amount of $100 ÷ 15 years = 6.67 per year on the bond.

21. **Answer A is correct.** Standard & Poor's highest credit rating is considered AAA because it uses all capital letters in its ratings. Moody's uses uppercase and lowercase letters for its highest rating of Aaa.

22. **Answer C is correct.** The lowest credit rating that Moody's gives to a security that is still considered investment grade is Baa.

23. **Answer C is correct.** The highest rating that Standard & Poor's and Fitch give to a speculative security is BB. Moody's has a comparable rating of Ba.

24. **Answer C is correct.** The lowest rating listed is Ba, and it is the only choice that would be considered a speculative security. BBB, Baa, and A are all considered investment grade ratings.

25. **Answer B is correct.** Similarly rated companies that issue debt with different terms to maturity pay different interest rates on their issues. The 30-year bonds expose the investor to an additional 10 years of interest rate exposure, so they pay a higher interest rate than the 20-year bonds.

Quick Check

Corporate Bonds

1. Of the following types of corporate debt, which are considered a secured debt?

   I. Commercial paper

   II. First mortgage bonds

   III. Second mortgage bonds

   IV. Debenture bonds

   ❍ A. I and II
   ❍ B. I, II, and III
   ❍ C. II and III
   ❍ D. I, II, III, and IV

Quick Answer: **63**
Detailed Answer: **64**

2. All the following characteristics of secured debt are true except for which one?

   ❍ A. Secured debt pays a lower interest rate.
   ❍ B. Secured debt receives a higher credit rating.
   ❍ C. The risk of default is nonexistent.
   ❍ D. Tangible assets are pledged.

Quick Answer: **63**
Detailed Answer: **64**

3. Collateral trust certificates are secured debt that is backed by which of the following collateral?

   ❍ A. A pledge of real property owned by the issuer
   ❍ B. A portfolio of negotiable securities owned by the issuer
   ❍ C. The good faith and credit worthiness of the issuer
   ❍ D. The product that the company is producing

Quick Check

4. A debenture bond issued by a company is backed by which of the following?

❍ A. A debit on the assets of the company
❍ B. The good faith and credit worthiness of the issuer
❍ C. The property pledged on the bond
❍ D. The plant and equipment of the issuer

Quick Answer: 63
Detailed Answer: 64

5. Of the following securities that could be issued by a company, which one has the highest borrowing costs?

❍ A. First mortgage bonds
❍ B. Debenture bonds
❍ C. Subordinate debentures
❍ D. Second mortgage bonds

Quick Answer: 63
Detailed Answer: 64

6. What is the conversion ratio on TNT convertible bonds issued at par that can be converted into TNT common shares for a price of $25.00?

❍ A. 25 to 1
❍ B. 50 to 1
❍ C. 40 to 1
❍ D. 4 to 1

Quick Answer: 63
Detailed Answer: 64

7. JTC convertible bonds are selling in the market at 110. The conversion ratio for the bonds is set at 25 to 1. At what price would the common stock be selling at parity with the convertible bonds?

❍ A. $40
❍ B. $42
❍ C. $44
❍ D. $46

Quick Answer: 63
Detailed Answer: 64

8. DDT Corporation issued convertible bonds with an interest rate of 7.10% with a conversion ratio of 18 to 1. The common shares of DDT are currently trading in the market at 57 1/4. At what price would the convertible bonds be selling in the market?

❍ A. 100
❍ B. 103
❍ C. 107
❍ D. 109

Quick Answer: 63
Detailed Answer: 64

Quick Check

9. The King Company issued convertible bonds with a conversion ratio of 22 to 1 in the market. The bonds are currently selling at 114 1/2 in the market. The common stock of King Company is selling at $52.50 in the market. An arbitrage dealer is closely watching the price movements of both securities. What would he do at this point?

   ❍ A. Wait for the stock to go down in value.
   ❍ B. Buy the convertible bond and convert to the common shares.
   ❍ C. Buy the common shares and wait for the conversion.
   ❍ D. Sell the stock short and go long on the bonds.

Quick Answer: 63
Detailed Answer: 65

10. RTC Company issued a convertible bond with a 7.44% coupon rate and a conversion ratio of 20 to 1 in the market. RTC convertible bonds are selling in the market at 100 1/2, and the stock is selling in the market at 50 1/4. RTC received approval to perform a 2-for-1 forward split on its stock. How does this affect the convertible bond?

   ❍ A. It does not affect the bond at all.
   ❍ B. The bond drops in value to 50 1/8.
   ❍ C. The conversion ratio goes to 10 to 1.
   ❍ D. The conversion ratio goes to 40 to 1.

Quick Answer: 63
Detailed Answer: 65

11. HTH Corporation issued convertible bonds in the market with a conversion ratio of 25 to 1. The bonds are currently selling at 102 1/2 in the market, and the stock is selling in the market at $41. HTH Corporation declares a stock dividend of 10% to all shareholders. What effect does this have on the convertible bonds?

   ❍ A. It has no effect on the bonds.
   ❍ B. It has no effect on the stock price.
   ❍ C. It lowers the conversion ratio to 22.5 to 1.
   ❍ D. It increases the conversion ratio to 27.5 to 1.

Quick Answer: 63
Detailed Answer: 65

12. STS Corporation issued callable convertible bonds in the market with a 7.34% coupon. The conversion ratio on the bonds is 24 to 1. The bonds were issued at par and are currently selling at 104 in the market. The stock is currently selling at $44 in the market, and the bonds are callable at 105. STS elects to call in the bonds per the call provision of the indenture. What should the investor do?

   ❍ A. Convert his bonds to common shares immediately.
   ❍ B. Allow the company to call his bonds at 105.
   ❍ C. Wait for the bonds to go up in value to 107.
   ❍ D. Wait for the stock to go up in value further.

Quick Answer: 63
Detailed Answer: 65

Quick Check

13. Which of the following types of bonds pays interest to bondholders on a regular semi-annual basis?
   - ❍ A. Moral obligation bonds
   - ❍ B. Adjustment bonds
   - ❍ C. Debenture bonds
   - ❍ D. Zero coupon bonds

Quick Answer: **63**
Detailed Answer: **65**

14. If a foreign company issues American dollar–denominated bonds in the United States and sells these bonds to U.S. investors, they are defined as which of the following?
   - ❍ A. Eurodollar bonds
   - ❍ B. Yankee bonds
   - ❍ C. Sovereign bonds
   - ❍ D. Foreign exchange bonds

Quick Answer: **63**
Detailed Answer: **65**

15. List in order from highest to lowest the following bonds and the interest rates they pay to investors in the market.

   Junk bonds, guaranteed bonds, debenture bonds, zero bonds
   - ❍ A. Junk bonds, debenture bonds, guaranteed bonds, zero bonds
   - ❍ B. Zero bonds, guaranteed bonds, debenture bonds, junk bonds
   - ❍ C. Debenture bonds, junk bonds, guaranteed bonds, zero bonds
   - ❍ D. Guaranteed bonds, junk bonds, debenture bonds, zero bonds

Quick Answer: **63**
Detailed Answer: **65**

16. Corporate bonds that are traded on the Over-the-Counter market print the latest prices on the bonds in which of the following publications?
   - ❍ A. Pink sheets
   - ❍ B. Blue list
   - ❍ C. Yellow sheets
   - ❍ D. *The Daily Bond Buyer*

Quick Answer: **63**
Detailed Answer: **66**

Quick Check

17. The following bond is listed in the newspaper. Which of the following statements are true regarding this bond?

    BAB Bonds 7% Debent. 02/10 Jan/July 96 1/8 unchgd.

    I. The bond is backed by the good faith and credit worthiness of BAB.

    II. The bonds are callable.

    III. The bond is selling at a premium.

    IV. The bond has not moved in price from the previous day.

    ❍ A. I and II
    ❍ B. I and III
    ❍ C. I, III, and IV
    ❍ D. I, II, and IV

Quick Answer: **63**
Detailed Answer: **66**

18. Accrued interest on a corporate bond is computed on which of the following basis?

    ❍ A. Actual day/actual year
    ❍ B. Actual month/360-day year
    ❍ C. 30-day month/360-day year
    ❍ D. 30-day month/365-day year

Quick Answer: **63**
Detailed Answer: **66**

19. Which of the following is true about accrued interest on a corporate bond?

    ❍ A. Accrued interest is paid by the seller.
    ❍ B. Accrued interest is paid on settlement date.
    ❍ C. Accrued interest is computed on an actual/actual basis.
    ❍ D. Accrued interest is computed on an actual month/360-day year.

Quick Answer: **63**
Detailed Answer: **66**

20. Alexander purchases 10 HTH bonds with a coupon rate of 6.5% January 1/July 1 on Monday, June 15, from Jerry. The trade settles regular way. How many days of interest is Jerry entitled to be paid in this transaction?

    ❍ A. 168 days of interest
    ❍ B. 169 days of interest
    ❍ C. 167 days of interest
    ❍ D. 177 days of interest

Quick Answer: **63**
Detailed Answer: **66**

Quick Check

21. Harry purchases the following bonds from Rich on September 11 in a cash settlement transaction: 5 GHI convertible bonds 8.10% January 1/July 1 maturing 2009. How many days of interest is Rich entitled to receive in this transaction?

   ❍ A. 70 days of interest
   ❍ B. 71 days of interest
   ❍ C. 72 days of interest
   ❍ D. 251 days of interest

Quick Answer: 63
Detailed Answer: 66

22. Zero coupon bonds that are sold at a deep discount pay which of the following to bondholders?

   ❍ A. The interest rate of the issue
   ❍ B. Phantom interest
   ❍ C. Amortized interest
   ❍ D. None of the above

Quick Answer: 63
Detailed Answer: 67

23. An investor purchasing a corporate bond is exposed to all the following risks except for which one?

   ❍ A. Interest rate risk
   ❍ B. Purchasing power risk
   ❍ C. Liquidity risk
   ❍ D. Actuarial risk

Quick Answer: 63
Detailed Answer: 67

24. If the U.S. government changes the tax structure of capital gains, it exposes a bondholder to what type of risk?

   ❍ A. Liquidity risk
   ❍ B. Market risk
   ❍ C. Legislative risk
   ❍ D. Reinvestment risk

Quick Answer: 63
Detailed Answer: 67

25. A flat yield curve affects short- and long-term bonds in which of the following ways?

   ❍ A. Short-term rates drop and long-term rates drop.
   ❍ B. Short-term rates rise and long-term rates drop.
   ❍ C. Short-term rates rise and long-term rates rise.
   ❍ D. Short-term rates remain stable and long-term rates remain stable.

Quick Answer: 63
Detailed Answer: 67

Quick Check Answer Key

1. C
2. C
3. B
4. B
5. C
6. A
7. C
8. B
9. B
10. D
11. D
12. A
13. C
14. B
15. A
16. C
17. D
18. C
19. B
20. C
21. B
22. B
23. D
24. C
25. C

Answers and Explanations

1. **Answer C is correct.** First and second mortgage bonds are examples of secured debt. They are backed by real property pledged by the issuer. Commercial paper is short term borrowing by a corporation and is considered debentures or is simply backed by the good faith and credit worthiness of the issuer.

2. **Answer C is correct.** Secured debt issued by a corporation pays a lower interest rate to bondholders than the same security that is unsecured. Because of the collateral or tangible assets that are pledged, the rating agencies give the issue a higher credit rating. Despite the bonds being secured, it does not mean that the bonds could not default. If they do default, the pledged assets are liquidated to pay off the bondholders.

3. **Answer B is correct.** Collateral trust certificates are issued by a company that pledges a portfolio of securities to secure the debt. First mortgage bonds are an example of real property being pledged, and a debenture bond is backed by the good faith and credit worthiness of the issuer.

4. **Answer B is correct.** Debenture bonds are issued by fairly stable companies who are able to borrow in the debt market based strictly on the issuer's good faith and credit worthiness. This type of issue does not have any specific collateral backing it. Property, plant, and equipment that are pledged to secure an issue are considered secured debt.

5. **Answer C is correct.** Secured debt is issued at a lower rate than unsecured debt because of the tangible assets backing the issue. Investors are willing to accept a lower interest rate, knowing that the issue is secured in some fashion. First and second mortgage bonds are considered secured debt. Debentures and subordinate debentures are considered unsecured debt. Subordinate debt is graded lower than the original debenture and thus incurs higher borrowing costs for the issuer.

6. **Answer A is correct.** A convertible bond issued at par value of $1000 that can be converted into common shares valued at $25 has a conversion ratio of 40 to 1. The equation is 40 shares × $25 = $1000.

7. **Answer C is correct.** A convertible bond selling at $1100 in the market with a conversion ratio of 25 to 1 needs the common shares to sell at $44 per share to be trading at parity. The equation is 44 × 25 = 1100.

8. **Answer B is correct.** A convertible bond with a conversion ratio of 18 to 1 and the common shares selling at 57 1/4 in the market mean that convertible bonds should sell very close to parity, which is 103, or $1030. The equation is 57 1/4 × 18 = $1030.50.

9. **Answer B is correct.** The King Company bonds are selling in the market at 114 1/2, or $1145 each. With the conversion ratio set at 22 to 1 and the common shares selling at $52.50, the shares are worth $1155, or $10 more than the bonds. An arbitrage dealer would watch this closely, buy the bonds at 114 1/2, and then convert them to the common shares for a $10 profit on each bond.

10. **Answer D is correct.** When a company has convertible bonds in the market and then declares a 2-for-1 forward stock split, the bond indenture requires that the conversion ratio be adjusted accordingly to bring the bonds in line with the after-split price of the common shares. The conversion ratio in this case is adjusted to 40 to 1.

11. **Answer D is correct.** A company with convertible bonds in the market that declares a stock dividend to be paid to shareholders requires that the conversion ratio be adjusted accordingly to reflect the stock dividend paid. In this example, the new conversion ratio is $25 \times 1.10 = 27.5$ to 1.

12. **Answer A is correct.** In this example, the bonds are selling at 104 or $1040 in the market with a conversion ratio of 24 to 1. With the common shares valued at $44 in the market, the bondholder can convert into shares that are worth a total of $1056 ($44 \times 24 = 1056$). If the bonds are called, the bondholder receives $1050 for each bond due to the call premium. It is to the bondholder's advantage to convert his bonds immediately to avoid the call and make a profit of $6.00 more on each bond.

13. **Answer C is correct.** All the examples except for debenture bonds trade flat in the market, that is, without interest payments. Debenture bonds are unsecured debt that is backed by the good faith and credit worthiness of the issuer. They pay interest semi-annually to holders. Moral obligation bonds are issued by municipalities with a moral obligation, but not a legal obligation, to pay. Adjustment bonds are issued by corporations in distress and pay interest when the company rebounds. Zero coupon bonds are sold at a deep discount and mature at par, without semi-annual interest payments.

14. **Answer B is correct.** A foreign company issuing American dollar–denominated bonds in the United States is issuing Yankee bonds. Each of the other choices are nonexistent.

15. **Answer A is correct.** In this question, you must decide which of the following bonds would pay the highest interest costs and then sequentially down to the lowest costs. Zero coupon bonds pay no interest, so they are the lowest. Guaranteed bonds are considered secured debt, so they pay the second lowest rate. Debenture bonds are backed by the good faith and credit worthiness of the issuer, so they pay the second highest. Junk bonds, even though they are also considered debenture bonds, are considered to be speculative, so they pay the highest interest rate.

16. **Answer C is correct.** Because there is no real-time reporting of corporate bond prices, they are printed daily in the yellow sheets. The blue list details municipal bonds. The pink sheets quote OTC stocks, and *The Daily Bond Buyer* services the municipal markets. The only other color is red for red herrings on prospectuses.

17. **Answer D is correct.** This bond is listed as a debenture bond and is backed by the good faith and credit worthiness of the issuer. The bonds are callable, which is discernable from the 02/10, which means the bonds are callable in the year 2002 and mature in 2010. The bond is not selling at a premium but rather at a discount (96 1/8). The current reported price is the same as the previous day price as indicated by the unchgd. designation.

18. **Answer C is correct.** Corporate bonds accrue interest on a 30-day month and a 360-day year (the same as municipal bonds). Government bonds accrue on an actual/actual basis.

19. **Answer B is correct.** The only true statement is that accrued interest is paid to the seller on settlement date. The buyer pays accrued interest to the seller. Corporate bonds accrue interest on a 30-day month/ 360-day year.

20. **Answer C is correct.** The HTH bonds pay interest on January 1 and July 1. Jerry buys the bonds on June 15 in a regular-way transaction (trade date + 3 days). The bonds last paid interest on January 1. Corporate bonds accrue interest on a 30-day month/360-day year. Harry owes interest on the following:

    January = 30 days
    February = 30 days
    March = 30 days
    April = 30 days
    May = 30 days
    June = 15 days + regular way settlement of 3 days – 1 (because you do not count settlement date)
    Total = 167 days of accrued interest owed

21. **Answer B is correct.** The GHI bonds pay interest on January 1 and July 1. Harry purchases the bonds on September 11 in a cash settlement trade (same day payment by 2:30 p.m.). The bonds last paid interest on July 1. Corporate bonds accrue interest on a 30-day month/360-day year. Harry is owed accrued interest for the following:

    July = 30 days
    August = 30 days
    September = 11 days (due to the cash settlement)
    Total = 71 days of accrued interest is owed

22. **Answer B is correct.** Zero coupon bonds sell at a deep discount and mature at par value. The bonds do not pay any interest (trade flat). Because of the fact that zero bonds sell at a deep discount and mature at par, the holder claims what is commonly referred to as phantom interest each year on the accretion of the bond. By claiming this phantom interest each year, the holder is actually accreting the bond so that when it matures, there is no capital gain on the bond.

23. **Answer D is correct.** Purchasers of corporate bonds are exposed to many different risks. They include interest rate risk (changing rates), purchasing power risk (inflation eats away at bond value), and liquidity risk (the transaction costs to sell the bond). Actuarial risk is associated to the insurance industry and does not affect bonds.

24. **Answer C is correct.** Changes in government policy or tax policy affect a bond through what is known as legislative risk. For instance, if the government increases taxes or changes the rules on capital gains, it could affect the price of the corporate bond.

25. **Answer C is correct.** A flat yield curve is caused by the tightening of money in the markets, making it harder to borrow. This causes interest rates to rise sharply. If this situation were to happen, then short term borrowing could pay a rate of interest close to that of the already existing long-term borrowers.

Quick Check

The Money Market

1. Instruments of the money market include which of the following securities?

   I. Jumbo certificates of deposit

   II. Treasury bills

   III. Commercial paper

   IV. Banker's acceptances

   ❍ A. I and III
   ❍ B. I, II, and III
   ❍ C. II, III, and IV
   ❍ D. I, II, III, and IV

Quick Answer: **76**
Detailed Answer: **77**

2. The role of the Federal Reserve Bank in the money markets is best described by which of the following statements?

   ❍ A. The Fed utilizes the money markets to sell its direct government obligations.
   ❍ B. The Fed utilizes the money markets to control the management of the nation's money supply.
   ❍ C. The Fed has no role in the money markets.
   ❍ D. The Fed is the only participant in the money markets.

Quick Answer: **76**
Detailed Answer: **77**

3. A rise in the discount rate impacts the overall economy in which of the following ways?

   ❍ A. A rise in the discount rate makes interest rates on loans increase.
   ❍ B. A rise in the discount rate makes banks lower their reserve requirements.
   ❍ C. A rise in the discount rate makes it easier for banks to borrow money.
   ❍ D. A rise in the discount rate gives a needed boost to a stagnant economy.

Quick Answer: **76**
Detailed Answer: **77**

Quick Check

4. If the Federal Reserve Bank raises the reserve requirement in the current market, how does this action affect the overall economy?
   - ❍ A. It sparks the economy.
   - ❍ B. It slows down the economy.
   - ❍ C. It makes borrowing cheaper.
   - ❍ D. It allows member banks to lend more.

Quick Answer: **76**
Detailed Answer: **77**

5. The Federal Reserve Bank uses which of the following money market instruments to fine-tune or contract the nation's overall money supply?
   - ❍ A. Issues banker's acceptances
   - ❍ B. Conducts repurchase agreements
   - ❍ C. Purchases certificates of deposit
   - ❍ D. Buys commercial paper

Quick Answer: **76**
Detailed Answer: **77**

6. If the Federal Reserve enters into a reverse repurchase agreement, which statements are true?

   I. The reverse repo expands the money supply.

   II. The reverse repo constricts the money supply.

   III. The reverse repo has the Fed purchasing securities.

   IV. The reverse repo has the Fed selling securities.

   - ❍ A. I only
   - ❍ B. II only
   - ❍ C. I and III
   - ❍ D. II and IV

Quick Answer: **76**
Detailed Answer: **77**

7. What is the most common type of security typically used in repurchase agreements and reverse repurchase agreements?
   - ❍ A. Commercial paper
   - ❍ B. Fed deposit
   - ❍ C. Treasury bill
   - ❍ D. Banker's acceptance

Quick Answer: **76**
Detailed Answer: **77**

Quick Check

8. If a commercial bank conducts a repurchase agreement with a large corporation, which of the following statements are considered true?

    I. Only the Federal Reserve can conduct repurchase agreements.

    II. The bank has sold securities through the repurchase agreement.

    III. The bank has purchased securities through the repurchase agreement.

    IV. The corporation could only do a repurchase agreement with the Fed.

    ❍ A. I only
    ❍ B. II only
    ❍ C. III only
    ❍ D. I and IV

Quick Answer: **76**
Detailed Answer: **77**

9. Which statement is not true regarding commercial paper?
    ❍ A. Commercial paper is issued by established companies with solid credit ratings.
    ❍ B. Commercial paper is redeemed at par value.
    ❍ C. Commercial paper can never be issued for longer than 270 days.
    ❍ D. It is cheaper for a corporation to borrow from a bank at the prime rate.

Quick Answer: **76**
Detailed Answer: **78**

10. Commercial paper that is traded in the money markets is considered which type of investment?
    ❍ A. An unsecured debt
    ❍ B. A secured debt
    ❍ C. A long-term debt
    ❍ D. A guaranteed debt

Quick Answer: **76**
Detailed Answer: **78**

11. All the following entities purchase jumbo certificates of deposit in the money market except for which one?
    ❍ A. The Federal Reserve Bank
    ❍ B. Pension funds
    ❍ C. Commercial banks
    ❍ D. Money market funds

Quick Answer: **76**
Detailed Answer: **78**

Quick Check

12. A foreign corporation receiving a banker's acceptance from an American importer for payment can do which of the following with the banker's acceptance?

    I. Ship the goods after the banker's acceptance matures

    II. Ship the goods upon a guarantee from the American bank

    III. Sell the banker's acceptance at a discount before it matures

    IV. It must wait for the banker's acceptance to mature before it can be redeemed.

    ❍ A. I only
    ❍ B. II only
    ❍ C. I and IV
    ❍ D. II and III

Quick Answer: **76**
Detailed Answer: **78**

13. Which statements are true regarding the Federal funds rate?

    I. Federal funds are not a money market instrument.

    II. The Federal funds rate is set by the Federal Reserve Bank.

    III. The Federal funds rate is the least volatile rate in the market.

    IV. The Federal funds rate is set by large commercial banks.

    ❍ A. I and II
    ❍ B. II and III
    ❍ C. II only
    ❍ D. IV only

Quick Answer: **76**
Detailed Answer: **78**

14. Overnight borrowing between commercial banks that are part of the Federal Reserve system is representative of which rate?

    ❍ A. Fed funds rate
    ❍ B. Discount rate
    ❍ C. Prime rate
    ❍ D. Broker loan rate

Quick Answer: **76**
Detailed Answer: **78**

15. Which of the following interest rates is most affected by the Federal Reserve Bank raising reserve requirements on member banks?

    ❍ A. Prime rate
    ❍ B. Fed funds rate
    ❍ C. Broker loan rate
    ❍ D. Discount rate

Quick Answer: **76**
Detailed Answer: **78**

Quick Check

16. LIBOR is an acronym for which of the following?

Quick Answer: 76
Detailed Answer: 79

- ❍ A. Long-Term Interest Bearing Option on Repurchase agreements
- ❍ B. London Interbank Offered Rate
- ❍ C. Lisbon Interbank Offered Rate
- ❍ D. Long-Term Interest Bearing Offered Rate

17. What regulation governs the broker loan rate established by the Federal Reserve Bank on the interest rate at which brokers can borrow from banks to finance margin accounts?

Quick Answer: 76
Detailed Answer: 79

- ❍ A. Regulation T
- ❍ B. Regulation G
- ❍ C. Regulation U
- ❍ D. Regulation Q

18. Which of the following rates are not set by the Federal Reserve Bank in the market?

Quick Answer: 76
Detailed Answer: 79

I. Discount rate

II. Prime rate

III. Broker loan rate

IV. Fed funds rate

- ❍ A. I and II
- ❍ B. I and III
- ❍ C. II and III
- ❍ D. II and IV

19. A money market fund has all the following characteristics except for which of the following?

Quick Answer: 76
Detailed Answer: 79

I. Shares are sold at the net asset value.

II. Shares are maintained at $1.00.

III. Money market funds are considered to be exempt securities and do not have to file with the SEC.

IV. Money market funds are sold by an open-ended investment company.

- ❍ A. I only
- ❍ B. II only
- ❍ C. I and III
- ❍ D. II and IV

Quick Check

20. If Elite bank has extensive amounts of customer withdrawals on a given day and falls below the 10% mandatory Federal Reserve Bank reserve requirement, where can it borrow the necessary funds to meet its requirement?
   - ❍ A. The discount window
   - ❍ B. Other commercial banks
   - ❍ C. The U.S. Treasury
   - ❍ D. A broker dealer

Quick Answer: **76**
Detailed Answer: **79**

21. Which method of borrowing is considered the core of the money markets?
   - ❍ A. Repurchase agreements
   - ❍ B. Reverse repos
   - ❍ C. Commercial paper
   - ❍ D. Federal funds

Quick Answer: **76**
Detailed Answer: **79**

22. Most instruments of the money market are considered what type of an investment to investors?
   - ❍ A. Speculative
   - ❍ B. Derivative based
   - ❍ C. Investment grade
   - ❍ D. Equity securities

Quick Answer: **76**
Detailed Answer: **79**

23. Which of the following money market instruments has the longest life expectancy in the money markets?
   - ❍ A. Fed funds
   - ❍ B. Repurchase agreements
   - ❍ C. Commercial paper
   - ❍ D. Eurodollar loans

Quick Answer: **76**
Detailed Answer: **80**

24. Which of the following interest rates changes most frequently in the market?
   - ❍ A. Discount rate
   - ❍ B. Fed funds rate
   - ❍ C. Prime rate
   - ❍ D. LIBOR rate

Quick Answer: **76**
Detailed Answer: **80**

Quick Check

25. Deposits that are kept at the Federal Reserve Bank to meet the member bank reserve requirements have which of the following characteristics?

Quick Answer: 76
Detailed Answer: 80

I. Deposited funds earn interest.

II. Deposited funds pay no interest.

III. This amount changes on a daily basis.

IV. Reserve amounts are set for a bank's fiscal year.

- ❍ A. I only
- ❍ B. II only
- ❍ C. II and III
- ❍ D. I and IV

Quick Check Answer Key

1. D
2. B
3. A
4. B
5. B
6. D
7. C
8. B
9. D
10. A
11. A
12. D
13. D
14. A
15. B
16. B
17. C
18. D
19. D
20. A
21. D
22. C
23. C
24. B
25. C

Answer and Explanations

1. **Answer D is correct.** All the securities listed are considered instruments of the money market. They are all debt securities that have a limited maturity of less than one year, and all trade actively as negotiable securities.

2. **Answer B is correct.** The Federal Reserve is the largest player in the money market because it uses repurchase and reverse repurchase agreements, as well as Treasury bills, to control the nation's money supply. It buys and sells these securities with the primary dealers it has appointed. The Fed does not use the money markets to directly issue government obligations.

3. **Answer A is correct.** If the Federal Reserve Bank raises the discount rate, it is more expensive for member banks to borrow directly from the Fed at the discount window. This action makes it more expensive for banks to borrow and, in turn, makes it more expensive for corporations to borrow from banks. This slows down borrowing and the overall economy.

4. **Answer B is correct.** A rise in reserve requirements by the Fed forces member banks to deposit additional funds with the Fed. This takes available funds out of the market, making interest rates for borrowing rise. This method is a common way for the Fed to slow down an overheated economy.

5. **Answer B is correct.** When the Fed wants to either fine-tune or slow down the economy, it can enter into repurchase agreements, where it sells securities to banks with the prospect of buying them back at a later date. This action takes funds out of the market, causing the economy to slow down. Banker's acceptances, CDs, and commercial paper are not used by the Fed to control the money supply.

6. **Answer D is correct.** When the Fed uses a reverse repurchase agreement, it is selling securities to primary dealers with the plan to buy them back at a later date. This action takes funds out of the markets (by the sale), shrinking the money supply and constricting the overall economy.

7. **Answer C is correct.** Repurchase agreements and reverse repos are conducted by the Fed with the purchase and sale of government securities. This includes Treasury bills. The other instruments of commercial paper and banker's acceptances are corporate and bank securities and are not used by the Fed. Fed fund deposits are funds that are held by the Fed from member banks meeting reserve requirements.

8. **Answer B is correct.** When a bank does a repurchase agreement, it sells securities to a corporation with the plan to buy them back at a later date. This brings funds into the bank, making it easier for the bank to lend additional funds.

9. **Answer D is correct.** Commercial paper is high-grade, short-term borrowing by major companies that is sold at a discount and redeemed at par. It has a maturity of 7 to 270 days. Corporations issue commercial paper because they can do so at a better rate than if they went to a bank and borrowed at the prime rate.

10. **Answer A is correct.** Commercial paper is an unsecured debt or debenture issued by a corporation. The only guarantee is based on the credit worthiness of the issuer. It is a short-term money market instrument with a maximum maturity of 270 days, to avoid having to register with the SEC.

11. **Answer A is correct.** Jumbo CDs are actively traded in the money markets by banks, pension funds, and money market mutual funds. The Fed does not actively trade these securities because it deals primarily with T-bills when conducting repurchase agreements and reverse repurchase agreements.

12. **Answer D is correct.** A banker's acceptance allows the exporter to ship the goods when it knows that the banker's acceptance has been guaranteed by the issuing bank. The exporter can hold the security to maturity or sell it at a discount after it is guaranteed.

13. **Answer D is correct.** Federal funds are a money market instrument. They are funds that are used for overnight borrowing between commercial banks needing to meet Federal Reserve requirements. The rate of interest on these loans changes almost daily and is the most volatile rate in the market.

14. **Answer A is correct.** The Fed funds rate is the rate that banks use to lend to each other to meet reserve requirements of the Federal Reserve Bank. They are known as overnight loans because each day, some banks need extra reserves to meet the requirement set by the Fed, but other banks have excess reserves. The banks with an excess lend to the banks in need of reserves. It is a very volatile rate that changes daily, and it is set by the major commercial banks in the country.

15. **Answer B is correct.** If the Federal Reserve Bank raises reserve requirements, it is requiring member banks to keep additional funds in reserve at the Fed. This causes some banks to have to borrow overnight to meet the additional reserve requirements. Member banks with excess reserves are willing to loan their excess reserves at the Fed funds rate. This is the most volatile rate in the market because it changes almost daily. So an increase in reserve requirements raises the volatile Fed funds rate.

16. **Answer B is correct.** LIBOR stands for the London Interbank Offered Rate. It is the rate that most international banks in need of loans charge each other to borrow. The less credit worthy a borrower, the higher the LIBOR rate, because it adds points to the loan. For example, it could be determined that a third-world country can borrow at the LIBOR rate + 1 when borrowing.

17. **Answer C is correct.** The regulation that governs the amount that banks are permitted to lend to customers buying securities on margin is established under Regulation U. Regulation T governs the amount that brokerages can lend to customers, as well as the amount of margin a customer must put up. Regulation G governs the institutions other than banks, brokers, or dealers that extend credit to individuals to purchase or carry securities. Regulation Q is the Federal Reserve Board ceiling that banks and other lending institutions can pay on savings and other time deposits.

18. **Answer D is correct.** The Federal Reserve Bank sets the discount rate and the broker loan rate. The prime rate is set by major commercial banks in lending to their best corporate customers, and the Fed funds rate is set by commercial banks lending to other banks to meet reserve requirements for overnight borrowing.

19. **Answer D is correct.** Money market funds are large mutual funds that invest primarily in money market instruments for their safety and relative ease of trading. The shares of money market funds are set at $1.00 each with fractional shares allowed. They are sold as an open-end investment company that can continually issue new shares. They are not exempt securities because they are considered a mutual fund that is required to register with the SEC.

20. **Answer A is correct.** A member bank in need of reserves can borrow as a last resort from the Federal Reserve Bank discount window. This is a privilege and not a right of member banks, and it is discouraged by the Fed. The first place where the bank would go would be the Fed funds market, but that was not a choice. The bank could not borrow from another commercial bank at the prime rate because that rate is set for corporate borrowers.

21. **Answer D is correct.** Although all the choices are important instruments of the money markets, the core of the money markets is considered Fed funds. Banks that must meet their changing reserve requirements do so in the money market by borrowing and lending Fed funds daily.

22. **Answer C is correct.** Money market instruments are considered high-grade, high-quality investments that have a maturity under one year. They are not derivative based as options are, nor do they trade equity securities such as common stocks in the money markets.

23. **Answer C is correct.** Commercial paper has a maximum maturity of 270 days. Fed funds are usually used for overnight borrowing to meet Federal Reserve Bank requirements. Eurodollar loans are also very short term in duration, when banks who are in need of meeting reserve requirements as a last resort go for overnight borrowing. Repurchase agreements are the selling of T-bills by a dealer with the plan to buy them back at future date that is typically 15 to 30 days in the future.

24. **Answer B is correct.** The most volatile of all interest rates is the Fed funds rate, which is used for overnight borrowing by banks in need of meeting reserve requirements. This rate is established by large commercial banks and can change daily.

25. **Answer C is correct.** Reserves that are deposited with the Federal Reserve Bank are non–interest-bearing funds for commercial banks. Because of this, the Fed funds market is important to banks that have excess funds which they can lend at a rate of interest to those banks in need of reserves. The amount of reserves changes daily for each bank as deposits come in and payments go out of the bank.

Quick Check

Government Debt Securities

1. Which securities are considered a direct obligation of the United States government:

   I. T-bills

   II. T-notes

   III. FNMA bonds

   IV. Strips

   ❍ A. I and II
   ❍ B. I, II, and III
   ❍ C. I, II, and IV
   ❍ D. I, II, III, and IV

Quick Answer: **89**
Detailed Answer: **90**

2. T-bills can be issued in all the following maturities except for which one?

   ❍ A. 13 weeks
   ❍ B. 26 weeks
   ❍ C. 39 weeks
   ❍ D. 52 weeks

Quick Answer: **89**
Detailed Answer: **90**

Quick Check

3. Which of the following government securities pay an investor interest for the time that she holds the security?

Quick Answer: 89
Detailed Answer: 90

I. T-bills

II. T-notes

III. T-bonds

IV. Strips

- ❍ A. I and IV
- ❍ B. I, II, and III
- ❍ C. II and III
- ❍ D. I, II, III, and IV

4. Which statements are true about the issuance of Treasury bills by the United States government?

Quick Answer: 89
Detailed Answer: 90

I. The T-bill has a maturity of up to one year maximum.

II. The T-bill pays the holder interest once per year.

III. The T-bill is sold on a discounted yield basis.

IV. The T-bill is sold on a competitive versus a noncompetitive bid basis.

- ❍ A. I and II
- ❍ B. I, II, and III
- ❍ C. I, III, and IV
- ❍ D. I, II, III, and IV

Quick Check

5. An investor decides to invest a recent inheritance he has received in the latest government issued T-bill being auctioned the following week. Which statements are true about the purchase?

I. The minimum purchase must be for $1000.

II. The investor receives a physical certificate on his purchase.

III. The investor must submit a bid on the rate he wants to receive.

IV. The T-bill pays the holder interest up front.

❍ A. I only
❍ B. I and III
❍ C. I, II, and III
❍ D. I, II, III, and IV

Quick Answer: **89**
Detailed Answer: **90**

6. The United States government has decided to issue $5 billion worth of T-bills in the coming week. There are $3 billion worth of competitive bids and $4 billion worth of noncompetitive bids for the issue. How does the government allocate the T-bills that were bid on?

❍ A. The $3 billion of competitive bids are filled, and $2 billion of the noncompetitive bids are filled.
❍ B. The government changes the auction to issue $7 billion worth of T-bills.
❍ C. The $4 billion of noncompetitive bids are filled and $1 billion of the competitive bids are filled.
❍ D. The government allows $2.5 billion of the competitive bids to be filled and $2.5 billion of the noncompetitive bids to be filled.

Quick Answer: **89**
Detailed Answer: **90**

Quick Check

7. The United States government received $5 billion worth of noncompetitive bids in a recent T-bill auction. Which of the following statements is true regarding these bids?

   I. All the bids are filled by the government.

   II. The minimum noncompetitive bid must be for $100,000.

   III. The bids are executed at the average price of all accepted competitive bids.

   IV. The T-bills issued in the noncompetitive bid offer pay interest once for the holding period.

   ❍ A. I and II
   ❍ B. I and III
   ❍ C. I, II, and III
   ❍ D. I, II, III, and IV

Quick Answer: **89**
Detailed Answer: **90**

8. T-bills are offered each Monday by the U.S. government to competitive bidders and noncompetitive bidders. An individual has $500,000 in cash she wants to invest in T-bills. What type of tender can she conduct?

   ❍ A. She can enter a competitive bid for $500,000.
   ❍ B. She can enter 5 separate noncompetitive bids for $100,000 each.
   ❍ C. She can enter one noncompetitive bid for $500,000.
   ❍ D. She can enter bids for $500,000 on both the competitive side and the noncompetitive side and take the best price.

Quick Answer: **89**
Detailed Answer: **90**

9. All the following securities pay federal income taxes on interest earned for the holder except which one?

   ❍ A. Corporate bonds
   ❍ B. T-bonds
   ❍ C. Preferred stock
   ❍ D. Common stock

Quick Answer: **89**
Detailed Answer: **91**

10. All the following issues pay a holder interest on a semi-annual basis except which one?

   ❍ A. A 52-week T-bill
   ❍ B. A 1-year T-note
   ❍ C. A 30-year T-bond
   ❍ D. A 20-year municipal bond

Quick Answer: **89**
Detailed Answer: **91**

Quick Check

11. Eric purchased a 10-year T-note in the market. The note has all the following characteristics except for which one?

Quick Answer: **89**
Detailed Answer: **91**

- ❍ A. It is callable with five years left to maturity.
- ❍ B. It is quoted in 32nds.
- ❍ C. It pays interest on a semi-annual basis.
- ❍ D. It can be purchased in denominations of $1000.

12. A Treasury note that is quoted at 92.10 in the market has a market value of which of the following?

Quick Answer: **89**
Detailed Answer: **91**

- ❍ A. $920.10
- ❍ B. $921.00
- ❍ C. $923.13
- ❍ D. $920.13

13. Steve owns five T-notes that are currently priced in the market at $102.18. If he sells his holdings at this price, what does he receive on settlement, excluding accrued interest?

Quick Answer: **89**
Detailed Answer: **91**

- ❍ A. $5010.90
- ❍ B. $5100.90
- ❍ C. $5114.05
- ❍ D. $5128.15

14. Owen purchased 10 30-year 6.44% Treasury bonds in the market at par value. Which statements are true regarding the purchase of these bonds?

Quick Answer: **89**
Detailed Answer: **91**

I. Owen receives a physical certificate for his purchase from the transfer agent.

II. The bonds are redeemed at par.

III. The bonds are callable after 25 years.

IV. The bonds pays interest semi-annually.

- ❍ A. I, III, and IV
- ❍ B. I, II, and III
- ❍ C. II, III, and IV
- ❍ D. I, II, III, and IV

Quick Check

15. Which of the following entities can bid on T-bills in a competitive bidding process known as a Dutch auction?

    I. Primary dealers

    II. Secondary dealers

    III. The general public

    IV. All of the above

    ❍ A. IV
    ❍ B. I only
    ❍ C. I and II
    ❍ D. I and III

Quick Answer: **89**
Detailed Answer: **91**

16. An individual received $1000 as a bonus from his employer that he wants to use to purchase government securities. Which of the following securities can he purchase with his $1000?

    I. A 52-week T-bill

    II. A 2-year T-note

    III. A 20-year T-bond

    IV. A 30-year T-bond

    ❍ A. I only
    ❍ B. I and II
    ❍ C. II and III
    ❍ D. I, II, III, and IV

Quick Answer: **89**
Detailed Answer: **91**

17. U.S. government securities trade in which of the following markets after they are issued?

    I. NYSE

    II. AMEX

    III. Over the Counter

    IV. Directly from the Fed

    ❍ A. I only
    ❍ B. I and II
    ❍ C. III
    ❍ D. I, II, III, and IV

Quick Answer: **89**
Detailed Answer: **91**

Quick Check

18. Jose has $10,000 that he wants to use to purchase a 26-week T-bill. The T-bill has a discounted yield of 5.50%. What does he pay for the T-bill?
    - ❍ A. $10,000
    - ❍ B. $9450
    - ❍ C. $9725
    - ❍ D. $9945

Quick Answer: 89
Detailed Answer: 91

19. Larry purchased a 13-week $10,000 T-bill on a noncompetitive bid basis with a discounted yield of 6%. What price did he pay for the T-bill, and what amount will he receive at maturity?
    - ❍ A. He paid $10,000; it matures at $10,600
    - ❍ B. He paid $10,000; it matures at $10,150
    - ❍ C. He paid $9850; it matures at $10,000
    - ❍ D. He paid $9850; it matures at $10,150

Quick Answer: 89
Detailed Answer: 92

20. If the U.S. government issues $10 billion of 52-week T-bills paying a discounted yield of 5%, what does the government receive in usable funds at the conclusion of the auction?
    - ❍ A. $10 billion
    - ❍ B. $9.5 billion
    - ❍ C. $10.5 billion
    - ❍ D. None of the above

Quick Answer: 89
Detailed Answer: 92

21. Eddie purchased a 52-week $10,000 T-bill with a discounted yield of 5.50% in the market. Three weeks later, the T-bill is quoted in the financial papers at 5.30%. What happened to the T-bill value?
    - ❍ A. The value increased.
    - ❍ B. The value decreased.
    - ❍ C. The value did not change.
    - ❍ D. It matures at an amount less than $10,000.

Quick Answer: 89
Detailed Answer: 92

22. Which of the following securities has the highest yield for an investor in a bull market with stable interest rates?
    - ❍ A. 52-week T-bills
    - ❍ B. 10-year T-notes
    - ❍ C. 20-year T-bonds
    - ❍ D. 30-year T-bonds

Quick Answer: 89
Detailed Answer: 92

Quick Check

23. A 30-year T-bond is quoted as a percentage of par in the newspaper. It is selling at a small discount. Which of the following quotes is representative of the bond quote?
    - ❍ A. 90 1/8
    - ❍ B. 95 7/8
    - ❍ C. 97.08
    - ❍ D. 101.08

Quick Answer: **89**
Detailed Answer: **92**

24. Regular way settlement on government-issued Treasury securities is which of the following?
    - ❍ A. Trade date + 3
    - ❍ B. Trade date + 1
    - ❍ C. Trade date + 5
    - ❍ D. Same-day settlement

Quick Answer: **89**
Detailed Answer: **92**

25. Accrued interest on Treasury bonds is calculated on which of the following terms?
    - ❍ A. 30-day month/360-day year
    - ❍ B. 30-day month/365-day year
    - ❍ C. Actual month/360-day year
    - ❍ D. Actual month/365-day year

Quick Answer: **89**
Detailed Answer: **92**

Quick Check Answer Key

1. A
2. C
3. C
4. C
5. A
6. C
7. B
8. C
9. B
10. A
11. A
12. C
13. D
14. C
15. C
16. D
17. C
18. B
19. C
20. B
21. A
22. D
23. C
24. B
25. D

Answers and Explanations

1. **Answer A is correct.** The Federal National Mortgage Association is considered agency debt that is implicitly backed by the federal government but is not considered a direct government obligation. T-notes and strips are not direct government obligations.

2. **Answer C is correct.** Treasury bills can be purchased by investors in either 13-week, 26-week, or 52-week durations. T-bills are not issued for a duration of 39 weeks by the government.

3. **Answer C is correct.** T-notes and T-bonds pay an investor interest on a semi-annual basis. T-bills are considered non–interest-bearing securities because they are sold at a discount to yield basis. Strips are actually zero coupon issues that have been created by stripping a pool of T-bonds into separate issues. They do not pay interest but rather are sold at a deep discount, and they mature at par.

4. **Answer C is correct.** T-bills are issued with a maximum maturity of 52 weeks. They are considered non–interest-bearing securities because they are sold at a discount to yield basis. They are also sold on a competitive versus a noncompetitive bid basis, with the average winning yields from the competitive side being the yield that all holders receive.

5. **Answer A is correct.** T-bills are sold at a discount to yield basis in a minimum denomination of $1000. They are issued in book entry form, so there is no physical certificate. Investors enter a noncompetitive bid that is based on the average winning bid on the competitive side. They are considered non–interest-bearing securities because they are sold at a discount to investors, maturing at par.

6. **Answer C is correct.** The U.S. government fills all noncompetitive bids on T-bills first before any competitive bids are filled. If the offering is for $5 billion and there is $4 billion of noncompetitive bids, they are all filled at the average winning competitive bid. Only $1 billion of the competitive bids is filled.

7. **Answer B is correct.** All noncompetitive bids entered in a T-bill offering must be filled. The minimum denomination on T-bills is for $1000, and the noncompetitive bids are issued at the winning average for all competitive bids. T-bills sell at a discount to yield and are considered non–interest-bearing securities.

8. **Answer C is correct.** Individual investors can only enter a noncompetitive bid for T-bills. An investor with $500,000 to invest tenders the entire amount in a noncompetitive bid.

9. **Answer B is correct.** Direct government issues such as T-bonds do not pay state or local income taxes on interest earned. The federal government and state governments have a reciprocating agreement not to tax each other in respect to debt issues.

10. **Answer A is correct.** Treasury bills are non–interest-bearing securities that are sold at a discount to yield basis. T-notes, T-bonds, and municipal bonds all pay interest on a semi-annual basis to bondholders.

11. **Answer A is correct.** The only direct government debt obligations that are callable are T-bonds, which are callable by the government in the last five years of their maturity.

12. **Answer C is correct.** A T-note that is quoted at 92.10 in the market sells for $923.13. Each point on a T-note has a value of $10. This is computed by multiplying 92 × $10 = $920 and then dividing 10 by 32, which equals .3125, or $3.13. Added together, the value is $923.13 for the T-note.

13. **Answer D is correct.** The T-notes are quoted at 102.18. The easiest way to compute this is to look at the 102 first; it means that the notes are worth $1020. (Each point is worth $10 = 102 × 10 = 1020.) To compute the 18/32nds you divide 18 by 32, which equals .5625, or $5.63. Add the two together, and the notes are worth $1025.63 each × 5 notes = $5128.15.

14. **Answer C is correct.** T-bonds are issued in book entry form only, so there is no physical certificate. They are redeemable at par upon maturity. They can be called in the last five years prior to maturity, and they pay semi-annual interest payments to holders.

15. **Answer C is correct.** Treasury competitive bids are held in a Dutch auction process. Both primary and secondary dealer competitive bids are accepted. The public enters their bids in a noncompetitive process, willing to accept the average winning bid on the competitive side.

16. **Answer D is correct.** An investor with $1000 to invest can purchase a T-bill, T-note, or T-bond from the U.S. Treasury. As of 1998, T-bills have a $1000 denomination, from a previous $10,000 minimum.

17. **Answer C is correct.** U.S. direct obligations trade in the Over-the-Counter market after being issued by the Federal Reserve Bank for the U.S. government. The secondary market for government securities is very active with more than 40 primary dealers maintaining inventories in government issues.

18. **Answer B is correct.** T-bills are issued on a discount to yield basis. A T-bill with a discounted yield of 5.50% with a 52-week maturity sells at $10,000 – $550 = $9450. The $10,000 T-bill costs $9450 and matures at par for the holder.

19. **Answer C is correct.** A T-bill is sold at a discount to yield basis. In this example, the T-bill is for 13 weeks, so you need to compute the amount of the discount and multiply by .25 (to represent 1/4 of a year). The equation is $10,000 × 6% = $600. Then, $600 × .25 = $150. The bill sells for $9850 and matures at a par value of $10,000.

20. **Answer B is correct.** T-bills are sold at a discount to yield basis. In this example, the U.S. government issued $10 billion worth of 52-week T-bills with a discounted yield of 5%. The bills are discounted 5%, or $500,000,000, leaving the government with $9.5 billion that matures in 52 weeks at 10 billion dollars.

21. **Answer A is correct.** T-bills sell at a discounted yield basis. A 52-week $10,000 T-bill selling at a discounted yield of 5.5% sells for $9450 and matures at par. A T-bill selling at a discounted yield basis of 5.3% sells for $9470 and matures at par. Thus, the bill has gone up in value. T-bills are quoted in discounted yields, with the lower the yield representing a higher value. This is counterintuitive, but as you can see, a discounted yield of 5.3% is worth more than a discounted yield of 5.5%.

22. **Answer D is correct.** Debt instruments typically follow a normal or ascending yield curve. This means that the longer the maturity, the higher the expected yield to an investor. In a stable economy, with normal reacting interest rates, the 30-year T-bond pays the highest yield to an investor.

23. **Answer C is correct.** Treasuries are quoted in 32nds, but corporate issues and municipal issues are quoted in 1/8ths. The only discounted quote representing 32nds is answer C for 97.08 (97 8/32nds) or a dollar value of $972.50.

24. **Answer B is correct.** Treasury securities settle regular way on a trade date + 1 basis. Corporate securities settle regular way on a trade date + 3 basis.

25. **Answer D is correct.** Accrued interest on Treasury securities is computed on an actual-month basis and a 365-day year. Corporate securities are quoted on a 30-day month and a 360-day year.

Agency Debt

Quick Check

1. All the following statements regarding agency debt issues are true except for which one?

   ❍ A. Agency debt is designed to assist the housing sector.
   ❍ B. Agency debt is designed to assist the farming sector.
   ❍ C. Agency debt is a direct obligation of the U.S. Government.
   ❍ D. Agency debt can be issued from a privatized company.

Quick Answer: **99**
Detailed Answer: **100**

2. Which of the following agency debt obligations has a AAA credit rating in the market?

   I. GNMA obligations

   II. FNMA obligations

   III. FHLMC obligations

   IV. None of the above

   ❍ A. I only
   ❍ B. II and III
   ❍ C. I, II, and III
   ❍ D. IV

Quick Answer: **99**
Detailed Answer: **100**

3. Income earned on notes and bonds that are issued by the Federal Farm Credit Bank is taxed in which manner for the holder?

   ❍ A. All income is taxed as ordinary income for the holder.
   ❍ B. Income is taxed at the state and local levels but not the federal level.
   ❍ C. Income is taxed at the federal level but not the state and local levels.
   ❍ D. All income earned is exempt from federal, state, and local taxes.

Quick Answer: **99**
Detailed Answer: **100**

Quick Check

4. Sallie Mae bonds that are issued to the public have all the following features except for which of the following?
   - ❍ A. They pay interest semi-annually.
   - ❍ B. They are rated AAA.
   - ❍ C. They are taxed only on the state and local levels.
   - ❍ D. They are a NYSE-listed company that is quoted in 32nds.

Quick Answer: 99
Detailed Answer: 100

5. Which of the following types of mortgages is backed by a guarantee from the U.S. Government?

   I. Veterans Administration

   II. Farmers Home Administration

   III. Conventional mortgages purchased by FNMA

   IV. Federal Housing Administration

   - ❍ A. I and II
   - ❍ B. I, II, and III
   - ❍ C. I, III, and IV
   - ❍ D. I, II, and IV

Quick Answer: 99
Detailed Answer: 100

6. The main role of the Federal Home Loan Bank system is to provide which of the following services?
   - ❍ A. Issue low rate mortgages to borrowers
   - ❍ B. Provide credit reserves to S&Ls and other mortgage lenders
   - ❍ C. Purchase mortgages from regional lending institutions
   - ❍ D. Guarantee mortgages that they directly issue

Quick Answer: 99
Detailed Answer: 100

7. The Federal National Mortgage Association was created to perform which of the following functions?

   I. Issue low-rate mortgages to the public

   II. Issue low-rate mortgages to Veterans

   III. Purchase FHA and VA guaranteed mortgages

   IV. Purchase conventional mortgages

   - ❍ A. I only
   - ❍ B. I and II
   - ❍ C. II and III
   - ❍ D. III and IV

Quick Answer: 99
Detailed Answer: 100

Quick Check

8. Which of the following statements are true regarding the issuing of debt securities by Fannie Mae?

   I. All issues are directly guaranteed by the U.S. Government.

   II. Income earned is exempt from federal taxes.

   III. Income earned is exempt from state and local taxes.

   IV. Fannie Mae securities are quoted in 32nds.

   ❍ A. I only
   ❍ B. I and II
   ❍ C. I, II, and III
   ❍ D. IV

Quick Answer: 99
Detailed Answer: 100

9. The Government National Mortgage Association is the only lending agency that is a direct part of the U.S. Government. Under what part of the government was the GNMA created?

   ❍ A. General Accounting Office
   ❍ B. Department of the Treasury
   ❍ C. Department of Housing and Urban Development
   ❍ D. Federal Deposit Insurance Company

Quick Answer: 99
Detailed Answer: 101

10. Income that is earned on Federal Home Loan mortgage company debt obligations is considered to be taxable in which manner?

   ❍ A. Exempt from federal taxes
   ❍ B. Exempt from state and local taxes
   ❍ C. Triple tax exempt
   ❍ D. Claimed on Federal, state, and local taxes as ordinary income

Quick Answer: 99
Detailed Answer: 101

11. Regular way settlement for agency-issued securities occurs on which of the following dates?

   ❍ A. Trade date + 3
   ❍ B. Trade date + 1
   ❍ C. Trade date + 5
   ❍ D. Same day settlement

Quick Answer: 99
Detailed Answer: 101

12. Agency debt obligations actively trade in which of the following secondary markets?

   ❍ A. NYSE
   ❍ B. AMEX
   ❍ C. Over the Counter
   ❍ D. Institutional network

Quick Answer: 99
Detailed Answer: 101

Quick Check

13. Pass-through certificates have all the following characteristics except which one?

Quick Answer: 99
Detailed Answer: 101

- ❍ A. The underlying mortgages are pooled.
- ❍ B. The mortgages are repackaged.
- ❍ C. The mortgages have been securitized.
- ❍ D. The mortgages are government guaranteed.

14. Which of the following government agencies issue pass-through certificates?

Quick Answer: 99
Detailed Answer: 101

I. GNMA

II. FNMA

III. Freddie Mac

IV. Export/import bank

- ❍ A. I only
- ❍ B. II and III
- ❍ C. IV only
- ❍ D. I, II, and III

15. The proceeds raised from a sale of pass-through certificates to the public by a government agency are used to perform which of the following functions?

Quick Answer: 99
Detailed Answer: 101

- ❍ A. Issue guaranteed mortgages to prospective homeowners
- ❍ B. Buy mortgages from lending institutions
- ❍ C. Sell guaranteed mortgages to low-income individuals
- ❍ D. Create a government lending institution

16. Ginnie Mae pass-through certificates that pay holders an interest rate of 7% have all the earned income that is received taxed in which manner?

Quick Answer: 99
Detailed Answer: 101

- ❍ A. Exempt from federal taxes
- ❍ B. Exempt from state and local taxes
- ❍ C. Exempt from federal and state taxes
- ❍ D. Fully taxable as ordinary income

17. A modified pass-through certificate has which of the following features?

Quick Answer: 99
Detailed Answer: 101

- ❍ A. It is guaranteed by the issuing agency.
- ❍ B. It is guaranteed by the lending institution.
- ❍ C. It is guaranteed by the homeowner.
- ❍ D. It is guaranteed by all of the above.

Quick Check

18. Which of the following risks are associated with mortgages that are part of pass-through certificates that have been issued by government agencies?

Quick Answer: 99
Detailed Answer: 101

I. Prepayment risk

II. Extension risk

III. Default risk

IV. Liquidity risk

- ❍ A. I only
- ❍ B. II only
- ❍ C. I, II, and III
- ❍ D. I, II, III, and IV

19. A collateralized mortgage obligation (CMO) has all the following characteristics except which one?

Quick Answer: 99
Detailed Answer: 102

- ❍ A. They are considered a derivative product.
- ❍ B. CMOs can be purchased in $1000 denominations.
- ❍ C. CMOs make payments to investors on a monthly basis.
- ❍ D. A CMO is exposed to the greatest prepayment risk.

20. To effectively deal with prepayment and extension risks associated to CMOs, brokers have created which of the following systems to deal with these risks?

Quick Answer: 99
Detailed Answer: 102

- ❍ A. The tranch system
- ❍ B. The repurchase system
- ❍ C. The collateral system
- ❍ D. The deferred system

21. Collateralized mortgage obligations that place mortgages in a limited-purpose finance subsidiary to retain ownership and then issue securities collateralized by these mortgages are known as what?

Quick Answer: 99
Detailed Answer: 102

- ❍ A. Pass-through bonds
- ❍ B. Pay-through bonds
- ❍ C. Collateral bonds
- ❍ D. Cash flow bonds

Quick Check

22. A 15-year CMO with five separate tranches retires which of the following tranches first?

    ❍ A. Tranch 1, representing years 1 through 3
    ❍ B. Tranch 2, representing years 4 through 6
    ❍ C. Tranch 3, representing years 7 through 9
    ❍ D. Tranch 4, representing years 10 through 12

Quick Answer: **99**
Detailed Answer: **102**

23. Because mortgage pools that are associated with CMOs are broken down into various cash flow streams, this allows the issuer to do which of the following?

    I. Issue CMOs with varying maturities

    II. Issue CMOs with varying interest rates

    III. Distribute prepayments to each tranch equally

    IV. Distribute prepayments to the earlier tranches first

    ❍ A. I and II
    ❍ B. I and III
    ❍ C. I, II, and III
    ❍ D. I, II, and IV

Quick Answer: **99**
Detailed Answer: **102**

24. A planned amortization class CMO has which of the following cash flow characteristics?

    I. A companion tranch to absorb prepayment risk

    II. A companion tranch to absorb extension risk

    III. Regular monthly payments are distributed to all tranches equally.

    IV. Prepayments are applied to earlier tranches first.

    ❍ A. I and II
    ❍ B. I, II, and III
    ❍ C. I, III, and IV
    ❍ D. I, II, III, and IV

Quick Answer: **99**
Detailed Answer: **102**

25. What is the current selling price of the agency debt bond maturing in May 2001?

    ❍ A. $1,020.12
    ❍ B. $1,020.09
    ❍ C. $1,021,20
    ❍ D. $1,023.75

Quick Answer: **99**
Detailed Answer: **102**

Quick Check Answer Key

1. C
2. C
3. C
4. C
5. D
6. B
7. D
8. D
9. C
10. D
11. B
12. C
13. D
14. D
15. B
16. D
17. A
18. C
19. D
20. A
21. B
22. A
23. C
24. B
25. D

Answers and Explanations

1. **Answer C is correct.** The government sponsors certain agency debt to assist both the housing and farming sectors of the economy. Certain agency debt is a direct obligation or guaranteed by the government. This includes GNMA issues and those of the export/import bank. All other agencies have an implied backing of the government.

2. **Answer C is correct.** All agency debt of GNMA, FNMA, and FHLMC have either a direct backing or, in the case of FNMA and FHLMC, the implicit backing of the U.S. Government. They are considered high-quality debt issues, and all have AAA ratings in the market.

3. **Answer C is correct.** The interest income that is earned on Federal Farm Credit Bank issues is exempt from state and local taxes but is required to be claimed on an investor's federal tax filing.

4. **Answer C is correct.** Income from Student Loan Marketing Association issues is paid semi-annually, and is exempt from state and local taxes but is included in federal taxes.

5. **Answer D is correct.** Certain mortgages that are issued by arms of the U.S. Government are guaranteed by the government. They include Veteran Administration mortgages to members of the armed forces, Farmers Home Administration mortgages offered in low-income rural areas, and Federal Housing Administration mortgages on residential properties. Conventional mortgages are issued from lending institutions such as banks, mortgage brokers, and S&Ls and are not guaranteed by the government.

6. **Answer B is correct.** The Federal Home Loan Bank system is designed to provide credit reserves to savings and loans and other mortgage lenders. They do not issue mortgages, nor do they guarantee mortgages. Unlike other agencies in the housing sector, they do not purchase mortgages from lenders, but rather they supply credit reserves for these lenders.

7. **Answer D is correct.** Fannie Mae provides needed funds in the mortgage market by purchasing Veterans Administration mortgages, FHA mortgages, and a large amount of conventional mortgages. Fannie Mae does not issue mortgages but rather provides funds to the mortgage market by purchasing existing mortgages.

8. **Answer D is correct.** Fannie Mae issues are quoted in 32nds. All interest earned on Fannie Mae bonds is taxable to the holder because the homeowners have already taken tax deductions on their mortgages. Fannie Mae bonds are implicitly backed by the government but are not considered to be guaranteed, as GNMA bonds are.

9. **Answer C is correct.** The Government National Mortgage Association is a government-owned corporation that was created as an agency under the Department of Housing and Urban Development or (HUD) in 1968.
10. **Answer D is correct.** All income that is earned by investors on Freddie Mac securities is taxed on the federal, state, and local levels. The homeowners have already taken deductions on their mortgages that Freddie Mac has purchased.
11. **Answer B is correct.** Regular way settlement for agency debt is the same as direct government obligations such as T-bonds. The regular way settlement is trade date + 1 for agency-issued securities.
12. **Answer C is correct.** Agency debt is actively traded in the Over-the-Counter market after the original issuance is sold out. The OTC secondary market is a very active market for agency debt issues.
13. **Answer D is correct.** Pass-through certificates are created by the pooling of mortgages that have been purchased from lending institutions. These mortgages are repackaged and securitized (made into a negotiable security). The mortgages are not government guaranteed.
14. **Answer D is correct.** Pass-through certificates can be issued by GNMA, FNMA, and Freddie Mac. They are not issued by the export/import bank. The agencies purchase mortgages, repackage them into pools, and use the cash flow generated from the mortgages to issue pass-through certificates against.
15. **Answer B is correct.** Pass-through certificates are issued to the public to raise funds that are used to purchase mortgages in the market. The agencies do not issue mortgages to homeowners.
16. **Answer D is correct.** All income realized from pass-through certificates is fully taxed to the holder on the federal, state, and local levels. The mortgages that are purchased by the agency have already taken a tax deduction on the mortgage interest, so the income earned from these pass-through certificates is fully taxable.
17. **Answer A is correct.** A modified pass-through certificate is backed by the purchase of a government-guaranteed mortgage through the government agency. In a sense, all modified pass-throughs are backed by the agency issuing them. The lending institution (bank) or homeowner is not guaranteeing the issued mortgage.
18. **Answer C is correct.** Agency-backed mortgage obligations have all the following risks except for liquidity risk. Liquidity risk is the ability to quickly sell an asset. Mortgages, however, have prepayment risk, which is the risk that a homeowner will pay off his mortgage prior to maturity. Extension risk is when interest rates have risen and mortgage holders decide to hold their better rate mortgages. Default risk is the risk that a homeowner will not be able to pay her mortgage and would default on the loan.

19. **Answer D is correct.** A collateralized mortgage obligation is a derivative product that was created to deal with prepayment and extension risks that are associated with mortgages. They are designed to deflect prepayment risk on mortgages that made pass-through certificates mature sooner than anticipated. There is still a certain level of prepayment risk associated to CMOs, but it is far less than that of a pass-through certificate.

20. **Answer A is correct.** The tranch system was created by brokers to deal with the prepayment and extension risks that are associated with pass-through certificates. By breaking maturities into separate "slices" or tranches, the brokers are able to deflect prepayment and extension risks on a less of an impact basis. The tranch system enables payments to be directed to a certain tranch and gives an investor the opportunity to purchase a mortgage-backed security with a specific maturity and interest rate.

21. **Answer B is correct.** Pay-through bonds are a collateralized mortgage obligation that places the mortgages in a limited-purpose finance subsidiary with the CMO holder having no ownership in the mortgages directly. They then issue mortgage-backed bonds to CMO holders with specific maturity dates and interest payments.

22. **Answer A is correct.** A 15-year mortgage with five separate tranches designed to manage the cash flow as well as the prepayment and extension risks associated to mortgages retires the tranch with the shortest maturity first. In this question, that is tranch 1, which represents years 1 through 3.

23. **Answer C is correct.** A CMO allows the broker to issue CMOs with varying maturities and varying interest rates. It can do so by effectively managing the existing cash flow. Prepayment risk is somewhat deflected because it is distributed to each tranch equally.

24. **Answer B is correct.** A planned amortization class CMO creates a separate companion tranch to absorb prepayment risk and a separate companion tranch to absorb extension risk. All regular monthly payments are distributed to all tranches equally or on a pro-rata basis.

25. **Answer D is correct.** The Federal agency bond listed with a maturity date of May 2001 has a selling price of the lowest asking price of 102.12, or 102 12/32nds. Each point is worth $10.00. Thus, 102 points × $10.00 = $1,020.00 and 12/32nds = $3.75, for a total value of $1,023.75.

Quick Check

Municipal Debt

1. Which of the following authorities could raise capital through a municipal bond issue?

   I. School districts

   II. Water districts

   III. Public utilities

   IV. Sewage treatment plants

   ❍ A. I and II
   ❍ B. I, II, and III
   ❍ C. I, II, and IV
   ❍ D. I, II, III, and IV

Quick Answer: 110
Detailed Answer: 111

2. If an investor living in Arizona purchases $10,000 worth of municipal bonds issued by the U.S. Virgin Islands, how is the interest income taxed?

   ❍ A. It is exempt from federal taxes.
   ❍ B. It is exempt from Arizona state and local taxes.
   ❍ C. It is triple-tax-exempt.
   ❍ D. It is included in federal, state, and local taxes.

Quick Answer: 110
Detailed Answer: 111

3. Which of the following investments gives an investor the highest yield?

   ❍ A. A Californian resident in the 30% tax bracket purchases a 6% Puerto Rico municipal bond.
   ❍ B. A Florida resident in the 25% tax bracket purchases a 6.5% U.S. Virgin Island municipal bond.
   ❍ C. A New York resident in the 33% tax bracket purchases a 6.9% Washington, D.C., municipal bond.
   ❍ D. A Colorado resident in the 20% tax bracket purchases a 6.2% 30-year U.S. Treasury bond.

Quick Answer: 110
Detailed Answer: 111

Quick Check

4. Which of the following statements is characteristic of a general obligation bond issue?

   I. Ad valorem taxes are used to pay the debt.

   II. Residents are able to vote on the approval of the bond issue.

   III. Bondholders could force an issuing municipality to raise taxes to meet its debt obligation.

   IV. Funds from the project being built are used to service the debt.

   ❍ A. I only
   ❍ B. I and II
   ❍ C. I, II, and III
   ❍ D. I, II, III, and IV

Quick Answer: 110
Detailed Answer: 111

5. A home in a municipality has an assessed value of $200,000. The local property tax rate for the municipality is 24 mills. This homeowner owes how much in property taxes?

   ❍ A. $240
   ❍ B. $2400
   ❍ C. $480
   ❍ D. $4800

Quick Answer: 110
Detailed Answer: 111

6. Fred Granger is interested in purchasing a home in the town of Friarville, Georgia. The house is being sold for $118,000. The town has a local property tax rate of 16 mill on residential homes. What are the property taxes on the home he is considering buying?

   ❍ A. $1880
   ❍ B. $1088
   ❍ C. $1888
   ❍ D. $737.50

Quick Answer: 110
Detailed Answer: 111

Quick Check

7. Which of the following protective covenants written into a municipal bond indenture protects bondholders?

   I. No sale covenant

   II. Rate covenant

   III. Maintenance covenant

   IV. Additional bonds covenant

   ❍ A. I and II
   ❍ B. I, II, and III
   ❍ C. II, III, and IV
   ❍ D. I, II, III, and IV

Quick Answer: 110
Detailed Answer: 111

8. A net revenue pledge has which of the following flow-of-funds priorities in disbursing pledged revenues from the project?

   ❍ A. Bondholder interest and principal are paid first.
   ❍ B. Operation and maintenance of the facility come first.
   ❍ C. Debt service reserve fund comes first.
   ❍ D. Sinking fund comes first.

Quick Answer: 110
Detailed Answer: 112

9. Which of the following statements is true of a gross revenue pledge for a revenue bond?

   I. Interest and principal are paid to bondholders first.

   II. Operation and maintenance of the project are paid first.

   III. Most revenue bonds issued have a net revenue pledge.

   IV. Most revenue bonds issued have a gross revenue pledge.

   ❍ A. I only
   ❍ B. II only
   ❍ C. I and III
   ❍ D. II and IV

Quick Answer: 110
Detailed Answer: 112

Quick Check

10. Which of the following short-term financing needs of a municipality are backed by a general obligation pledge?

Quick Answer: 110
Detailed Answer: 112

I. Bond anticipation notes

II. Tax anticipation notes

III. Revenue anticipation notes

IV. Grant anticipation notes

❍ A. I and II
❍ B. II and III
❍ C. III and IV
❍ D. I, II, III, and IV

11. A municipality issuing a double-barreled bond has all the following characteristics except for which one?

Quick Answer: 110
Detailed Answer: 112

❍ A. The bond is backed by the revenue from the project being built.
❍ B. The bond is backed by ad valorem taxes.
❍ C. The bond is backed by taxes other than property taxes.
❍ D. It would be considered a general obligation bond issue.

12. If an investor in the 35% tax bracket can purchase a AAA-rated municipal bond with a triple-tax–free yield of 5.44%, what does she need to receive on a comparable corporate issue to earn the same rate of return?

Quick Answer: 110
Detailed Answer: 112

❍ A. 7.34%
❍ B. 8.36%
❍ C. 9.04%
❍ D. 9.12%

13. Daniel is considering purchasing a municipal bond that pays an interest rate of 5.17%. Daniel is in the 29% tax bracket. What does he need to receive on a corporate bond to attain the same equivalent yield?

Quick Answer: 110
Detailed Answer: 112

❍ A. 6.67%
❍ B. 7.28%
❍ C. 8.07%
❍ D. 8.24%

Quick Check

14. Martha is a Texas resident who has purchased a municipal bond from American Samoa. The bond pays 5.24%. Martha is in the 20% tax bracket. What does Martha need to earn on a comparable corporate bond to receive the same rate of return?
    - ❍ A. 6.55%
    - ❍ B. 7.24%
    - ❍ C. 6.26%
    - ❍ D. 4.19%

Quick Answer: 110
Detailed Answer: 112

15. Richard is thinking of investing in triple-exempt municipal bonds that have a yield of 6.04%. He is in the 37% tax bracket. What yield does he need on a corporate bond to give him the same effective yield?
    - ❍ A. 6.41%
    - ❍ B. 8.27%
    - ❍ C. 8.77%
    - ❍ D. 9.59%

Quick Answer: 110
Detailed Answer: 113

16. Thomas Crown owns 10 TNT Corporate bonds that have a coupon rate of 7.89%. He is in the 32% tax bracket. What yield does he need to receive on a triple-tax–exempt municipal bond to equal the TNT bonds?
    - ❍ A. 5.37%
    - ❍ B. 6.44%
    - ❍ C. 8.57%
    - ❍ D. 11.19%

Quick Answer: 110
Detailed Answer: 113

17. A municipal bond that is purchased at an original issue discount and then held to maturity has which of the following tax consequences?
    - ❍ A. The discounted amount can be accreted for the bondholder.
    - ❍ B. The discounted amount can be amortized for the bondholder.
    - ❍ C. The discounted amount can be appreciated for the bondholder.
    - ❍ D. The discounted amount has no tax consequences.

Quick Answer: 110
Detailed Answer: 113

18. Jordan purchased $10,000 worth of municipal bonds in the secondary market with a price of 96. He held the bonds to maturity and redeemed them for par value. What are the tax consequences on the bonds?
    - ❍ A. There are no tax consequences because the bonds are tax free.
    - ❍ B. He has a $400 capital gain on the bonds.
    - ❍ C. He has a $400 capital loss on the bonds.
    - ❍ D. He has no gain on the bonds because he amortizes the discount over the life of the bond.

Quick Answer: 110
Detailed Answer: 113

Quick Check

19. An investor purchased 10 municipal bonds in the secondary market at a $100 premium for each. After holding the bonds for four years, he sold the bonds with an adjusted cost basis of $10,400. Which of the following tax consequences is true regarding the bonds?

Quick Answer: 110
Detailed Answer: 113

- ❍ A. If the bonds were sold for more than $10,400, the investor would incur a capital loss on the bonds.
- ❍ B. If the bonds were sold at par, the investor would have a capital gain on the bonds.
- ❍ C. If the bonds were sold for less than $10,400, the investor would incur a capital gain on the bonds.
- ❍ D. If the bonds were sold for more than $10,400, the investor would have a capital gain on the bonds.

20. A Maine resident purchased 10 Guam territorial bonds with an interest rate of 6%. The investor is in the 25% tax bracket. How much in income will the investor earn each year on the bonds after tax considerations?

Quick Answer: 110
Detailed Answer: 113

- ❍ A. $600 per year
- ❍ B. $450 per year
- ❍ C. $800 per year
- ❍ D. $850 per year

21. Which of the following types of investors are most active in purchasing municipal bonds in the market?

Quick Answer: 110
Detailed Answer: 114

I. A wealthy individual with a net worth of $10,000,000

II. A retired individual living on Social Security, with $500,000 in savings

III. An individual who is married with three children, earning $50,000 per year, with limited savings

IV. An individual who invests only in her self-directed individual retirement account

- ❍ A. I only
- ❍ B. I and II
- ❍ C. I, II, and IV
- ❍ D. II and IV

Quick Check

22. Which of the following municipal bond issues is considered the safest for an investor?

Quick Answer: 110
Detailed Answer: 114

- ❍ A. A 10-year 6% revenue bond to build a new airport
- ❍ B. A 20-year 6.5% G.O. bond issued to build a new school
- ❍ C. A 20-year 7% revenue bond issued to build a new toll highway
- ❍ D. A 20-year 7% revenue bond issued to build a new bridge

23. A homeowner purchased a home for $225,000 in Dade County, Florida. The local mill rate for taxes in the county is 26 mill. What are the assessed taxes on this property?

Quick Answer: 110
Detailed Answer: 114

- ❍ A. $585.00
- ❍ B. $5850.00
- ❍ C. $58,500.00
- ❍ D. $8653.00

24. Peter is a resident of the state of Michigan and is currently in the 29% tax bracket. Which of the following bonds gives him the highest rate of return as an investment?

Quick Answer: 110
Detailed Answer: 114

- ❍ A. Guam territorial bonds paying 6.4%
- ❍ B. Michigan G.O. bonds paying 6.6%
- ❍ C. Washington, D.C., bonds paying 6.77%
- ❍ D. U.S. Virgin Island bonds paying 7.0%

25. Which of the following statements are true in respect to revenue bonds issued by a municipality?

Quick Answer: 110
Detailed Answer: 114

I. The bonds are considered safer than G.O. bonds.

II. Bondholders are safeguarded by protective covenants.

III. Income from the project services the debt issue.

IV. Revenue bonds that derive income from a project could never default.

- ❍ A. I and II
- ❍ B. II and III
- ❍ C. I and III
- ❍ D. I, II, III, and IV

Quick Check Answer Key

1. D
2. C
3. C
4. C
5. D
6. C
7. D
8. B
9. C
10. D
11. B
12. B
13. B
14. A
15. D
16. A
17. D
18. B
19. D
20. A
21. B
22. B
23. B
24. D
25. B

Answers and Explanations

1. **Answer D is correct.** Municipal bonds can be issued through any state, county, township, or village. They can also be issued for a municipal entity such as a school district. This could include public utilities, water and sewage districts, and other municipal debt.

2. **Answer C is correct.** Interest earned on a municipal bond from an American territory such as the U.S. Virgin Islands is triple-tax–exempt, regardless of whether the investor resides in the territory. Thus, an individual living in Arizona who purchases a Virgin Island municipal issue has triple-tax–exempt status.

3. **Answer C is correct.** The highest yield is realized from the purchase of a 6.9% Washington, D.C., municipal bond by a New York resident. Territorial municipal bond issues are triple-tax–exempt for any resident of any state. Territory bonds include the U.S. Virgin Islands; American Samoa; Puerto Rico; Washington, D.C.; and Guam. The 6.2% U.S. Treasury bond is exempt from state and local taxes but pays the 20% federal tax in this example.

4. **Answer C is correct.** A general obligation bond is backed by the full faith and taxing ability of the issuer. Ad valorem taxes (property taxes) are used to back many G.O. bond issues. When a municipality is taking on additional debt, it is quite common that taxpayers have the right to vote on the approval of the debt through a referendum. G.O. bonds are considered the most secure municipal debt because the issuer could be required to raise taxes if the debt service cannot be met.

5. **Answer D is correct.** A home with an assessed value of $200,000 and a property tax rate of 24 mills pays $4800 per year in property taxes. A mill is 1/10th of 1%. You multiply 200,000 × .024 = $4,800 to compute the tax rate.

6. **Answer C is correct.** A mill is 1/10th of 1%. Therefore, a house with an assessed value of $118,000 and a mill rate of 16 has property taxes of 118,000 × .016 = $1888 for the prospective homeowner.

7. **Answer D is correct.** Protective covenants are written into a bond indenture to protect bondholders. A no-sale covenant prevents the issuer from selling a project that is backing a revenue bond. A rate covenant requires that an issuer raise user rates on the project if it is unable to service the debt. An additional bonds covenant requires that the issuer not use the project as collateral to issue additional bonds against without bondholder approval. A maintenance covenant requires that the issuer maintain the project in good working order so user fees that are collected will continue to be paid.

8. **Answer B is correct.** A net revenue pledge allows for the operation and maintenance of the revenue project to be paid first. After the operating costs are paid, the bondholders receive interest and principal payments.

9. **Answer C is correct.** A gross revenue pledge requires that the bondholder interest and principal be paid first before operation and maintenance costs. Most municipal revenue bonds have a net revenue pledge, where operation and maintenance costs are paid first.

10. **Answer D is correct.** A municipality can issue short-term financing in the form of tax anticipation notes (ad valorem taxes), revenue anticipation notes (taxes other than ad valorem), bond anticipation notes (to start construction of a project and then later retire with a takeout loan), and government grant anticipation notes (future receipt of a government grant or subsidy). Each of these short-term means of financing is backed by a general obligation pledge of the issuer.

11. **Answer B is correct.** A double-barreled bond is backed by both revenue generated from the project being built and taxes other than ad valorem taxes collected by the issuing municipality.

12. **Answer B is correct.** An investor that is in the 35% tax bracket has 35% of her interest income go to pay taxes. You divide a triple-tax–exempt municipal bond that pays 5.44% by .65, which is the complement number of .35 (1 – .35 = .65), to determine the amount you need to receive on a corporate bond to receive the same tax equivalent yield. (The equation is 5.44 ÷ .65 = 8.36.) Thus, the investor needs a corporate bond earning 8.36% to receive the same tax equivalent yield as that of the 5.44% municipal bond.

13. **Answer B is correct.** An investor in the 29% tax bracket has 29% of his interest income earned on a corporate bond go to pay taxes. The municipal bond that pays 5.17% tax-free interest is divided by .71, which is the complement of .29 (1 – .29 = .71) to determine the amount needed on a corporate bond to receive the same tax equivalent yield. (The equation is 5.17 ÷ .71 = 7.28.) The investor needs a corporate bond that pays 7.28% to receive the same yield as the 5.17% municipal bond.

14. **Answer A is correct.** A territorial municipal bond purchased by a Texas resident still receives triple-tax–exempt status on the interest earned for the investor. Martha is in the 20% tax bracket, and any income earned on a corporate bond is taxed at 20%. To calculate the taxable equivalent yield that the 5.24% municipal bond earns, you take .80, which is the complement of the 20% tax bracket (1 – .20 = .80) and divide that number into the municipal return of 5.24%. (The equation is 5.24 ÷ .80 = 6.55%.) Thus, Martha needs to purchase a 6.55% corporate bond to give her the same tax-equivalent yield that she can earn on the municipal bond.

15. **Answer D is correct.** An investor in the 37% tax bracket that purchases a triple-tax–exempt bond that earns 6.04% needs a 9.59% corporate bond to earn the same tax-equivalent yield earned on the municipal issue. To compute this, you take the complement of the 37% tax bracket, which is .63 (1 - .37 = .63), and divide that number into the municipal yield of 6.04%. (The equation is 6.04 ÷ .63 = 9.59%.) Richard needs to purchase a corporate bond that pays 9.59% to earn the same yield that the 6.04% municipal bond would earn.

16. **Answer A is correct.** Thomas owns 10 TNT bonds that pay an interest rate of 7.89%. He is in the 32% tax bracket. To find the same tax-equivalent yield a municipal bond would have to pay, you multiply the complement of the tax bracket, which is .68 (1 – .32 = .68), times the rate of the corporate bond of 7.89%. (The equation is 7.89 × .68 = 5.37%.) Thus, Thomas needs to earn 5.37% yield on a municipal bond to give him the same after-tax rate of return that he would earn on the corporate bond.

17. **Answer D is correct.** An original issue discount municipal bond is a bond that has been issued by the municipality at a discount. An investor purchasing an original issue discount and holding the bond to maturity does not have any tax consequences on the discounted amount. It is important to note that this is not true on a discounted bond that was purchased at a discount in the secondary market and held to maturity. In that case, the adjusted cost basis is determined to see whether the investor has earned a capital gain or incurred a capital loss.

18. **Answer B is correct.** The purchase of the municipal bonds in the secondary market at a discount of $400 (100 – 96 = 4) and held to maturity gives the investor a $400 capital gain on the bonds. The interest on the bonds is tax exempt, but the discounted amount cannot be accreted because of the tax status of the bond. Thus, the investor must claim a $400 capital gain on the bonds.

19. **Answer D is correct.** An investor who purchases a municipal bond at a premium in the secondary market and then sells the bond prior to maturity with an adjusted cost basis of $10,400 has a capital gain if the bonds are sold for more than $10,400. He has a capital loss if the bonds are sold for less than $10,400.

20. **Answer A is correct.** An investor living in Maine can purchase Guam municipal bonds and still receive a triple-tax–exempt status on the bonds. Guam is a territory of the United States, and investors do not lose their tax-exempt status when buying these bonds. The investor in this example purchased 10 bonds, or $10,000 worth. They pay 6%, or $600 per year, to the investor (10,000 × .06 = $600).

21. **Answer B is correct.** The typical buyer of municipal bonds is an individual attempting to shelter his or her investments from having to pay taxes. In most cases, municipal bonds offer triple-tax–exempt status to investors. The wealthy individual with a $10 million net worth would probably consider purchasing municipal bonds to earn tax-free income. The retired individual with $500,000 in savings and collecting Social Security would also want to shelter her income from taxes while not affecting her Social Security benefits.

22. **Answer B is correct.** This question is tricky. The investor who purchases a municipal bond is safest if she purchases general obligation bonds over revenue bonds. G.O. bonds are backed by the taxing power of the issuing municipality. If the bonds could not meet its debt service, the municipality could be forced to raise taxes to meet its debt. Revenue bonds have defaulted in the past, so they are not considered as safe an investment as G.O. bonds.

23. **Answer B is correct.** The owner owes $5850 in property taxes for a house that is assessed at $225,000 with a mill rate of 26. A mill is 1/10th of 1%. To calculate the property tax, the equation is $225{,}000 \times .026 = \$5850$ in property taxes.

24. **Answer D is correct.** A resident of Michigan who purchases a U.S. territory municipal bond still receives the triple-tax exemption on the interest earned on the bonds. Guam; Washington, D.C.; and the U.S. Virgin Islands are all territories of the United States. If the investor purchases a Michigan bond, he receives 6.6% tax free, but this is less than the U.S. Virgin Island bonds paying 7.0%.

25. **Answer B is correct.** Revenue bonds are not safer than general obligation bonds because G.O. bonds are backed by the taxing power of the issuing municipality. (It can raise taxes.) Revenue bonds are only backed by the revenue generated from the project and could default. Most revenue bonds do have protective covenants written into the indenture to protect bondholders, but the success of these covenants depends on the way they are worded and how they can be enforced to protect bondholders.

Quick Check

Judging Municipal Debt

1. What is the highest rating that Standard & Poor's assigns to a security?

Quick Answer: **122**
Detailed Answer: **123**

- ❍ A. Aaa
- ❍ B. A+
- ❍ C. AAA
- ❍ D. Aaa+

2. Which of the following figures are used by a credit-rating agency to analyze the debt of a municipality?

Quick Answer: **122**
Detailed Answer: **123**

   I. The total outstanding debt of the issuer

   II. The amount of debt that is self-supporting

   III. The sinking fund provision of the debt

   IV. The collected tax revenues of the municipality and the ability to collect

- ❍ A. I and II
- ❍ B. II and III
- ❍ C. I, II, and III
- ❍ D. I, II, III, and IV

Quick Check

3. Which of the following municipal bond issues is considered self-supporting debt issued by a municipality?

   I. Water treatment bonds

   II. Bridge and tunnel bonds

   III. School district bonds

   IV. Capital improvement bonds

❍ A. I and II
❍ B. II and III
❍ C. I, II, and III
❍ D. I, II, III, and IV

Quick Answer: 122
Detailed Answer: 123

4. Which of the following factors are used by a credit analyst to determine the quality of a general obligation bond issued by a municipality?

   I. The economic and employment conditions in the municipality

   II. The income level of the municipality

   III. The public's general attitude toward the municipality's debt and taxes

   IV. The ability of the project to be self-supporting in servicing its debt

❍ A. I and II
❍ B. I, II, and III
❍ C. II and IV
❍ D. I, II, III, and IV

Quick Answer: 122
Detailed Answer: 123

5. The protective covenants of a municipal revenue bond issue are worded to protect investors primarily against which of the following?

❍ A. The chance that a natural disaster could destroy the project
❍ B. The tax collection ratio meets debt service coverage
❍ C. The assessed value ratio meets debt service coverage
❍ D. The risk of the default of the bond issue

Quick Answer: 122
Detailed Answer: 123

Quick Check

6. The municipality of Ditch Plains received a credit rating of BBB on its debt. It decides to issue additional debt in the market that will be insured by an independent municipal bond insurance company. All the following are true about the new issue except for which one?

Quick Answer: 122
Detailed Answer: 123

❍ A. The new issue receives a AAA credit rating on the insured bonds.
❍ B. The municipality can issue the new bonds at a lower interest rate.
❍ C. The credit rating of the municipality is now AAA.
❍ D. The cost of the insurance will be paid by the issuer.

7. A revenue bond that is issued with a serial maturity has which of the following characteristics?

Quick Answer: 122
Detailed Answer: 123

❍ A. The bonds have different interest rates and mature on the same date.
❍ B. The bonds have the same interest rate and mature on various dates.
❍ C. The bonds have varying interest rates and different maturity dates.
❍ D. The bonds have the same interest rate and mature on the same date.

8. When an issuing municipality redeems a small portion of the bonds on a serial basis and the remainder of the bonds at maturity, this is known as which of the following?

Quick Answer: 122
Detailed Answer: 123

❍ A. A sinking fund
❍ B. A serial takeout
❍ C. A balloon maturity
❍ D. Level debt service

9. If a municipality issues a municipal bond with a mandatory redemption feature, which of the following statements is true?

Quick Answer: 122
Detailed Answer: 124

❍ A. The bonds have a term maturity.
❍ B. Bondholders know exactly when they will have the bonds redeemed.
❍ C. The bonds have a call schedule that will be conducted on a random basis.
❍ D. The redemption of the issue is always done on an equal basis.

Quick Check

10. A municipality issued general obligation bonds with a mandatory redemption. Which of the following statements are true about this issue?

    I. The bonds are called on a preset schedule.

    II. The bonds are called on a random basis.

    III. The bonds pay a higher interest rate than bonds without a redemption feature.

    IV. The bonds decrease in value as they are called.

    ❍ A. I only
    ❍ B. I and II
    ❍ C. I, II, and III
    ❍ D. I, II, III, and IV

Quick Answer: **122**
Detailed Answer: **124**

11. Which of the following bonds pays the highest rate of interest to an investor?

    ❍ A. A 20-year AAA-rated G.O. bond with a mandatory redemption feature after 10 years
    ❍ B. A 20-year AAA-rated G.O. bond that is not callable
    ❍ C. A 20-year AAA-rated G.O. bond that has an optional redemption feature in its last 5 years
    ❍ D. A 20-year AAA-rated G.O. bond that has an extraordinary mandatory redemption feature

Quick Answer: **122**
Detailed Answer: **124**

12. Which of the following redemption features are required to be written into a bond indenture?

    I. An optional redemption

    II. A mandatory redemption

    III. Extraordinary optional redemption

    IV. A bond refunding

    ❍ A. I and II
    ❍ B. II and III
    ❍ C. I, II, and III
    ❍ D. I, II, III, and IV

Quick Answer: **122**
Detailed Answer: **124**

Quick Check

13. A municipality that issued noncallable debt at 9% and saw interest rates drop sharply in the market to 6% could perform which of the following refinancing methods?
    - ❍ A. An optional redemption
    - ❍ B. A refunding or rollover redemption
    - ❍ C. A mandatory redemption
    - ❍ D. There would be no way for the issuer to refinance its debt

Quick Answer: 122
Detailed Answer: 124

14. When a municipality has outstanding debt that it wants to remove from its balance sheet by the use of government securities purchased and then deposited with a trustee, this is known as which of the following?
    - ❍ A. A rollover
    - ❍ B. A debt nullification
    - ❍ C. A defeasance
    - ❍ D. A discharge of debt

Quick Answer: 122
Detailed Answer: 124

15. Which of the following securities could be used by a municipality to defease an outstanding bond issue?

    I. High-grade commercial paper

    II. Government agency issues

    III. Direct government obligations

    IV. Interest rate options

    - ❍ A. I and II
    - ❍ B. II and III
    - ❍ C. III and IV
    - ❍ D. I, II, III, and IV

Quick Answer: 122
Detailed Answer: 124

16. A municipality with a credit rating of Ba has $100,000,000 of debt outstanding in the market. It has reached its allowable debt ceiling and wants to retire the outstanding debt. It purchases $68,000,000 worth of FNMA bonds in the market and deposits them with a trustee. What is the credit rating of the $100,000,000 worth of debt that is outstanding?
    - ❍ A. AAA
    - ❍ B. AA
    - ❍ C. A
    - ❍ D. Ba

Quick Answer: 122
Detailed Answer: 124

Quick Check

17. A municipality with a BBB credit rating has $200,000,000 worth of outstanding debt in the market, which places it at its maximum debt ceiling. The municipality performs a defeasance of its current outstanding debt by purchasing $135,000,000 worth of agency debt. What is the municipality's debt ceiling after the defeasance?

   - ❍ A. It is still at its maximum debt limit.
   - ❍ B. It has a debt ceiling of $135,000,000.
   - ❍ C. It has a debt ceiling of $65,000,000.
   - ❍ D. It has a debt ceiling of $200,000,000.

Quick Answer: **122**
Detailed Answer: **125**

18. A debt instrument that allows a bondholder to put his bonds back to the issuer is permitted under which of the following features in the indenture?

   - ❍ A. A call feature
   - ❍ B. A reverse call
   - ❍ C. A rights offer
   - ❍ D. A tender offer

Quick Answer: **122**
Detailed Answer: **125**

19. Erie County issued 20-year G.O. bonds in the market with a 5.44% interest rate. The bond indenture has a put provision that allows the holder to tender the bonds to the issuer at 100. Which of the following scenarios best describes when the bondholders exercise their put provision?

   - ❍ A. Interest rates go to 5.03% and the bonds are redeemed at a premium.
   - ❍ B. Interest rates go to 7.77% and the bonds are redeemed at par.
   - ❍ C. Interest rates go to 5.55% and the bonds are redeemed at a discount.
   - ❍ D. Interest rates go to 5.05% and the bonds are redeemed at par.

Quick Answer: **122**
Detailed Answer: **125**

Answer questions 20 through 22 using the following information:

In 1992, the cities of St. Paul and St. Mary issued the following municipal bonds in the market: $200,000,000 worth of 20-year G.O. 7.10% redevelopment bonds, January 1/July 1 callable 02 at 104. The bonds are rated AA, and the debt service is set at 50/50.

20. What type of municipal debt is this issue considered?

   - ❍ A. Net direct debt
   - ❍ B. Overlapping debt
   - ❍ C. Industrial development bonds
   - ❍ D. Industrial revenue bonds

Quick Answer: **122**
Detailed Answer: **125**

Quick Check

21. If the bonds are called, what amount is the city of St. Mary required to come up with to redeem the issue?

Quick Answer: 122
Detailed Answer: 125

- ❍ A. $104,000,000
- ❍ B. $208,000,000
- ❍ C. $100,000,000
- ❍ D. $200,000,000

22. If a municipality issues a serial bond, all the following statements are true except for which one?

Quick Answer: 122
Detailed Answer: 125

- ❍ A. The bonds are issued with the same interest rates.
- ❍ B. The bonds are issued with various maturities.
- ❍ C. Some of the bonds could be redeemed prior to maturity.
- ❍ D. The bonds will have a AAA rating.

23. A municipality that wants to defease $50,000,000 worth of debt obligations paying a 7.62% interest rate is allowed to purchase all the following securities except for which type?

Quick Answer: 122
Detailed Answer: 125

- ❍ A. U.S. Treasury bonds
- ❍ B. FNMA debt obligations
- ❍ C. Bank certificates of deposit
- ❍ D. Corporate bonds of blue chip companies

24. What is the difference between a rating on a municipal bond that has been done by Moody's and one done by White's?

Quick Answer: 122
Detailed Answer: 125

- ❍ A. Moody's measures credit worthiness, and White's measures default probability.
- ❍ B. Moody's measures credit worthiness, and White's measures marketability.
- ❍ C. Moody's measures debt service coverage, and White's measures credit worthiness.
- ❍ D. Moody's measures marketability, and White's measures credit worthiness.

25. Which of the following municipal issues has the least chance of default for a bondholder?

Quick Answer: 122
Detailed Answer: 125

- ❍ A. 20-year municipal revenue bond
- ❍ B. 20-year municipal G.O. bond
- ❍ C. 20-year municipal G.O. bond that has been defeased
- ❍ D. Tax anticipation notes

Quick Check Answer Key

1. C
2. D
3. A
4. B
5. D
6. C
7. B
8. C
9. C
10. C
11. A
12. C
13. B
14. C
15. B
16. A
17. C
18. D
19. B
20. B
21. A
22. D
23. D
24. B
25. C

Answers and Explanations

1. **Answer C is correct.** Standard & Poor's uses all capital letters in its ratings of municipal bonds, with its highest rating depicted as AAA. Moody's uses uppercase and lowercase letters, with its highest rating being Aaa.

2. **Answer D is correct.** An analyst who is rating municipal debt looks at the total amount of outstanding debt that the municipality has issued and the amount of the total debt that is considered to be self-supporting (backed by project revenues). The analyst determines whether any of the debt has a sinking fund provision that requires money to be set aside for early debt retirement. The analyst also determines the ability of the issuer to collect the taxes that it has levied.

3. **Answer A is correct.** Self-supporting debt is considered debt that provides its own revenue stream for debt coverage. This includes water treatment bonds and bridge and tunnel bonds, where fees or tolls could be charged.

4. **Answer B is correct.** A credit analyst uses many factors to determine the quality of a G.O. bond. This includes the overall economic condition of the municipality, the level of income in the area, and the perception of the public regarding taxes being assessed.

5. **Answer D is correct.** Protective covenants are included in a bond indenture to protect the revenue bondholder against the possible risk of default of the issue. Depending on how the protective covenants are worded, a municipal bond uses the protective covenants to protect against the issue defaulting.

6. **Answer C is correct.** Insured municipal issues receive a AAA credit rating by S&P and Moody's because of the insurance coverage. This insurance allows an issuer to issue the bonds at a lower interest rate as it pays for the cost of the bond insurance. It does not raise the credit rating of the issuer, but the insured issue receives a AAA rating due to the insurance.

7. **Answer B is correct.** Serial bonds that are issued by a municipality have the same interest rates and a maturity schedule on varying dates. Term bonds have the same interest rate and mature on the same date.

8. **Answer C is correct.** Serial bonds that are redeemed on a specific call schedule with the remaining bonds redeemed at maturity are considered to have a balloon maturity. For instance, after a set 10-year waiting period, a municipality could redeem 5% of a $10,000,000 issue every year, with a final balloon maturity on the bonds of $5,000,000.

9. **Answer C is correct.** A municipality that issued a bond with a mandatory redemption feature redeems a portion of the bonds on a regular basis, according to a specific call schedule. In this case, the bonds have a serial maturity, not a term maturity. The bondholders do not know when they will be redeemed because the redemption is done on a random basis as determined by the trustee.
10. **Answer C is correct.** G.O. bonds that have a mandatory redemption feature are considered serial bonds. They are redeemed on a preset call schedule, which is conducted on a random basis. Callable bonds also typically pay a higher interest rate to investors to compensate for the call feature.
11. **Answer A is correct.** This is a tricky question. You first have to realize that bonds with a call feature typically pay a higher rate of interest to investors to compensate for the call feature. The 20-year AAA has a mandatory redemption feature after 10 years begins redemption after the 10th year. This bond issue has the greatest chance to be redeemed and would probably pay the highest interest rate to bondholders.
12. **Answer C is correct.** Any type of redemption feature that calls in the bonds prior to maturity must be written into the bond indenture so that the investor is aware of the feature. A refunding is not written into the indenture for the bond.
13. **Answer B is correct.** An issue without a mandatory or optional redemption feature written into the bond indenture could still retire debt by performing a rollover or refunding of the issue. They issue bonds at a lower interest rate and then purchase the outstanding bonds with the higher rate already in the market.
14. **Answer C is correct.** When an issuer purchases government obligations such as T-bonds or agency debt to be deposited with a trustee to remove a debt from its balance sheet, this is known as defeasance. The issuer purchases higher-paying government securities, deposits them with a trustee, and uses the interest and principal payments to defease the current outstanding issue.
15. **Answer B is correct.** An issuer that decides to defease the current outstanding debt that it has in the market could do so by purchasing direct government obligations such as T-bonds or agency debt such as FNMA obligations to be deposited with a trustee.
16. **Answer A is correct.** If an issuer uses direct government obligations or agency debt securities to defease an issue, the municipality in effect removes the debt from its balance sheet. Because the outstanding debt is deposited with a trustee, and the future interest and principal payments are used to pay off the existing debt, the bonds are defeased. The older debt also takes on the credit rating of the government securities being used, which is always a AAA rating.

17. **Answer C is correct.** A municipality that has defeased an outstanding $200,000,000 issue has, in effect, removed the liability from its balance sheet. If the municipality purchases $135,000,000 worth of government obligations to defease the outstanding issue, it effectively wipes out the $200,000,000 debt. If its debt ceiling was set at $200,000,000, it now has $65,000,000 of room under its debt ceiling. Remember, it had to purchase $135,000,000 worth of government securities, and it still has to pay it back eventually to bondholders.

18. **Answer D is correct.** When a bondholder has the right to put bonds back to the issuer after a certain date due to rising interest rates, this is known as a tender offer or a put provision.

19. **Answer B is correct.** In this question, the 5.44% Erie County bonds have a put provision that allow the holder to tender the bonds back to the issuer after a certain date. The best time to do so is if interest rates rise and the bonds are tendered at par back to the issuer.

20. **Answer B is correct.** When two municipalities come together to issue bonds to fund a project, this is known as overlapping debt.

21. **Answer A is correct.** If the bonds are called, they pay each bondholder a premium of 104 on each bond held. This makes the entire $200,000,000 issue callable at $208,000,000, of which 50% is the responsibility of the city of St. Mary, totaling $104,000,000.

22. **Answer D is correct.** Serial bonds that are issued by a municipality have the same interest rate and varying maturity dates. The call schedule allows the issuer to call back certain bonds after a set period of time prior to full maturity of the issue. The bonds have a credit rating that is determined by the issuers' credit standings, which is not necessarily a AAA rating.

23. **Answer D is correct.** A municipality that has elected to defease an outstanding issue is not able to use corporate debt securities as a choice in defeasing the issue.

24. **Answer B is correct.** White's measures the marketability of a municipal issue, whereas Moody's measures the credit worthiness of the underlying issue.

25. **Answer C is correct.** The 20-year municipal bond that is defeased by the issuer with the purchase of government obligations (direct or agency debt) and deposited with a trustee has the least chance of default. The bonds are now backed by AAA government obligations and are no longer an obligation of the issuing municipality.

Quick Check

Issuing and Trading Municipal Debt

1. The financial advisor to a municipality performs which of the following duties for a municipality that is considering a bond issue?

    I. Analyze the municipality's debt statement

    II. Advise the municipality on how the bond issue will affect its credit rating

    III. Recommend the type of bonds the municipality should issue

    IV. Recommend the interest rate at which the municipality should offer the bonds in the market

    ❍ A. I and II
    ❍ B. II and III
    ❍ C. I, II, and III
    ❍ D. I, II, III, and IV

Quick Answer: **136**
Detailed Answer: **137**

2. The role of a bond counsel in a municipal bond underwriting includes which of the following duties?

    I. Render a legal opinion on the bond issue

    II. Draw up the bond contract between the municipality and bondholder

    III. Appoint a trustee for the bond issue

    IV. Become the trustee for the bond issue

    ❍ A. I only
    ❍ B. I and II
    ❍ C. I, II, and III
    ❍ D. I, II, and IV

Quick Answer: **136**
Detailed Answer: **137**

Quick Check

3. A municipality decides to build a new bridge to service a connecting area. Which of the following statements are true of the bond issue that will finance the new bridge?

Quick Answer: **136**
Detailed Answer: **137**

I. The municipality needs a referendum vote of residents before it can issue bonds to finance the project.

II. A feasibility study will be commissioned to study the project.

III. The cost of the project must be determined.

IV. Property taxes will be reassessed in the community.

❍ A. I and II
❍ B. II and III
❍ C. I, II, and III
❍ D. I, II, III, and IV

4. A feasibility study that is commissioned by a municipality for a new bond issue has which of the following characteristics?

Quick Answer: **136**
Detailed Answer: **137**

I. The study is done by the issuing municipality's engineers.

II. The study is done by an independent engineering firm.

III. The study determines the cost of the project.

IV. The study reassesses local property taxes.

❍ A. I and III
❍ B. I and IV
❍ C. II and III
❍ D. II and IV

5. The notice of sale placed by a municipality in *The Daily Bond Buyer* has all the following information except for which item?

Quick Answer: **136**
Detailed Answer: **137**

❍ A. The amount of the bond issue
❍ B. The type of bond to be offered
❍ C. The interest rate for the bonds
❍ D. The type of tax backing the issue

Quick Check

6. A municipal bond underwriter determines its submitted competitive bid on a new issue by using all the following except for which factor?

   ❍ A. Pre-sale orders
   ❍ B. The credit rating of the issuer
   ❍ C. The municipality's debt per capita ratio
   ❍ D. The anticipated revenues from the proposed project

Quick Answer: **136**
Detailed Answer: **137**

7. Which of the following statements are true of pre-sale orders for a municipal bond offering?

   I. Pre-sale orders can be taken on municipal bond issues but not on corporate issues.

   II. Pre-sale orders give the underwriter a better gauge of investor interest.

   III. Pre-sale orders must be filled by the municipal bond underwriter.

   IV. Pre-sale orders enable the underwriter to make a competitive bid on the issue.

   ❍ A. I and II
   ❍ B. I, II, and III
   ❍ C. I, III, and IV
   ❍ D. II, III, and IV

Quick Answer: **136**
Detailed Answer: **138**

8. When a municipal bond underwriter "writes the scale," it is in effect doing which of the following?

   ❍ A. Comparing interest rates with other municipal bond issues
   ❍ B. Determining whether taxes collected by the municipality can meet the debt obligation
   ❍ C. Assessing the market demand for the bond offering
   ❍ D. Comparing its submitted bid to other underwriters' bids

Quick Answer: **136**
Detailed Answer: **138**

Quick Check

9. A bank acting as a municipal bond underwriter submitted a sealed bid on an official bid form to a municipality for a bond offering. When the issuer opens the final bids, it immediately throws out the underwriter's bid. What is a reason for the issuer to throw out the bid?

   - ❍ A. The underwriter does not have a contract with the municipality.
   - ❍ B. The underwriter did not send a good faith deposit with its bid.
   - ❍ C. The underwriter is a bank, and banks are not permitted to underwrite municipal bonds.
   - ❍ D. The underwriter did not get its bid in on time.

Quick Answer: **136**
Detailed Answer: **138**

10. The lead underwriter for a municipal bond underwriting syndicate has which of the following characteristics?

    I. It is considered the syndicate manager.

    II. It makes all investment decisions for the bond underwriting.

    III. It earns a management fee on each bond sold.

    IV. It chooses all syndicate members.

   - ❍ A. I and II
   - ❍ B. II and III
   - ❍ C. I, II, and III
   - ❍ D. I, II, III, and IV

Quick Answer: **136**
Detailed Answer: **138**

11. A municipal bond syndicate is established as an Eastern account. J.J. Reed is a member of the syndicate and is allocated 10% of the $100,000,000 bond offering. J.J. Reed has sold its allocated amount. There are $20,000,000 worth of bonds remaining. What is its total commitment for the issue?

   - ❍ A. $10,000,000
   - ❍ B. $12,000,000
   - ❍ C. $20,000,000
   - ❍ D. $30,000,000

Quick Answer: **136**
Detailed Answer: **138**

Quick Check

12. Which of the following statements are true of Western account municipal bond offerings?

    I. Western accounts are divided accounts.

    II. Western accounts are undivided accounts.

    III. In a Western account, any unsold bonds are the responsibility of all syndicate members.

    IV. In a Western account, a syndicate member is responsible only for the amount it is allocated.

    ❍ A. I and III
    ❍ B. I and IV
    ❍ C. II and III
    ❍ D. II and IV

Quick Answer: 136
Detailed Answer: 138

13. Cord & James is a large municipal bond underwriter who is the lead manager of a $100,000,000 municipal bond offering. The bond offering has a 1/2 point spread. The lead underwriter receives a management fee of 1/8th of a point for each bond sold. Lakeland Securities is a syndicate member that has sold $10,000,000 worth of the issue. What does Cord & James earn on the amount of the issue that Lakeland has sold?

    ❍ A. $12,500 management fee
    ❍ B. $37,500 management fee
    ❍ C. $50,000 management fee
    ❍ D. $50,000 takedown fee

Quick Answer: 136
Detailed Answer: 139

14. Determine which of the following types of brokers in a municipal syndicate takes on the most risk and the least risk of the bond offering. Choose the correct order from most risk to least risk.

    ❍ A. Lead underwriter, selling group member, syndicate member, outside broker
    ❍ B. Lead underwriter, syndicate member, selling group member, outside broker
    ❍ C. Syndicate member, lead underwriter, selling group member, outside broker
    ❍ D. Syndicate member, selling group member, outside broker, lead underwriter

Quick Answer: 136
Detailed Answer: 139

Quick Check

15. All the following are responsibilities of the syndicate manager in a municipal bond syndicate except for which one?

Quick Answer: 136
Detailed Answer: 139

- ❍ A. Announcing the syndicate's winning bid on the Munifacts wire
- ❍ B. Closing the books on the sold-out issue and paying syndicate members their shares of the spread
- ❍ C. Making sure that any one customer did not purchase too many bonds of the issue
- ❍ D. Becoming a market maker of the sold-out issue in the secondary market

16. Which of the following statements are true of municipal bonds that trade in the secondary market?

Quick Answer: 136
Detailed Answer: 139

I. Municipal bonds trade in increments of $5,000 minimums.

II. A round lot for institutional traders is $100,000.

III. A round lot for retail investors is five bonds.

IV. Municipal bonds are quoted in points.

- ❍ A. I and II
- ❍ B. II and III
- ❍ C. I, II, and III
- ❍ D. I, II, III, and IV

17. Which statement is true of municipal bonds that are trading in the secondary market?

Quick Answer: 136
Detailed Answer: 139

- ❍ A. The municipal bond market is a thinly traded illiquid market.
- ❍ B. The municipal bond market provides real-time reporting of all municipal bond trades.
- ❍ C. All municipal bonds trade on the American Stock Exchange.
- ❍ D. The municipal bond market is considered an auction market.

Quick Check

Choose from the following types of municipal bond quotes to answer Questions 18 and 19. An answer may be used once, more than once, or not at all.

- ❍ A. Firm offer
- ❍ B. Firm offer with recall
- ❍ C. Municipal workable
- ❍ D. Nominal bid

18. A municipal bond dealer that quotes to another dealer a price that is considered a good price for a certain period of time is giving what type of quote to the dealer?

Quick Answer: **136**
Detailed Answer: **139**

19. A municipal bond dealer that quotes a price at which it would be willing to buy or sell the bonds is giving what type of quote?

Quick Answer: **136**
Detailed Answer: **139**

20. Which of the following statements are true of the role that a broker's broker plays in the municipal bond market?

Quick Answer: **136**
Detailed Answer: **140**

   I. The broker's broker maintains an inventory in most municipal bonds offered.

   II. A broker's broker deals only with the public in trading municipal bonds.

   III. A broker's broker deals with the public and institutions in the municipal bond market.

   IV. The broker's broker secures the best possible price for its client on an anonymous basis.

- ❍ A. I and II
- ❍ B. I and III
- ❍ C. I and IV
- ❍ D. IV only

21. First Nation Bank has an extremely large block of municipal bonds that it wants to sell in the market. Where does it go to get the best possible price for its bonds?

Quick Answer: **136**
Detailed Answer: **140**

- ❍ A. It offers the bonds for sale in the OTC market.
- ❍ B. It goes to a municipal broker's broker to have it sell the bonds.
- ❍ C. It offers the bonds for sale in the blue list.
- ❍ D. It offers the bonds for sale in the pink sheets.

Quick Check

22. Municipal bond dealers looking to find the best possible price for their retail customers who want to buy or sell look in which of the following publications for their customers?

❍ A. The pink sheets
❍ B. The yellow sheets
❍ C. The blue list
❍ D. *The Daily Bond Buyer*

Quick Answer: **136**
Detailed Answer: **140**

23. *The Bond Buyer* is a trade paper for municipal bond issues. Which of the following characteristics are true of *The Bond Buyer*?

I. It tracks the visible supply of municipal bond issues.

II. It offers placement ratios for all issues placed in the secondary market.

III. It lists all competitive and negotiated offerings of 13 months or longer expected to reach the market in the next 30 days.

IV. It is supported by the Munifacts wire that gives dealers information on new issues and on the secondary market.

❍ A. I and II
❍ B. II and III
❍ C. I, II, and III
❍ D. I, II, III, and IV

Quick Answer: **136**
Detailed Answer: **140**

24. The Bond Buyer Index has which of the following characteristics in the municipal bond market?

I. It is an index compiled by *The Bond Buyer* each week.

II. It is the average yield of 20 municipal issues each with a maturity of 20 years and a rating of single A or better.

III. It is the average yield of 30 municipal issues each with a maturity of 30 years and a credit rating of AAA.

IV. The index lists all AAA-rated municipal bonds that are for sale in the secondary market that week.

❍ A. I and II
❍ B. II and IV
❍ C. I and IV
❍ D. III and IV

Quick Answer: **136**
Detailed Answer: **140**

Quick Check

25. Use the following municipal bond offering to answer the question:

    50 California Highway 6.175% 1/1/15 C05 6.485% Merrill Lynch

    Which of the following statements are true of the preceding municipal bond offering?

    I. The bonds have a nominal yield of 6.485%.

    II. The bonds are revenue bonds.

    III. The bonds are callable.

    IV. The bonds mature in the year 2015.

    ❍ A. I and II
    ❍ B. II and III
    ❍ C. II, III, and IV
    ❍ D. I, II, III, and IV

Quick Answer: 136
Detailed Answer: 140

Quick Check Answer Key

1. D
2. C
3. B
4. C
5. C
6. D
7. C
8. C
9. B
10. D
11. B
12. B
13. A
14. B
15. D
16. D
17. A
18. B
19. A
20. D
21. B
22. C
23. D
24. A
25. C

Answers and Explanations

1. **Answer D is correct.** The financial advisor for a municipality is a firm that has typically worked with the municipality in the past. It analyzes the municipality's debt statement to ensure that it has room under its debt ceiling to issue additional bonds. It advises the municipality on how the issue will impact its credit rating. It also recommends the target interest rate the municipality should seek in the bond issue and the type of bonds that it should issue to meet its needs.

2. **Answer C is correct.** A bond counsel is a law firm that the municipality has done business with in the past. The primary charge of the bond counsel is to render an impartial legal opinion on the bond. The bond counsel also draws up the bond contract between municipality and bondholder and appoints a trustee, which is typically a bank, to oversee the issue.

3. **Answer B is correct.** A municipality considering a building a revenue-producing project finances the project with revenue bonds. The first thing that a municipality does is commission a feasibility study to determine the cost, expected use, and whether the revenue-producing project can service the debt. Revenue bonds are backed by project revenues and are not backed by property taxes. G.O. bonds are backed by taxes and often need a voter approval to be issued.

4. **Answer C is correct.** A feasibility study is done for a revenue bond issue only. The municipality hires an outside independent consulting firm to determine the cost of the project, expected usage, projected revenues, and whether the project can support the debt issue that will be used to finance the project.

5. **Answer C is correct.** The notice of sale for a general obligation bond that is placed in *The Daily Bond Buyer* by a municipality states the amount of the issue, the type of bond being offered, and the type of tax that will be backing the bonds. It does not state the interest rate of the bonds because it is determined by the bidding process.

6. **Answer D is correct.** A competitive bid is almost always used exclusively for general obligation bond issues. In determining its bid, the underwriter gauges investor demand by pre-sale orders that are taken. The bid also considers the credit rating of the municipality and the risk it will incur. Tax collection ratios are also used to help determine the lowest possible bid. Anticipated project revenues come from revenue bonds and are not considered in a competitive bid (G.O. bonds) but rather on a negotiated basis between one underwriter chosen by the issuing municipality.

7. **Answer C is correct.** Pre-sale orders are permitted on municipal bond issues but not corporate issues. This allows an underwriter to pre-sell bonds prior to even winning the bid for the bonds. The pre-sale orders help an underwriter gauge investor demand for new bonds. It helps the underwriter determine its lowest possible final competitive bid on the issue. Obviously, pre-sale orders are not required to be filled, in the event that the underwriter does not win the bond issue with its bid.

8. **Answer C is correct.** Writing the scale is a process used by municipal bond underwriters when entering a bid for a general obligation bond issue. The scale is a schedule of interest rates for pre-sale orders. This rate represents the underwriter's assessment of the market demand for the bond issue. It shows the rate at which investors are willing to buy the bonds. It is not the final submitted bid that the underwriter submits to the issuer.

9. **Answer B is correct.** An underwriter for a general obligation competitive bid is required to follow the instructions of the issuer when submitting its bid. Competitive bids require that an underwriter submit a 2% good faith deposit with the sealed submitted bid. Remember, banks are permitted to underwrite municipal bond issues as long as they are G.O. bonds.

10. **Answer D is correct.** The lead underwriter for a municipal bond syndicate is considered the syndicate manager. It chooses all members of the syndicate and makes all investment decisions on the issue. For each bond that is sold, the lead underwriter earns a management fee as part of the total spread charged.

11. **Answer B is correct.** In an Eastern account, the syndicate members agree to enter into an undivided account. This means that they are responsible for their allocated percentage of the entire bond issue as well as the same percentage portion of any unsold bonds in the syndicate. In this question, J.J. Reed is responsible for the 10% of the $100,000,000 offering ($10,000,000) plus 10% of any unsold bonds. There were $20,000,000 of unsold bonds, and J.J. Reed is responsible for $2,000,000 or 10% of that amount. Its total commitment is $10,000,000 + $2,000,000 = $12,000,000.

12. **Answer B is correct.** In a Western account for a bond underwriting, the account is considered to be divided. This means that each syndicate member is responsible only for the allocated amount of the total offering it is assigned. Any unsold bonds remain the responsibility of the member that was unable to sell the bonds. Each syndicate member knows its total commitment to the overall issue exactly.

13. **Answer A is correct.** As the lead underwriter, Cord & James earns 1/4 of the 1/2 point spread that Lakeland earns on the sale of its bonds. $10,000,000 × 1/2 point spread = a $50,000 takedown on the bonds. Cord & James earns 1/8th on each bond sold. Remember that 1/8th is 1/4 of the 1/2 point spread. $10,000,000 × 1/8th (.125) = a $12,500.00 management fee earned by Cord & James for the bonds that Lakeland has sold.

14. **Answer B is correct.** An established underwriting syndicate has varying levels of risk for each broker that is associated to the syndicate. The greatest risk is borne by the lead underwriter. Next comes the syndicate members, who are responsible for selling a percentage of the issue. After that comes the selling group members, who, even though they have no liability for selling a certain amount of the issue, still take on more risk than any outside broker/dealer.

15. **Answer D is correct.** A syndicate manager is not necessarily required to become a market maker in the underlying bonds that it brings to the public. In many cases, it holds some bonds in inventory if they remain unsold. Otherwise, there is no obligation to be a market maker for the bonds.

16. **Answer D is correct.** Municipal bonds trade in increments of five bonds, with a round lot for retail customers being five bonds and a round lot for institutional investors being 100 bonds. Prices for municipal bonds are quoted in points, with each point equaling one percent of the bond. Most municipal bonds trade in increments of $5,000. Thus, one bond actually totals $5,000.

17. **Answer A is correct.** The municipal market is considered a thinly traded market and is rather illiquid. The reason is that municipal bonds are only purchased by residents of the state of issuance. There is no physical trading floor for municipal bonds, nor is there any real-time reporting of the up-to-the-minute prices on municipals.

18. **Answer B is correct.** A municipal bond dealer that gives a quote on a bond while the interested dealer decides to "shop around" for a better price modifies its quote to a firm offer with recall. The recall means that the dealer has given a price to the interested dealer, but only for a specified period of time. If the bonds are not sold within that time, then the quoting dealer can sell the bonds to a higher bidder.

19. **Answer A is correct.** A firm offer by a municipal dealer is a good price at which it is willing to buy or sell the bonds. The firm quote is honored by the quoting dealer if it is accepted.

20. **Answer D is correct.** A broker's broker serves as a conduit for large institutional clients in the sale of large blocks of municipal bonds. It does not deal with the public, nor does it maintain an inventory in any bonds. The broker's broker sells the bonds for its large institutional clients on an anonymous basis to avoid putting downward pressure on the price of the bonds that would happen if they were sold directly by a large institution.

21. **Answer B is correct.** A municipal broker's broker assists large institutional clients in selling municipal bonds in the market. Because the municipal market is a thinly traded market, a large block of bonds for sale by an institutional client could drive the price on the bonds down. A broker's broker represents the institution on an anonymous basis and moves the bonds bit by bit. By providing this service, the broker's broker is able to get the best possible price for the bonds.

22. **Answer C is correct.** The blue list is a daily publication by Standard & Poor's that is printed on blue paper, in which dealers advertise their available municipal offerings to other dealers. These dealers often find bonds for their retail clients in the blue list.

23. **Answer D is correct.** *The Bond Buyer* is a trade paper for municipal issues. It also tracks the visible supply of bonds, supplies information on new issues, and gives placement ratios for all issues that dealers have placed in the secondary market. *The Bond Buyer* visible supply reflects the total known competitive and negotiated offerings of 13 months or longer expected to reach the market within the next 30 days. The placement ratio compares the dollar volume of bonds sold each week to the volume of the week's new competitive issues of $5,000,000 or more.

24. **Answer A is correct.** The Bond Buyer Index is a closely watched index printed by *The Bond Buyer* that gives the average yield of 20 municipals, each with a maturity of 20 years and a rating of single A or better.

25. **Answer C is correct.** In a municipal bond offering, the first interest rate quoted is considered the nominal yield for the bond. The second interest rate is the yield to maturity for the bond. These are California Highway bonds that are more than likely to be revenue bonds supported by tolls from the project. The bonds are callable, starting in the year 2005 (C 05), and the bonds mature on 1/1/15.

The Municipal Securities Rulemaking Board

Quick Check

1. The Municipal Securities Rulemaking Board (MSRB) falls under the jurisdiction of which of the following organizations?

Quick Answer: 149
Detailed Answer: 150

- ❍ A. Federal Reserve
- ❍ B. Securities and Exchange Commission
- ❍ C. National Association of Securities Dealers
- ❍ D. New York Stock Exchange

2. Which of the following agencies enforces Municipal Securities Rulemaking Board rules and regulations?

Quick Answer: 149
Detailed Answer: 150

I. SEC

II. NASD

III. Federal Reserve Board

IV. Federal Deposit Insurance Company

- ❍ A. I and II
- ❍ B. II and III
- ❍ C. I, II, and III
- ❍ D. I, II, III, and IV

3. The Securities and Exchange Commission enforces MSRB rules for municipal dealers in which of the following?

Quick Answer: 149
Detailed Answer: 150

- ❍ A. Securities broker/dealers
- ❍ B. Commercial banks
- ❍ C. Savings banks
- ❍ D. State chartered banks

Quick Check

4. To be considered licensed under MSRB rules to deal in the municipal market, which of the following licenses are acceptable?

Quick Answer: 149
Detailed Answer: 150

I. Series 7

II. Series 62

III. Series 52

IV. Series 8

❍ A. I and II
❍ B. II and III
❍ C. I and III
❍ D. I and IV

5. Which of the following individuals are not permitted to be licensed under current MSRB standards?

Quick Answer: 149
Detailed Answer: 150

I. An individual who has been expelled from the futures market

II. An individual who has been expelled from the Chicago Board of Options

III. An individual who been out of the municipal market for more than two years

IV. An individual who has made a false statement on an application to the NASD

❍ A. I and II
❍ B. II and III
❍ C. I, II, and III
❍ D. I, II, and IV

Quick Check

6. Which of the following actions taken by a municipal broker is a violation of MSRB rules?

Quick Answer: **149**
Detailed Answer: **150**

I. Not paying a customer accrued interest on the date when issued bonds

II. Failing to tell a customer of a call feature on a municipal bond that he or she purchased

III. Giving a gift to a customer of two $50 tickets to a Broadway show

IV. Sending a customer a confirm for a trade on the next business day

❍ A. I and II
❍ B. II and III
❍ C. III and IV
❍ D. I, II, III, and IV

7. Victor goes to his neighborhood municipal broker/dealer to open a discretionary account. When filling out his new account form, Victor declines to disclose his financial holdings to the broker. What must the broker do under MSRB rules for this account?

Quick Answer: **149**
Detailed Answer: **150**

❍ A. He must decline to open the account under Rule 405, the "know your customer" rule.
❍ B. He can open the account and perform discretionary trades for the client.
❍ C. He can open the account but cannot make trading recommendations to the customer.
❍ D. He must receive a waiver from the branch manager of the office to open the account without any restrictions.

8. Which of the following documents are needed for a municipal broker to open a discretionary account for a client?

Quick Answer: **149**
Detailed Answer: **150**

I. Notarized power of attorney

II. Trading authorization

III. Customer agreement

IV. Hypothecation agreement

❍ A. I only
❍ B. I and II
❍ C. I, II, and III
❍ D. I, II, III, and IV

Quick Check

9. A municipal broker that has discretion over a customer account must adhere to which of the following procedures?

   I. Enter the order as discretionary

   II. Have each order approved by the operations manager

   III. Have each order approved by a manager

   IV. Have each order approved by a principal

   ❍ A. I only
   ❍ B. I and II
   ❍ C. I and III
   ❍ D. I and IV

Quick Answer: 149
Detailed Answer: 151

10. Joe works for a large securities broker in Richmond, Virginia. He decides to open a municipal trading account at a local municipal broker/dealer that has no affiliation with the firm where he works. How is the account handled?

   ❍ A. Joe can open the account without any restrictions.
   ❍ B. Joe can only open the account if it is a discretionary account.
   ❍ C. Joe can open the account as long a duplicate confirm is sent to his employer.
   ❍ D. Joe is not permitted to open the account because he already works for a broker/dealer.

Quick Answer: 149
Detailed Answer: 151

11. What is a bona fide quote that has been given by a municipal broker/dealer to another dealer?

   ❍ A. An absolute guaranteed price
   ❍ B. A good price only if it is accepted immediately
   ❍ C. A price that cannot change unless the market moves
   ❍ D. A price that can only change if it is for more than 10 bonds

Quick Answer: 149
Detailed Answer: 151

12. If a municipal bond dealer is cited by the MSRB for “painting the tape” on a transaction, what occurred?

   ❍ A. The dealer moved a large block of bonds in an illiquid market and is being commended by the MSRB.
   ❍ B. The municipal bond dealer purchased the bonds in excess for its own inventory.
   ❍ C. The municipal bond dealer reported a trade that did not occur.
   ❍ D. The municipal bond dealer sold more bonds than permitted under MSRB rules.

Quick Answer: 149
Detailed Answer: 151

Quick Check

13. A customer purchases 10 municipal G.O. bonds that are delivered to him within the prescribed time frame with nine coupons that are inexplicably mutilated. Which of the following best describes the customer's next action?

   ❍ A. Accept the bonds and notify the issuer of the mutilated coupons
   ❍ B. Accept the bonds as a good delivery but notify the broker/dealer of the mutilated coupons
   ❍ C. Refuse the bonds as a bad delivery and request his funds back
   ❍ D. Notify the MSRB that the broker/dealer sent him a bad delivery of bonds

Quick Answer: 149
Detailed Answer: 151

14. The receipt of municipal bonds with missing or mutilated coupons results in the client exercising her right to return the bonds. What is this known as?

   ❍ A. Refunding
   ❍ B. Reclamation
   ❍ C. Right of refusal
   ❍ D. Redemption recourse

Quick Answer: 149
Detailed Answer: 151

15. A syndicate member municipal dealer that has purchased newly issued municipal bonds is required under MSRB rules to disclose which of the following?

   I. Disclose to the lead underwriter if the bonds are going into its own inventory

   II. Disclose to the lead underwriter if the bonds are going into a related dealer account

   III. Disclose to the dealer if the bonds are going into an allocation account

   IV. Disclose to the dealer if the bonds are going into a municipal investment trust

   ❍ A. I only
   ❍ B. I and II
   ❍ C. I, II, and III
   ❍ D. I, II, III, and IV

Quick Answer: 149
Detailed Answer: 151

Quick Check

16. Municipal order tickets are required under MSRB rules to be retained by a broker/dealer for a time period of how long?
    - A. 1 year
    - B. 2 years
    - C. 3 years
    - D. 6 years

Quick Answer: 149
Detailed Answer: 151

17. Under MSRB rules, customer correspondence with a municipal broker/dealer is required to be retained for a period of how long?
    - A. 1 year
    - B. 2 years
    - C. 3 years
    - D. 6 years

Quick Answer: 149
Detailed Answer: 151

18. A municipal broker/dealer is required under MSRB rules to retain its corporate minute books for a period of how long?
    - A. 3 years
    - B. 5 years
    - C. 6 years
    - D. Permanently

Quick Answer: 149
Detailed Answer: 151

19. When advertising municipal bonds, a dealer must use which of the following yields, according to MSRB rules?
    - A. Nominal yield
    - B. Current yield
    - C. Yield to maturity
    - D. Any yield is acceptable

Quick Answer: 149
Detailed Answer: 152

20. Which of the following information is required by a municipal dealer when advertising municipal bonds, according to MSRB rules?

    I. The price of the bonds on publication date

    II. The current yield

    III. The nominal yield

    IV. The yield to maturity

    - A. I only
    - B. I and II
    - C. I and III
    - D. I and IV

Quick Answer: 149
Detailed Answer: 152

Quick Check

21. Ace Securities is a broker/dealer that is currently acting in a fiduciary role for a municipality. The dealer, due to its fiduciary role, has become privilege to certain information that other broker/dealers do not have about the municipality. Which of the following statements is true in this situation?

Quick Answer: 149
Detailed Answer: 152

- ❍ A. Ace Securities must make this information available to all other municipal dealers.
- ❍ B. The issuer must make this information available to all other municipal dealers.
- ❍ C. Ace Securities must have written permission from the municipality to use the information.
- ❍ D. Ace Securities can use the information without any restrictions.

22. Harold Applebee is a senior partner at Grange Securities, a large municipal bond dealer. Harold is close friends with Ken Vincent, who is an elected official of Hudson township. Under MSRB rules, what is the maximum contribution that Harold could make to Ken's campaign?

Quick Answer: 149
Detailed Answer: 152

- ❍ A. $100
- ❍ B. $250
- ❍ C. $500
- ❍ D. $1000

23. Which of the following contributions is considered a violation of MSRB rules pertaining to excessive political contributions to municipal officials?

Quick Answer: 149
Detailed Answer: 152

I. A broker/dealer who contributes $500 to a political action committee

II. A $1000 anonymous contribution to an elected municipal official

III. A $1000 contribution that a broker/dealer principal gives to his brother and then is sent to an elected official

IV. A $200 contribution that is given directly to an official running for reelection

- ❍ A. I and II
- ❍ B. II and III
- ❍ C. I, II, and III
- ❍ D. I, II, III, and IV

Quick Check

24. Under MSRB rules, a broker/dealer that receives a customer complaint against its firm in writing is required to do which of the following?

Quick Answer: 149
Detailed Answer: 152

❍ A. Resolve the complaint with the customer

❍ B. Resolve the complaint with the customer in arbitration

❍ C. Resolve the complaint with the customer in arbitration only if the client signed the arbitration agreement when opening the account

❍ D. Pay the client back any losses he had incurred

25. Which of the following gifts to a client is considered a violation of MSRB rules?

Quick Answer: 149
Detailed Answer: 152

I. A $75 autographed baseball

II. Two $40 tickets to a football game

III. $100 in cash

IV. Two $75 tickets to a Broadway play

❍ A. I, II, and III

❍ B. III and IV

❍ C. III only

❍ D. IV only

Quick Check Answer Key

1. B
2. D
3. A
4. C
5. D
6. A
7. C
8. B
9. D
10. C
11. B
12. C
13. C
14. B
15. D
16. A
17. C
18. D
19. C
20. D
21. C
22. B
23. C
24. C
25. D

Answers and Explanations

1. **Answer B is correct.** The MSRB is considered a self-regulatory organization that sets the rules which govern the municipal market place. The rules that are designed to regulate the dealers of these securities fall under the final jurisdiction of the Securities and Exchange Commission.

2. **Answer D is correct.** The underwriting of municipal securities can be conducted by securities dealers, commercial banks, and savings banks. Various enforcement agencies have the responsibility of enforcing MSRB rules as they apply to the various municipal dealers. They includes the SEC for securities broker/dealers, the NASD for broker/dealers that are NASD members, the Federal Reserve Board for commercial or savings banks that are members of the Federal Reserve system, and the FDIC for enforcing the rules on state chartered banks that are not members of the Federal Reserve system.

3. **Answer A is correct.** The Securities and Exchange Commission is the enforcement arm of MSRB rules as they apply to municipal securities broker/dealers.

4. **Answer C is correct.** Municipal brokers are required to be licensed by the NASD by way of either the Series 7 General Securities Registration or the Series 52 Municipal Securities Representative registration.

5. **Answer D is correct.** The MSRB would decline to register an individual who has been expelled or banished from another self-regulatory body, such as the futures market or options exchange. If an individual supplies false or misleading information on his qualifying application, he would also be refused a license qualification. Any individual who has been away from the municipal industry for a period longer than two years is required to reregister with the NASD and pass the Series 7 or Series 52 examination again.

6. **Answer A is correct.** MSRB rules cover a range of areas in the industry. Failure to pay accrued interest to a customer on the date when he issued bonds is considered a violation of the customer's rights. Failure to notify a customer of a call feature on a bond she purchases is also a violation of the customer's rights.

7. **Answer C is correct.** The refusal of a client to provide the necessary financial information to a municipal broker/dealer does not prohibit the account from being opened. The broker can open the account but is prohibited from making any trading recommendations to the customer. The client must make all investment decisions in the account, and each trade entered is marked "unsolicited."

8. **Answer B is correct.** A municipal discretionary account is required under MSRB rules to have a notarized legal power of attorney on file as well as a trading authorization from the customer.

9. **Answer D is correct.** Discretionary orders in a municipal account are required under MSRB rules to be marked discretionary for each order entered and to have the approval of a municipal principal by the end of the business day.

10. **Answer C is correct.** An employee of another securities firm is permitted to open an account at a second firm, as long as duplicate confirms on all transactions performed in the account are sent to the employer. This is done for security purposes to prevent embezzlement or fraud by an individual.

11. **Answer B is correct.** A bona fide quote is a good price if the broker accepts the quoted price immediately. The quoting broker is required to deliver the security at this quoted price as long as the contra broker accepts it.

12. **Answer C is correct.** Painting the tape is a violation of MSRB rules where a municipal dealer reports a trade in the market that did not actually occur. Remember, the municipal market is a thin market, and there is no real-time reporting of trades. To report trades in error or on purpose can affect prices in the marketplace.

13. **Answer C is correct.** A good delivery is considered a right of the customer. If bonds are mutilated or have missing coupons as part of the delivery, the client has the right to refuse delivery under reclamation and has the right to receive his funds back from the dealer.

14. **Answer B is correct.** Reclamation is the right of a customer to refuse a bad delivery of bonds that have missing coupons or have been mutilated in some manner. Under MSRB rules, the dealer is required to take the bonds back and refund the client her funds.

15. **Answer D is correct.** A syndicate member that purchases newly issued municipal bonds is required to disclose to the lead underwriter where all the bonds are going. This information is required under MSRB rules so the lead underwriter can make sure that too many bonds are not going to any one individual or account. The municipal market is a thin market, and this rule protects the trading of the bonds once they reach the secondary market.

16. **Answer A is correct.** Under MSRB rules, a broker/dealer is required to retain order tickets that are entered for clients for a period of three years, keeping the tickets readily accessible for two years.

17. **Answer C is correct.** Under MSRB rules, customer correspondence must be retained by a broker/dealer for a period of three years, keeping the correspondence readily accessible for two years.

18. **Answer D is correct.** A municipal broker/dealer under MSRB rules is required to maintain the corporate minute books on a permanent basis.

19. **Answer C is correct.** When advertising municipal bonds, a broker/dealer under MSRB rules is required to use the yield to maturity as the advertised yield. The yield to maturity is a more accurate indicator of a bond's value compared to current yield or nominal yield.

20. **Answer D is correct.** When advertising municipal bonds, a broker/dealer is required to list the price of the bonds as of the date of the advertisement, as well as the yield to maturity, which is a more accurate indicator of a bond's value in the market.

21. **Answer C is correct.** A municipal dealer that becomes privileged to certain inside information about a municipality while acting in a fiduciary role for the municipality is permitted under MSRB rules to use the information, as long as it receives permission from the municipality to do so. It is not required to share this information with other broker/dealers.

22. **Answer B is correct.** MSRB rules state that a broker/dealer cannot make a political contribution in excess of $250, either directly to a candidate or subversively through a political action committee. If the contribution is in excess of $250, the broker/dealer is prohibited from conducting a negotiated bid underwriting with the municipality for a period of two years.

23. **Answer C is correct.** Any political contribution that a broker/dealer makes in excess of $250 to a political candidate of a municipality is considered a violation of MSRB rules. This includes a direct contribution, an anonymous contribution, or any other subversive contribution that finds its way to the candidate from other sources associated to the broker/dealer.

24. **Answer C is correct.** With a customer complaint, the broker/dealer is required to submit the case to either simplified or binding arbitration, depending on the amount of the complaint. This depends on whether the client signed the arbitration agreement when opening his account.

25. **Answer D is correct.** Gifts to clients under MSRB rules are restricted to a maximum of $100 per year per client. The only violation in this question is the two Broadway tickets whose value totals in excess of $150.

Quick Check

The New York Stock Exchange

1. Which of the following statements are true regarding the New York Stock Exchange?

   Quick Answer: **161**
   Detailed Answer: **162**

   I. The NYSE is an auction market.

   II. The NYSE is a negotiated market.

   III. The NYSE is also known as the Curb Market.

   IV. The NYSE is also known as the Big Board.

   ❍ A. I and III
   ❍ B. II and IV
   ❍ C. I and IV
   ❍ D. II and III

2. For a company to be listed on the NYSE, which of the following requirements must be met?

   Quick Answer: **161**
   Detailed Answer: **162**

   I. The stock must have at least 2000 shareholders minimum with at least 100 shares.

   II. The company must have at least 1.1 million outstanding shares.

   III. The company must have earnings of at least $2.5 million before taxes.

   IV. The company must have a monthly trading volume of 1,000,000 shares.

   ❍ A. I and II
   ❍ B. II and III
   ❍ C. I, II, and III
   ❍ D. I, II, III, and IV

Quick Check

3. Which of the following instances cause the NYSE to delist a security?

Quick Answer: 161
Detailed Answer: 162

I. The company files for bankruptcy.

II. The company fails to issue an annual report.

III. The company issues nonvoting common stock.

IV. The company has losses in a given year in excess of $10,000,000.

- ❍ A. I and II
- ❍ B. II and III
- ❍ C. I, II, and III
- ❍ D. I, II, III, and IV

4. A seat on the New York Stock Exchange must be in the name of which of the following?

Quick Answer: 161
Detailed Answer: 162

- ❍ A. The member firm
- ❍ B. The individual floor broker
- ❍ C. The senior board member
- ❍ D. The seat can be in the name of any of the preceding choices.

5. Which of the following statements are considered true regarding a seat on the NYSE?

Quick Answer: 161
Detailed Answer: 162

I. The seat must be in the name of the member firm.

II. There are 1366 seats on the exchange.

III. A seat can only be purchased if an owner puts it up for auction.

IV. A member firm can have more than one seat on the exchange.

- ❍ A. I and II
- ❍ B. II and III
- ❍ C. I, II, and III
- ❍ D. II, III, and IV

Quick Check

6. NYSE Rule 77 states all the following to be true except for which one?

Quick Answer: 161
Detailed Answer: 162

- ❍ A. Member firms cannot buy or sell dividends.
- ❍ B. Member firms cannot bet on movements in the market.
- ❍ C. Member firms can only have one seat on the floor of the exchange.
- ❍ D. Member firms cannot buy or sell privileges to receive or deliver securities.

7. New York Stock Exchange Rule 405 is best described as which of the following?

Quick Answer: 161
Detailed Answer: 162

- ❍ A. A member firm cannot buy or sell dividends.
- ❍ B. A member firm cannot bet on market movements.
- ❍ C. A broker is required to know its customer.
- ❍ D. A firm is prohibited from buying or selling stock for a customer with a prearranged agreement to sell or buy them back at the same price.

8. All NYSE member firms are required to provide which of the following to prevent against fraud or embezzlement by the firm's employees?

Quick Answer: 161
Detailed Answer: 162

- ❍ A. A surety bond
- ❍ B. A blanket fidelity bond
- ❍ C. A flower bond
- ❍ D. A zero tolerance bond

9. Aaron Novell is currently studying for his Series 7 licensing exam. When filing his paperwork for the exam, he neglected to mention that he was expelled from the Chicago Board of Options Exchange five years earlier. Aaron will not trade any type of options when he is licensed. Which of the following statements is true?

Quick Answer: 161
Detailed Answer: 163

- ❍ A. Aaron can still earn the Series 7 license but is restricted from ever doing options again.
- ❍ B. Aaron must receive a waiver from the CBOE to be allowed to be registered as a licensed broker.
- ❍ C. Aaron would be disqualified as a candidate and immediately dismissed by his firm.
- ❍ D. Aaron has been out of the business for five years and is now qualified to reregister himself by passing the Series 7 Exam.

Quick Check

10. Lester currently works for a NYSE member firm as a broker. He is just getting started in the business, and to make ends meet, he needs to take on a second job at a local retailer. Which of the following statements is true?

- ❍ A. Lester can have a second job without any problems.
- ❍ B. Lester is prohibited from having a second job.
- ❍ C. Lester needs the approval of the broker to take on a second position.
- ❍ D. Lester needs duplicate confirms sent to the second employer if he takes on the job.

Quick Answer: 161
Detailed Answer: 163

11. New York Stock Exchange Rules 80A and 80B are designed specifically to do which of the following?

- ❍ A. They act as circuit breakers for the market.
- ❍ B. They prevent brokers from buying or selling dividends.
- ❍ C. They dictate that to open an account, a broker must know its customer.
- ❍ D. They concern the opening of long margin and short margin accounts.

Quick Answer: 161
Detailed Answer: 163

12. When institutions set certain parameters on their portfolios that strategically react to market movements and automatically buy or sell certain holdings, this is known as which of the following?

- ❍ A. Stop loss orders
- ❍ B. Buy limit orders
- ❍ C. Sell limit orders
- ❍ D. Program trading orders

Quick Answer: 161
Detailed Answer: 163

13. As of early 1998, circuit breakers are designed to automatically kick in when the Dow Jones Industrial Average drops what amount?

- ❍ A. 250 points
- ❍ B. 500 points
- ❍ C. 5% of the total Dow average
- ❍ D. 10% of the total Dow average

Quick Answer: 161
Detailed Answer: 163

Quick Check

14. A 50-point movement in the Dow Jones Industrial Average in either direction causes which of the following to occur?

    I. Shuts down the market to institutions for 1/2 hour

    II. Shuts down the Super Dot system to institutions for the day

    III. Directs all orders to the floor reporter

    IV. Directs all orders to the specialist

❍ A. I only
❍ B. II only
❍ C. I and III
❍ D. II and IV

Quick Answer: 161
Detailed Answer: 163

15. Which of the following statements is true about specialists on the NYSE floor?

    I. A specialist makes a market in all NYSE-listed securities.

    II. A specialist makes a market in certain NYSE-listed securities.

    III. A specialist is required to maintain an inventory in all NYSE-listed securities.

    IV. A specialist is required to maintain an inventory in certain NYSE-listed securities.

❍ A. I only
❍ B. II only
❍ C. I and III
❍ D. II and IV

Quick Answer: 161
Detailed Answer: 163

16. A specialist is required to handle which of the following types of orders?

    I. Market orders

    II. Limit orders

    III. Market orders to sell short

    IV. Stop orders

❍ A. I and II
❍ B. II and III
❍ C. I, II, and III
❍ D. II, III, and IV

Quick Answer: 161
Detailed Answer: 163

Quick Check

17. Competitive traders on the floor of the NYSE are required to make what percentage of their trades in a stabilizing fashion to ensure the integrity of the market?

   - ❍ A. 25% of their trades in a stabilizing manner
   - ❍ B. 50% of their trades in a stabilizing manner
   - ❍ C. 75% of their trades in a stabilizing manner
   - ❍ D. 100% of their trades in a stabilizing manner

Quick Answer: **161**
Detailed Answer: **164**

18. Which of the following statements is true regarding competitive traders on the floor of the NYSE?

   I. Fifty percent of their purchases of stock must be done on a negative tick.

   II. Seventy-five percent of their purchases of stock must be done on a negative tick.

   III. Fifty percent of their sales of stock must be done on a plus tick.

   IV. Seventy-five percent of their sales of stock must be done on a plus tick.

   - ❍ A. I only
   - ❍ B. II only
   - ❍ C. I and III
   - ❍ D. II and IV

Quick Answer: **161**
Detailed Answer: **164**

19. New York Stock Exchange Rule 92 states which of the following to be true?

   - ❍ A. Member firms must complete at least 50% of their trades after they execute a customer order first.
   - ❍ B. Member firms must complete at least 75% of their trades after they execute a customer order first.
   - ❍ C. Member firms must complete at least 90% of their trades after they execute a customer order first.
   - ❍ D. Member firms must complete 100% of their trades after they execute a customer order first.

Quick Answer: **161**
Detailed Answer: **164**

20. The role of the $2 broker on the floor of the New York Stock Exchange is best described as which of the following?

   - ❍ A. It handles any trades for stock valued under $5.
   - ❍ B. It handles any trades for stock valued under $2.
   - ❍ C. It handles market orders that the specialist cannot execute.
   - ❍ D. It handles market orders for member firms that have an overflow of orders.

Quick Check

21. A specialist that has quoted the market on GM at 70 1/4 × 70 1/2, 800 × 500, is stating which of the following?

Quick Answer: 161
Detailed Answer: 164

❍ A. The market for GM is 70 1/4 ask and 70 1/2 bid with sellers for 800 shares and buyers for 500 shares.
❍ B. The market for GM is 70 1/4 bid and 70 1/2 ask with sellers for 800 shares and buyers for 500 shares.
❍ C. The market for GM is 70 1/4 bid and 70 1/2 ask with buyers for 800 shares and sellers for 500 shares.
❍ D. The market for GM is 70 1/4 ask and 70 1/2 bid with buyers for 800 shares and sellers for 500 shares.

22. A customer entered a GTC order to purchase 500 shares of XYZ stock at a price of $55 in the market. The price of XYZ stock is currently at $59 per share. Which of the following handles this order?

Quick Answer: 161
Detailed Answer: 164

❍ A. The $2 broker
❍ B. The floor broker
❍ C. The specialist
❍ D. The competitive trader

23. A trade that is executed on the floor of the NYSE between a broker and a contra broker typically appears on the consolidated tape how quickly?

Quick Answer: 161
Detailed Answer: 164

❍ A. Within 5 seconds
❍ B. Within 30 seconds
❍ C. Within 60 seconds
❍ D. Within 90 seconds

24. The consolidated tape reports trades to the public for which of the following?

Quick Answer: 161
Detailed Answer: 164

❍ A. Network A reports NYSE trades, and Network B reports OTC trades.
❍ B. Network A reports NYSE trades, and Network B reports off-the-floor trades.
❍ C. Network A reports NYSE trades, and Network B reports AMEX trades.
❍ D. Network A reports NYSE trades, and Network B reports all other exchange trades.

Quick Check

25. NYSE Rule 411 states that if a customer enters an order to buy a stock at $50 and the trade is reported back to the customer at $51, which of the following is true?

   ❍ A. The customer can kill the trade by his right of reclamation.
   ❍ B. The customer is required to settle the trade at $50.
   ❍ C. The customer is required to settle the trade at $51.
   ❍ D. The customer asks for the trade to be held in a suspense account.

Quick Answer: **161**
Detailed Answer: **164**

Quick Check Answer Key

1. C

2. C

3. C

4. B

5. D

6. C

7. C

8. B

9. C

10. C

11. A

12. D

13. D

14. D

15. D

16. D

17. C

18. D

19. D

20. D

21. C

22. C

23. D

24. C

25. B

Answers and Explanations

1. **Answer C is correct.** The NYSE is considered the largest auction market in the world. The OTC market is considered a negotiated market. The NYSE is commonly nicknamed the Big Board, and the AMEX is known as the Curb Market.

2. **Answer C is correct.** NYSE listing requirements include 2000 shareholders, each with at least 100 shares of stock. The company must have at least 1.1 million outstanding shares and earnings before taxes of $2.5 million. The trading volume for the stock must be at least a minimum of 100,000 shares traded on the stock in the last six months.

3. **Answer C is correct.** A company that is listed on the NYSE can be delisted if it files for bankruptcy, fails to provide full financial disclosure to shareholders, or issues nonvoting common shares of stock. Being profitable is not a requirement to remain listed on the NYSE. A company can incur losses and still remain listed.

4. **Answer B is correct.** Each seat that is owned must be in the name of an individual. The seat is typically in the name of the floor broker of the member firm. It would not be in the member firm's name or a senior broker's name.

5. **Answer D is correct.** The last three choices are all correct; only A is not correct. The 1366 seats on the NYSE are required to be in the names of individuals. A seat can only be purchased if someone who currently owns a seat elects to auction off the seat. Member firms are allowed as many seats on the floor as needed to meet the amount of business.

6. **Answer C is correct.** Rule 77 prevents member firms from betting on movement in the market, buying or selling dividends, or buying and selling privileges to receive or deliver securities. No rule states that a member is only permitted one seat on the floor of the exchange. Many large broker/dealers can have numerous seats to execute their volume of business on the NYSE.

7. **Answer C is correct.** Rule 405 is the "Know Your Customer" rule. This rule is designed to ensure that a broker is familiar with its customer, his investment objectives, and his ability to handle risk.

8. **Answer B is correct.** NYSE member firms are required to provide a blanket fidelity bond to guard against fraud and embezzlement by employees when becoming a member of the NYSE.

9. **Answer C is correct.** An individual who has lied or misrepresented himself on a U-4 application to become registered as a broker is summarily dismissed by the firm and disqualified from becoming a registered representative. If an individual willfully lies, deceives, or is guilty of being expelled from any other securities exchange, he cannot be licensed.

10. **Answer C is correct.** Individuals who are employed by a broker/dealer need to notify their employers of their desire to take on a second job and receive approval of the broker/dealer to accept the additional position.

11. **Answer A is correct.** Rules 80A and 80B were created after the market crash of 1987. They were known as circuit breakers for the market. Many believed that program trading was a major contributor to the market meltdown in 1987, and these circuit breakers were instituted to prevent a freefall of the market. Rule 80B makes provisions to shut down the market for a prescribed period of time if the market drops more than 250 points in one day. This guideline has since been changed to a 10% drop in the Dow. Rule 80A states that if the S&P rises or falls more than 12 points in a given day, the Super Dot trading system used by institutions is shut off to institutional clients, and their orders are directed to the specialist for execution.

12. **Answer D is correct.** Program trading is the use of computers to execute the investment decisions of large institutions. When prescribed parameters are met, a programmed trading plan kicks into effect and the computer enters orders designed to follow the plan.

13. **Answer D is correct.** Rule 80B originally stated that if the market declines 250 points or more, the market shuts down for a prescribed period of time. This rule was updated in 1998 to require a 10% drop in the value of the Dow Jones Industrial Average to halt trading.

14. **Answer D is correct.** A 50-point drop in the Dow or a movement of 12 points in either direction for the S&P 500 Index shuts down the NYSE computerized trading system, known as the Super Dot system, to institutions and directs these orders directly to the floor specialist.

15. **Answer D is correct.** A specialist on the floor of the NYSE makes a market in certain securities by maintaining an inventory in those securities to which he has been assigned to be the market maker. Each market maker must maintain an inventory in his assigned securities.

16. **Answer D is correct.** Specialists on the floor of the NYSE handle limit orders or orders that are away from the market. They also handle market orders to sell short a stock and any protective stop order that is entered by an investor.

17. **Answer C is correct.** The NYSE requires that 75% of all trades conducted by a competitive trader be done in a stabilizing manner. That is, on a purchase of a security, they must buy the stock 75% of the time when it is moving downward in price, and on a sale of a stock, they must sell 75% of the time when the stock is moving upward in price. Because competitive traders are considered insiders, the NYSE requires that they act in a stabilizing manner to ensure the integrity of the market.

18. **Answer D is correct.** Competitive traders must buy 75% of their sales on a negative tick and sell 75% of the trades on a plus tick. The NYSE considers competitive traders insiders and implemented this rule to ensure the integrity of the market.

19. **Answer D is correct.** NYSE Rule 92 requires that a customer order always take priority over a NYSE member's own trading account when being handled for execution.

20. **Answer D is correct.** A $2 broker on the floor of the NYSE executes orders for member firms and floor brokers that have been inundated with orders. The $2 broker also executes trades for members who do not have seats on the floor of the exchange.

21. **Answer C is correct.** The specialist quote of GM 70 1/4 × 1/2 8 × 5 means that there are buyers who have a bid of 70 1/4 for the stock totaling 800 shares and sellers who have an asking price of 70 1/2 on the stock for 500 shares.

22. **Answer C is correct.** The floor broker leaves these orders that are marked GTC (good till cancelled) with the specialist. When the limit is reached, the specialist executes the trade that has been sitting in her specialist book. Orders that are away from the market are considered limit orders, and these orders might not necessarily be executed on the day they are entered.

23. **Answer D is correct.** Normal trade reporting from the time of execution to reporting on the consolidated tape takes an average of 90 seconds to be disseminated to the public forum.

24. **Answer C is correct.** The consolidated tape consists of Network A and Network B. Network A consists of trades conducted on the NYSE, and Network B consists of trades conducted on the American Stock Exchange.

25. **Answer B is correct.** Rule 411 states that a trade reported in error to a client holds the client responsible only for the actual price on the trade. In this question, the customer is required to pay $50 for the stock.

NASDAQ and OTC Markets

Quick Check

1. The Over-the Counter-stock exchange has all the following characteristics except for which one?
   - ❍ A. It is considered a negotiated market place.
   - ❍ B. It maintains a physical trading floor.
   - ❍ C. It uses market makers to maintain the market.
   - ❍ D. It is controlled by the NASD.

Quick Answer: 172
Detailed Answer: 173

2. An OTC market maker in an underlying OTC security that must be a member of which of the following markets to trade the stock?
   - ❍ A. NASDAQ
   - ❍ B. NASD
   - ❍ C. NYSE
   - ❍ D. SEC

Quick Answer: 172
Detailed Answer: 173

3. Non-NASDAQ listed securities are reported each day in which of the following publications?
   - ❍ A. Yellow sheets
   - ❍ B. Blue list
   - ❍ C. Pink sheets
   - ❍ D. White sheets

Quick Answer: 172
Detailed Answer: 173

4. The National Market System is considered the largest of the NASDAQ marketplace. How many different securities are listed on the NMS?
   - ❍ A. 1000
   - ❍ B. 2500
   - ❍ C. 4500
   - ❍ D. 10,000

Quick Answer: 172
Detailed Answer: 173

Quick Check

5. Aaron is an investor who is constantly searching for small emerging stocks coming out as new issues. He can find quotes on these types of stocks from which of the following?

Quick Answer: 172
Detailed Answer: 173

- ❍ A. The blue list
- ❍ B. The pink sheets
- ❍ C. The NASDAQ system
- ❍ D. The yellow sheets

6. The difference between a market maker's bid quote and ask quote is considered the what?

Quick Answer: 172
Detailed Answer: 173

- ❍ A. Market
- ❍ B. Spread
- ❍ C. Workable
- ❍ D. Firm quote

7. The NASDAQ system that is used by NASD member firms consists of which of the following?

Quick Answer: 172
Detailed Answer: 173

I. Level one

II. Level two

III. Level three

IV. Level four

- ❍ A. I only
- ❍ B. I and II
- ❍ C. I, II, and III
- ❍ D. I, II, III, and IV

8. What is the NASDAQ Level screen that is available for market makers to change their quotes on securities?

Quick Answer: 172
Detailed Answer: 173

- ❍ A. Level I
- ❍ B. Level II
- ❍ C. Level III
- ❍ D. Level IV

Quick Check

9. Which of the following quotes by an OTC market maker are considered a good price at which a dealer can buy stock?

Quick Answer: 172
Detailed Answer: 173

I. Firm quote

II. Nominal quote

III. Subject quote

IV. Workable quote

- ❍ A. I only
- ❍ B. I and II
- ❍ C. I, II, and III
- ❍ D. I, II, and IV

10. An OTC dealer that is interested in selling a stock could ask a potential buyer for a price on the stock. What is this is known as?

Quick Answer: 172
Detailed Answer: 174

- ❍ A. Offer wanted
- ❍ B. Bid wanted
- ❍ C. Spread wanted
- ❍ D. Workout wanted

11. An OTC broker/dealer that trades stock out of its own inventory acts as which of the following in the transaction?

Quick Answer: 172
Detailed Answer: 174

- ❍ A. Registered trader
- ❍ B. Specialist
- ❍ C. Principal
- ❍ D. Competitive trader

12. A dealer that sells securities out of its own inventory account to a client must report which of the following information to the customer on the confirmation?

Quick Answer: 172
Detailed Answer: 174

I. Whether it acted as a principal in the trade

II. Any markup it charged

III. The security purchased

IV. The price of the security

- ❍ A. I only
- ❍ B. I and II
- ❍ C. I, II, and III
- ❍ D. I, II, III, and IV

Quick Check

13. A riskless trade that is conducted by an OTC broker/dealer occurs when it does which of the following?

Quick Answer: 172
Detailed Answer: 174

- ❍ A. Sells a stock from its inventory to a customer
- ❍ B. Buys a stock for its inventory and immediately sells it to a customer for a profit
- ❍ C. Sells a stock short for the customer when the customer is short against the box
- ❍ D. Buys a married put for a customer on the same day that it buys shares for the customer

14. An OTC dealer received identical buy and sell market orders from two of its customers. The dealer elects to cross the orders of the two customers. What can the dealer charge on the trade?

Quick Answer: 172
Detailed Answer: 174

- ❍ A. The dealer cannot charge anything because crossing orders is prohibited on OTC securities.
- ❍ B. The dealer can only charge one commission on the trade.
- ❍ C. The dealer can charge a commission to each side of the crossed order.
- ❍ D. The dealer can only charge a markup.

15. Which of the following acts of Congress was designed specifically to regulate the Over-the-Counter market?

Quick Answer: 172
Detailed Answer: 174

- ❍ A. Securities Act of 1933
- ❍ B. Securities Act of 1934
- ❍ C. Maloney Act of 1938
- ❍ D. Investment Act of 1940

16. The National Association of Securities Dealers (NASD) bylaws consist of which of the following?

Quick Answer: 172
Detailed Answer: 174

I. Uniform Practice Code

II. Rules of Fair Practice

III. Code of Procedure

IV. Code of Arbitration

- ❍ A. I only
- ❍ B. I and II
- ❍ C. I, II, and III
- ❍ D. I, II, III, and IV

Quick Check

17. The NASD bylaws and rules that govern member firms and their dealings with customers are covered by which of the following NASD bylaws?
    - ❍ A. Code of Arbitration
    - ❍ B. Code of Procedure
    - ❍ C. Rules of Fair Practice
    - ❍ D. Uniform Practice

Quick Answer: **172**
Detailed Answer: **174**

18. The NASD 5% policy states that member firms are required to perform in which of the following manners?
    - ❍ A. The firm is required to limit its markups on trades to 5% on all transactions handled by the office.
    - ❍ B. The firm should aim to charge 5% on transaction fees on all transactions handled by the office, but if justified, it is permitted to charge more.
    - ❍ C. The NASD requires that 5% of the trades in any member office be conducted in a stabilizing manner.
    - ❍ D. The NASD requires that commissions on trades never exceed 5%.

Quick Answer: **172**
Detailed Answer: **174**

19. An OTC broker/dealer that trades for its own inventory account ahead of a customer's order for the same security is guilty under NASD rules of which of the following?
    - ❍ A. Reclamation
    - ❍ B. Interpositioning
    - ❍ C. Front running
    - ❍ D. Backdoor trading

Quick Answer: **172**
Detailed Answer: **175**

20. An OTC broker/dealer that trades a security with one of its customers from its own inventory is permitted to charge which of the following?
    - ❍ A. A markup only
    - ❍ B. A commission only
    - ❍ C. Both a markup and a commission
    - ❍ D. None of the above

Quick Answer: **172**
Detailed Answer: **175**

Quick Check

21. Under the Code of Procedure rules set forth by the NASD, a customer with a complaint is required to do which of the following?
    - ❍ A. Call the branch manager of the member firm and formally complain.
    - ❍ B. Call the District Business Conduct Committee of the NASD to formally complain.
    - ❍ C. Submit a formal written complaint to the District Business Conduct Committee.
    - ❍ D. Hire a lawyer and sue the member firm in a court of civil law.

Quick Answer: **172**
Detailed Answer: **175**

22. The District Business Conduct Committee of the NASD has the power to handle customer complaints in which of the following manners?

    I. It can dismiss a complaint that it feels is unwarranted.

    II. It can censure a member firm in response to the complaint.

    III. It acts as legal counsel for the customer.

    IV. It acts as legal counsel for the member firm.

    - ❍ A. I and II
    - ❍ B. II and III
    - ❍ C. I, II, and III
    - ❍ D. I, II, III, and IV

Quick Answer: **172**
Detailed Answer: **175**

23. A client who feels that he has been unfairly treated by his broker and defrauded of a monetary amount of $5,000 can resolve this dispute in the quickest way by doing which of the following?
    - ❍ A. Submit to simplified arbitration
    - ❍ B. Submit to binding arbitration
    - ❍ C. Go to civil court
    - ❍ D. Go to the National Security Council

Quick Answer: **172**
Detailed Answer: **175**

Quick Check

24. A customer who has been solicited by an OTC member firm to purchase a penny stock is required to sign which of the following agreements before the trade can be entered?

    I. A suitability form

    II. A margin agreement

    III. A hypothecation agreement

    IV. A broker loan agreement

    - A. I only
    - B. I and II
    - C. I, II, and III
    - D. I, II, III, and IV

Quick Answer: 172
Detailed Answer: 175

25. Which of the following securities actively trades on the OTC market?

    I. Government securities

    II. Agency securities

    III. Corporate bonds

    IV. Municipal bonds

    - A. I only
    - B. I and II
    - C. I, II, and III
    - D. I, II, III, and IV

Quick Answer: 172
Detailed Answer: 175

Quick Check Answer Key

1. B

2. B

3. C

4. B

5. B

6. B

7. C

8. C

9. A

10. B

11. C

12. D

13. B

14. C

15. C

16. D

17. C

18. B

19. C

20. A

21. C

22. A

23. A

24. A

25. D

Answers and Explanations

1. **Answer B is correct.** The OTC market is a computerized marketplace that is regulated by the NASD. There is no physical trading floor for the OTC market, but rather a negotiated market utilizing computer links.

2. **Answer B is correct.** A market maker of an OTC stock is required to be a member of the NASD, which regulates the market for active participants.

3. **Answer C is correct.** The smaller OTC securities that are not part of the NASDAQ system appear in the daily publication of the pink sheets.

4. **Answer B is correct.** The National Market System includes the largest of the securities that are listed on the NASDAQ system. Currently, about 2500 different stocks compose the NMS system, and another 3000 make up the Small Cap Market of NASDAQ.

5. **Answer B is correct.** The pink sheets list small emerging initial public offerings to investors who like to speculate in these securities. The NASDAQ system lists all NMS stocks as well as Small Cap Market securities.

6. **Answer B is correct.** The difference between the bid and ask quote that a market maker gives is known as the spread. The bid is the highest anyone is willing to pay, and the ask is the lowest anyone is willing to sell at. The difference between the two prices is known as the spread on the security.

7. **Answer C is correct.** The NASDAQ system has three levels of reporting for securities. Level I provides the bid and ask on a security and is used by brokers. Level II gives a list of all market makers and their quotes, and Level III is used by the member firm trader that wants to change a quote on the security it makes a market in.

8. **Answer C is correct.** The NASDAQ system allows market makers to change their daily quotes on underlying securities by using Level III of the reporting system. This is a limited-access level that is only used by traders which make the market for the underlying security for the OTC member firm.

9. **Answer A is correct.** A firm quote is considered a good quote by a market maker. In essence, this is a quote at which the market maker is willing to sell or buy the security. A nominal quote requires a reconfirmation by the market maker and thus is not considered firm. A workable quote is a feeler quote that a dealer uses to try to ascertain the market. A workable quote is a quote that a dealer gives but needs to check with a market maker to see whether that price is good.

10. **Answer B is correct.** A dealer that is looking to sell stock in the market requests bids on the stock by potential buyers. This is known as bid wanted. The bid is the highest anyone is willing to pay for the security, and the ask is the lowest anyone is willing to sell at.
11. **Answer C is correct.** An OTC broker/dealer that is trading stock out of its own inventory is considered a principal in the trade.
12. **Answer D is correct.** When a broker/dealer sells the security out of its own inventory, it must report to the client its role as principal. The trade confirmation has the price of the security, the stock purchased, and any markup charged if the stock was a NASDAQ-listed security only. Non-NASDAQ securities do not require the markup to be disclosed.
13. **Answer B is correct.** A riskless trade is when a broker/dealer purchases a stock for its own inventory and immediately sells it for a profit to a customer.
14. **Answer C is correct.** When an OTC broker/dealer conducts a crossed order at the current market price, it is permitted to charge two separate commissions on the transaction: one for the buyer and one for the seller. It is permitted to cross the orders only if it offers the stock at the current market price.
15. **Answer C is correct.** Congress implemented the Maloney Act of 1938 to deal with the Over-the-Counter securities market when it realized that this market was not being adequately regulated. It gave the NASD the authority to set the rules and enforce them on member firms.
16. **Answer D is correct.** The NASD was empowered by the Maloney Act of 1938 to design, regulate, and enforce the rules on OTC member firms. The NASD is a self-regulatory body that created the NASD bylaws, which includes the Uniform Practice Code, Rules of Fair Practice, and the Codes of Procedure and Arbitration.
17. **Answer C is correct.** The Rules of Fair Practice cover the dealings that OTC member firms have with customers. The code holds dealers to the highest ethical standards in their dealings with customers. This includes "knowing their customers" and how they handle markups and markdowns on stocks.
18. **Answer B is correct.** The NASD 5% markup policy states that a member firm should follow the 5% guideline set forth by the NASD on customer markups. This is only a guideline and is not considered a rule. If certain details of a trade cause a member firm to go to extraordinary measures to execute a trade for a client, then it is permitted to charge a markup in excess of 5%.

19. **Answer C is correct.** An OTC member firm that executes a transaction for its own trading account ahead of a customer order is guilty of front running under NASD rules. A customer order always takes precedence over a firm order.

20. **Answer A is correct.** A broker that trades a security out of its own inventory is only permitted to charge that customer one transaction fee under NASD rules. This is typically a markup. It is not permitted to charge both a markup and a commission on the same transaction.

21. **Answer C is correct.** Per NASD rules, all customer complaints are required to be sent in writing to a District Business Conduct Committee for initial review. The DBCC can either dismiss the complaint as frivolous or censure the broker/dealer against which the complaint is entered.

22. **Answer A is correct.** The District Business Conduct Committee can either dismiss the complaint as unwarranted or censure the broker/dealer for its actions. The DBCC never represents either the member or the client as legal counsel in any formal complaint.

23. **Answer A is correct.** When a client declares monetary damages, the dispute goes to the NASD Code of Arbitration. Depending upon the size of the dispute, it either goes to simplified arbitration or binding arbitration. For amounts under $10,000, clients enter into simplified arbitration. For larger amounts, they could go to binding arbitration. Most clients sign an arbitration agreement when opening their accounts to agree to resolve disputes in this fashion.

24. **Answer A is correct.** OTC broker/dealers that solicit penny stock trades from a prospective client are required to have the customer sign a suitability form prior to the trade being executed. The suitability form states that the customer is considered suitable for such a speculative stock.

25. **Answer D is correct.** The Over-the-Counter market trades NASDAQ stocks and other OTC stocks. It is also the secondary market for corporate bonds, municipal bonds, government obligations, and agency debt obligations.

Quick Check

Call Options

1. How much does an investor pay to purchase 10 call option contracts at a premium of $4?
   - ❍ A. $4.00
   - ❍ B. $400.00
   - ❍ C. $4000.00
   - ❍ D. $40,000.00

Quick Answer: **183**
Detailed Answer: **184**

2. All the following statements are true regarding option premiums except for which one?
   - ❍ A. An option premium can have a zero intrinsic value.
   - ❍ B. An option premium can have a zero time value.
   - ❍ C. An option premium can change in value.
   - ❍ D. An option premium is multiplied by the number of shares in a contract.

Quick Answer: **183**
Detailed Answer: **184**

3. All the following statements are true regarding the option contract 1 PDQ April 70 Call @ 2, with a market price of PDQ at 71 7/8, except for which one?
   - ❍ A. The option is at the money.
   - ❍ B. The option is in the money.
   - ❍ C. The option contract is not out of the money.
   - ❍ D. The option has intrinsic value.

Quick Answer: **183**
Detailed Answer: **184**

4. What is the breakeven point on the following option contract?

   Buy 1 TNT October 60 Call @ 3 with a market price of TNT at 60 1/2
   - ❍ A. 57
   - ❍ B. 60 1/2
   - ❍ C. 62 1/2
   - ❍ D. 63

Quick Answer: **183**
Detailed Answer: **184**

Quick Check

5. What is the breakeven point on the following option contract?

   Buy 10 AOL November 70 Calls @ 5 with a market price of AOL at $73

   ❍ A. $65
   ❍ B. $68
   ❍ C. $73
   ❍ D. $75

Quick Answer: 183
Detailed Answer: 184

6. What is the breakeven point of the following option contract?

   Buy 5 KLM August 55 Calls @ 3 1/2 with KLM having a market price of $56

   ❍ A. 51 1/2
   ❍ B. 52 1/2
   ❍ C. 58 1/2
   ❍ D. 59 1/2

Quick Answer: 183
Detailed Answer: 184

7. What is the maximum loss the holder of the following contract could incur?

   Buy 1 HTH October 60 Call @ 4 with a market price of HTH at $62

   ❍ A. $400
   ❍ B. $5600
   ❍ C. $5800
   ❍ D. $6400

Quick Answer: 183
Detailed Answer: 185

8. On what side of the market is the writer and what side is the holder for the following option contract?

   1 LTV April 60 Call @ 4

   ❍ A. Writer is bearish; holder is bullish.
   ❍ B. Holder is bullish; writer is bullish.
   ❍ C. Holder is bearish; writer is bullish.
   ❍ D. Writer is bullish; holder is bearish.

Quick Answer: 183
Detailed Answer: 185

9. What is the writer's breakeven point on the following option contract?

   1 FTD April 70 Call @ 5 with FTD having a market price of $73

   ❍ A. $65
   ❍ B. $68
   ❍ C. $70
   ❍ D. $75

Quick Answer: 183
Detailed Answer: 185

Quick Check

10. What is the breakeven point for the writer on the following option contract?

    1 TNT September 55 Call @ 4 with TNT having a market price of $57

    ❍ A. $51
    ❍ B. $53
    ❍ C. $59
    ❍ D. $61

Quick Answer: 183
Detailed Answer: 185

11. What is the maximum loss potential for the writer of the following option contracts?

    2 GHI May 50 Calls @ 5

    ❍ A. $1000
    ❍ B. $4500
    ❍ C. $9000
    ❍ D. Unlimited

Quick Answer: 183
Detailed Answer: 185

12. What is the maximum potential gain for the writer of the following option contract?

    Write 3 FTD October 80 Calls @ 5

    ❍ A. $1500
    ❍ B. $22,500
    ❍ C. $24,000
    ❍ D. Unlimited

Quick Answer: 183
Detailed Answer: 185

13. What is the maximum potential gain and the maximum potential loss the writer of the following option contract could incur?

    Write 1 STP May 60 Call @ 4

    ❍ A. Maximum gain is $400; maximum loss is $5600.
    ❍ B. Maximum gain is $5600; maximum loss is $400.
    ❍ C. Maximum gain is $400; maximum loss is unlimited.
    ❍ D. Maximum gain is $5600; maximum loss is unlimited.

Quick Answer: 183
Detailed Answer: 185

14. What is the maximum potential gain and the maximum potential loss the writer of the following option could incur?

    Write 10 CBC June 50 Calls @ 3

    ❍ A. Maximum gain is $300; maximum loss is $4700.
    ❍ B. Maximum gain is $4700; maximum loss is $300.
    ❍ C. Maximum gain is $3000; maximum loss is $47,000.
    ❍ D. Maximum gain is $3000; maximum loss is unlimited.

Quick Answer: 183
Detailed Answer: 186

Quick Check

15. What is the maximum potential gain and the maximum potential loss for the holder of the following option contract?

    Buy 1 ACE May 50 Calls @ 4

    - A. Maximum gain is $400; maximum loss is $4600.
    - B. Maximum gain is $4600; maximum loss is $400.
    - C. Maximum gain is unlimited; maximum loss is $400.
    - D. Maximum gain is unlimited; maximum loss is $4600.

Quick Answer: **183**
Detailed Answer: **186**

16. What is the maximum potential loss for the writer and the holder of the following option contract?

    1 RCA November 60 Call @ 4

    - A. Writer could lose $5600; holder could lose $400.
    - B. Writer could lose $400; holder could lose $5600.
    - C. Writer could lose an unlimited amount; holder could lose $5600.
    - D. Writer could lose an unlimited amount; holder could lose $400.

Quick Answer: **183**
Detailed Answer: **186**

17. What is the maximum potential loss for the writer and the maximum potential gain for the holder of the following option contract?

    2 FTD May 60 Calls @ 4

    - A. Writer can lose $800; holder can gain $800.
    - B. Writer can lose $5600; holder can gain $5600.
    - C. Writer can lose an unlimited amount; holder can gain $800.
    - D. Writer can lose an unlimited amount; holder can gain an unlimited amount.

Quick Answer: **183**
Detailed Answer: **186**

18. The writer of the following option is considered covered with which of the following positions?

    Write 1 ABC May 65 Call @ 4?

    I. The writer is long 100 shares of ABC stock.

    II. The writer owns a call on ABC stock with a strike price of $70.

    III. The writer is short 100 shares of ABC stock.

    IV. The writer owns warrants on ABC stock with a price of $58.

    - A. I only
    - B. I and II
    - C. II and III
    - D. I and IV

Quick Answer: **183**
Detailed Answer: **186**

Quick Check

19. Rick has purchased 1 FTD May 70 Call @ 3 in the option market. FTD rises in the market to $94. What is Rick's profit or loss?
   - ❍ A. A profit of $2100
   - ❍ B. A profit of $2400
   - ❍ C. A loss of $300
   - ❍ D. A loss of $2400

Quick Answer: 183
Detailed Answer: 186

20. Steve has purchased the following option contracts: 7 JGE April 70 Calls @ 4. JGE stock has risen in the market to $88. What is Steve's profit or loss on this option?
   - ❍ A. A loss of $9800
   - ❍ B. A gain of $12,600
   - ❍ C. A loss of $2800
   - ❍ D. A gain of $9800

Quick Answer: 183
Detailed Answer: 186

21. Peter has written 5 ARK October 35 Calls @ 3 in the market. What is the breakeven point for the writer (Peter) and the breakeven point for the purchaser of these options?
   - ❍ A. The writer's breakeven point is $32; the holder's breakeven point is $38.
   - ❍ B. The writer's breakeven point is $38; the holder's breakeven point is $32.
   - ❍ C. The writer's breakeven point is $32; the holder's breakeven point is $32.
   - ❍ D. The writer's breakeven point is $38; the holder's breakeven point is $38.

Quick Answer: 183
Detailed Answer: 187

Answer the remaining questions based on the following option position:

10 TNT April 60 Calls @ 3

22. What is the maximum exposure to loss for the writer of this option?
   - ❍ A. $3000
   - ❍ B. $57,000
   - ❍ C. $60,000
   - ❍ D. Unlimited

Quick Answer: 183
Detailed Answer: 187

Quick Check

23. What is the maximum gain the writer of this option can make on the sale of the contract?

Quick Answer: 183
Detailed Answer: 187

- ❍ A. $3000
- ❍ B. $57,000
- ❍ C. $60,000
- ❍ D. Unlimited

24. What are the breakeven points for the writer and the buyer of this option contract?

Quick Answer: 183
Detailed Answer: 187

- ❍ A. Writer's breakeven is $57; buyer's breakeven is $63.
- ❍ B. Writer's breakeven is $57; buyer's breakeven is $57.
- ❍ C. Writer's breakeven is $63; buyer's breakeven is $57.
- ❍ D. Writer's breakeven is $63; buyer's breakeven is $63.

25. The 10 TNT options affect open interest on TNT stock in which of the following ways?

Quick Answer: 183
Detailed Answer: 187

- ❍ A. Open interest increases by 1.
- ❍ B. Open interest increases by 10.
- ❍ C. Open interest increases by 100.
- ❍ D. Open interest increases by 1000.

Quick Check Answer Key

1. C
2. D
3. A
4. D
5. D
6. C
7. A
8. A
9. D
10. C
11. D
12. A
13. C
14. D
15. C
16. D
17. D
18. B
19. A
20. D
21. D
22. D
23. A
24. D
25. B

Answers and Explanations

1. **Answer C is correct.** The 10 option contracts represent 10 contracts × 100 shares per contract, or 1000 shares. The premium paid of $4.00 is for each share in the contract, or in this question, $4,000 for the 10 call options at $4.00.

2. **Answer D is correct.** Premiums are determined by time value, intrinsic value (the in-the-money amount of the contract), and the quality of the underlying security. The volatility of the stock represented by the option also affects the premium paid. Stocks that have high trading volumes and a tendency to move in the market affect the premium more than a stock with a low trading volume and little volatility. The number of contracts could affect the premium, but for the most part, the number of contracts affects the premium the least of all the choices.

3. **Answer A is correct.** The option 1 PDQ April 70 Call @ 2 is in the money if the market price of the underlying security is above $70. In this example, the market price is 71 7/8, so the option has an intrinsic value of 1 7/8 and a time value of 1/8th (1 7/8 + 1/8 = $2 premium paid). The option is in the money. It is not at the money, which is represented by a market price equal to the $70 strike price.

4. **Answer D is correct.** Call options have a breakeven point determined by the strike price plus the premium paid. In this option, the strike price is $60 and the premium paid is $3 for a $63 breakeven point. At $63, the holder breaks even. He is able to purchase a $63 stock in the market at a $60 strike price. This realizes a profit of $3.00, which is exactly what he paid for the contract; thus, the holder breaks even.

5. **Answer D is correct.** Call options have a breakeven point determined by the strike price plus the premium paid. In this option, the strike price is $70 and the premium paid is $5, for a breakeven point of $75. The holder has the right to purchase AOL stock at $70 when it is actually selling in the market at $75. The holder paid $5 for this right, so he regained the premium paid and broke even at $75.

6. **Answer C is correct.** A call option has a breakeven point determined by the strike price plus the premium paid. In this example, the strike price is $55 and the premium paid is $3 1/2, for a breakeven point of $58 1/2. The holder has the right to buy KLM stock at $55, and that right cost her 3 1/2 for a breakeven point of $58 1/2.

7. **Answer A is correct.** The maximum loss the holder can incur is the premium paid of $400.00. The purchaser of a call option contract of 1 HTH Oct. 60 Call @ 4 is hoping that HTH stock rises well above the strike price of $60 in the market so she can purchase the stock for $60 and realize a profit. If she is correct and the stock rises above $60 plus the premium paid of $4, or her breakeven point of $64, she realizes a profit. If the stock's market price drops below the strike price, the option is out of the money and the holder would not exercise her contract.
8. **Answer A is correct.** A writer of a call option is bearish. He hopes that the underlying stock decreases in value below the strike price so that he can keep the premium received. The holder of the call option hopes that the market price of the underlying security rises above the strike price so that he can purchase the stock at the lower strike price. The holder or buyer is considered bullish.
9. **Answer D is correct.** A call option of 1 FTD Apr. 70 Call @ 5 has a breakeven point of the strike price plus the premium paid. The breakeven point for this option contract is the strike price of $70 plus the premium of $5, or $75. The buyer of the option wants the stock to rise in value above the strike price so she can purchase the stock at the lower strike price. Remember, the breakeven point for the buyer and the seller are exactly the same. When one makes money, the other loses money.
10. **Answer C is correct.** A call option has a breakeven point of the strike price of the option plus the premium paid. For 1 TNT Sept. 55 Call @ 4, the breakeven point is the $55 strike price plus $4 premium paid, or $59. Remember, the breakeven point is the same for both the writer and the buyer.
11. **Answer D is correct.** A writer of call options has unlimited loss potential on the option contract. In theory, the market price of the underlying security could rise to any amount above the strike price. This exposure subjects an uncovered writer to an unlimited loss potential.
12. **Answer A is correct.** The maximum potential gain that a writer could realize on a call option is the premium received from the buyer. In this example, for the 3 FTD October 80 Calls @ 5, the writer receives the entire $5 premium for the three contracts he has written. 300 shares × $5 premium = $1500 maximum potential gain for the writer.
13. **Answer C is correct.** The maximum gain for a writer of a call option is the premium received. In this question, the premium received is $4.00 × 100 shares in the contract = $400. The maximum exposure to loss that the writer can have is the amount that the market price of the stock could go above the strike price. In theory, the maximum loss is unlimited because the stock could rise to any price.

14. **Answer D is correct.** The maximum gain for a writer of a call option is the premium received. In this question, the premium received is $3.00 × 1000 shares (10 contracts) = $3,000. The maximum exposure to loss that the writer of an uncovered option has is the amount that the market price of the stock could go above the strike price. In theory, the maximum loss is unlimited because the stock could rise to any price.

15. **Answer C is correct.** The buyer of 1 ACE May 50 Call @ 4 has a maximum exposure to loss of the premium paid, which in this example is $400. The maximum possible gain on a long call option is unlimited because the stock's market price could rise to an unlimited amount above the strike price of $50.

16. **Answer D is correct.** The maximum exposure to loss for the writer of 1 RCA Nov. 60 Call @ 4 is an unlimited amount because the stock could rise in price to an unlimited amount above the strike price of the option. The maximum potential loss for the buyer or holder of the option is the premium paid, which is $4.00 × 100 shares = $400.

17. **Answer D is correct.** The maximum potential loss to the writer of 2 FTD May 60 Calls @ 4 is the unlimited amount that the market price of the underlying stock could rise above the strike price of the option. If the writer has an unlimited potential loss, then the holder of the option has an unlimited potential gain. Remember, when one side makes money, the other side loses that amount!

18. **Answer B is correct.** The riskiest option position that can be taken by an investor is to write uncovered calls. The market price of the underlying security could go up to an unlimited amount, thus causing an unlimited loss for the writer. Uncovered puts have a finite loss because the stock represented by the option could only go to zero. Buying calls or puts has a maximum loss potential of the premium paid by the buyer.

19. **Answer A is correct.** The purchase of 1 FTD May 70 Call @ 3 has the holder of the contract wanting the stock to rise above the lower strike price. An increase in the market price to $94 is 24 points higher than the strike price of $70. The buyer paid $3.00 for the option contract, thus he has a gain of 24 – 3 = 21 points × 100 shares in the contract = $2100.

20. **Answer D is correct.** The purchase of 7 JGE April 70 Calls @ 4 costs the holder $2800 (700 shares × $4 premium = $2800). The holder of this call option wants the market price of the stock to increase in value above the strike price. It went to $88, which is 18 points higher than the strike price of $70. The holder makes an 18-point profit less her $4 premium paid = $14 profit × 700 shares = $9800 profit for the long call option.

21. **Answer D is correct.** Breakeven points on a call option are the same for both the writer and the holder. The breakeven point for a call option is the strike price plus the premium paid. In this question, the breakeven point is $38 ($35 strike + $3 premium = $38).

22. **Answer D is correct.** The maximum exposure to loss for the writer of these 10 calls is an unlimited amount. The market price of the underlying security (TNT) could in theory go to any price above the strike price of $60.

23. **Answer A is correct.** The maximum gain that a writer can have on an option that he has written is the premium received. The writer received a $3.00 premium for 1000 shares (10 contracts) = $3000 maximum potential profit as a writer.

24. **Answer D is correct.** The breakeven point for a call option is the same for both the writer and the holder. When one side makes money, the other side loses money. The breakeven point for a call option is the strike price plus the premium paid. In this question, the strike price is $60 and the premium is $3.00, which equals a breakeven point of $63 for both the writer and the buyer.

25. **Answer B is correct.** The 10 option contracts that were purchased from the writer increase open interest on TNT stock by a total of 10 contracts. The writer sold 10 options on TNT and the holder purchased 10. They offset each other, and open interest increases by the matched 10 contracts.

Quick Check

Put Options

1. The purchaser of a put option and the seller of a put option want the market price of the underlying security to go which way?
   - ❍ A. Purchaser wants it to go down; seller wants it to go down.
   - ❍ B. Purchaser wants it to go down; seller wants it to go up.
   - ❍ C. Purchaser wants it to go up; seller wants it to go up.
   - ❍ D. Purchaser wants it to go up; seller wants it to go down.

Quick Answer: **195**
Detailed Answer: **196**

2. Which of the following sides of the market is correct for these options?
   - ❍ A. Buy call and sell put are bearish.
   - ❍ B. Sell call and buy put are bullish.
   - ❍ C. Buy call and sell put are bullish.
   - ❍ D. Sell call and sell put are bearish.

Quick Answer: **195**
Detailed Answer: **196**

3. What is the maximum loss a seller of the following option is exposed to?

   Sell 1 DTT May 55 Put @ 3
   - ❍ A. Unlimited
   - ❍ B. $300
   - ❍ C. $5200
   - ❍ D. $5500

Quick Answer: **195**
Detailed Answer: **196**

4. What is the maximum possible loss and the maximum possible gain the writer of the following option can have?

   Sell 10 HTH September 30 Puts @ 2
   - ❍ A. Maximum loss is $28,000; maximum gain is $2000.
   - ❍ B. Maximum loss is unlimited; maximum gain is $2000.
   - ❍ C. Maximum loss is $30,000; maximum gain is unlimited.
   - ❍ D. Maximum loss is unlimited; maximum gain is $28,000.

Quick Answer: **195**
Detailed Answer: **196**

Quick Check

5. What is the maximum possible gain that the holder of the following put option contract can make?

   Buy 15 GHI May 60 Puts @ 5

   - ❍ A. $5500
   - ❍ B. $7500
   - ❍ C. $8250
   - ❍ D. $82,500

Quick Answer: 195
Detailed Answer: 196

6. Which of the following formulas is used to compute the intrinsic value for a put option contract?
   - ❍ A. Intrinsic value = strike price + market price
   - ❍ B. Intrinsic value = strike price – market price
   - ❍ C. Intrinsic value = market value – strike price
   - ❍ D. Intrinsic value = market value + strike price

Quick Answer: 195
Detailed Answer: 196

7. Donald owns 5 IRT April 50 Puts @ 4. If the market price of IRT was $51 when he purchased these options, what is the intrinsic value of the premium?
   - ❍ A. Zero
   - ❍ B. $1
   - ❍ C. $2
   - ❍ D. $4

Quick Answer: 195
Detailed Answer: 196

8. Robert purchased 5 HTH May 70 Puts @ 5. What is the breakeven point on this put option?
   - ❍ A. $75
   - ❍ B. $76
   - ❍ C. $65
   - ❍ D. $64

Quick Answer: 195
Detailed Answer: 196

9. Iris purchased the following put option from a writer: 1 FTD June 75 Put @ 6. What is the breakeven point for Iris and the breakeven point for the writer of this option?
   - ❍ A. Iris's breakeven point is $81; the writer's breakeven point is $69.
   - ❍ B. Iris's breakeven point is $69; the writer's breakeven point is $81.
   - ❍ C. Iris's breakeven point is $69; the writer's breakeven point is $69.
   - ❍ D. Iris's breakeven point is $81; the writer's breakeven point is $81.

Quick Answer: 195
Detailed Answer: 197

Quick Check

10. Steve purchases 5 RPM June 70 Puts @ 6 with DTT selling at $68 in the market. What is the breakeven point for the writer of this option, and what is the breakeven point for Steve?
   - ❍ A. The writer's breakeven point is $76; Steve's breakeven point is $64.
   - ❍ B. The writer's breakeven point is $74; Steve's breakeven point is $62.
   - ❍ C. The writer's breakeven point is $64; Steve's breakeven point is $64.
   - ❍ D. The writer's breakeven point is $62; Steve's breakeven point is $62.

Quick Answer: **195**
Detailed Answer: **197**

11. An investor purchases 10 ARK January 60 Puts @ 5 with a market value of ARK at $58. What is the maximum potential profit on this contract?
   - ❍ A. $5,000
   - ❍ B. $5,500
   - ❍ C. $55,000
   - ❍ D. $58,000

Quick Answer: **195**
Detailed Answer: **197**

12. Edward writes 7 HTH May 70 Puts @ 6. HTH goes to $79 in the market. What is his profit or loss?
   - ❍ A. A loss of $4200
   - ❍ B. A gain of $4200
   - ❍ C. A loss of $2100
   - ❍ D. A gain of $2100

Quick Answer: **195**
Detailed Answer: **197**

13. Rick purchased 12 XYZ April 60 Puts @ 7. XYZ goes to $42 in the market. What is his profit or loss on these options?
   - ❍ A. A profit of $1800
   - ❍ B. A profit of $13,200
   - ❍ C. A loss of $8400
   - ❍ D. A loss of $21,600

Quick Answer: **195**
Detailed Answer: **197**

14. A writer sells 5 XYZ May 70 Puts @ 4. To be a covered writer, what does the investor need to have in his account?
   - ❍ A. Long 5000 shares of XYZ stock
   - ❍ B. Long 500 shares of XYZ stock
   - ❍ C. Short 500 shares of XYZ stock
   - ❍ D. Short 5000 shares of XYZ stock

Quick Answer: **195**
Detailed Answer: **197**

Quick Check

Answer Questions 15 through 19 regarding the following option contract:

12 ARK November 75 Puts @ 7

15. How many shares of ARK does the writer of this put contract control?
    - ❍ A. None
    - ❍ B. 120 shares
    - ❍ C. 1200 shares
    - ❍ D. 12,000 shares

Quick Answer: 195
Detailed Answer: 197

16. What is the breakeven point for the writer on these 12 puts of ARK?
    - ❍ A. $82
    - ❍ B. $83
    - ❍ C. $68
    - ❍ D. $67

Quick Answer: 195
Detailed Answer: 198

17. What is the breakeven point for the holder of these 12 ARK puts?
    - ❍ A. $67
    - ❍ B. $68
    - ❍ C. $82
    - ❍ D. $83

Quick Answer: 195
Detailed Answer: 198

18. If the market price of ARK goes to $60, what is the profit or loss for the holder of the options?
    - ❍ A. $1500 profit
    - ❍ B. $1500 loss
    - ❍ C. $9600 profit
    - ❍ D. $9600 loss

Quick Answer: 195
Detailed Answer: 198

19. If the market price of ARK goes to $81 what is the profit or loss for the seller of the options?
    - ❍ A. Profit of $7200
    - ❍ B. Profit of $8400
    - ❍ C. Loss of $7200
    - ❍ D. Loss of $8400

Quick Answer: 195
Detailed Answer: 198

20. Joseph writes 20 KLM September 85 Puts @ 6. KLM's market price goes to $91. What is the profit or loss for Joseph?
    - ❍ A. He broke even.
    - ❍ B. He made a profit of $12,000.
    - ❍ C. He lost $12,000.
    - ❍ D. He lost $6,000.

Quick Answer: 195
Detailed Answer: 198

Quick Check

21. Hector purchases 2 TCI December 35 Puts @ 6. What is the breakeven point for the writer and the breakeven point for Hector?

Quick Answer: **195**
Detailed Answer: **198**

I. Hector's breakeven point is $41.

II. The writer's breakeven point is $29.

III. Hector's breakeven point is $29.

IV. The writer's breakeven point is $41.

❍ A. I and II
❍ B. II and III
❍ C. III and IV
❍ D. I and IV

22. How many shares of stock does the writer of this contract control?

Quick Answer: **195**
Detailed Answer: **198**

50 TCI March 75 PUTS @ 6

❍ A. None
❍ B. 500
❍ C. 5000
❍ D. 50,000

23. Tom purchases 5 TNT May 60 Puts @ 4. TNT announces a 2-for-1 forward stock split in the market place. How does this affect Tom's option contracts?

Quick Answer: **195**
Detailed Answer: **198**

❍ A. It does not affect the options.
❍ B. Tom now has 10 TNT May 60 Puts @ 4.
❍ C. Tom now has 10 TNT May 30 Puts @ 4.
❍ D. Tom now has 10 TNT May 30 Puts @ 2.

24. Martha owns 5 PDQ May 60 Puts @ 4. PDQ declares a 5-for-4 forward stock split. How does this affect the options on PDQ?

Quick Answer: **195**
Detailed Answer: **199**

❍ A. It does not affect the options.
❍ B. Martha now has 5 PDQ May 48 Puts @ 3 1/4.
❍ C. Martha now has 4 PDQ May 48 Puts @ 3 1/4.
❍ D. Martha now has 5 PDQ May 48 Puts @ 3 1/4 with each contract representing 125 shares.

Quick Check

25. Harry owns 1 KLM May 55 PUT @5. KLM stock declares a 10% stock dividend to shareholders. How does this affect the option Harry holds?

Quick Answer: **195**
Detailed Answer: **199**

- ❍ A. It does not affect his option.
- ❍ B. He now has 1 KLM May 60 Put @ 5.
- ❍ C. He now has 1 KLM May 60 Put @ 5 1/2.
- ❍ D. He now has 1 KLM May 50 Put @ 4 1/2.

Quick Check Answer Key

1. B

2. C

3. C

4. A

5. D

6. B

7. A

8. C

9. C

10. C

11. C

12. B

13. B

14. D

15. A

16. C

17. B

18. C

19. B

20. B

21. B

22. A

23. D

24. D

25. D

Answers and Explanations

1. **Answer B is correct.** The purchaser of a put option hopes that the underlying security goes down in value below the strike price of the put option. This enables the holder to put the stock back to the writer at the higher strike price. The writer hopes that the underlying security goes up in value above the strike price so that the put option goes unexercised and the writer keeps the premium received.

2. **Answer C is correct.** The buyer of a call wants the market to go up in value so that he can purchase the stock at the lower strike price. The seller of a put also hopes that the stock goes up in value so that the put option goes unexercised and the writer can keep the premium received.

3. **Answer C is correct.** Te maximum loss that a seller of a put is exposed to is the value of the underlying security dropping to zero. 1 DDT May 55 Put @ 3 could go to zero from the strike of $55 for a 55-point loss + the premium received of $3 = $52 maximum loss × 100 shares = $5200.

4. **Answer A is correct.** The maximum potential loss on 10 HTH September 30 Puts @ 2 is the stock going to zero from the strike of $30. A $30 loss + $2 premium received = $28 possible loss × 1000 shares = $28,000 maximum possible loss. The most the writer of the put option can make is the premium received. The premium of $2 ×1000 shares = $2000 maximum potential gain.

5. **Answer D is correct.** The holder of 15 GHI May 60 Puts @ 5 can make the strike price less the premium paid as a profit (60 – 5 = 55 × 1500 shares = $82,500). This is because the stock could go to zero and then be put back to the writer at the higher strike price of $60.

6. **Answer B is correct.** The formula to determine the intrinsic value of an option premium for a put is to take the strike price – market price. A strike price of $50 – $48 market price = $2 in the money amount, or intrinsic value.

7. **Answer A is correct.** The 5 IRT April 50 Puts @ 4 with a market price of $51 is out of the money by $1 for the holder. The holder will not put a $51 stock to someone at $50. The option has a zero intrinsic value and a time value of the entire $4 premium.

8. **Answer C is correct.** The breakeven point on 5 HTH May 70 Puts @ 5 is the strike price less the premium. The $70 strike – $5 premium = a $65 breakeven point. When the stock reaches $65, both the holder and the writer break even.

9. **Answer C is correct.** It is important to remember that the breakeven point on an option is always the same for both the writer and the holder. In this example, the strike price of $75 less the premium of $6 is a $69 breakeven point for the put option. The holder wants the option to go down in value, but the writer wants it to go above $75. When it reaches $69, the writer is out of the money by $6, which wipes out the premium received for a breakeven point on the contract.

10. **Answer C is correct.** The breakeven point on a put option contract is the strike price less the premium. The strike price of $70 – the $6 premium = a $64 breakeven point. Remember, the breakeven point for the writer and the holder is always the same. When one starts to make money, the other starts to lose money.

11. **Answr C is correct.** The maximum profit that can made on 10 ARK January 60 Puts @ 5 is for the stock to decline to zero and then be put back to the writer at $60, less the premium paid of $5. The equation is $55 × 1000 shares = $55,000 total potential profit for the holder.

12. **Answer B is correct.** The writer of a put option wants the stock to rise in value above the strike price of the contract so the option is not exercised against him. The HTH stock went to $79, which is above the strike price of $70. The option expires worthless to the holder and the writer keeps the premium received as a profit. The $6 premium × 700 shares = $4200 profit for the writer.

13. **Answer B is correct.** The holder of a put option wants the stock to fall below the strike price of the contract. The strike of $60 – a $7 premium paid = a $53 breakeven point. The stock went to $42 for a difference of $11 per share from the breakeven. The equation is $11 × 1200 shares = $13,200 profit to the holder.

14. **Answer D is correct.** To be covered when writing put options, the seller needs to be short the number of shares indicated by the option contract. In this case, Ryan needs to be short 5000 shares of NCR stock to be a covered writer. If the put options go down in value, the loss is offset by the gain from the shorted shares of NCR stock. Remember, a writer wants the market price of the put option to rise above the strike price so that he can keep the premium received and the put expires worthless to the holder. A put writer loses money if the stock declines in value. A short seller makes money on the decline in market value of the stock. The two positions cancel each other out, and the writer is considered covered.

15. **Answer A is correct.** The writer of an option contract does not control any shares. The holder controls the shares of stock in the contract. The holder determines when the option is exercised, not the writer.

16. **Answer C is correct.** The breakeven point on a put option is determined by the strike price – the premium paid. The strike of $75 – a $7 premium = a $68 breakeven point. Remember, the breakeven point for the writer and the holder of the option is the same. When one starts to make money, the other starts to lose money.

17. **Answer B is correct.** The breakeven point on a put option is determined by the strike price – the premium paid. The strike of $75 – a $7 premium paid = a $68 breakeven point. Once again, it is important to realize that the breakeven point on all options is the same for the writer and the holder of the contract. When one starts to make money, the other starts to lose money.

18. **Answer C is correct.** The breakeven point on these options is $68, which is determined by the strike price of $75 less the premium of $7. The stock drops to $60 in market price. The breakeven point – market price = $8 profit per share to the holder. The equation is $8 × 1200 shares (12 contracts) = $9600 for the holder as a profit.

19. **Answer B is correct.** If the market price of the stock rises above the strike price of the put option, the option is out of the money for the holder. The writer keeps the premium received, and the put options expire worthless. The holder is not going to put a $81 stock to a writer at a $75 strike price. The contract expires worthless and the writer keeps the $7 premium × 1200 shares = $8400 profit to the writer.

20. **Answer B is correct.** On 20 KLM September 85 Puts @ 6, the writer wants the stock to stay above the strike price of $85 so the holder does not put the lower price of the stock back to the writer. If this does occur, the writer in this case keeps the premium received of $6 × 2000 shares = $12,000 profit.

21. **Answer B is correct.** The breakeven point on a put option is the strike price less the premium. A strike of $35 less the $6 premium is a $29 breakeven point. Remember, the breakeven point on the option is the same for both the writer and the buyer.

22. **Answer A is correct.** The writer of an option contract does not control any shares of the underlying security. The holder controls the shares because she decides when and if to exercise the option contract.

23. **Answer D is correct.** A 2-for-1 stock split gives the holder twice as many contracts at half the strike price and half the premium. Tom now has 10 TNT May 30 Puts @ 2. The total value of the contracts remains the same. It was an even split, so the contract number doubled and the strike and premium are halved. The 500 shares × a 60 strike = $30,000, which is the same as 1000 shares × a 30 strike.

24. **Answer D is correct.** A 5-for-4 forward stock split alters the option contract by leaving the number of contracts the same but changing the size of the contract to 125 shares. (For every 4 Martha had, she now has 5 = 25 × 5 = 125.) The strike price of $60 is now multiplied by 4/5ths: $60 × .80 = $48 strike price. The premium of $4 is multiplied by 4/5ths: $4 × .80 = $3.20. Martha now has 5 contracts of 125 shares each with a strike price of $48 and a premium of $3 1/4.

25. **Answer D is correct.** A stock dividend affects Harry's option contract accordingly. A 10% stock dividend changes the 1 KLM May 55 Put @ 5 to > 1 KLM May 50 Put @ 4 1/2, with each contract now representing 110 shares.

Quick Check

Equity Options and Trading Rules

1. Which of the following entities issues, guarantees, and clears all option contracts in the market?

Quick Answer: **208**
Detailed Answer: **209**

- ❍ A. NASD
- ❍ B. OCC
- ❍ C. SEC
- ❍ D. Specialist

2. Which of the following are characteristics of the Options Clearing Corporation?

Quick Answer: **208**
Detailed Answer: **209**

I. It clears all option trades.

II. It sets the strike price and expiration on contracts.

III. It sets maximum position limits on options.

IV. It guarantees all contracts.

- ❍ A. I and II
- ❍ B. II and III
- ❍ C. I, II, and III
- ❍ D. I, II, III, and IV

3. A new client goes to a broker to open an option account with the member firm. The client meets all the profile requirements to open the account. At the time of opening the account, the client does not sign the options agreement. Which of the following statements is true?

Quick Answer: **208**
Detailed Answer: **209**

- ❍ A. The client is prohibited from opening the account.
- ❍ B. The client can conduct option trades in the account as long as the agreement is signed within 15 days.
- ❍ C. The client can start trading in the option account only after she signs the option agreement.
- ❍ D. The client has a 30-day waiting period before she can trade options.

Quick Check

4. All the following are required when opening an option account except for which one?

Quick Answer: 208
Detailed Answer: 209

- ❍ A. The account must be approved by a registered options principal.
- ❍ B. The client must receive the risk disclosure document, "Characteristics and Risks of Standardized Options."
- ❍ C. The client must sign the option agreement before any trades can be entered.
- ❍ D. A determination of the client's financial position is required.

5. Which of the following options are part of the same option series?

Quick Answer: 208
Detailed Answer: 209

- ❍ A. GM April 55 Calls and GM May 55 Calls
- ❍ B. GM May 55 Calls and GM May 60 Calls
- ❍ C. GM May 60 Calls and GM June 60 Calls
- ❍ D. GM June 60 Calls and GM June 60 Calls

6. The strike prices for options are set by the OCC. All the following are possible strike price intervals except for which interval?

Quick Answer: 208
Detailed Answer: 209

- ❍ A. 2 1/2 point intervals
- ❍ B. 5 point intervals
- ❍ C. 10 point intervals
- ❍ D. 20 point intervals

7. An option that has been assigned a January, April, July, October expiration cycle can have options that trade in which of the following months?

Quick Answer: 208
Detailed Answer: 209

I. January

II. February

III. April

IV. July

- ❍ A. I only
- ❍ B. I and IV
- ❍ C. I, II, and III
- ❍ D. I, II, III, and IV

Quick Check

8. Options that are currently trading in June (spot) for an underlying security also have options trading in which of the following months?

   Quick Answer: 208
   Detailed Answer: 210

   I. July

   II. September

   III. December

   IV. March

   - ❍ A. I only
   - ❍ B. II and III
   - ❍ C. I, II, and III
   - ❍ D. I, II, III, and IV

9. Which of the following exchanges actively trade equity option contracts?

   Quick Answer: 208
   Detailed Answer: 210

   I. NYSE

   II. AMEX

   III. CBOE

   IV. Pacific Stock Exchange

   - ❍ A. I only
   - ❍ B. I and II
   - ❍ C. I, II, and III
   - ❍ D. II, III, and IV

10. An individual who is an employee of the CBOE and holds the public limit orders to be executed when the limit is reached is known as a what?

    Quick Answer: 208
    Detailed Answer: 210

    - ❍ A. Floor broker
    - ❍ B. Competitive trader
    - ❍ C. Market maker
    - ❍ D. Order book official

Quick Check

11. The number of option contracts that an investor can have on an underlying security depends on which of the following?

Quick Answer: 208
Detailed Answer: 210

I. The number of shares outstanding on the stock

II. The trading volume of the underlying security

III. The side of the market the contract is on

IV. The expiration cycle of the security

❍ A. I only
❍ B. I and II
❍ C. I, II, and III
❍ D. I, II, III, and IV

12. Arlis performed an opening sale of 3000 KLM June 75 Puts. The position limit on KLM options is set at 4500 contracts. Which of the following options is he permitted to do?

Quick Answer: 208
Detailed Answer: 210

I. Sell 2000 KLM June 75 Puts

II. Buy 2000 KLM June 75 Puts

III. Buy 2000 KLM June 75 Calls

IV. Sell 2000 KLM June 75 Calls

❍ A. I only
❍ B. I and III
❍ C. III and IV
❍ D. II and IV

13. Kerry sells 10 BTO October 75 Calls @ 4. What is the maximum profit and maximum loss Kerry can have on these options?

Quick Answer: 208
Detailed Answer: 210

A. Maximum profit is $400; maximum loss is $71,000.
B. Maximum profit is $4,000; maximum loss is $71,000.
C. Maximum profit is $4,000; maximum loss is unlimited.
❍ D. Maximum profit is unlimited; maximum loss is $4,000.

14. George wants to purchase the following options in a margin account: Buy 10 HTH May 50 Calls @ 4. What amount must George deposit in the account for the trade?

Quick Answer: 208
Detailed Answer: 210

❍ A. $2000
❍ B. $4000
❍ C. $25,000
❍ D. $50,000

Quick Check

15. Trudy writes 5 ACE November 80 Puts @ 4. Which of the following positions make her a covered writer?

Quick Answer: 208
Detailed Answer: 211

I. Long 500 shares of ACE stock

II. Short 500 shares of ACE stock

III. Long 5 ACE November 80 Puts @ 1

IV. A letter of guarantee from a bank securing any losses in the account

- A. I only
- B. II only
- C. I and IV
- D. II, III, and IV

16. Nelson writes 4 HTH September 35 Puts @ 3 in his margin account. He also sells 400 shares of HTH stock short at $36 in his margin account. What is the amount he is required to deposit in his account?

Quick Answer: 208
Detailed Answer: 211

- A. $1200
- B. $6000
- C. $7200
- D. $14,400

17. Oscar sells 700 shares of TNT stock short in his margin account at $84. Oscar also writes 7 TNT November 85 Puts @ 6 in his margin account. What is he required to deposit in his account on these transactions?

Quick Answer: 208
Detailed Answer: 211

- A. $25,200
- B. $29,400
- C. $54,600
- D. $58,800

18. Oliver writes 12 BCI March 50 Calls @ 4 in his margin account. He also purchases 1200 shares of BCI at $46 in his margin account. What is he required to deposit to meet his Regulation T requirement?

Quick Answer: 208
Detailed Answer: 211

- A. $22,800
- B. $27,600
- C. $32,400
- D. $55,200

Quick Check

19. Norton writes 1 GHI October 50 Call @ 4 that is uncovered. What is his margin requirement on the call option if GHI has a market value of $48?

    ❍ A. $400
    ❍ B. $880
    ❍ C. $1160
    ❍ D. $1360

Quick Answer: 208
Detailed Answer: 211

20. Referring to the previous question, what is the amount of cash that Christine is required to bring into the margin account when writing the uncovered JVC May 80 Put @ 7 and a market value of $77?

    ❍ A. $700
    ❍ B. $1470
    ❍ C. $1540
    ❍ D. $2240

Quick Answer: 208
Detailed Answer: 212

21. An out-of-the-money call that is written by an option writer has which of the following characteristics?

    I. A market price higher than the strike price

    II. A market price lower than the strike price

    III. A margin requirement if uncovered

    IV. A margin requirement if covered

    ❍ A. I only
    ❍ B. II only
    ❍ C. I and IV
    ❍ D. II and III

Quick Answer: 208
Detailed Answer: 212

22. The Options Clearing Corporation will automatically exercise an option on the expiration date that is in the money by what amount?

    ❍ A. 1/4 point
    ❍ B. 1/2 point
    ❍ C. 3/4 point
    ❍ D. 1 point

Quick Answer: 208
Detailed Answer: 212

Quick Check

23. When the Options Clearing Corporation sets a limit on the number of options that any individual can exercise over a set period of time, that time period is typically for how long?
    - ❍ A. 5 business days
    - ❍ B. 7 business days
    - ❍ C. 30 business days
    - ❍ D. 90 days

Quick Answer: 208
Detailed Answer: 212

24. Which of the following options has an expiration term longer than nine months?
    - ❍ A. 1 HTH October 50 Call
    - ❍ B. 1 RDE November 70 Call
    - ❍ C. 1 DISNEY May 40 Call Leap
    - ❍ D. 1 KLM June 60 Call

Quick Answer: 208
Detailed Answer: 212

25. All option trades are settled with the Options Clearing Corporation in how many days?
    - ❍ A. Same-day settlement
    - ❍ B. Next-day settlement
    - ❍ C. Three business days
    - ❍ D. Five business days

Quick Answer: 208
Detailed Answer: 212

Quick Check Answer Key

1. B
2. D
3. B
4. C
5. D
6. D
7. D
8. C
9. D
10. D
11. C
12. D
13. C
14. B
15. D
16. B
17. A
18. A
19. C
20. C
21. D
22. C
23. A
24. C
25. B

Answers and Explanations

1. **Answer B is correct.** The Options Clearing Corporation was created by the option exchanges to issue, guarantee, and act as a clearing agent for all option contracts.

2. **Answer D is correct.** The Options Clearing Corporation has a wide variety of responsibilities over option contracts. It sets the parameters on all options such as the strike price, expiration, and initial premium. It guarantees all contracts and handles the clearing of all trades on the next business day. The OCC also sets the limits on the number of contracts that any one investor can exercise in any five-day period.

3. **Answer B is correct.** When opening an option account, a customer is required to sign the option agreement within 15 days. The client can enter orders for options during this time period. If the client does not sign the agreement by the 15th day, the client is restricted to closing transactions in the option account.

4. **Answer C is correct.** When opening an option account, the customer is required to sign the option agreement within a 15-day period. The client's financial position should be determined to make sure she can take on the risks involved with options. The client must receive the "Risks of Standardized Options" brochure, and the account must be approved by a registered options principal before it can be opened. The customer is permitted to enter trades in an option account, even if she has not signed the option agreement.

5. **Answer D is correct.** All call or put options on the same underlying security with the same expiration date and strike price represent one series of options. Only choice D shows the same exact option. Different strike prices represent different series. Different expirations represent different series.

6. **Answer D is correct.** Options have spaced strike price intervals that start from 2 1/2 points for stock trading at less than $25. A $5 strike interval is assigned to stocks trading between $25 and $200. A $10 strike interval is assigned to stocks that trade for more than $200. There are no strike intervals that exceed $10.

7. **Answer D is correct.** The OCC can issue options with an expiration for the current month, which is known as spot. It can also issue options on a stock for the following month and the next two months of the option cycle it has been assigned. In this question, the cycle is January, April, July, October. The OCC can issue options on the stock for January, the next month (February), and then the next two months of the cycle, which are April and July. Thus, options on any security are limited to four expiration dates.

8. **Answer C is correct.** If June is the current, or spot, month for an option, the security can have an expiration date for the current month (June), the next month (July), and then the next two months of the assigned cycle, which are September and December. The March expiration occurs only when July expires. The OCC limits an option to four expiration dates at any given time.

9. **Answer D is correct.** The most active markets for equity options exist on the Chicago Board of Options Exchange, the American Stock Exchange, and the Pacific Stock Exchange. The NYSE no longer trades equity options. It sold this business to the CBOE in 1997 because it never really had much impact in the option market.

10. **Answer D is correct.** An order book official handles public limit orders on options that are away from the market. When the price is reached, he executes the orders. A market maker trades for its own account, as well as steps in to be the other side of an option transaction if sellers and buyers do not match up in number.

11. **Answer C is correct.** The OCC has set parameters for the number of contracts that any one investor is permitted to have on an underlying security on either side of the market. The number of contracts permitted is determined by the number of outstanding shares, the trading volume, and which side of the market the option is on (bullish or bearish). An investor who buys calls and sold puts on the same security is actually on the same side of the market (bullish). Selling calls and buying puts are also on the same side of the market (bearish).

12. **Answer D is correct.** Arlis wrote 3000 KLM June 75 Puts, which places him on the bullish side of the market. He cannot exceed 4500 contracts on either side of the market. Selling puts and buying calls are both considered bullish. If he did 2000 of either, he exceeds the limit. Choices I and III exceed the limit of 4500 contracts on either side of the market. He is permitted to conduct the bearish options of buying puts or selling calls, as long as they do not exceed the 4500 limit.

13. **Answer C is correct.** The maximum gain that a writer can make is the premium received. In this case, the premium is $4 × 1000 shares, or $4000. The maximum loss to a call writer is an unlimited amount. The underlying security could go up in value to any price and then be purchased at the lower strike.

14. **Answer B is correct.** This is a tricky question. Options can be purchased in a margin account, but the buyer must put up 100% of the cost. In essence, options cannot be purchased on margin. However, uncovered writers must put up margin to write uncovered options. George purchased 10 HTH options @ 4, a $4000 cost. He is required to deposit the full amount.

15. **Answer D is correct.** The writer of 5 ACE November 80 Puts is a covered writer if he is short 500 shares of ACE stock. The writer of a put wants the stock to go up in value. The short position on ACE offsets any decline on the put options. A bank guarantee also covers the writer of these puts because the bank is guaranteeing the customer's uncovered options. The writer is also considered covered if he is long the same puts with the same strike price or higher. Being long, the shares do not cover the writer of puts because they lose on the short puts and they also lose on the decline in value of the long shares. Thus, they lose twice as much money if the stock declines in value.

16. **Answer B is correct.** Nelson sold 400 shares of HTH stock short at $36 in his account. The Regulation T requirement on this short sale is 50%. The equation is 400 shares × $36 = $14,400 × 50% = $7200 required. He also wrote 4 HTH September 35 Puts @ 3 in the account, taking in $1200 in premiums. This money is already in the account, so Nelson is required to deposit the remaining amount of $6000 ($7200 – $1200 = $6000) to meet the Regulation T requirement.

17. **Answer A is correct.** Oscar sold short 700 shares of TNT stock at $84 in his account. The Regulation T requirement on this is 50%. The equation is 700 shares × $84 = $58,800 × 50% = $29,400. Oscar also wrote 7 TNT Puts @ 6 in his account, taking in $4200 in premiums to the account. The money is already in the account, so he is required to deposit the remaining amount of $25,200 in the account ($29,400 – $4200 = $25,200).

18. **Answer A is correct.** Oliver purchased 1200 shares of BCI stock in his margin account at $46. His Regulation T requirement on the 1200 shares is 50%. The equation is 1200 shares × $46 = $55,200 × 50% = $27,600 required by Regulation T. Oliver also wrote 12 BCI March 50 Calls @ 4 and took in $4800 in premiums to the account. This money is in the account, so he is required to deposit $27,600 – $4800 = $22,800 to meet his Regulation T requirement.

The following explanation applies to the Questions 19 and 20:

The margin requirement on writing uncovered options is the greater of either the basic requirement or the minimum requirement. The basic requirement is the premium received plus 20% of the market value of the stock, less any amount out of the money for the option. The minimum requirement is the premium received plus 10% of the market value of the underlying security.

19. **Answer C is correct.** Norton writes 1 uncovered GHI October 50 Call @ 4. He took in $400 as the premium for the sale of the call. The underlying market price for GHI is $48. The equation is 100 shares × $48 = $4800 × 20% required = $960. The option is out of the money by $2. (The strike price = $50 – $48 market price.) Thus, he is required to deposit $400 + $960 = $1360 – $200 (100 × $2 out of the money) = $1160.

20. **Answer C is correct.** The previous question calculated the margin requirement on the JVC May 80 Put to be a total of $2240. This question asks how much of that amount is required to be deposited into the account. The account already has the $700 premium in the account. Thus, the remaining amount of $1540 is needed to meet the $2240 margin requirement.

21. **Answer D is correct.** An out-of-the-money call option has a strike price that is higher than the current market price. Only uncovered options require a margin deposit when they are written. (See the preceding explanation.)

22. **Answer C is correct.** The Options Clearing Corporation automatically exercises any option contract that is in the money by more than 3/4 point on the expiration date.

23. **Answer A is correct.** The Options Clearing Corporation puts exercise limit restrictions on investors in options. These limits restrict any option holder from exercising too many of the contracts he owns over a five-day period. Each option varies as to the maximum number of contracts that can be exercised. The time limit is set over a five business day period.

24. **Answer C is correct.** Leaps are long-term equity anticipation options. They are equity options that have an expiration date of up to 36 months. Most other options have a maximum expiration of nine months.

25. **Answer B is correct.** All options must settle with the Options Clearing Corporation on the next business day. The broker may give a client up to five business days to settle her option account.

Quick Check

Options Strategies

1. An investor who conducts an opening purchase of an option to protect his long position of a stock in an account has conducted which of the following?
   - ❍ A. Protective put
   - ❍ B. Protective call
   - ❍ C. Protective straddle
   - ❍ D. Protective spread

Quick Answer: **219**
Detailed Answer: **220**

2. An investor purchased 200 shares of TNT stock at $44 on May 20. The investor also purchased 2 TNT Puts on May 20. This investor conducted which of the following?
   - ❍ A. Protective put option
   - ❍ B. Married put option
   - ❍ C. Settled put option
   - ❍ D. Tandem put option

Quick Answer: **219**
Detailed Answer: **220**

3. Which of the following best describes the strategy of a short call option writer?
   - ❍ A. Hopes the market rises to buy the stock at the lower strike
   - ❍ B. Hopes the market rises to keep the premium on the expiring worthless option
   - ❍ C. Hopes the market drops to be able to sell the stock at the higher strike price
   - ❍ D. Hopes the market drops to keep the premium on the expiring worthless option

Quick Answer: **219**
Detailed Answer: **220**

Quick Check

4. Which of the following best describes the strategy of a long call option holder?

Quick Answer: 219
Detailed Answer: 220

- ❍ A. Hopes the market declines in value to sell the stock at the higher strike price
- ❍ B. Hopes the market declines to keep the premium on the expiring worthless option
- ❍ C. Hopes the market rises to keep the premium received on the expiring worthless option
- ❍ D. Hopes the market rises to purchase the stock at the lower strike price

5. Which of the following option contracts determine the breakeven point by adding the premium to the strike price?

Quick Answer: 219
Detailed Answer: 220

I. Long call

II. Short call

III. Long put

IV. Short put

- ❍ A. I and II
- ❍ B. I and III
- ❍ C. I and IV
- ❍ D. I, II, III, and IV

6. A long put holder could have a maximum potential loss of which of the following on the option contract?

Quick Answer: 219
Detailed Answer: 220

- ❍ A. The premium paid
- ❍ B. The premium received
- ❍ C. The amount the market price falls below the strike price
- ❍ D. The amount the market price rises above the strike price

7. Which of the following statements is true about a covered put writer?

Quick Answer: 219
Detailed Answer: 221

- ❍ A. The writer is long the underlying shares of the option contract.
- ❍ B. The writer is long the underlying shares of the option contract as long as the shares are purchased below the strike price.
- ❍ C. The writer is short the number of shares of the security represented by the option contract.
- ❍ D. The writer needs the exact opposite call option contract to be covered.

Quick Check

8. The maximum potential loss for an opening sale of a call option is realized when which of the following occurs?

   Quick Answer: 219
   Detailed Answer: 221

   ❍ A. The stock drops to zero in the market.
   ❍ B. The stock rises in value to an unlimited amount.
   ❍ C. The market price falls below the strike and the premium is retained.
   ❍ D. The market price rises above the strike and the premium is retained.

9. An investor performs a long call option in the market for an underlying security. Which of the following statements is not true about a long call option?

   Quick Answer: 219
   Detailed Answer: 221

   ❍ A. The investor doing the call is bullish.
   ❍ B. The maximum potential loss is limited to the premium paid.
   ❍ C. The maximum potential gain is limited to the stock dropping to zero.
   ❍ D. The investor conducted an opening purchase.

10. An investor performs a long put option in the market for an underlying security. Which of the following statements is not true about a long put option?

   Quick Answer: 219
   Detailed Answer: 221

   ❍ A. The breakeven point is the strike price minus the premium.
   ❍ B. The maximum potential loss occurs if the market price rises above the strike price.
   ❍ C. The maximum potential gain occurs if the stock falls to zero.
   ❍ D. The maximum gain that could be realized is the premium received.

11. Ira purchases 100 shares of TNT stock in the market at $86 per share. He also purchases 1 TNT October 85 Put @ 2 in the market. TNT stock goes to $79 in the market at expiration. What is Ira's profit or loss on these positions?

   Quick Answer: 219
   Detailed Answer: 221

   ❍ A. Profit of $400
   ❍ B. Profit of $600
   ❍ C. Loss of $300
   ❍ D. Loss of $700

Quick Check

12. Walter sells 100 shares of BTO stock short in the market at $47. He also purchases 1 BTO May 50 Call @ 4 in the market. BTO market price goes to $33 at expiration. What is Walter's profit or loss on these positions?

   ❍ A. Gain of $1400
   ❍ B. Gain of $1000
   ❍ C. Loss of $500
   ❍ D. Loss of $1300

Quick Answer: 219
Detailed Answer: 221

13. Eddie purchases 500 shares of LTV stock in the market at $44. He also purchases 5 LTV September 45 Puts @ 5 in the market. LTV stock goes to $83 in the market at expiration. What is the profit or loss for this account?

   ❍ A. Profit of $17,000
   ❍ B. Profit of $19,500
   ❍ C. Loss of $100
   ❍ D. Loss of $500

Quick Answer: 219
Detailed Answer: 222

14. An investor sells 1000 shares of MTV stock short in the market at $44. The investor also purchases 10 MTV September 45 Calls @ 4 in the market. MTV stock goes to $67 in the market at expiration. What is the profit or loss for this account?

   ❍ A. Gain of $18,000
   ❍ B. Gain of $23,000
   ❍ C. Loss of $23,000
   ❍ D. Loss of $5000

Quick Answer: 219
Detailed Answer: 222

15. An investor purchases 100 shares of DTT stock in the market at $33. The investor also purchases 1 DTT October 30 Put @ 3 in the market. What is the maximum potential loss this account could have?

   ❍ A. $300
   ❍ B. $600
   ❍ C. $3300
   ❍ D. $3600

Quick Answer: 219
Detailed Answer: 222

16. An investor is long 100 shares of RCA stock at $45 in the market. The investor also writes 1 RCA May 50 Call @ 3 in the market. What is the maximum possible gain this account could have?

   ❍ A. Unlimited amount
   ❍ B. $300
   ❍ C. $500
   ❍ D. $800

Quick Answer: 219
Detailed Answer: 222

Quick Check

17. An investor purchases 200 shares of QVC in the market at $50. The same investor also purchases 2 QVC April 50 Puts @ 4 in the market. What is the maximum potential gain and maximum potential loss this account could have?

   ❍ A. The maximum gain is $10,000; the maximum loss is $400
   ❍ B. The maximum gain is $10,000; the maximum loss is $800
   ❍ C. The maximum gain is an unlimited amount; the maximum loss is $400
   ❍ D. The maximum gain is an unlimited amount; the maximum loss is $800

Quick Answer: **219**
Detailed Answer: **222**

18. To effectively hedge a long stock position, an investor uses which of the following options?

   ❍ A. Short call
   ❍ B. Long call
   ❍ C. Short put
   ❍ D. Long put

Quick Answer: **219**
Detailed Answer: **222**

19. An investor is long 100 shares of ACE stock in his account. The current market price for ACE is $55. The investor wants to increase his portfolio income on this position. What is the best way to enhance the portfolio income?

   ❍ A. Buy ace calls
   ❍ B. Sell ace calls
   ❍ C. Buy ace puts
   ❍ D. Sell ace puts

Quick Answer: **219**
Detailed Answer: **223**

20. Stuart is long 100 shares of VTV stock in the market at $52. He also sells 1 VTV January 55 Call @ 3. What is the breakeven point on the VTV stock that he holds?

   ❍ A. $49
   ❍ B. $52
   ❍ C. $55
   ❍ D. $58

Quick Answer: **219**
Detailed Answer: **223**

Quick Check

Use the following account positions to answer the next five questions:

Sell 400 shares of PDQ Stock short @ $59 per share

Purchase 4 PDQ July 60 Calls @ 5

21. What price must PDQ stock have for the investor to break even?
    - ❍ A. $54
    - ❍ B. $55
    - ❍ C. $64
    - ❍ D. $65

Quick Answer: **219**
Detailed Answer: **223**

22. What is the maximum potential loss for this account?
    - ❍ A. $100
    - ❍ B. $600
    - ❍ C. $2400
    - ❍ D. Unlimited

Quick Answer: **219**
Detailed Answer: **223**

23. What is the maximum possible gain for this account?
    - ❍ A. $5400
    - ❍ B. $5900
    - ❍ C. $21,600
    - ❍ D. $23,600

Quick Answer: **219**
Detailed Answer: **223**

24. If the market price of PDQ stock goes to $43, what is the profit or loss on this account?
    - ❍ A. A profit of $6400
    - ❍ B. A profit of $4400
    - ❍ C. A loss of $2000
    - ❍ D. A loss of $4800

Quick Answer: **219**
Detailed Answer: **223**

25. If the market price of PDQ stock goes to $71 in the market, what is the profit or loss in the account?
    - ❍ A. Profit of $600
    - ❍ B. Profit of $2400
    - ❍ C. Loss of $2400
    - ❍ D. Loss of $4800

Quick Answer: **219**
Detailed Answer: **223**

Quick Check Answer Key

1. A
2. B
3. D
4. D
5. A
6. B
7. C
8. B
9. C
10. D
11. C
12. B
13. A
14. D
15. B
16. D
17. D
18. D
19. B
20. C
21. A
22. C
23. C
24. B
25. C

Answers and Explanations

1. **Answer A is correct.** An investor with a long position in his account wants to protect against a decline in the market for the stock. A put option allows the holder to put the stock back to the writer at the higher strike price. A protective put option is an opening purchase of a put that reflects the long position in the account.

2. **Answer B is correct.** The investor in this question purchased 200 shares of stock and 2 puts on that stock on the same day (May 20). This is known as a married put. The married put must be done on the same day as the long position because it allows the investor to add the cost basis of the put to the cost basis of the long stock position. In this example, the investor has a cost basis of $44 plus the cost of the puts.

3. **Answer D is correct.** A short call writer is bearish on the underlying security. The short call writer hopes that the price of the underlying security falls below the strike price of the call option she has written. If the market price is below the strike price, then the call writer keeps the premium received on the sale of the calls.

4. **Answer D is correct.** The holder of a long call option is bullish on the underlying security. She hopes that the market price of the stock rises above the strike price of the option so that she can purchase the stock at the lower strike price. The most that she can lose is the premium paid, and the most she can make is the amount that the stock rises above the strike price of the option contract.

5. **Answer A is correct.** The breakeven point of a put option is determined by subtracting the premium from the strike price. In this question, the breakeven point of the call option is determined by adding the premium to the strike price. Remember, the breakeven point for the buyer and seller is always the same for options. That is why the long calls and the short calls have the same breakeven point.

6. **Answer B is correct.** A holder of a put option (a long position or opening purchase) has a maximum potential loss of the premium that has been paid on the option contract. The holder of a put wants the market price of the stock to decline below the strike price of the option. If it rises above the strike price, the option expires worthless, and the put holder loses the premium paid.

7. **Answer C is correct.** A covered put writer is considered "covered" when she is short the number of shares represented by the option contract. A put writer loses money when the stock declines below the strike price of the option. When long, the shares actually lose twice as much for the writer if the stock falls below the strike price. When short, the shares offset the loss on a put that has a market value which declines below the strike price. Short sellers make money on a decline in the market price of the shares.

8. **Answer B is correct.** The writer of a call option has a maximum loss exposure for the amount the market price rises above the strike price of the option. This possible loss could be any price above the strike, so it is considered an unlimited loss potential.

9. **Answer C is correct.** The stock dropping to zero does not make money for the long call option. The holder would lose the premium paid. The holder of a call option is bullish on the underlying security when he does an opening purchase of a call option. The most that he can lose is the amount he paid in premium to the writer. The most he can make is the amount that the market price of the underlying security rises above the strike price, which is considered an unlimited amount.

10. **Answer D is correct.** The maximum gain on a long put option is if the stock drops to zero and is put back to the writer at the higher strike price. The holder of a long option has a breakeven point of the strike price minus the premium paid. The most the holder can lose is the premium paid if the market price rises above the strike price and the option expires worthless. The maximum gain for the holder is if the stock declines to zero and is then put back to the writer at the higher strike price. The maximum gain for the writer is the premium received.

11. **Answer C is correct.** Ira purchases 100 shares of TNT stock at $86. The stock goes to $79 in the market and he loses $700 on the stock. He also bought 1 TNT Oct 85 Put that allows him to put the stock back to a writer at $85. He can take the $79 stock and put it to the writer at $85 for a $600 profit. The put cost him $200, which equals a $400 profit on the option. He lost $700 on stock and made $400 on the put, for a total loss of $300.

12. **Answer B is correct.** Walter sells 100 shares of BTO stock short at $47. The stock went to $33 for a gain on the short position of $1400. He also bought 1 BTO May 50 Call @ 4. The holder of a call option only makes money if the market price of the stock rises above the strike price. It did not. He thus lost the premium paid of $400. He has a total gain of $1400 less the premium loss of $400 = $1000 total gain for the account.

13. **Answer A is correct.** Eddie purchased 500 shares of LTV stock at $44. The stock went to $83 in the market for a profit of $39 per share × 500 shares = $19,500. He also purchased 5 LTV Sept 45 Puts @ 5. The puts allow him to put LTV stock to the writer at $45. He will not exercise the puts and they will expire worthless, losing the premium he paid. He paid $5 × 500 shares = $2500 premium lost. He made $19,500 on the stock and lost $2500 on the options, for a total gain in the account of $17,000.

14. **Answer D is correct.** The investor sells short 1000 shares of MTV at $44. The stock went to $67 in the market for a loss on the short sale of 23 points × 1000 shares = $23,000 loss. The investor also purchased 10 MTV Sept 45 Calls @ 4. The calls give the investor the right to buy MTV shares at $45. The stock is selling at $67 for a profit of $22 per share × 1000 shares = $22,000. The premium on the options was $4 × 1000 shares = $4000—so the total gain on the options is $18,000. She lost $23,000 and made $18,000 for a total loss of $5,000 in the account.

15. **Answer B is correct.** An investor purchasing 100 shares of DTT stock at $33 and 1 DTT Oct 30 Put @ 3 has a maximum potential loss in the account of $600 in the account. The DTT stock could in theory go down to zero. However, the protective put protects the investor down to $30 for a 3-point loss on the stock. The option cost $3 × 100 shares = $300. The total potential loss will not exceed $300 + $300 = $600.

16. **Answer D is correct.** An investor with 100 shares of RCA stock at $45 who also writes 1 RCA May 50 Call @ 3 has a maximum possible gain of $800 in the account. The 100 shares of RCA stock could go up in price to any amount. The investor also wrote a call on RCA. The stock can only go to $50 (the strike price of the option) before he has to give the stock up in the option. The $500 profit on the stock plus the premium of $300 received = a total $800 maximum profit.

17. **Answer D is correct.** The investor purchased 200 shares of QVC stock at $50. The same investor also protected his downside potential loss by purchasing the 2 QVC April 50 Puts @ 4 in the market. The maximum gain on the shares of QVC stock is unlimited, but the maximum potential loss is the $800 paid for the two QVC options.

18. **Answer D is correct.** A long stock position is hedged by protecting the downside of the long position. This is done with the purchase of a put option that allows the investor to put the stock back to the writer at the higher strike price.

19. **Answer B is correct.** An investor who is long 100 shares of ACE stock at $55 could increase his portfolio income on the ACE stock by writing covered calls on the ACE stock. The ACE calls enable the investor to receive the premium paid on the options, as well as hope the stock increases in value. Covered call writing enhances the income for the portfolio.

20. **Answer C is correct.** An investor who is long 100 shares of VTV stock at $52 and also sells 1 VTV Jan 55 Call @3 has a breakeven point in the account of $55. When the stock hits $55, he makes $3 per share on the long stock and he loses the $3 premium on the call option to break even.

21. **Answer A is correct.** The investor breaks even on this account when the price of PDQ stock goes to $54 per share. At $54 per share, the investor makes 5 points × 400 shares on the short sale = $2000 gain. The call options that the investor purchased to protect her upside loss potential would, at a market price of $54, lose the entire premium paid of $5 × 400 shares = $2000 loss.

22. **Answer C is correct.** The maximum loss the investor can have on this account is if the short shares go up in value to infinity. This is covered by the long calls at a strike price of $60. The most the investor can lose is the 1-point increase on the short shares to the maximum of the strike price, plus the premium of $5 per share on the calls = $6 total × 400 shares = $2400 possible loss.

23. **Answer C is correct.** The maximum gain that the investor can have is if the short shares decline in value to zero for a $59 per share gain × 400 shares = $23,600 gain. If this occurs, the 4 PDQ calls expire worthless and the investor loses the premium of $5 paid × 400 shares = $2,000 loss. The total maximum gain is thus $21,600.

24. **Answer B is correct.** If the market price goes to $43 per share, the investor makes 16 points per share on the short sale (59 – 43 = 16 point gain) × 400 shares = $6400 gain. The investor then loses the $5 per share on the PDQ calls that expire worthless because the market price is well below the strike price of the call options. The investor gains $6400 on the short sale and loses $2000 on the long calls, for a $4400 total gain.

25. **Answer C is correct.** If PDQ stock goes to $71, the investor loses 12 points per share on the short shares (71 – 59 = 12 loss) × 400 shares = $4800 loss on the short sale. However, the investor can exercise the call option at $60 for a stock selling at $71. This is an 11-point gain for the investor, less the premium of $5 paid = 6 point gain × 400 shares = $2400 gain. He has a loss of $4800 on the short sale and a gain of $2400 on the call options, so he has a total loss of $2400 for the account.

Quick Check

Spreads and Straddles

1. Which of the following is an example of a long option straddle position?

   Quick Answer: 231
   Detailed Answer: 232

   - ❍ A. Buy 1 ABC July 50 Call / Sell 1 ABC July 50 Call
   - ❍ B. Buy 1 ABC July 50 Call / Sell 1 ABC July 50 Put
   - ❍ C. Buy 1 ABC July 50 Call / Buy 1 ABC July 50 Put
   - ❍ D. Buy 1 ABC July 50 Put / Sell 1 ABC July 50 Call

2. Which of the following is an example of a long straddle option?

   Quick Answer: 231
   Detailed Answer: 232

   - ❍ A. Buy 1 TNT May 50 Call / Sell 1 TNT May 50 Call
   - ❍ B. Sell 1 TNT May 50 Call / Buy 1 TNT May 50 Put
   - ❍ C. Buy 1 TNT May 50 Call / Buy 1 TNT May 50 Put
   - ❍ D. Sell 1 TNT May 50 Call / Sell 1 TNT May 50 Put

3. A straddle position conducted by an investor has which of the following characteristics?

   Quick Answer: 231
   Detailed Answer: 232

   I. The purchase of a call and a put.

   II. The options have the same strike price.

   III. The options have the same expiration.

   IV. The investor is betting on the stocks' volatility.

   - ❍ A. I and II
   - ❍ B. I and III
   - ❍ C. I, II, and III
   - ❍ D. I, II, III, and IV

Quick Check

4. Which of the following best describes the beliefs of an investor who is utilizing long straddle positions?

Quick Answer: 231
Detailed Answer: 232

- ❍ A. Firmly believes the market is in a bullish trend
- ❍ B. Firmly believes the market is in a bearish trend
- ❍ C. Firmly believes the market will remain stable
- ❍ D. Firmly believes the market will move drastically but is unsure of which way

5. Cord purchases 1 HTH May 75 Call @ 5 and 1 HTH May 75 Put @ 2. What is the breakeven point on the HTH Call in this account?

Quick Answer: 231
Detailed Answer: 232

- ❍ A. $75
- ❍ B. $77
- ❍ C. $80
- ❍ D. $82

6. An investor purchases 1 TNT October 70 Call @ 4 and 1 TNT October 70 Put @ 3. What is the maximum possible loss this account can incur?

Quick Answer: 231
Detailed Answer: 232

- ❍ A. Unlimited
- ❍ B. $700
- ❍ C. $6700
- ❍ D. $6300

7. What is the breakeven point for the following straddle?

   Sell 1 TKP June 50 Call @ 3 and Sell 1 TKP June 50 Put @ 4

Quick Answer: 231
Detailed Answer: 232

- ❍ A. The call has a breakeven point of $53; the put has a breakeven point of $46.
- ❍ B. The call has a breakeven point of $43; the put has a breakeven point of $57.
- ❍ C. The call has a breakeven point of $57; the put has a breakeven point of $43.
- ❍ D. The call has a breakeven point of $57; the put has a breakeven point of $57.

8. Phillip writes 3 JNJ August 75 Calls @ 5 and 3 JNJ August 75 Puts @ 4 in the market. What is the maximum potential loss he can incur from the sale of this straddle?

Quick Answer: 231
Detailed Answer: 232

- ❍ A. $900 possible loss
- ❍ B. $2700 possible loss
- ❍ C. $22,500 possible loss
- ❍ D. Unlimited possible loss

Quick Check

9. An investor purchases 1 FTD May 50 Call @ 3 and purchases 1 FTD August 45 Put @ 4. This is an example of what type of option?

❍ A. A spread

❍ B. A combination

❍ C. A short straddle

❍ D. A diagonal straddle

Quick Answer: **231**
Detailed Answer: **233**

10. Allison writes 5 URC June 65 Calls @ 4 and also writes 5 URC June 65 Puts @ 3. URC stock goes to $77 in the market. What is the profit or loss on this account?

❍ A. Profit of $4000

❍ B. Profit of $2500

❍ C. Loss of $2500

❍ D. Loss of $4000

Quick Answer: **231**
Detailed Answer: **233**

11. Henry writes 2 JKE April 100 Calls @ 6 and also writes 2 JKE April 100 Puts @ 5. JKE stock goes to $137 in the market. What is the profit or loss for the account?

❍ A. Profit of $6200

❍ B. Profit of $5200

❍ C. Loss of $5200

❍ D. Loss of $1000

Quick Answer: **231**
Detailed Answer: **233**

12. Carol purchases 9 LTV April 65 Calls @ 7 and also purchases 9 LTV April 65 Puts @ 5. LTV stock goes to a price of $37 in the market. What is the profit or loss in the account?

❍ A. Profit of $20,700

❍ B. Profit of $14,400

❍ C. Loss of $10,800

❍ D. Loss of $20,700

Quick Answer: **231**
Detailed Answer: **233**

Quick Check

13. An investor conducts the following option position: Buy 1 TNT May 60 Call @ 5 and Sell 1 TNT May 70 Call @ 2. Which of the following statements are true about this position?

    I. The investor is bullish on TNT stock.

    II. The investor is bearish on TNT stock.

    III. This is considered a credit spread.

    IV. This is considered a debit spread.

    ❍ A. I only
    ❍ B. II only
    ❍ C. I and IV
    ❍ D. II and III

Quick Answer: **231**
Detailed Answer: **233**

14. Which of the following is an example of a long call debit bull spread?
    ❍ A. Buy 1 ACE May 60 Call @ 6 / Sell 1 ACE May 70 Call @ 3
    ❍ B. Buy 1 ACE May 60 Put @ 5 / Sell 1 ACE May 50 Put @ 2
    ❍ C. Buy 1 ACE May 60 Call @ 2 / Sell 1 ACE May 70 Call @ 5
    ❍ D. Buy 1 ACE May 60 Put @ 2 / Buy 1 ACE May 50 Put @ 4

Quick Answer: **231**
Detailed Answer: **233**

15. Which of the following are bullish on the underlying security?

    I. Long call spread

    II. Short call spread

    III. Long put spread

    IV. Short put spread

    ❍ A. I only
    ❍ B. II only
    ❍ C. I and IV
    ❍ D. II and III

Quick Answer: **231**
Detailed Answer: **234**

16. An investor received a tip that the market price of VTV stock will be increasing in market value shortly. The investor is still somewhat wary of the "tip" he received. What is the best spread position to do in his account?
    ❍ A. Do a long call debit spread.
    ❍ B. Do a long call credit spread.
    ❍ C. Do a short call debit spread.
    ❍ D. Do a short put debit spread.

Quick Answer: **231**
Detailed Answer: **234**

Quick Check

17. Arthur writes 2 STP August 65 Calls @ 6 and also writes 2 STP August 65 Puts @ 4. What is the breakeven point on the STP put in this account if STP has a market price of $64?

   - ❍ A. $61
   - ❍ B. $60
   - ❍ C. $59
   - ❍ D. $55

Quick Answer: 231
Detailed Answer: 234

18. Matt Sells 1 KLM June 60 Call @ 5 and also Buys 1 KLM June 70 Call @ 1. What is the breakeven point on this short call spread?

   - ❍ A. $60
   - ❍ B. $64
   - ❍ C. $65
   - ❍ D. $74

Quick Answer: 231
Detailed Answer: 234

19. George purchases 1 HTH July 70 Put @ 6 and also Sells 1 HTH July 60 Put @ 2. What is the breakeven point on this long put spread?

   - ❍ A. $58
   - ❍ B. $64
   - ❍ C. $66
   - ❍ D. $74

Quick Answer: 231
Detailed Answer: 234

20. An investor Sells 1 GHI June 50 Call @ 5 and also Purchases 1 GHI June 60 Call @ 2. What is the maximum possible profit that this short call spread can have?

   - ❍ A. Unlimited
   - ❍ B. $300
   - ❍ C. $400
   - ❍ D. $700

Quick Answer: 231
Detailed Answer: 234

Answer Questions 21 through 25 with the following spread option information.

Investor Buys 1 STP September 70 Call @ 5

Investor Sells 1 STP September 80 Call @ 2

21. What type of spread is this STP option?

   - ❍ A. Short call debit spread
   - ❍ B. Long call credit spread
   - ❍ C. Short call credit spread
   - ❍ D. Long call debit spread

Quick Answer: 231
Detailed Answer: 234

Quick Check

22. What is the maximum possible gain that the investor can have on this spread?
    - A. $200
    - B. $500
    - C. $700
    - D. Unlimited

Quick Answer: 231
Detailed Answer: 235

23. What is the maximum possible loss the investor can have on this spread?
    - A. $200
    - B. $300
    - C. $700
    - D. Unlimited

Quick Answer: 231
Detailed Answer: 235

24. If the market price of STP stock goes to $87 in the market, what is the profit or loss for this spread?
    - A. Profit of $1200
    - B. Profit of $700
    - C. Loss of $700
    - D. Loss of $1500

Quick Answer: 231
Detailed Answer: 235

25. If the market price of STP stock goes to $61 in the market, what is the profit or loss for the spread?
    - A. Profit of $200
    - B. Profit of $700
    - C. Loss of $300
    - D. Loss of $500

Quick Answer: 231
Detailed Answer: 235

Quick Check Answer Key

1. C
2. C
3. D
4. D
5. D
6. B
7. C
8. D
9. B
10. C
11. C
12. B
13. C
14. A
15. C
16. A
17. D
18. B
19. C
20. B
21. D
22. C
23. B
24. B
25. C

Answers and Explanations

1. **Answer C is correct.** A straddles position is the purchase and sale of a put or a call option with the same underlying security, same expiration, and same strike price. A long straddle is to Buy 1 ABC July 50 Call and also Buy 1 ABC July 50 Put.

2. **Answer C is correct.** A long straddle is when the option investor purchases both a call and put option on the same underlying security. A short straddle is the writer of the same options. The only choice that shows two purchases is C.

3. **Answer D is correct.** Straddles are used by option investors because they are convinced the stock will move substantially, but they are unsure of which way (up or down). The purchase of a put and a call enables the long straddle holder to cover both sides of the market. The straddle position has the same strike price and expiration.

4. **Answer D is correct.** Straddle options are used by an investor who is convinced that the market will move sharply but is unsure of which way. The purchase of a put and a call option enables the investor to cover both sides of the market, with the premiums paid as the most they risk losing.

5. **Answer D is correct.** The purchase of 1 HTH May 75 Call @ 5 and 1 HTH May 75 Put @ 2 has a breakeven point on the call of $82 ($75 + 5 + 2 = $82). If the holder is right on the call side (bullish), then he has to be wrong on the put side (bearish). Both premiums paid are added to the call strike price to determine the breakeven point. Both premiums paid are deducted from the strike price to determine the breakeven point on the put.

6. **Answer B is correct.** The investor who is long 1 TNT October 70 Call @ 4 and also long 1 TNT October 70 Put @ 3 has a maximum possible loss of the premiums paid on the straddle position (total premiums $7 × 100 shares = $700). The worse case scenario for the long straddle is if the market price of the stock remains constant at the strike price of the straddle.

7. **Answer C is correct.** The breakeven point on 1 TKP June 50 Call @ 3 and TKP June 50 Put @ 4 is determined by adding the two premiums ($3 + $4 = $7) and adding it to the call option strike price ($50 + $7 = $57). Conversely, you subtract the combined premiums from the strike of the put option to determine the breakeven points, ($50 – $7 = $43).

8. **Answer D is correct.** The writer of a straddle position option has a maximum exposure to loss of the call option rising to an unlimited amount. The put side can only decline to zero, but the call options can go up to an unlimited amount.

9. **Answer B is correct.** An investor who purchases 1 FTD May 50 Call @ 3 and 1 FTD August 45 Put @ 4 conducts a combination straddle. A combination can have a different strike price and a different expiration for the underlying security. The investor is betting that time will affect the price of the underlying security.

10. **Answer C is correct.** The writer of 5 URC June 65 Calls @ 4 and 5 URC June 65 Puts @3 has a maximum potential gain of the premiums received ($4 + $3 = $7) × 500 shares = $3500. The price of URC stock at $77 gives the holder of the calls the right to buy the stock at $65 for a $12 gain, less the premiums of $7, which is a $5 gain to the holder and a loss to the writer. The writer loses $5 × 500 shares = $2500 loss.

11. **Answer C is correct.** Henry writes 2 JKE April 100 Calls @ 6 and also 2 JKE April 100 Puts @ 5. The stock goes to $137 in the market. The put option expires worthless to the holder. The call option enables the holder to buy the stock from the writer (Henry) at $100, for a 37 point loss to Henry. The combined premiums of $6 + $5 = $11 are deducted from the loss to give Henry a 26 point loss × 200 shares = $5200 total loss for Henry.

12. **Answer B is correct.** Carol purchases 9 LTV April 65 Calls @ 7 and also purchases 9 LTV April 65 Puts @ 5. If LTV stock goes to $37 in the market, the long calls expire worthless for Carol, but the long puts enable her to put the stock back to the writer at $65 for a 28 point gain, less the two premiums paid of $12. The total gain to Carol is $26 – $12 premiums = $16 gain per share × 900 shares = $14,400 gain in the account.

13. **Answer C is correct.** The investor who buys 1 TNT May 60 Call @ 5 and also Sells 1 TNT May 70 Call @ 2 has done a long call debit spread. The investor wants the price of TNT stock to increase in value so the spread makes him money. The investor is bullish and not bearish on TNT stock. The investor paid more for the call than he took in for the put, so this is a debit spread.

14. **Answer A is correct.** A long call debit bull spread is the purchase of a call that costs more than the sale of the call in the spread. The debit means the investor paid more than she took in, so that becomes the dominant option in the spread. It's a bull spread because the investor would rather see the market go up in value to make money than go down in value. The best example is in choice A. It costs the investor more than the option in choice C, which creates the debit we are looking for. The other choices have puts in them and do not apply here.

15. **Answer C is correct.** The long call spread and the short put spread are both bullish for the investor in the market. In a long spread, the investor buys a call that makes him money if the market increases in value. In the short put spread, the investor sells a put and only keeps the premium if the market price of the stock rises above the strike price of the put. In both cases, and for different reasons, the long call and short put spreads are both considered bullish.

16. **Answer A is correct.** The investor with the "hot tip" on a stock is best served by buying a call on the underlying stock in a debit spread (the cost is more than the short call) in the market. The long call is bullish because the investor makes money if the stock goes up in value. The call that he sells in the long spread limits his potential profits but also limits his potential losses.

17. **Answer D is correct.** Arthur sells 2 STP August 65 Calls @ 6 and also writes 2 STP August 65 Puts @ 4. The breakeven point on the put in this straddle is the strike price less the combined premiums of the straddle position. The equation is $65 strike – $6 call premium + $4 put premium = $55 breakeven point on the put.

18. **Answer B is correct.** Matt sold 1 KLM June 60 Call @ 5 and bought 1 KLM June 70 Call @ 1. The breakeven point is $64 on the options. At a market price of $64, the short June 60 calls lose $4, but he keeps the $5 premium for a net gain of $1. The long June 70 Calls expire worthless, and Matt loses the $1 premium paid for a net gain of zero.

19. **Answer C is correct.** The breakeven point on the long put spread is $66. If the market price of HTH goes to $66, the long HTH July 70 Put @ 6 makes $4 but costs $6, for a net loss of $2. The short HTH July 60 Put @ 2 expires worthless to the holder, and George retains the $2 premium received for a $2 gain. The loss is cancelled out by the gain, and the account breaks even.

20. **Answer B is correct.** An investor who sells 1 GHI June 50 Call @ 5 and also buys 1 GHI June 60 Call @ 2 has a maximum gain of $3 points on each share, or $300. The investor took in $500 in premiums and paid out $200 in premiums for a net gain of $300. If the stock goes to 60, she keeps the $500 premium on the sale of the June 50 Calls but loses $500 on the increase to $60. The loss is $500, and the additional loss on the expiring worthless long June 60 Call costs her $200 more for a total loss of $700. If the stock falls below $50, she keeps the $500 premium received on the June 50 call but loses the $200 premium paid on the June 60 Call for a profit of $300.

21. **Answer D is correct.** This is an example of a long call debit spread. The investor paid more for the September 70 call than she took in on the September 80 Call, making it a debit spread. The more important option is the one she purchased for the higher price, so it is a long spread.

22. **Answer C is correct.** The maximum gain is the spread of $10 less the difference in the premiums ($5 – $2 = $3). The equation is $10 – $3 = $7 × 100 shares = $700 maximum gain. If STP goes to $90, she makes 20 points on the long call less the $5 premium = $15 profit × 100 shares = $1500 gain. She loses $10 on the short call less the premium received of $2 = $8 loss × 100 shares = $800 loss. Therefore, she makes $1500 and loses $800, for a gain of $700.

23. **Answer B is correct.** The most that the investor could lose on this spread is the difference in premiums. The equation is $5 premium paid – $2 premium received = $3 total cost. If the stock goes below $70, then both options expire worthless and she loses $500 on one while making $200 on the other, for a net loss of $300.

24. **Answer B is correct.** If the market price of STP stock goes to $87, the long September 70 Call is in the money by 17 points, less the $5 premium paid, for a $12 profit per share × 100 shares = $1200 profit. The short call option is in the money by 7 points for the holder, less the $2 premium received, for a $5 loss per share × 100 shares = $500 loss. The difference is a $700 profit for the investor.

25. **Answer C is correct.** If the market price goes to $61, both the long call and the short call in the spread are out of the money, and the investor sees both expire worthless. She loses $500 on the September 70 Call and makes $200 on the September 80 call for a net loss of $300.

Quick Check

Stock Index Options

1. All the following statements are true except for which one?

    ❍ A. Indexes measure change in a larger group of data.

    ❍ B. Indexes can indicate the current state of a market.

    ❍ C. Indexes can be established only for stocks.

    ❍ D. Indexes are typically weighted for each component in the index.

Quick Answer: **244**
Detailed Answer: **245**

2. Which of the following statements are considered true of stock indexes?

    I. The index measures the current value of the stock.

    II. The index measures the percentage change of a stock from a set point in the past.

    III. The volume of outstanding shares is used to weight a stock index.

    IV. A stock with 1 million shares has the same impact on an index as a stock with 2 million shares.

    ❍ A. I and II

    ❍ B. I, II, and III

    ❍ C. II, III, and IV

    ❍ D. I, II, III, and IV

Quick Answer: **244**
Detailed Answer: **245**

Quick Check

3. A broad-based index is characteristic of which of the following?

Quick Answer: 244
Detailed Answer: 245

I. A major stock index.

II. Indexes that include a small number of stocks from very large companies.

III. A large number of stocks from a variety of companies and sectors.

IV. The index mirrors the movements of the market as a whole.

- A. I and II
- B. II and III
- C. I, II, and III
- D. I, II, III, and IV

4. The New York Stock Exchange composite index represents which of the following?

Quick Answer: 244
Detailed Answer: 245

- A. A select 100 stocks listed on the NYSE
- B. A select 500 stocks listed on the NYSE
- C. All common and preferred stocks listed on the NYSE
- D. All common stocks listed on the NYSE

5. Each of the following is considered a narrow-based index except for which one?

Quick Answer: 244
Detailed Answer: 245

- A. Mexico index
- B. Technology index
- C. Gold/silver index
- D. S&P 100 index

6. A narrow-based index has all the following characteristics except for which one?

Quick Answer: 244
Detailed Answer: 245

- A. It tracks stock movements in one segment of the market.
- B. It tracks stocks in one particular country.
- C. It tracks all stocks on the NYSE.
- D. It tracks stocks for one sector or industry.

7. An option contract for a index option is represented by which of the following in computing the contract?

Quick Answer: 244
Detailed Answer: 245

- A. Each contract represents 100 shares.
- B. Each contract represents a multiplier of 100.
- C. Each contract represents $100.
- D. Each contract represents $1000.

Quick Check

8. An investor purchased five S&P 500 index options with a strike price of 940. The investor paid a premium of 3 1/2 for the options. What dollar amount did the investor pay?
   - ❍ A. $350
   - ❍ B. $1750
   - ❍ C. $3500
   - ❍ D. $17,500

Quick Answer: **244**
Detailed Answer: **245**

9. An investor purchased 10 S&P 500 call index options with a strike price of 920. The S&P index goes to 980 in the market, and the investor exercises the option. What is the profit or loss?
   - ❍ A. A profit of $600
   - ❍ B. A profit of $6000
   - ❍ C. A profit of $60,000
   - ❍ D. A loss of $6000

Quick Answer: **244**
Detailed Answer: **245**

10. An investor purchases the following index options: 4 OEX January 910 Calls @ 3. The S&P 100 goes to 980 in the market, and the investor exercises the contract. What is the profit or loss?
    - ❍ A. A profit of $7000
    - ❍ B. A profit of $26,800
    - ❍ C. A profit of $27,700
    - ❍ D. A profit of $28,000

Quick Answer: **244**
Detailed Answer: **246**

11. An investor sells the following index options: 3 XMI June 970 Calls @ 4. The XMI index goes to 960 at expiration. What is the seller's profit or loss?
    - ❍ A. A profit of $1200
    - ❍ B. A profit of $12,000
    - ❍ C. A loss of $1800
    - ❍ D. A loss of $3000

Quick Answer: **244**
Detailed Answer: **246**

12. A portfolio manager writes 200 SPX April 930 Calls @ 4 1/2. The underlying S&P 500 index rises to 939 in the market. What is the profit or loss on the index options for the writer?
    - ❍ A. A profit of $9000
    - ❍ B. A profit of $90,000
    - ❍ C. A loss of $9000
    - ❍ D. A loss of $90,000

Quick Answer: **244**
Detailed Answer: **246**

Quick Check

13. A portfolio manager writes 325 SPX June 950 Calls @ 3 1/2. What is the maximum possible gain of the writer?
   - ❍ A. Unlimited potential gain
   - ❍ B. A maximum gain of $1137.50
   - ❍ C. A maximum gain of $113,750
   - ❍ D. A maximum gain of $1,137,500

Quick Answer: **244**
Detailed Answer: **246**

14. An investor who is hedging a portfolio with index options is protecting against which type of risk?
   - ❍ A. Systematic risk
   - ❍ B. Unsystematic risk
   - ❍ C. Interest rate risk
   - ❍ D. Liquidity risk

Quick Answer: **244**
Detailed Answer: **246**

15. The use of index options as a hedge does not protect an investor from which type of risk?
   - ❍ A. Systematic risk
   - ❍ B. Market risk
   - ❍ C. Liquidity risk
   - ❍ D. Unsystematic risk

Quick Answer: **244**
Detailed Answer: **246**

16. The number of open stock index options on an underlying security is represented by which of the following?
   - ❍ A. Short interest positions
   - ❍ B. Open interest
   - ❍ C. Special memorandum account
   - ❍ D. Beta coefficiency

Quick Answer: **244**
Detailed Answer: **246**

17. The S&P 500 index has a beta of 1. An investment advisor manages a portfolio with a beta of 2. The S&P index increases 10%. The portfolio should react in which manner?
   - ❍ A. The portfolio value rises 10%.
   - ❍ B. The portfolio value rises 20%.
   - ❍ C. The portfolio value decreases 10%.
   - ❍ D. The portfolio value decreases 20%.

Quick Answer: **244**
Detailed Answer: **246**

Quick Check

18. An investor owns two SPX April 950 Calls @ 4. The investor enters an order to exercise his two index options at the opening of the market. The market opens at 970 and then rises three hours later to 980. The market eventually closes at 985. At what price will the index options be exercised for the investor?

❍ A. 950
❍ B. 970
❍ C. 980
❍ D. 985

Quick Answer: **244**
Detailed Answer: **247**

19. Which of the following statements are true of American-style options?

I. All equity options are American-style options.

II. All stock index options are American-style options.

III. All stock index options are European-style options.

IV. Index options can be American-style or European-style options.

❍ A. I and II
❍ B. I and III
❍ C. I and IV
❍ D. IV only

Quick Answer: **244**
Detailed Answer: **247**

20. Which of the following statements are characteristic of long-term equity anticipation securities?

I. They have expiration terms of up to 3 years.

II. They can be American-style options.

III. They can be European-style options.

IV. They expire in December of each year.

❍ A. I and II
❍ B. I and III
❍ C. I, II, and III
❍ D. I, II, III, and IV

Quick Answer: **244**
Detailed Answer: **247**

Quick Check

21. Capped index options have all the following characteristics except for which one?

Quick Answer: **244**
Detailed Answer: **247**

- ❍ A. They are American style options.
- ❍ B. The maximum profit is capped at 30 points.
- ❍ C. When the option reaches its cap, it is automatically exercised.
- ❍ D. They can only be exercised at expiration or when they reach the cap.

22. An investor purchases the following capped index option: 1 OEX June 450 Call @ 4. Halfway through the expiration cycle, the option goes to 475, and the holder wants to exercise the option. What is the profit on the option?

Quick Answer: **244**
Detailed Answer: **247**

- ❍ A. $2100 profit
- ❍ B. $2500 profit
- ❍ C. $4000 profit
- ❍ D. The option cannot be exercised at this time.

23. Which of the following are characteristic of unsystematic risk on an index option?

Quick Answer: **244**
Detailed Answer: **247**

I. A security declines in the market due to poor management.

II. A security declines in the market due to more competitors in the industry.

III. A security declines in the market due to general market declines.

IV. A security declines in the market because of loss of market share taken by a new product.

- ❍ A. I and II
- ❍ B. I, II, and III
- ❍ C. I, II, and IV
- ❍ D. I, II, III, and IV

Quick Check

24. An investment advisor manages a $10,000,000 portfolio that closely mirrors the major market index. He decides to buy options on the XMI index with a strike price of 400. How many contracts will he have to purchase to effectively hedge his position?

Quick Answer: 244
Detailed Answer: 247

- ❍ A. 100 contracts
- ❍ B. 200 contracts
- ❍ C. 250 contracts
- ❍ D. 2500 contracts

25. Which of the following statements is considered true of a stock's beta?

Quick Answer: 244
Detailed Answer: 248

I. Beta measures volatility.

II. Beta measures volume.

III. A stock with a beta of 2 is twice as volatile as the market.

IV. A stock with a beta of 2 has half the volume of the market.

- ❍ A. I only
- ❍ B. II only
- ❍ C. I and III
- ❍ D. II and IV

Quick Check Answer Key

1. C

2. B

3. D

4. D

5. D

6. C

7. B

8. B

9. B

10. B

11. A

12. D

13. C

14. A

15. D

16. B

17. B

18. D

19. C

20. D

21. A

22. D

23. C

24. C

25. C

Answers and Explanations

1. **Answer C is correct.** Indexes are typically established for stocks and markets. They can also be established for other measures. The Consumer Price Index is an example of an index that is not a stock index. It measures the changing prices of important consumer goods.

2. **Answer B is correct.** An index does not simply just measure the current value of a stock, but rather the percentage change in the stock's value from some arbitrary point in the past. Indexes are typically weighted according to the number of outstanding shares for the stock. A stock with twice as many shares as another has a greater impact on the overall index.

3. **Answer D is correct.** A broad-based index includes all the major market indexes. It includes a small number of stocks from very large companies or a large number of stocks from a variety of companies and sectors. Broad-based indexes tend to mirror the movements of the market as a whole.

4. **Answer D is correct.** The New York Composite Index measures all the common stocks listed on the NYSE. It is a broad-based index that measures about 75% of all the stocks listed on the NYSE.

5. **Answer D is correct.** The S&P 100 index is calculated from 100 of the larger stocks listed on the NYSE. It is a broad-based index that tends to mirror the market as a whole.

6. **Answer C is correct.** A narrow-based index tracks stock movements in only one segment of the market. It can be for a particular industry, country, or sector. The index that tracks all NYSE-listed securities is considered broad based because it mirrors the market as a whole.

7. **Answer B is correct.** Stock index options use a multiplier of 100 when computing the value of the contract and the premium for the contract. Thus, an index that cost an investor a premium of 3 1/2 is multiplied by 100 to equal a dollar amount of $350 for the premium.

8. **Answer B is correct.** An investor who purchased five S&P 500 index options @ 3 1/2 paid a total of $1750 for the options. This is computed as 3 1/2 premium × 5 contracts × a multiplier of 100 = 17 1/2 × 100 = 1750.

9. **Answer B is correct.** An investor with 10 S&P 500 call index options with a strike price of 920 saw the index rise to 980. This is a 60-point increase. The stock index option has a multiplier of 100 that is used to compute the value. The equation is a 60 point increase × 10 contracts = 600 × multiplier of 100 = $6000 profit.

10. **Answer B is correct.** An investor with four OEX January 910 Calls @ 3 of stock index options saw the index rise to 980. This is a 70-point increase × the number of contracts of 4 = 280 × the multiplier of 100 = a $28,000 profit. You must also deduct the premium paid of 3. A premium of 3 × 4 contracts × the multiplier of 100 = $1200. Thus, the investor made a profit of $28,000 – $1200 = a $26,800 profit.

11. **Answer A is correct.** An investor selling 3 XMI June 970 Calls @ 4 hopes the index value will drop below the strike price of 970 so that he can retain the premium received. The index drops to 960 in the market, and the index option expires worthless for the holder. The seller keeps the premium of 4 × 3 contracts = 12 × the multiplier of 100 = a $1200 profit from the premium received.

12. **Answer D is correct.** A portfolio manager writes 200 SPX April 930 Calls @ 4 1/2. He takes in a total premium of 4 1/2 × 200 contracts = 900 × the multiplier of 100 = a $90,000 premium received. The call options rise to 939, which is a 9-point increase. The 9-point increase × 200 contracts = 1800 × the multiplier of 100 = $180,000. Thus, the writer lost $180,000 but retained the premium of $90,000, for a total loss of $90,000.

13. **Answer C is correct.** The writer of stock index call options has a maximum potential gain of the premiums received. The portfolio manager writes 325 SPX June 950 Calls @ 3 1/2. The total premium received is 3 1/2 × 325 contracts = 1137.50 × the multiplier of 100 = a $113,750 total premium received for the 325 contracts.

14. **Answer A is correct.** Hedging with index options protects a portfolio from what is known as systematic risk or market risk. It is the risk that the value of the stocks might decrease as part of a more general market movement.

15. **Answer D is correct.** Hedging with index options protects an investor against systematic risk. It does not protect the investor against unsystematic risk, which is the risk that a stock will fall in value for reasons other than a general market movement or decline. The reasons can include poor management decisions or new competitors in the market.

16. **Answer B is correct.** Open interest is the number of contracts existing on an index that have not yet been closed out. Short interest represents the number of shorted shares on a particular security in the market.

17. **Answer B is correct.** Beta is a measure of price volatility of a stock or a group of stocks. If a security has a beta of 2, the portfolio is twice as volatile as the benchmark it is being compared to (an index). The S&P 500 index has a beta of 1 because it is the benchmark. A portfolio with a beta of 2 is twice as volatile and should have twice the movement of the index. In this question, the stock portfolio should increase by 20%.

18. **Answer D is correct.** Stock index options that are exercised receive the closing value of the index for the day and not its value at the moment of exercise. In this example, the investor receives a closing value of 985, which is far better than the market opening value of 970.

19. **Answer C is correct.** Equity options are all considered American-style options that can be exercised at any time by the holder. Stock index options can either be American style or European style in their ability to exercise. European-style options can only be exercised at expiration, and some index options have this designation.

20. **Answer D is correct.** LEAPS, or long-term equity anticipation securities, have terms of up to three years, allowing investors to create long-term options strategies. LEAPS can either be American style or European style in their exercise. All LEAPS have expirations in the month of December.

21. **Answer A is correct.** Capped index options are European-style options that can only be exercised at expiration or if the set cap is reached. Capped index options are set at a predetermined cap typically at a maximum profit of 30 points. When the cap is met, they are automatically exercised; if the cap is not reached, they are exercised for the in-the-money amount at expiration.

22. **Answer D is correct.** A capped index option is typically set at a 30-point maximum cap that must be met before the option can be exercised. If the cap is not reached, then the option cannot be exercised because the option is European style. In this question, the option halfway through the expiration went up 25 points, but it did not reach the cap. It cannot be exercised at this time by the holder because it is a European-style option. If the option expires and it is 25 points in the money, the investor receives the 25-point profit.

23. **Answer C is correct.** Unsystematic risk is the risk that a security might fall in value for reasons other than a general market decline. They can include declines caused by poor management, more competitors in the market, or a loss of market share and business by a new product in the market.

24. **Answer C is correct.** To answer this question, you must remember that stock index options use a multiplier of 100. The $10,000,000 portfolio is hedged by an investment advisor with a strike price of 400. The strike price in effect has a value of 400 × the 100 multiplier = $40,000. Thus, each index option with a strike price of 400 has a value of $40,000. The value of the index divided into the value of the portfolio of $10,000,000 = $10,000,000 ÷ 40,000 = 250 contracts.

25. **Answer C is correct.** Beta is a measure of a stock's or portfolio's volatility in the market as compared to a benchmark, typically a broad-based index. The benchmark index has a beta of 1 assigned to it. The stock with a beta of 2 is considered twice as volatile as the index and moves up or down twice as fast as the index it is compared to.

Quick Check

Interest Rate Options

1. The pricing method that is used by the U.S. Treasury when pricing Treasury bills is commonly known as which of the following?
   - ❍ A. Competitive basis
   - ❍ B. Noncompetitive basis
   - ❍ C. Discount to yield basis
   - ❍ D. Premium yield basis

Quick Answer: **255**
Detailed Answer: **256**

2. A 52-week $10,000 Treasury bill that is quoted in the financial newspapers at a discount to yield of 5.20% sells in the market for which of the following amounts?
   - ❍ A. $10,520
   - ❍ B. $10,480
   - ❍ C. $9520
   - ❍ D. $9480

Quick Answer: **255**
Detailed Answer: **256**

3. A 26-week $10,000 Treasury bill that is quoted in the financial newspapers at a discount to yield of 5.15% sells in the market for which of the following amounts?
   - ❍ A. $10,515.00
   - ❍ B. $10,257.50
   - ❍ C. $9742.50
   - ❍ D. $9485.00

Quick Answer: **255**
Detailed Answer: **256**

4. A 13-week $10,000 Treasury bill that is quoted in the financial newspapers at a discount to yield of 5.04% sells in the market for which of the following amounts?
   - ❍ A. $10,504.00
   - ❍ B. $10,126.00
   - ❍ C. $9874.00
   - ❍ D. $9496.00

Quick Answer: **255**
Detailed Answer: **256**

Quick Check

5. A 52-week $25,000 Treasury bill that is quoted at a discount to yield of 5.50% in the financial newspapers sells in the market for which of the following amounts?

   ❍ A. $26,625.00
   ❍ B. $25,678.50
   ❍ C. $23,643.00
   ❍ D. $24,321.50

Quick Answer: 255
Detailed Answer: 256

6. A strike price of 93.24 on a price-based option means that the Treasury security can be purchased or sold at which of the following prices?

   ❍ A. $930.24
   ❍ B. $932.40
   ❍ C. $903.24
   ❍ D. $937.50

Quick Answer: 255
Detailed Answer: 256

7. A customer holds a price-based put option on 10-year Treasury notes with a strike price of 102. The market price on the 10-year T-Note declines to 98. What is the customer's profit or loss on this option?

   ❍ A. Gain of $2000
   ❍ B. Gain of $4000
   ❍ C. Loss of $2000
   ❍ D. Loss of $4000

Quick Answer: 255
Detailed Answer: 256

8. A customer sells a price-based call option on a 10-year T-note with a strike price of 105.16 and a premium of 1.16. The market price on the 10-year T-note goes to 104.08. What is the profit or loss on the call option for the writer?

   ❍ A. A loss of $1500
   ❍ B. A gain of $1500
   ❍ C. A loss of $1250
   ❍ D. The writer breaks even.

Quick Answer: 255
Detailed Answer: 256

9. Rick writes 10 price-based put options on a 5-year T-note with a strike price of 98.08 and a premium of 1.24. The market price on the notes goes to 102. What is the profit or loss to the writer?

   ❍ A. A loss of $3750
   ❍ B. A loss of $37,500
   ❍ C. A gain of $17,500
   ❍ D. A gain of $37,500

Quick Answer: 255
Detailed Answer: 257

Quick Check

10. A money market fund currently holds $1,000,000 worth of 13-week Treasury bills in its portfolio that it purchased at a discount to yield basis of 5.5%. What did the fund pay for these T-bills?

   - ❍ A. $986,100
   - ❍ B. $945,000
   - ❍ C. $1,055,000
   - ❍ D. $1,000,000

Quick Answer: **255**
Detailed Answer: **257**

11. The settlement terms on price-based options are set at which of the following terms?

   - ❍ A. Same-day settlement
   - ❍ B. Next-day settlement
   - ❍ C. Trade date + 3
   - ❍ D. Trade date + 5

Quick Answer: **255**
Detailed Answer: **257**

12. Which of the following statements are considered true regarding price-based option contracts?

   I. Price-based options are American-style options.

   II. The expiration date for price-based options is the same as for equity options.

   III. Settlement on price-based options is next-day settlement.

   IV. Uncovered writers are required to put up a margin for price-based options.

   - ❍ A. I and II
   - ❍ B. II and III
   - ❍ C. I, II, and III
   - ❍ D. I, II, III, and IV

Quick Answer: **255**
Detailed Answer: **257**

13. A dealer owns $5,000,000 worth of 30-year T-bonds with an interest rate of 6.40%. The dealer believes that interest rates will rise in the next six months. The dealer wants to hedge his position by purchasing call options on the yield with a strike price of 6.50%. How many call options does the dealer need to purchase to protect his current position?

   - ❍ A. 5 call contracts
   - ❍ B. 50 call contracts
   - ❍ C. 500 call contracts
   - ❍ D. 5000 call contracts

Quick Answer: **255**
Detailed Answer: **257**

Quick Check

14. Georgia is the fund manager for a large money market fund that is long $10,000,000 worth of 30-year Treasury bonds with a yield of 6.85%. Georgia believes that interest rates will drop sharply in the next six months. She purchases 100 put options on 30-year T-bonds with a strike price of 69 and a premium of 1 1/4 in the market. What was the cost of these protective puts to the fund?

   ❍ A. $125
   ❍ B. $1250
   ❍ C. $12,500
   ❍ D. $125,000

Quick Answer: 255
Detailed Answer: 257

15. Which of the following statements is true about price-based options?

   I. T-bill options have a face value of $1,000,000.

   II. T-note options have a face value of $1,000,000.

   III. T-bond options have a face value of $100,000.

   IV. All contracts have a face value of $1,000,000.

   ❍ A. I only
   ❍ B. IV only
   ❍ C. I and III
   ❍ D. II and III

Quick Answer: 255
Detailed Answer: 257

16. Which of the following statements is considered true about yield-based options?

   I. Yield-based options are American style.

   II. A multiplier of 1000 is used to compute the value of the contract.

   III. Settle in cash when exercised.

   IV. Settle in the underlying security being delivered or sold.

   ❍ A. I and II
   ❍ B. II and III
   ❍ C. III only
   ❍ D. III and IV

Quick Answer: 255
Detailed Answer: 257

Quick Check

17. A price-based option for a T-bill with a premium quoted at 1.10 has which value?
   - ❍ A. $110
   - ❍ B. $1100
   - ❍ C. $1000.10
   - ❍ D. $1312.50

Quick Answer: 255
Detailed Answer: 258

18. Interest rate options on Treasury bills are issued for purchase or sale how frequently?
   - ❍ A. Once per week
   - ❍ B. Once per month
   - ❍ C. Once every 60 days
   - ❍ D. Once every 90 days

Quick Answer: 255
Detailed Answer: 258

19. New interest rate options on Treasury notes are issued by the OCC how often?
   - ❍ A. Weekly
   - ❍ B. Every month
   - ❍ C. Every quarter
   - ❍ D. Every 60 days

Quick Answer: 255
Detailed Answer: 258

20. An investor purchases 10 yield base call options on a 30-year T-bond with a strike price of 65. The yield on the 30-year bonds goes to 6.92% in the market. What has the investor made or loss on these options.
   - ❍ A. gain of $4,200
   - ❍ B. gain of $42,000
   - ❍ C. loss of $4,200
   - ❍ D. loss of $42,000

Quick Answer: 255
Detailed Answer: 258

21. A large broker dealer is holding $25,000,000 worth of U.S. government T-bonds in their inventory with interest rates between 5.77% and 5.89%. The dealer wishes to hedge their T-bond holdings against a decline in interest rates. Which of the following would the broker dealer purchase?
   - ❍ A. Buy 25 T-bond Puts
   - ❍ B. Buy 25 T-bond Calls
   - ❍ C. Buy 250 T-bond Puts
   - ❍ D. Buy 250 T-bond Calls

Quick Answer: 255
Detailed Answer: 258

Quick Check

22. Which of the following option contracts can be exercised by the holder at any given time?

I. European-style options

II. American-style options

III. Price-based interest rate options

IV. Yield-based interest rate options

- ❍ A. I only
- ❍ B. II only
- ❍ C. I and IV
- ❍ D. II and III

Quick Answer: 255
Detailed Answer: 258

23. A price-based option for a T-bill with a premium quoted at 1.10 has a value of which of the following amounts?

- ❍ A. $110
- ❍ B. $1100
- ❍ C. $1000.10
- ❍ D. $1312.50

Quick Answer: 255
Detailed Answer: 258

24. If the premium on an interest rate option on a T-bill moves 25 basis points in one day, the value of the contract moves which of the following amounts?

- ❍ A. $25
- ❍ B. $250
- ❍ C. $625
- ❍ D. $2500

Quick Answer: 255
Detailed Answer: 258

25. How frequently are interest rate options on Treasury bills issued for purchase or sale?

- ❍ A. Once per week
- ❍ B. Once per month
- ❍ C. Once every 60 days
- ❍ D. Once every 90 days

Quick Answer: 255
Detailed Answer: 258

Quick Check Answer Key

1. C
2. B
3. C
4. C
5. A
6. D
7. B
8. B
9. C
10. A
11. B
12. D
13. B
14. D
15. C
16. C
17. D
18. A
19. B
20. A
21. C
22. D
23. D
24. C
25. A

Answers and Explanations

1. **Answer C is correct.** Treasury bills are purchased on a discount to yield basis. Instead of actually paying interest as T-notes and T-bonds do, Treasury bills are discounted and based on the maturity of either 13, 26, or 52 weeks. The T-bill matures at par value.

2. **Answer B is correct.** A $10,000 T-bill with a discounted yield of 5.20% and a maturity of 52 weeks is discounted by an amount of $520. In effect, the investor purchases the T-bill at $9480, and in 52 weeks, it matures at the face value of $10,000.

3. **Answer C is correct.** A 5.15% discounted $10,000 T-bill with a 26-week maturity is purchased for a discount of $257.50. ($10,000 – $257.50 = $9742.50). To compute the discount, multiply $10,000 × 5.15% = $515 for one year. The T-bill has a maturity of 26 weeks, so you divide this amount by 2 to get $257.50. Subtract $257.50 from $10,000 to get $9742.50.

4. **Answer C is correct.** A 13-week $10,000 T-bill that is quoted at a discount to yield basis of 5.04% sells in the market for $$9,874. Following is the math: $10,000 × 5.04% = $504 ÷ 4 = $126. Remember that it is a 13-week T-Bill, so you need to take 1/4 of this amount, which is $126. $10,000 minus the $126 discount gives you $9874.

5. **Answer A is correct.** A 52-week $25,000 T-bill that is discounted 5.50% sells for $23,625. The equation begins $25,000 × 5.50% = $1375. $25,000 – $1375 = $23,625. The investor can purchase the $25,000 T-bill for the discounted sum of $23,625.

6. **Answer D is correct.** A strike price of 93.24 on a price-based option is actually representative of a price of 93 and 24/32, which totals $937.50 per actual bond being quoted: 24 ÷ 32 = $7.50. Then, 930 + $7.50 = $937.50. Each point is worth $10.

7. **Answer B is correct.** A 10-year T-note put with a strike price of 102 with a market price of 98 is considered in the money by 4 points, or a profit of $4000. Remember that each point is worth $1000. So 4 points × $1000 = a $4000 gain.

8. **Answer B is correct.** A writer sells a call option on a 10-year T-note for 1.16 or 1 1/2 points × $1000 = $1500 premium received. The option has a strike price of 105.16. The market price goes to 104.08, which is below the strike price of the call for the buyer. The option expires out of the money, and the writer retains the premium of $1500 received.

9. **Answer C is correct.** Ten price-based put options on a 5-year T-note with a strike price of 98.08 that goes to 102 for the purchaser is out of the money because it went above the strike price of 98.08. The writer retains the premium received of 1.24 per contract. The equation is 1.24 = $1750 per contract (each premium point is worth $1000) and $1750 × 10 contracts = a $17,500 profit for the writer.

10. **Answer A is correct.** A money market fund that has purchased $1,000,000 worth of 13-week T-bills at a discount yield of 5.50% would have paid 5.50% × 91/360 = 1.39%. The money market fund purchased the T-bills at a discount of 1.39%, or at a price of 100 – 1.39 = 98.61%. So $1,000,000 worth of T-bills × 98.61 = a $986,100 purchase price.

11. **Answer B is correct.** The settlement date on price-based options is set at the next business day. Thus, regular-way settlement for price-based options is considered next-day settlement.

12. **Answer D is correct.** Price-based options are considered American-style options that settle on the next business day. They have the same expiration as equity-based options, which is the first Saturday after the third Friday of the expiration month. Uncovered writers are required to put up a margin requirement if they are writing puts or calls.

13. **Answer B is correct.** A dealer with $5,000,000 worth of T-bonds with a yield of 6.40% needs to purchase 50 call contracts to hedge against an increase in the interest rate of 6.40%. By purchasing 50 calls with a strike price of 6.50, the dealer locks in a price of 6.50 on his future yield. Each contract is worth $100,000, so 50 contracts are needed to hedge $5,000,000 worth of T-bonds.

14. **Answer D is correct.** The fund manager of $10,000,000 worth of T-bonds needs to purchase 100 put contracts to cover her portfolio. Each T-bond contract is valued at $100,000 × 100 contracts = $10,000,000. If the fund manager pays 1 1/4 for each contract, it costs her $1250 per contract × 100 contracts = $125,000 for the purchase of the 100 puts.

15. **Answer C is correct.** Price-based options have a face value for T-bills of $1,000,000. The face value of the option contracts for T-notes and T-bonds is $100,000.

16. **Answer C is correct.** Yield-based interest rate options settle in cash when exercised. There is no physical security to be purchased or sold. The option is written only on the underlying yield of the instrument that it is tied into (such as a T-bill or T-note). A multiplier of 100 is used to compute the contracts, and yield-based options are considered European style.

17. **Answer D is correct.** A T-bill price-based option with a premium of 1.10 costs the buyer 1 = $1000 + 10/100ths. The total premium on this price-based option is 1000 + 10/100ths. Each point on a price-based T-bill option is worth $2500 because the size of the contract is $1,000,000 for a T-bill. The equation is 1.10 × 2500 = $2750 total premium.

18. **Answer A is correct.** T-bill interest rate options are available for purchase or sale every week as the latest version of issued T-bills comes out from the Federal Reserve Bank. The price-based option is tied directly to the issue price of the T-bill.

19. **Answer B is correct.** Treasury note price-based options are issued monthly by the Options Clearing Corporation. This coincides with its issuance from the Federal Reserve Bank.

20. **Answer A is correct.** An investor who purchased 10 yield-based calls with a strike price of 65 that goes to a yield of 6.92 in the market has a profit of 4.20. The multiplier is 100 × 4.2 = 420 × 10 call contracts = a $4200 profit.

21. **Answer C is correct.** A dealer that holds a $25,000,000 position of T-bonds in its portfolio and wants to protect its downside risk purchases puts on the T-bonds as a hedge. Each contract is valued at $100,000, so the dealer needs to purchase 250 contracts to effectively hedge the $25,000,000 worth of long T-bonds being held. So 250 contracts × $100,000 per contract = $25,000,000 in value.

22. **Answer D is correct.** American-style options can be exercised at any given time. Price-based options are also considered American style, so they can also be exercised at any given time. European-style options, which also include yield-based options, can only be exercised at the expiration date.

23. **Answer D is correct.** A T-bill price-based option with a premium of 1.10 costs the buyer 1 = $1,000 + 10/100ths. (The equation is 10 ÷ 100 = 0.1.) The total premium on this price-based option is 1000 + 10/100ths. Each point on a price-based T-bill option is worth $2500 because the size of the contract is $1,000,000 for a T-bill. The equation is 1.10 × 2500 = a $2750 total premium.

24. **Answer C is correct.** A price-based T-bill option for the premium is quoted in points and basis points, which are 1/100 of a point. For the premium, each point is worth $2500. Thus, an option premium that has moved 25 basis points has moved 25 × $25 = $625 in value.

25. **Answer A is correct.** T-bill interest rate options are available for purchase or sale every week as the latest version of issued T-bills come out from the Federal Reserve Bank. The price-based option is tied directly to the issue price of the T-bill.

Quick Check

Foreign Currency Options

1. The unregulated international market for trading foreign currencies between major money center banks is known as what?

   ❍ A. The Libor market
   ❍ B. The Interbank market
   ❍ C. The European currency market
   ❍ D. The Floating Exchange market

Quick Answer: **266**
Detailed Answer: **267**

2. When the foreign currency exchange rate fluctuates in response to economic and political forces, it is commonly known as which of the following?

   ❍ A. Floating exchange rate
   ❍ B. Fixed exchange rate
   ❍ C. Economic exchange rate
   ❍ D. Lead exchange rate

Quick Answer: **266**
Detailed Answer: **267**

3. Which of the following factors affects the rate of exchange of currencies in the world markets?

   I. The supply and demand of foreign currencies

   II. The fiscal policies of a country

   III. The monetary policies of a country

   IV. The inflation rate of a country

   ❍ A. I only
   ❍ B. II and III
   ❍ C. I, II, and III
   ❍ D. I, II, III, and IV

Quick Answer: **266**
Detailed Answer: **267**

Quick Check

4. A drop in a country's exchange rate affects the country's exports in which of the following ways?

   ❍ A. The exports of the country increase.
   ❍ B. The exports of the country decrease.
   ❍ C. The exports of the country are not affected.
   ❍ D. The exports of the country basically stop.

Quick Answer: 266
Detailed Answer: 267

5. The exchange rate of foreign currencies that is set at a date in the future is known as which of the following?

   ❍ A. The spot rate
   ❍ B. The forward rate
   ❍ C. The call rate
   ❍ D. The put rate

Quick Answer: 266
Detailed Answer: 267

6. Currency options on foreign currencies are issued by which of the following entities?

   ❍ A. The Interbank market
   ❍ B. The Options Clearing Corporation
   ❍ C. The NASD
   ❍ D. The SEC

Quick Answer: 266
Detailed Answer: 267

7. An investor believes that the currency rate of the Japanese yen is going to drop in value considerably. Which of the following options supports his belief?

   ❍ A. Sell J-yen calls
   ❍ B. Sell J-yen puts
   ❍ C. Buy J-yen calls
   ❍ D. Buy J-yen puts

Quick Answer: 266
Detailed Answer: 267

8. Which of the following statements is considered true regarding foreign currency options that are traded?

   I. Foreign currency options can be American style.

   II. Foreign currency options can be European style.

   III. Foreign currency options are at a fixed rate.

   IV. Foreign currency options are at a floating rate.

   ❍ A. I only
   ❍ B. II only
   ❍ C. I, II, and III
   ❍ D. I, II, and IV

Quick Answer: 266
Detailed Answer: 267

Quick Check

9. An American importer is currently buying Swiss-made watches that he will pay the exporter for in U.S. dollars. The current exchange rate of a Swiss franc to the U.S. dollar is 2.10. To protect against a rise in the value of the Swiss franc that he must pay, the importer must do which of the following?

Quick Answer: 266
Detailed Answer: 267

- A. Buy Swiss franc calls
- B. Buy Swiss franc puts
- C. Buy U.S. dollar calls
- D. Buy U.S. dollar puts

10. Henry is an investor who believes that the Japanese economy is going to become a lot worse before it finally recovers. Which of the following exchange rate strategies is considered wise for him?

Quick Answer: 266
Detailed Answer: 268

I. Buy J-yen calls

II. Buy J-yen puts

III. Sell J-yen calls

IV. Sell J-yen puts

- A. I and II
- B. II and III
- C. I and IV
- D. II and IV

11. If a country sees that its currency is undervalued, the country conducts which of the following measures?

Quick Answer: 266
Detailed Answer: 268

I. Buys its own currency

II. Sells its own currency

III. Devalues its own currency

IV. Does nothing and lets the market run its course

- A. I only
- B. II only
- C. I and III
- D. IV only

Quick Check

12. The Canadian dollar is currently at 81.22 to the U.S. dollar. If the option contract size of Canadian dollars is 50,000, how much does it cost in American dollars to purchase one Canadian dollar contract?
   - ❍ A. $615.61
   - ❍ B. $9390
   - ❍ C. $40,610
   - ❍ D. $50,000

Quick Answer: 266
Detailed Answer: 268

13. An investor purchases 1 Canadian dollar May 84 Put @ 1.31. The size of a Canadian dollar contract is 50,000. What did the investor pay for this put option?
   - ❍ A. $655
   - ❍ B. $1310
   - ❍ C. $2620
   - ❍ D. $5240

Quick Answer: 266
Detailed Answer: 268

14. An investor purchases one Japanese yen October 74 Put @ 1.44 in the market. The yen contract size is set at 6,250,000 and quoted in 1/100ths of a cent. What did this investor pay for the Japanese yen put?
   - ❍ A. $106.56
   - ❍ B. $144
   - ❍ C. $900
   - ❍ D. $9000

Quick Answer: 266
Detailed Answer: 268

15. An investor purchases 1 Canadian dollar April 86 Put @ 1.44 in the market. The size of the Canadian dollar contract is 50,000. The Canadian dollar declines in value to 82.22 in the market. What is the profit or loss on the call?
   - ❍ A. A loss of $720
   - ❍ B. A loss of $1890
   - ❍ C. A gain of $1170
   - ❍ D. A gain of $1890

Quick Answer: 266
Detailed Answer: 268

16. An investor buys 8 British pound May 164 Calls @ 1.61 in the market. The size of the British pound contract is 31,250. The pound goes to 167.33 in the market. What is the profit or gain on this contract?
   - ❍ A. $537.50 gain
   - ❍ B. $4300 gain
   - ❍ C. $503.13 loss
   - ❍ D. $4025 loss

Quick Answer: 266
Detailed Answer: 268

Quick Check

17. An investor purchases 3 Australian dollar July 80 Calls @ .88 in the market. The contract size on Australian dollars is 50,000 AD. The Australian dollar goes to 82.65 in the market. What is the profit or loss on this contract?

   ❍ A. $885 profit
   ❍ B. $2655 profit
   ❍ C. $1320 loss
   ❍ D. $885 loss

Quick Answer: 266
Detailed Answer: 268

18. An investor writes 15 European currency unit May 92 Calls @ 1.03 in the market. The ECU contract size is 62,500 ECU. The ECU moves to 91.78 in the market. What is the profit or loss for the writer?

   ❍ A. A gain of $137.50
   ❍ B. A gain of $2062.50
   ❍ C. A gain of $9656.25
   ❍ D. A loss of $2062.50

Quick Answer: 266
Detailed Answer: 269

19. A dealer purchases 7 British pound May 190 Calls @ 2.11 in the market. The British pound contract size is 31,250 BP. The BP goes to 195.34 in the market. What was the profit or loss on the calls?

   ❍ A. $1009.38 gain
   ❍ B. $7065.63 gain
   ❍ C. $4615.63 loss
   ❍ D. $1668.75 loss

Quick Answer: 266
Detailed Answer: 269

20. An investor purchases 4 Australian dollar June 80 Puts @ .69 in the market. The Australian dollar contract size is 50,000 AD. The Australian dollar goes to 77.58 in the market. The profit or loss on the puts is which of the following?

   ❍ A. $1210 gain
   ❍ B. $4840 gain
   ❍ C. $3460 gain
   ❍ D. $1380 loss

Quick Answer: 266
Detailed Answer: 269

Quick Check

21. A large steel manufacturer in the United States ships steel to Germany and is paid in Deutschemarks. The steel manufacturer wants to protect against a drop in the Deutschemark. The steel manufacturer is owed 9.8 million Deutschemarks for a recent order. To protect against the drop in the Deutschemark, the steel company decides to purchase Deutschemarks puts. How many puts does it need to hedge the amount owed?

   ❍ A. 157 put contracts
   ❍ B. 196 put contracts
   ❍ C. 211 put contracts
   ❍ D. 314 put contracts

Quick Answer: **266**
Detailed Answer: **269**

22. Joel wants to protect the value of the Deutschemark until he is able to purchase his car in Germany. To protect against a rise in the Deutschemark, he decides to buy 1 Deutschemark March 67 Call @ 1.77. What does this call on the Deutschemark currency cost him?

   ❍ A. $885
   ❍ B. $1077
   ❍ C. $1106.25
   ❍ D. $1770

Quick Answer: **266**
Detailed Answer: **269**

23. David writes 1 Australian dollar May 55 Call @ 0.27 in the market. He is an uncovered writer on the call for Australian dollars. What is his margin requirement if the Australian dollar was trading at 55.77?

   ❍ A. $135
   ❍ B. $385
   ❍ C. $865.40
   ❍ D. $1115.40

Quick Answer: **266**
Detailed Answer: **269**

24. Arthur writes one uncovered Canadian dollar October 82 Call @ .94 in the market. The Canadian dollar is trading at 82.54 in the market. What is his margin requirement on this CD Call?

   ❍ A. $470
   ❍ B. $1850.80
   ❍ C. $2200
   ❍ D. $2470

Quick Answer: **266**
Detailed Answer: **270**

Quick Check

Quick Answer: **266**
Detailed Answer: **270**

25. The foreign exchange rate that is quoted in American terms has which of the following characteristics?

I. The number of foreign currency units needed to buy one U.S. dollar.

II. The number of U.S. dollars needed to buy one foreign currency unit.

III. Spot rates can use American terms.

IV. Forward rates can use American terms.

- ❍ A. I only
- ❍ B. II only
- ❍ C. I, III, and IV
- ❍ D. II, III, and IV

Quick Check Answer Key

1. B

2. A

3. D

4. A

5. B

6. B

7. D

8. D

9. A

10. B

11. A

12. C

13. A

14. C

15. C

16. B

17. B

18. C

19. B

20. C

21. A

22. C

23. C

24. B

25. C

Answers and Explanations

1. **Answer B is correct.** The Interbank market is the unregulated market where major money center banks buy and sell foreign currencies. LIBOR stands for the London Interbank offered rate.

2. **Answer A is correct.** Foreign currency rates that react to political and economic forces are known as floating rate currency exchange rates. Fixed rates were the norm at one time, but now all currencies fluctuate to external forces.

3. **Answer D is correct.** Foreign exchange rates are affected by supply and demand and the rate of inflation in a country. Foreign governments also use their monetary and fiscal policies to control the rate of exchange of their currency. Monetary policy is the management of the supply of money in a country, whereas fiscal policy is the rate at which the country taxes its citizens.

4. **Answer A is correct.** If a country's exchange rate drops, it leads to an increase in the goods that they export. The drop in the value of the exporters' currency leads to foreign importers buying the cheaper goods with the more valuable currency of the importer.

5. **Answer B is correct.** The forward rate of exchange is an agreed-upon settlement and delivery at some time in the future. For instance, if a manufacturer is worried about the rise or fall of a currency that it gets paid in, it can buy forward contracts that settle at a set date in the future to protect the funds received. If it is worried about a drop in the currency, it purchases puts. If it thinks the currency is going to go up in value, it purchases calls.

6. **Answer B is correct.** Foreign currency options are issued and guaranteed by the Options Clearing Corporation. The Interbank market is an unregulated market that currencies trade in. The NASD and SEC are regulatory bodies over the equity and debt markets.

7. **Answer D is correct.** If an investor believes that the yen is going to drop in value to the dollar, the investor protects himself by purchasing yen puts. If the yen does drop, he can put the currency back to the seller at the higher exchange rate.

8. **Answer D is correct.** Foreign currency options can be American style, where they can be exercised at any time, or in some cases, they are European style, which are only exercisable at expiration. The foreign currency market is no longer set at a fixed rate of exchange, but rather at a floating rate.

9. **Answer A is correct.** An importer of Swiss watches sees that the Swiss franc is at 2.10 to the U.S. dollar. If it rises above 2.10, it costs the importer more in U.S. dollars for the same product. To protect against this fluctuation, the importer purchases Swiss franc calls with a strike price at or close to 2.10.

10. **Answer B is correct.** If Henry is confident that the Japanese currency market is going to drop in value, he can either buy yen puts or sell yen calls. Both benefit him if the Japanese yen drops in value. The sale of calls enables him to keep the premium received if the currency drops in value, and the long puts enable him to put the lower valued yen back to the writer at the higher strike price for a profit.

11. **Answer A is correct.** A country seeing its exchange rate dropping compared to other currencies moves into the market and purchases its own currency to stabilize the drop. It buy its currency in this scenario because it believes it is undervalued.

12. **Answer C is correct.** The Canadian contract size is 50,000 Canadian dollars quoted at 81.22. Next, multiply .8122 × 50,000 = $40,610 U.S. dollars to buy 50,000 Canadian dollars.

13. **Answer A is correct.** The Canadian dollar contract is quoted at a 1.31 premium. To compute the cost of the Canadian dollar contract, multiply .0131 × the size of the Canadian dollar contract of 50,000 = $655. (Canadian dollar contracts are quoted in cents.)

14. **Answer C is correct.** The Japanese yen contract is set at 6,250,000 yen. The investor purchased one put contract at 1.44. Because the yen contract is set at 6,250,000, move the decimal place four positions to the left, instead of the customary two, and then multiply by the contract size: .000144 × 6,250,000 yen = $900 premium paid.

15. **Answer C is correct.** The Canadian dollar contract size is 50,000 Canadian. The investor purchased 1 April 86 Put @ 1.44. The cost of the put was .0144 × 50,000 = $720. The currency option dropped to 82.22 for a profit : 86 – 82.22 = 3.78. We multiply the profit of .0378 × the contract size of 50,000, which equals $1890 profit less the premium of $720 = $1170 total profit.

16. **Answer B is correct.** An investor purchased 8 British pound May 164 Calls @ 1.61 in the market. The size of the BP contract is 31,250. The investor paid .0161 × 31,250 for the calls = $503.125 × 8 contracts = $4025 premium paid. The contract has a strike price of 164. The market went to 167.33. 167.33 – 164 = 3.33 profit. The equation is .0333 × 31,250 contract size = $1040.625 profit × 8 contracts = $8325 profit. The profit of $8325 less the premium paid of $4025 = $4300 gain.

17. **Answer B is correct.** An investor purchases 3 Australian dollar July 80 Calls @ .88 in the market. The contract size for Australian dollars is 50,000 and quoted in cents. The investor paid .0088 × 50,000 = $440 for each call × 3 calls = $1320 total premium. The calls went to 82.65. The equation is 82.65 – 80 = 2.65 gain. Next, multiply .0265 × the contract size 50,000 = $1325 gain per contract × 3 contracts = $3975 loss. The $3,975 loss – a premium paid of $1320 = $2655 gain for the investor.

18. **Answer C is correct.** An investor writes 15 European currency units (ECU) May 92 Calls @ 1.03. The ECU contract size is 62,500 in cents. The investor received a premium of .0103 × 62,500 = $643.75 per contract × 15 contracts = $9656.25 total premium received. The calls went to 91.78 in the market. They are out of the money for the holder and thus expire worthless. The writer of the 15 ECU calls retains the premium received of $9656.25.

19. **Answer B is correct.** A dealer purchases 7 British pound May 190 Calls @ 2.11. The British pound contract size is 31,250 and quoted in cents. The dealer paid a premium of .0211 × 31,250 = $659.375 per contract × 7 contracts = $4615.63 total premium paid. The BP calls went to 195.34 in the market. So 195.34 – 190 = 5.34 profit. Next, multiply .0534 × 31,250 contract size = $1668.75 profit per contract × 7 contracts = $11,681.25 profit. The profit $11,681.25 less the premium paid of $4615.63 = $7065.63, the total gain.

20. **Answer C is correct.** The investor purchased 4 Australian dollar June 80 Puts @ .69 in the market. The contract size for Australian dollars is 50,000 and quoted in cents. The puts went to 77.58 in the market. So 80 – 77.58 = 2.42 gain. The premium is subtracted from 2.42 – .69 = 1.73 profit. Next, multiply .0173 × 50,000 contract size = $865 per contract × 4 contracts = $3460 total profit.

21. **Answer A is correct.** The steel manufacturer wants to protect against a drop in the Deutschemark because it receives payment in Deutschemarks. The steel manufacturer is owed 9.8 million marks for steel delivered. The Deutschemark contract is set at 62,500 Deutschemarks. The equation is 9,800,000 ÷ 62,500 = 156.8 contracts. The steel manufacturer needs to purchase 157 put contracts to cover the possibility of the Deutschemark dropping in value.

22. **Answer C is correct.** To protect against a rise in the Deutschemark, Joel decides to purchase 1 Deutschemark March 67 Call @ 1.77. The size of the contract is 62,500 Deutschemarks quoted in cents. The equation is .0177 × 62,500 = $1106.25 total premium paid for the 1 call currency option.

23. **Answer C is correct.** The margin requirement on writing uncovered currency options is the current premium received + 4% of the current contract value (the total number of currency units covered by option × the current spot rate). For any amount, the option is out of the money. Thus, the premium received is .0027 × the contract size of 50,000 = $135. 4% of the current contract value is 50,000 × .04 ×the spot rate of .5577 = $1115.40 less any amount the option is out of the money. .0077 × 50,000 = $385 – $135 $250; $1115.40 – $250 = $865.40 total margin requirement.

24. **Answer B is correct.** Arthur writes 1 uncovered Canadian dollar October 82 Call @ .94. His margin requirement is the premium received of .0094 × 50,000 contract size = $470. Add 4% of the contract size = 50,000 × .04 = 2000 times the spot rate of 82.54 = 2000 × .8254 = $1650.80 less any amount out of the money for the writer = .0054 × 50,000 = $270. Thus, $470 + $1650.80 = $2120.80 minus $270 = $1850.80 total premium required.

25. **Answer C is correct.** The foreign currency exchange rate is the number of foreign currency units needed to buy one U.S. dollar. The spot rate and forward rate are in American terms.

Quick Check

Customer Accounts

1. The definition of what makes an individual an insider in a company includes which of the following requirements?

   I. An officer of the company

   II. A director of the company

   III. A 10% shareholder

   IV. A 5% bondholder

   ❍ A. I and II
   ❍ B. II and III
   ❍ C. I, II, and III
   ❍ D. I, II, III, and IV

Quick Answer: **278**
Detailed Answer: **279**

2. Which of the following information is consistent with what a broker needs to know about his customer when opening an account?

   I. The customer's net worth

   II. The customer's financial objectives

   III. The customer's age

   IV. The customer's marital status

   ❍ A. I only
   ❍ B. I and II
   ❍ C. I, II, and III
   ❍ D. I, II, III, and IV

Quick Answer: **278**
Detailed Answer: **279**

Quick Check

3. A broker who is not able to obtain financial information about a customer when opening a cash account for the customer is required to do which of the following?

Quick Answer: 278
Detailed Answer: 279

- ❍ A. The broker cannot open the account for the customer.
- ❍ B. The broker can only open the account if the customer provides the information.
- ❍ C. The broker can open the account but can only execute unsolicited trades.
- ❍ D. The broker must get a waiver from the customer's lawyer to open the account.

4. A broker opened an account for a customer. The client refused to give certain information to the broker. Which of the following information that was not given requires the broker to refuse to open the account?

Quick Answer: 278
Detailed Answer: 279

- ❍ A. The customer's age
- ❍ B. The customer's net worth
- ❍ C. The customer's Social Security number
- ❍ D. The customer's marital status

5. A client calls his broker to purchase 1000 shares of Fly By Night Industries. The broker feels that the order is extremely risky for the client and attempts to talk him out of the trade. The client persists. What should the broker do?

Quick Answer: 278
Detailed Answer: 279

- ❍ A. Refuse to enter the order for the client because it does not meet the customer suitability parameters for this client.
- ❍ B. Tell the client that he cannot enter the order for him and that he should try to enter the order at another brokerage.
- ❍ C. The broker should mark the trade solicited and enter the order.
- ❍ D. The broker should mark the trade unsolicited and enter the order.

6. A client goes to her broker to open an option account. The client has never traded options before. The broker realizes the customer is inexperienced in this type of trading. What should the broker do?

Quick Answer: 278
Detailed Answer: 279

- ❍ A. Tell the customer to take some option courses before she can be approved for trading.
- ❍ B. Design an appropriate options agreement with the client.
- ❍ C. Tell the customer he cannot open the account because the principal of the office would never approve the account.
- ❍ D. Talk the customer into opening a margin account first before she can trade options.

Quick Check

7. The standard option trading disclosure document titled "Characteristics and Risks of Standardized Options" is required to be sent to all clients dealing in options by which of the following?

Quick Answer: **278**
Detailed Answer: **279**

- ❍ A. NASD
- ❍ B. SEC
- ❍ C. CBOE
- ❍ D. OCC

8. A joint tenancy with rights of survivorship account was opened for John and Mary Clark. If one partner dies, what happens to the assets in the account?

Quick Answer: **278**
Detailed Answer: **279**

- ❍ A. The account must go to probate.
- ❍ B. The surviving partner takes control of the assets.
- ❍ C. The account is frozen by the IRS.
- ❍ D. The portion of the deceased partner's assets goes to his or her estate.

9. If a corporation wants to open a brokerage margin account, what is needed to open the account?

Quick Answer: **278**
Detailed Answer: **280**

I. A copy of the corporate resolution

II. A directive on who is permitted to trade in the account

III. A copy of the certificate of incorporation

IV. A copy of the corporate bylaws

- ❍ A. I only
- ❍ B. I and II
- ❍ C. I, II, and III
- ❍ D. I, II, III, and IV

Quick Check

10. If a custodian account is established for a minor, which of the following statements is true?

    I. The custodian must be related to the minor.

    II. The funds or securities in the account are considered irrevocable.

    III. At the age of majority, the account must be re-registered in the name of the new adult.

    IV. Margin trades are permitted in the account.

- ❍ A. II and III
- ❍ B. I, II, and III
- ❍ C. III only
- ❍ D. I, II, III, and IV

Quick Answer: **278**
Detailed Answer: **280**

11. If a custodian account generates $6000 of income for the year, and the parent of the minor is in the 40% tax bracket, what is the tax on the income in the account?

- ❍ A. There is no tax because the account is established for a minor.
- ❍ B. The account has a tax of $2400.
- ❍ C. The account has a tax of $1880.
- ❍ D. The account is taxed according to the normal IRS tax code for progressive income levels.

Quick Answer: **278**
Detailed Answer: **280**

12. A trade is considered a discretionary trade in an account when the broker decides on which of the following?

    I. The time of the trade

    II. The price of the trade

    III. The time and price of the trade

    IV. The time, price, and security

- ❍ A. I and II
- ❍ B. I, II, and III
- ❍ C. IV only
- ❍ D. I, II, III, and IV

Quick Answer: **278**
Detailed Answer: **280**

Quick Check

13. All trades that are marked discretionary for an account by a registered representative must have which of the following by the end of business each day?

Quick Answer: 278
Detailed Answer: 280

- ❍ A. The approval by the principal in the branch office
- ❍ B. The cash to settle the trade in the account by the end of the day
- ❍ C. The approval of the customer by the end of the day
- ❍ D. The approval of one other broker in the office

14. An omnibus account is best described as which of the following types of accounts?

Quick Answer: 278
Detailed Answer: 280

- ❍ A. An umbrella account where one investment advisor manages numerous client accounts
- ❍ B. An option account that is used to hold closing transactions
- ❍ C. A guardian account for a business in receivership
- ❍ D. A liquidating account for a bankrupt corporation managed by a trustee

15. A client is extremely wealthy with numerous investments. The client wants to open an account with a large brokerage house but not put his name on the account. Which of the following is true regarding his request?

Quick Answer: 278
Detailed Answer: 280

- ❍ A. The broker cannot open an unnamed account.
- ❍ B. The client is permitted to open a numbered account with the broker.
- ❍ C. Due to the IRS tax code, the client can only open an unnamed account if he is a foreign resident.
- ❍ D. The client can only open a numbered account if he is an accredited investor.

16. Which of the following statements is true regarding a trust account?

Quick Answer: 278
Detailed Answer: 280

I. A trustee manages the assets of the individual named in the account.

II. The court appoints a trustee.

III. The person named in the trust account can either be alive or deceased.

IV. Transactions in the account can only be performed according to what is outlined in the trust agreement.

- ❍ A. I and II
- ❍ B. II and III
- ❍ C. I, II, and III
- ❍ D. I, II, III, and IV

Quick Check

17. A fiduciary account that is established by a court appointment to manage the assets of an incompetent individual is known as which of the following?

❍ A. A guardian account
❍ B. A testamentary account
❍ C. A living trust account
❍ D. A conservator account

Quick Answer: **278**
Detailed Answer: **281**

18. A wealthy individual who dies without a will has his assets distributed through which of the following accounts?

❍ A. An executor account
❍ B. A receivership account
❍ C. A trust account
❍ D. An administrator account

Quick Answer: **278**
Detailed Answer: **281**

19. Which of the following governs the investments in a fiduciary account?

I. The Prudent Man Rule

II. The Legal List

III. The Probate List

IV. The NYSE approved list

❍ A. I only
❍ B. I and II
❍ C. I, II, and III
❍ D. I, II, III, and IV

Quick Answer: **278**
Detailed Answer: **281**

Answer the next two questions from the following choices on brokerage operation departments.

❍ A. Purchase and sales department
❍ B. Cashier department
❍ C. Proxy department
❍ D. Reorganization department

20. A client is long 500 shares of TNT stock in her account. TNT has recently merged with GHI Industries. Which brokerage department handles the merge of the two companies?

Quick Answer: **278**
Detailed Answer: **281**

21. A customer calls his broker to request that a recent dividend received in his account be paid to him directly. Which brokerage department distributes the funds to the client?

Quick Answer: **278**
Detailed Answer: **281**

Quick Check

22. Which of the following items are part of a customer confirm?

    I. The security and number of shares

    II. Trade and settlement dates

    III. The role of the broker as agent or principal

    IV. The commission charged to the client

- ❍ A. I and II
- ❍ B. I, II, and III
- ❍ C. II, III, and IV
- ❍ D. I, II, III, and IV

Quick Answer: **278**
Detailed Answer: **281**

23. A client with a brokerage account has recently passed away. Which of the following procedures are true in how the account is handled?

    I. All open orders are canceled.

    II. The account is marked with a deceased notice.

    III. The executor receives the proceeds of the account.

    IV. The broker awaits instructions from the executor.

- ❍ A. I and II
- ❍ B. I, II, and III
- ❍ C. I, II, and IV
- ❍ D. I, II, III, and IV

Quick Answer: **278**
Detailed Answer: **281**

24. A customer has an account at a broker/dealer that has recently failed due to fraud by management of the firm. The client has $200,000 in securities and $125,000 in cash in her account. What will she be covered for by SIPC insurance?

- ❍ A. $200,000 in stock and $125,000 in cash
- ❍ B. $100,000 in stock and $100,000 in cash
- ❍ C. $200,000 in stock and $100,000 in cash
- ❍ D. $200,000 in stock and $50,000 in cash

Quick Answer: **278**
Detailed Answer: **281**

25. The maximum coverage for a brokerage account by the Securities Investor Protection Corporation is set at which of the following?

- ❍ A. $1,000,000 in combined securities and cash
- ❍ B. $500,000 in securities and $100,000 in cash
- ❍ C. $400,000 in securities and $100,000 in cash
- ❍ D. $900,000 in securities and $100,000 in cash

Quick Answer: **278**
Detailed Answer: **281**

Quick Check Answer Key

1. C
2. C
3. C
4. C
5. D
6. B
7. D
8. B
9. D
10. A
11. C
12. C
13. A
14. A
15. B
16. D
17. D
18. D
19. B
20. D
21. B
22. D
23. C
24. C
25. B

Answers and Explanations

1. **Answer C is correct.** An insider is defined as an officer, director, or 10% shareholder of a company. Insiders are accessible to privileged information and are subject to limitations when trading.

2. **Answer C is correct.** A broker opening an account for a customer needs to know the customer's legal age, his financial objectives, and his approximate net worth to determine the appropriate investment objectives of the client. The client's marital status is not required if the customer does not want to disclose the information.

3. **Answer C is correct.** A customer who refuses to disclose financial information to the broker can still open an account. The broker is limited to executing unsolicited trades in the account for the customer. Not fully knowing the customer's financial position, the broker cannot make recommendations to the client. If there is no way to verify the customer's assets, the broker is limited to unsolicited trades in the account.

4. **Answer C is correct.** Failure to disclose a Social Security number for tax purposes forces a broker to refuse to open an account for a customer. The IRS requires this information, and a client cannot trade without this documentation.

5. **Answer D is correct.** If a customer persists in conducting an unsuitable trade in his account, the trade is marked unsolicited by the broker and entered for execution. The broker even goes as far as tape-recording the trade to protect against the client holding him responsible for the unsuitable trade.

6. **Answer B is correct.** A customer who is considered inexperienced in option trading works with the senior option principal to design an appropriate option agreement. The customer's inexperience does not restrict her from opening the account. The customer is assigned certain parameters to meet her ability in trading options.

7. **Answer D is correct.** The Options Clearing Corporation requires that all clients, whether experienced or not, receive a copy of "Characteristics and Risks of Standardized Options," prior to the approval of trading in the account.

8. **Answer B is correct.** When one partner dies, a joint tenancy with rights of survivorship account has the assets in the account revert to the surviving partner. The control of the assets by the surviving partner might or might not have to pay estate taxes or go to probate to be resolved.

9. **Answer D is correct.** A corporate margin account can be opened by an incorporated business at a brokerage. The account must have a copy of the corporate resolution that authorizes the opening of the account. In addition, it must provide a copy of the certificate of incorporation with the attached corporate bylaws permitting the margin account to be opened. The account also requires a directive about who is permitted to trade in the account.

10. **Answer A is correct.** A custodian account for a minor can be opened by either a parent or another adult. The assets in the account are considered irrevocable. After the minor reaches the age of majority, the account must be re-registered in the new adult's name. Custodial accounts operate under the principle of the Prudent Man Rule, and margin or option trading in the account is prohibited.

11. **Answer C is correct.** Under the IRS Tax Reform Act of 1986, a custodial account is subject to the Kiddie tax. Any income in excess of $1300 in an account is subject to tax at the tax rate of the parent or guardian. In this example, the account earned $6000 less $1300 maximum = $4700 taxable income at the parents' tax rate of 40% = $1880 tax liability.

12. **Answer C is correct.** A trade in a discretionary account is considered discretionary if the broker determines more than just the time and price of the trade. If the broker chooses the time, price, and security, it is considered a discretionary trade.

13. **Answer A is correct.** Discretionary trades require the approval of a principal in the office at the end of business each day. The principal of the office is responsible for making sure that the broker is conducting suitable trades and making sure that the broker is not churning the customer's account.

14. **Answer A is correct.** An omnibus account is a group of accounts that fall under one umbrella. The account is managed by an investment advisor who trades on behalf of numerous clients.

15. **Answer B is correct.** A client is permitted to open a numbered account at a broker/dealer providing that the identity of the account is known to the principal of the office where the account is opened. This type of account provides a client with anonymity on the investments he or she makes.

16. **Answer D is correct.** A trust account is typically established by a court appointment of a trustee to manage the account. The trustee has a duty to manage the assets in the account for the individual named in the account. That individual can be either alive or deceased. The trustee is required to follow the instructions set forth in the trust agreement.

17. **Answer D is correct.** An individual who is declared incompetent by a court can have his or her assets protected by the opening of a conservator account. The court appoints a trustee to oversee the assets of the individual to preserve the individual's estate.

18. **Answer D is correct.** An individual who has died without a will has died intestate. A court appoints an administrator who is designated to settle the affairs of the deceased individual through an administrator account.

19. **Answer B is correct.** Fiduciary accounts must follow the Prudent Man Rule or the Legal List of the corresponding state in respect to the investments that can be made in the account. A fiduciary account is controlled by someone other than the beneficial owner, and restrictions are placed on the account as to the investments that can be made.

20. **Answer D is correct.** The reorganization department of a brokerage handles the merging of two companies for customers who are long the corresponding shares. They credit the customers who are long the shares with the new company shares issued.

21. **Answer B is correct.** A customer who requests that a dividend payment be paid to him directly, rather than held in his account, notifies the cashier department. The cashier department prints a check for the available funds and mails it to the customer upon his request.

22. **Answer D is correct.** A customer confirm lists the security and number of shares bought or sold. It designates the trade date, settlement date, and any commission or markup charged to the customer. The broker also designates his role in the trade as either principal or agent.

23. **Answer C is correct.** Upon the death of a customer, the broker marks the account deceased and cancels any open orders in the account. The account is then frozen as it awaits further instructions from the executor of the estate.

24. **Answer C is correct.** The Securities and Investors Protection Corporation guarantees a customer account up to $500,000 in assets with a maximum of $100,000 in cash. The account is covered for the $200,000 in securities and $100,000 of the $125,000 in cash. The remaining cash assets become a general creditor of the firm.

25. **Answer B is correct.** The Securities and Investors Protection Corporation covers a customer account up to an amount of $500,000, of which $100,000 can be in cash. Most brokers offer an enhanced version of this insurance coverage, but the maximum coverage offered by SIPC is the $500,000 coverage of assets.

Margin

Quick Check

1. Customer margin is best defined as which of the following?

   ❍ A. The portion of the value of the securities that an investor must deposit in her account when she buys or sells securities on credit

   ❍ B. The portion of the value of the securities that an investor can borrow from the Federal Reserve Bank when buying or selling securities on credit

   ❍ C. The portion of the value of the securities that an investor can borrow from the broker when buying or selling securities on credit

   ❍ D. The portion of the value of the securities that an investor can borrow from the NYSE when buying or selling securities on credit

Quick Answer: **289**
Detailed Answer: **290**

2. Regulation T empowers which of the following to set margin requirements for securities trading?

   ❍ A. NASD

   ❍ B. New York Stock Exchange

   ❍ C. Securities and Exchange Commission

   ❍ D. Federal Reserve Bank

Quick Answer: **289**
Detailed Answer: **290**

3. Which of the following securities are considered marginable securities?

   I. New York Stock Exchange listed securities

   II. American Stock Exchange securities

   III. National Market System securities

   IV. All Over-the-Counter securities

   ❍ A. I and II

   ❍ B. I, II, and III

   ❍ C. I, II, and IV

   ❍ D. I, II, III, and IV

Quick Answer: **289**
Detailed Answer: **290**

Quick Check

4. Which of the following securities are permitted to be purchased on margin?

    I. Options

    II. NYSE listed securities

    III. American Stock Exchange listed securities

    IV. Over-the-Counter securities

    ❍ A. II and III
    ❍ B. I, II, and III
    ❍ C. II, III, and IV
    ❍ D. I, II, III, and IV

Quick Answer: **289**
Detailed Answer: **290**

5. A customer deposited $12,000 worth of fully owned marginable securities into his margin account. How much in additional stock is the investor able to purchase?

    ❍ A. $6000
    ❍ B. $12,000
    ❍ C. $24,000
    ❍ D. $48,000

Quick Answer: **289**
Detailed Answer: **290**

6. The term *fail to deliver* regarding a margin account is defined as which of the following?

    ❍ A. A customer sold securities in a margin account and did not deliver the securities within 10 days.
    ❍ B. A customer failed to meet his Regulation T requirement.
    ❍ C. A customer fell below the NYSE minimum maintenance requirement.
    ❍ D. A customer sold securities in a margin account and did not deliver the securities on the settlement date.

Quick Answer: **289**
Detailed Answer: **290**

7. An investor purchased $8000 worth of securities in a margin account. The securities increased in value to $9000. Which of the following happens to the $1000 increase?

    ❍ A. It is split between the brokerage and the customer.
    ❍ B. It increases the customer debit balance.
    ❍ C. It decreases the customer debit balance.
    ❍ D. It increases the customer equity.

Quick Answer: **289**
Detailed Answer: **290**

Quick Check

8. The main reason an investor utilizes a margin account is best described as which of the following?
   - ❍ A. It allows the investor to leverage her investment choice.
   - ❍ B. It allows the investor to purchase securities at a discount.
   - ❍ C. It allows an investor to own securities without having to pay for them.
   - ❍ D. It allows investors to play the stock market.

Quick Answer: 289
Detailed Answer: 291

9. Securities that are held in a margin account are required to be kept in which of the following?
   - ❍ A. Street name
   - ❍ B. Safekeeping
   - ❍ C. Segregation
   - ❍ D. Registered form

Quick Answer: 289
Detailed Answer: 291

10. Which agreement of a margin account allows the broker to pledge securities to secure a loan for a customer?
    - ❍ A. The broker loan agreement
    - ❍ B. The hypothecation agreement
    - ❍ C. The margin agreement
    - ❍ D. The credit agreement

Quick Answer: 289
Detailed Answer: 291

Choose from the following agreements to answer the next four questions. A choice can be used once, more than once, or not at all.

- ❍ A. Margin agreement
- ❍ B. Hypothecation agreement
- ❍ C. Credit agreement
- ❍ D. Loan consent agreement

11. The agreement that allows a broker to pledge customer securities to secure a loan for the customer is what?

Quick Answer: 289
Detailed Answer: 291

12. The agreement that allows a broker to lend customer securities to other clients selling securities short is what?

Quick Answer: 289
Detailed Answer: 291

13. The agreement that sets forth the terms of a loan that a brokerage can make to a customer, including the interest rate charged, is what?

Quick Answer: 289
Detailed Answer: 291

14. The agreement which states that margin account securities must be kept in street name is what?

Quick Answer: 289
Detailed Answer: 291

Quick Check

15. Securities that are held in street name in a margin account make the customer what type of owner?

Quick Answer: 289
Detailed Answer: 291

- ❍ A. Nominal owner
- ❍ B. Beneficial owner
- ❍ C. Street owner
- ❍ D. Stated owner

16. Which of the following regulations governs the broker loan that is secured for a customer from a bank?

Quick Answer: 289
Detailed Answer: 291

- ❍ A. Regulation T
- ❍ B. Regulation Q
- ❍ C. Regulation G
- ❍ D. Regulation U

17. A broker lends a client $5000 to purchase securities in a margin account. The broker pledges 140% of the debit balance to the bank to secure the loan. How much does the bank lend to the broker from the hypothecated securities?

Quick Answer: 289
Detailed Answer: 291

- ❍ A. $4900
- ❍ B. $5000
- ❍ C. $7000
- ❍ D. $10,000

18. The New York Stock Exchange can impose its own margin requirements on member firms. Which of the following statements is true?

Quick Answer: 289
Detailed Answer: 292

I. NYSE rules can be less strict than the Federal Reserve Bank rules.

II. NYSE rules also apply to NASD firms.

III. NYSE rules can be the same as the Federal Reserve Bank rules.

IV. NYSE rules can be more strict than the Federal Reserve Bank rules.

- ❍ A. I and II
- ❍ B. II and III
- ❍ C. I, II, and III
- ❍ D. III and IV

Quick Check

19. A customer has an initial transaction in a margin account of a purchase of 100 shares of XYZ stock at $38 per share. What is the Regulation T requirement on the account?

Quick Answer: 289
Detailed Answer: 292

- ❍ A. $1800
- ❍ B. $1900
- ❍ C. $2000
- ❍ D. $3800

20. A customer has an initial transaction in her margin account of a purchase of 100 shares of TNT stock at $28 per share. What is the customer's Regulation T requirement on the account?

Quick Answer: 289
Detailed Answer: 292

- ❍ A. $1400
- ❍ B. $2000
- ❍ C. $2100
- ❍ D. $2800

21. A customer purchased a $10,000 corporate bond in a margin account. Which of the following dictates a margin requirement on the purchase?

Quick Answer: 289
Detailed Answer: 292

- ❍ A. Federal Reserve Bank
- ❍ B. New York Stock Exchange
- ❍ C. MSRB
- ❍ D. SEC

22. A customer purchased a $10,000 NYSE listed corporate bond on margin. What is the margin requirement on the bond if it is selling at 98 in the market?

Quick Answer: 289
Detailed Answer: 292

- ❍ A. $700
- ❍ B. $1960
- ❍ C. $2000
- ❍ D. $9800

23. A client purchased $100,000 worth of Treasury bills in a margin account. What is the margin requirement on the purchase?

Quick Answer: 289
Detailed Answer: 292

- ❍ A. $1000
- ❍ B. $2000
- ❍ C. $10,000
- ❍ D. $100,000

Quick Check

24. Which of the following statements are considered true about a short sale of securities?

    I. The client makes money if the stock goes up in value.

    II. The margin requirement is higher for low-priced stocks.

    III. The margin requirement is set at 50% for higher-priced stocks.

    IV. The client borrows the shares from the broker/dealer through his margin account.

- ❍ A. I and II
- ❍ B. II and III
- ❍ C. I, II, and IV
- ❍ D. II, III, and IV

Quick Answer: **289**
Detailed Answer: **292**

25. Which of the following entities enforces its margin requirement on 100 shares of a NASDAQ security sold short at $3 per share?

- ❍ A. Federal Reserve Bank
- ❍ B. NASD
- ❍ C. NYSE
- ❍ D. SEC

Quick Answer: **289**
Detailed Answer: **292**

Quick Check Answer Key

1. A
2. D
3. B
4. A
5. B
6. A
7. D
8. A
9. A
10. B
11. B
12. D
13. C
14. A
15. B
16. D
17. A
18. D
19. C
20. B
21. B
22. B
23. A
24. D
25. B

Answers and Explanations

1. **Answer A is correct.** Margin is that portion of a margined investment that an investor must put up when either selling or purchasing securities in a margin account on credit.

2. **Answer D is correct.** The Federal Reserve Bank was empowered by the Securities Act of 1934 to set margin requirements for margin trading. The NYSE sets minimum maintenance requirements, but it is the Fed that sets the Regulation T rate.

3. **Answer B is correct.** All New York Stock Exchange listed securities, as well as American Stock Exchange securities and listed regional securities, are considered marginable securities. Only National Market System stocks that are part of the NASDAQ system are marginable securities. Other Over-the-Counter market securities must be listed on the Federal Reserve Bank's "margin list" to be considered marginable securities.

4. **Answer A is correct.** Only New York Stock Exchange securities and American Stock Exchange securities are permitted to be bought or sold on margin automatically. NASDAQ National Market System securities are also permitted to be bought or sold on margin. Over-the-Counter securities need the approval of the Federal Reserve Bank on its margin list to be considered a marginable security. Options can be purchased in a margin account but are not considered a marginable security.

5. **Answer B is correct.** A customer depositing fully owned marginable securities into a margin account is able to purchase additional securities in the same amount of the deposit. If the customer uses the securities to meet a margin requirement, then only 50% of the market value is considered. The question does not indicate whether the client is meeting a Regulation T Call, so the customer can purchase an additional $12,000 worth of securities.

6. **Answer A is correct.** A fail to deliver constitutes a customer selling securities in a margin account and not bringing the securities in to the brokerage for delivery within 10 days. If a fail to deliver occurs, the broker buys in the securities to cover the delivery.

7. **Answer D is correct.** An increase in the value of customer securities in a margin account increases the market value and the customer's equity position in the account. Customers receive full appreciation in the value of securities, as well as any loss incurred on a drop in market value. The broker does not benefit from market movement.

8. **Answer A is correct.** Sophisticated investors use margins to effectively leverage the market positions they take in underlying securities in the account. Customers are required to put up 50% of the market value to control twice as much in value of the underlying investment.

9. **Answer A is correct.** Securities that are purchased in a margin account are held in street name by the broker. The securities are considered owned by the customer and entitle the customer to dividends. They remain in street name until the debit balance is paid off by the customer for ease of selling.

10. **Answer B is correct.** The hypothecation agreement allows the broker to pledge securities in the account up to 140% of the debit balance (the loan) to the bank to secure a loan for a margin client.

11. **Answer B is correct.** The hypothecation agreement allows a broker to pledge customer securities in the account up to 140% of the debit balance (the loan) to secure a loan for a margin client.

12. **Answer D is correct.** The loan consent agreement is signed by a margin client, allowing the broker to use securities in the account to lend to other clients selling securities short. This agreement is not considered mandatory by many brokers.

13. **Answer C is correct.** The credit agreement sets the parameters of the secured loan to the margin customer. This includes the interest rate charged and the limits to receive a lower rate by the customer.

14. **Answer A is correct.** The margin agreement informs the customer that the securities in the margin account are held in street name. The client is the beneficial owner, and the broker remains the nominal owner.

15. **Answer B is correct.** Securities held in street name are in the name of the broker who acts as nominal owner, but the client is considered the beneficial owner. Dividends paid on street name securities go to the broker, who in turn credits the beneficial owner (the client).

16. **Answer D is correct.** Regulation U governs the amount that a broker can borrow from a bank using pledged securities to secure a margin loan for a customer. Brokers pledge 140% of the debit balance, and banks are permitted to lend 70% of that amount to the broker for a margin loan.

17. **Answer A is correct.** A broker that has pledged 140% of a debit balance of $5000 has pledged $7000 worth of securities to the lending bank to secure a loan. The bank is permitted under Regulation U to lend 70% of the pledged amount to the broker. The equation is $7000 pledged × 70% = $4900 as a loan. The broker must make up the $100 difference toward the loan to the margin customer.

18. **Answer D is correct.** The New York Stock Exchange margin rules can either be the same as the Federal Reserve Bank margin rules or stricter than the Fed's rules. NYSE rules can never be less lenient than the established Fed rules.

19. **Answer C is correct.** A customer who has purchased 100 shares of XYZ stock at $38 per share as his initial transaction in a margin account needs to meet the $2000 minimum. The client is required to deposit $2000 on the initial transaction.

20. **Answer B is correct.** An initial transaction in a margin account for 100 shares of TNT at $28 has a margin requirement of $2000. The broker can lend the remaining $800 to the client as the debit balance.

21. **Answer B is correct.** The NYSE requires that a margin of the greater of 7% of the face value or 20% of the market value be deposited in a margin account for the purchase of a corporate bond on margin.

22. **Answer B is correct.** The NYSE requires a margin of the greater of 7% of the face value of the corporate bond ($10,000 × 7% = $700) or 20% of the market value ($9800 × 20% = $1990) as margin for the purchase of a corporate bond in a margin account. The customer has a margin requirement of $1990.

23. **Answer A is correct.** Treasury bills require a margin deposit of 1% of the market value to be purchased on margin. A $100,000 T-bill requires a 1% deposit or $1,000 in the margin account.

24. **Answer D is correct.** A short sale of securities is done by an investor with the hope that the security will decline in value and be purchased back to cover the loaned stock at a lower value. The client makes money if the price declines. He borrows the shorted shares from his broker. The margin requirement is 50% but is more for riskier, lower-price stocks.

25. **Answer B is correct.** The National Association of Securities Dealers (NASD) enforces the margin requirement on a penny stock or cheap stock sold short in a margin account. The requirement is set at $2.50 per share or 100% of the sale proceeds, whichever is greater.

Quick Check

Margin Accounts

1. Which of the following statements are considered true of long and short margin accounts?

Quick Answer: 300
Detailed Answer: 301

I. The minimum maintenance on a long account is 25%.

II. The minimum maintenance on a short account is 30%.

III. An account that falls below the minimum maintenance receives a margin call.

IV. A broker can have stricter minimum maintenance requirements than the NASD and NYSE.

- A. I and II
- B. I and III
- C. I, II, and III
- D. I, II, III, and IV

2. An investor purchases 500 shares of TNT stock on margin at $44 per share. The stock rises in value to $48 per share. What is the new equity in the account?

Quick Answer: 300
Detailed Answer: 301

- A. $11,000
- B. $12,000
- C. $13,000
- D. $24,000

Quick Check

3. Which of the following statements are considered true of equity in a combined margin account?

Quick Answer: **300**
Detailed Answer: **301**

   I. Any increase in the long market value increases the equity by the same amount.

   II. Any decrease in the long market value decreases the equity by the same amount.

   III. Any increase in the short market value increases the equity by the same amount.

   IV. Any increase in the short market value decreases the equity by the same amount.

   - ❍ A. I and II
   - ❍ B. II and III
   - ❍ C. I, II, and IV
   - ❍ D. I, II, and III

4. All the following statements are true of a customer selling securities from a restricted margin account except for which one?

Quick Answer: **300**
Detailed Answer: **301**

   - ❍ A. Fifty percent of the proceeds must be used to decrease the debit balance.
   - ❍ B. The account is below the required Regulation T 50%.
   - ❍ C. The client is not permitted to purchase any additional securities.
   - ❍ D. The client is not required to bring the account up to Regulation T of 50%.

5. A client purchased $20,000 worth of TNT stock in her margin account. The account long market value falls to $16,000. The account is now which of the following?

Quick Answer: **300**
Detailed Answer: **301**

   - ❍ A. Regulation T restricted
   - ❍ B. At its NYSE minimum maintenance level
   - ❍ C. At the minimum retention requirement
   - ❍ D. In need of a margin call

Quick Check

6. A margin account has a long market value of $22,000, a debit balance of $11,000, and equity of $11,000. The market value of the account increases to $28,000. Which of the following statements are true?

   I. The account has a debit balance of $14,000.

   II. The account has equity of $17,000.

   III. The account has excess of $3000.

   IV. The account has excess of $6000.

   ❍ A. I and II
   ❍ B. II and III
   ❍ C. I, II, and III
   ❍ D. I, II, and IV

Quick Answer: 300
Detailed Answer: 301

7. A margin customer has an account with an SMA of $4000. If the client uses the entire SMA, which statements are considered true?

   I. The debit balance increases by $4000.

   II. The equity increases by $4000.

   III. The equity decreases by $4000.

   IV. The debit balance decreases by $4000.

   ❍ A. I only
   ❍ B. II only
   ❍ C. I and III
   ❍ D. II and IV

Quick Answer: 300
Detailed Answer: 302

Answer the following four questions with the margin information provided for the long margin account.

An investor purchases the following:

100 shares of X @ $34
100 shares of Y @ $42
100 shares of Z @ $62

8. The debit balance on the long margin account is set at which amount?

   ❍ A. $13,800
   ❍ B. $10,350
   ❍ C. $6900
   ❍ D. $3450

Quick Answer: 300
Detailed Answer: 302

Quick Check

9. What is the customer equity in the margin account after the purchase of the three securities?
   - ❍ A. $13,800
   - ❍ B. $10,350
   - ❍ C. $6900
   - ❍ D. $3450

Quick Answer: 300
Detailed Answer: 302

10. If the market price of Security Z increases to $75 per share and X and Y remain the same, what is the excess in the margin account?
   - ❍ A. Excess of $500
   - ❍ B. Excess of $650
   - ❍ C. Excess of $1300
   - ❍ D. Excess of $2600

Quick Answer: 300
Detailed Answer: 302

11. The client uses the SMA in the account that was created by the increase in the market value of Security Z. What is the client's buying power in the account?
   - ❍ A. $1000 buying power
   - ❍ B. $1300 buying power
   - ❍ C. $2600 buying power
   - ❍ D. $5200 buying power

Quick Answer: 300
Detailed Answer: 302

12. A long margin account has a market value of $18,000, a debit balance of $9000, and equity of $9000. How low can the market value fall before the account reaches the minimum maintenance?
   - ❍ A. $16,000
   - ❍ B. $12,000
   - ❍ C. $9000
   - ❍ D. $4500

Quick Answer: 300
Detailed Answer: 302

13. A margin account has a market value of $45,000 and equity in the account of $22,500. How low can the market value of this account fall before the account receives a margin call?
   - ❍ A. $42,000
   - ❍ B. $40,000
   - ❍ C. $35,000
   - ❍ D. $30,000

Quick Answer: 300
Detailed Answer: 303

Quick Check

14. George has a margin account with a long market value of $12,000, a debit balance of $5000, and equity of $7000. He wants to purchase another $2000 worth of securities in the account. How much cash is he required to deposit in the account?

 ❍ A. No cash is required.
 ❍ B. $1000 cash deposit
 ❍ C. $2000 cash deposit
 ❍ D. $4000 cash deposit

Quick Answer: **300**
Detailed Answer: **303**

15. A margin customer has a market value of $14,000, a debit balance of $6000, and equity of $8000. If the client uses the available created SMA in the account, how does it affect the equity in the account?

 ❍ A. The equity increases by $1000.
 ❍ B. The equity increases by $2000.
 ❍ C. The equity increases by $4000.
 ❍ D. The equity remains the same.

Quick Answer: **300**
Detailed Answer: **303**

Answer the next two questions regarding the following margin account information:

Long market value of $16,000
Debit balance of $12,000
Equity of $4000
SMA of $3500

16. What is the maximum buying power of the account as it currently sits?

 ❍ A. The account has buying power of $3500.
 ❍ B. The account has buying power of $7000.
 ❍ C. The account has unlimited buying power.
 ❍ D. The account has no buying power.

Quick Answer: **300**
Detailed Answer: **303**

17. What is the equity in the account after the client uses the permitted SMA available?

 ❍ A. Equity of $4000
 ❍ B. Equity of $5750
 ❍ C. Equity of $7500
 ❍ D. Equity of $11,000

Quick Answer: **300**
Detailed Answer: **303**

Quick Check

18. Which of the following statements are considered true of using SMA to buy additional securities in a margin account?

    I. Using SMA increases the market value of the account.

    II. Using SMA increases the debit balance of the account.

    III. Using SMA increases the equity in the account.

    IV. SMA can always be used by the customer.

    ❍ A. I and II
    ❍ B. II and III
    ❍ C. I, II, and III
    ❍ D. I, II, III, and IV

Quick Answer: 300
Detailed Answer: 304

19. What is the credit balance in a short margin account if the customer sells short 1000 shares of TNT @ $56 per share?

    ❍ A. $28,000
    ❍ B. $56,000
    ❍ C. $84,000
    ❍ D. $112,000

Quick Answer: 300
Detailed Answer: 304

20. What is the credit balance in a short margin account if the customer sells short 500 shares of XYZ @ $33 per share?

    ❍ A. $8250
    ❍ B. $16,500
    ❍ C. $24,750
    ❍ D. $33,000

Quick Answer: 300
Detailed Answer: 304

21. As his initial transaction in his short margin account, Tony sells short 100 shares of GHI @ $30 per share. What is his credit balance in the account for this transaction?

    ❍ A. $2000
    ❍ B. $3000
    ❍ C. $4500
    ❍ D. $5000

Quick Answer: 300
Detailed Answer: 304

Quick Check

22. All the following statements are true of long and short margin accounts except for which one?
    - ❍ A. The only constant in a long margin account is the debit balance.
    - ❍ B. The only constant in a short margin account is the credit balance.
    - ❍ C. The equity in a long account increases if the market value increases.
    - ❍ D. The equity in a short account increases if the market value increases.

Quick Answer: 300
Detailed Answer: 304

23. Frank sells 100 shares of KLM stock short @ $88 per share. The price of KLM stock rises to $92 per share. Which of the following statements are true?

    I. The equity in the account has risen.

    II. The equity in the account has fallen.

    III. The credit balance in the account has risen.

    IV. The credit balance in the account has fallen.

    - ❍ A. I and III
    - ❍ B. II only
    - ❍ C. II and IV
    - ❍ D. I and IV

Quick Answer: 300
Detailed Answer: 304

24. A short margin account has a credit balance of $14,000, a short market value of $5000, and equity of $9000. What is the SMA in the account?
    - ❍ A. The account has an SMA of $2500.
    - ❍ B. The account has an SMA of $4500.
    - ❍ C. The account has an SMA of $6500.
    - ❍ D. The account has an SMA of $7000.

Quick Answer: 300
Detailed Answer: 305

25. A short margin account has a credit balance of $35,000, a short market value of $15,000, and equity of $20,000. What is the SMA in the account?
    - ❍ A. The account has an SMA of $7500.
    - ❍ B. The account has an SMA of $10,000.
    - ❍ C. The account has an SMA of $12,500.
    - ❍ D. The account has an SMA of $15,000.

Quick Answer: 300
Detailed Answer: 305

Quick Check Answer Key

1. D
2. C
3. C
4. C
5. A
6. B
7. C
8. C
9. C
10. B
11. B
12. B
13. D
14. A
15. D
16. D
17. A
18. A
19. C
20. C
21. D
22. D
23. B
24. C
25. C

Answers and Explanations

1. **Answer D is correct.** The minimum maintenance requirements on a long margin account are 25% and 30% on a short margin account. Accounts falling below the minimum requirements receive a margin call from the broker. Brokerages can have requirements on margin accounts that are stricter than the NYSE and NASD but never more lenient than the prescribed minimum amounts.

2. **Answer C is correct.** A long margin account with 500 shares of TNT at $44 is established as LMV = 22,000 – debit balance ($11,000) = equity ($11,000). If the LMV increases to $48 per share, the result is LMV = $24,000 – debit balance ($11,000) = equity ($13,000).

3. **Answer C is correct.** Equity has a direct correlation to the long market value (LMV) of the margin account. If LMV increases, then equity increases by the same amount. If LMV decreases, then equity decreases by the same amount. Conversely, in a short margin account, if the short market value increases, then the equity in the account decreases by the same amount.

4. **Answer C is correct.** In a restricted margin account, the margin account fell below the required Regulation T 50% requirement. This means that the equity in the account is no longer at 50% of the market value. A customer is still permitted to purchase securities in the margin account as long as he meets the Regulation T Requirements of 50% on all new purchases.

5. **Answer A is correct.** With a long margin account that has the market value of the securities fall to a point where the equity in the account drops below the Regulation T 50% level, the account is considered Regulation T restricted. An account that had a market value of $20,000 which fell to $16,000 now has $4000 less in both market value and equity. The account is still above the minimum maintenance levels, but it is considered Regulation T restricted.

6. **Answer B is correct.** The account must be compared to determine what an increase in market value will do.

LMV	$22,000	LMV	$28,000
DB	$11,000	DB	$11,000
EQ	$11,000	EQ	$17,000
Reg T Req	$11,000	Reg T Req	$14,000
Excess	-0-	Excess	$3000

The account now has an equity of $17,000 and an excess or SMA created in the account by the market increase of $3000.

7. **Answer C is correct.** The SMA in a margin account is a credit line for the customer. When the investor uses the SMA, the amount is added to the debit balance and deducted from the equity in the account. Remember, this was an extension of credit used by the client that must now be paid back.

8. **Answer C is correct.** The investor purchased $13,800 worth of securities in his margin account. The Regulation T requirement demands that the client put up 50% in equity to the 50% he will borrow in the form of the debit balance. The debit balance in the account is 13,800 × .50 = $6900.

9. **Answer C is correct.** The customer purchased $13,800 worth of securities in the account. Under the Regulation T requirement, the customer must put up 50% of the value of the securities as equity in the account. In this case, the result is $13,800 × 50% = $6900 in equity.

10. **Answer B is correct.** Security Z increased by $13 per share for a $1300 increase in the market value of the account. The account is now compared as such:

	Original	After Increase
LMV	$13,800	$15,100
DB	$6900	$6900
EQ	$6900	$8200
Reg T Required	$6900	$7550
Excess	-0-	$650

11. **Answer B is correct.** With an excess of $650 in the account, the SMA is credited for that excess amount. The buying power for the account is the SMA ÷ .50 = $650 ÷ .50 = $1300 worth of additional buying power in the account.

12. **Answer B is correct.** To determine the amount that a long margin account can fall before it is required to bring in additional funds (through a margin call), an investor can simply divide the debit balance by the complement of the 25% minimum maintenance requirement for a long account, which is .75.

    A debit balance of $9000 ÷ .75 = $12,000. The account can fall in market value to $12,000 before it is at the minimum maintenance level.

    The next equation is a LMV of $12,000 – a debit balance of $9000 = equity of $3000. The account is now sitting at exactly 25%.

13. **Answer D is correct.** To determine the amount that a long margin account can fall before it is required to bring in additional funds (through a margin call), an investor can simply divide the debit balance by the complement of the 25% minimum maintenance requirement for a long account, which is .75. A debit balance of $22,500 ÷ .75 = $30,000. The account can fall to a market value of $30,000 before it is at the minimum maintenance level.

    The next equation is a LMV of $30,000 – a debit balance of $22,500 = equity of $7500. The account is now sitting exactly at 25%.

14. **Answer A is correct.** George is not required to deposit any cash in the account to purchase $2000 worth of additional securities. The account was sitting above the Regulation T 50% requirement and had created an SMA of $1000 in the account. With an SMA of $1000, the account has buying power of $2000. Thus, George can purchase $2000 worth of additional securities without having to bring in any funds by using the SMA available. The account afterward is the LMV = $14,000 – a debit balance of $5000 + $2000 ($7000) = equity of $7000.

15. **Answer D is correct.** The customer's margin account has an excess in the account of $1000, which is credited to the client's SMA. To use the entire SMA to buy additional securities, the customer has buying power of $2000 ($1000 SMA ÷ .50 = $2000). If the client purchases $2000 worth of additional securities in the account, the market value increases by $2000 and the debit balance increases by $2000. Because the credit line is used to buy securities for the account, the equity in the account remains the same.

16. **Answer D is correct.** Buying power is determined by the available credit line in the account. The SMA is the credit line for the account. An SMA of $3500 enables the investor to purchase twice as many securities in the account. To compute this, you determine buying power with SMA ÷ .50. The account has an SMA of $3500 ÷ .50 = $7000 buying power.

    This account, however, does not have any buying power because it has what is commonly known as a phantom SMA of $3500. It does have the credit line, but it cannot be used, because if it is, the account is sent into a margin call for falling below the 25% minimum maintenance requirement. An investor cannot use SMA if it sends the account into a margin call by doing so.

17. **Answer A is correct.** The equity in the account remains the same at $4000 because this account does not have any available buying power. The account is sitting at the NYSE minimum maintenance requirement of 25%. Using the SMA would make the account receive a margin call. The client therefore has SMA that is considered phantom SMA. (It is there but cannot be used.) The account remains the same with an equity of $4000.

18. **Answer A is correct.** The use of SMA in a margin account to buy additional securities increases the market value of the account by the amount of the additional shares purchased. Using SMA also increases the debit balance in the account. SMA is a credit line that once used must be paid back, so it is added to the debit balance.

19. **Answer C is correct.** A short margin account is established as credit balance – short market value = equity. To find the credit balance, you add the SMV and equity together. A client who sells short 1000 shares @ $56 has a short market value of $56,000. The required Regulation T on this short sale is 50%, or $28,000. These two numbers added together give you a credit balance of $56,000 SMV + $28,000 equity = a $84,000 credit balance.

20. **Answer C is correct.** A short margin account is established as credit balance – short market value = equity. To find the credit balance, we you the SMV and equity together. A client who sells short 500 shares @ $33 has a short market value of $16,500. The Regulation T requirement on this short sale is 50%, or $8250. These two numbers added together give you a credit balance of $16,500 SMV + $8250 equity = a $24,750 credit balance in the account.

21. **Answer D is correct.** Any initial transaction in a short margin account requires a $2000 deposit whether the transaction was for that amount or less. Tony sells short 100 shares GHI @ $30. This gives him a short market value of $3000. The Regulation T requirement in equity for this transaction is normally 50%, or $1500. This transaction is different because it is the initial transaction for the account. Tony deposits $2000 in equity. The SMV of $3,000 + $2000 equity = a credit balance of $5000.

22. **Answer D is correct.** Equity in a short account only increases by a decline in the short market value of the account. Short sellers make money when the securities drop in market value, not rise. If the market value increases in a short account, the equity decreases.

23. **Answer B is correct.** An increase in price of 100 shares of KLM stock from $88 to $92 makes the equity in the short account decrease. Short sellers want the price of the stock to decline in value to make money, not rise. The credit balance in a short account is the only constant, so it remains the same. Equity and SMV are the only variables in a short account.

24. **Answer C is correct.** To determine SMA in a short margin account you must construct the account:

Credit Balance	$14,000
Short Mkt Value	$5000
Equity	$9000
Reg T Req 50%	$2500
Excess	**=$6500**

The SMV of $5000 must have a Regulation T requirement of 50%, or $2500. The account has equity of $9000. The difference is the amount of the SMA in the account, or $6500.

25. **Answer C is correct.** To determine SMA in a short account, we must construct the account.

Credit Balance	$35,000
Short Mkt Value	$15,000
Equity	$20,000
Reg T Req 50%	$7500
Excess	**$12,500**

The SMV of $15,000 must have a Regulation T requirement of 50%, or $7500. The account has equity of $20,000. The difference is the amount of the SMA in the account, or $12,500.

Quick Check

Investment Companies

1. All the following are characteristics of an investment company except for which one?

   Quick Answer: **314**
   Detailed Answer: **315**

   ❍ A. It allows investors' holdings to remain liquid.
   ❍ B. It allows investors to make their own specific investment choices.
   ❍ C. It allows investors to diversify their holdings, regardless of size.
   ❍ D. It gives investors professional management of their holdings.

2. All the following contribute to an investor having liquidity in an investment company except for which one?

   Quick Answer: **314**
   Detailed Answer: **315**

   ❍ A. Investors can sell their shares in an investment company easily.
   ❍ B. There are a large number of investors in investment companies.
   ❍ C. Share prices for investment companies are low.
   ❍ D. Share prices for investment companies are high.

3. A face amount certificate company invests funds in all the following securities except for which one?

   Quick Answer: **314**
   Detailed Answer: **315**

   ❍ A. T-notes
   ❍ B. T-bonds
   ❍ C. Blue chip debt instruments
   ❍ D. Zero coupon bonds

Quick Check

4. Which statements are true regarding a unit investment trust?

I. A unit investment trust is considered an investment company.

II. It is governed by a board of trustees.

III. It is governed by a board of directors.

IV. A unit investment trust issues redeemable shares of beneficial interest.

❍ A. I and II
❍ B. II and III
❍ C. I, II, and IV
❍ D. I, III, and IV

Quick Answer: 314
Detailed Answer: 315

5. Shares of beneficial interest in an investment company represent which of the following?

❍ A. An investor's interest in income generated by an underlying portfolio of securities
❍ B. Direct ownership of the underlying securities
❍ C. Voting rights of an underlying portfolio of securities
❍ D. The holding of the securities in an underlying portfolio to maturity

Quick Answer: 314
Detailed Answer: 315

6. An investor purchases a fixed unit investment trust. Which of the following are true?

I. A select portfolio of securities is purchased.

II. The portfolio is set for the life of the trust.

III. Securities in the portfolio can be bought and sold.

IV. A fixed unit investment trust is self-liquidating.

❍ A. I and II
❍ B. II and III
❍ C. I, II, and III
❍ D. I, II, and IV

Quick Answer: 314
Detailed Answer: 315

7. Upon maturity of a fixed unit investment trust, which statements are considered true?

Quick Answer: 314
Detailed Answer: 315

   I. The fixed UIT is self-liquidating.

   II. Principal payments are made to the trust first.

   III. Principal payments are made directly to the unit holders.

   IV. The trust is liquidated.

   ❍ A. I and II
   ❍ B. II and IV
   ❍ C. I, II, and IV
   ❍ D. I, III, and IV

8. An investor owns 10 $1000 units in a fixed unit investment trust. The investor wants to sell his units. Which statement is considered true?

Quick Answer: 314
Detailed Answer: 315

   ❍ A. The investor must sell the units in the secondary market.
   ❍ B. The investor must find a buyer for the units.
   ❍ C. The investor can redeem the units with the sponsor.
   ❍ D. The investor is required to hold the units to maturity.

9. The net asset value for a unit investment trust is computed by which of the following formulas?

Quick Answer: 314
Detailed Answer: 315

   ❍ A. Market value of portfolio ÷ number of issued units
   ❍ B. Market value of portfolio ÷ number of outstanding units
   ❍ C. Market value of portfolio × number of outstanding units
   ❍ D. Market value of portfolio – number of outstanding units

10. Matt owns 100 units in Cortland Investments, a fixed unit investment trust. The UIT has 100,000 outstanding units with a portfolio value of $97,500,000. What is the net asset value of the 100 units that Matt owns?

Quick Answer: 314
Detailed Answer: 316

   ❍ A. $975
   ❍ B. $9750
   ❍ C. $97,500
   ❍ D. $975,000

Quick Check

11. Susan owns 25 units in Monroe Investments, a fixed unit investment trust. The trust has 150,000 outstanding units with a portfolio value of $153,300,000. What is the net asset value for the units that Susan owns?
    - ❍ A. $25,000
    - ❍ B. $25,550
    - ❍ C. $255,000
    - ❍ D. $255,500

Quick Answer: **314**
Detailed Answer: **316**

12. A participating trust is best described as which of the following?
    - ❍ A. The trust chooses securities that cannot be changed.
    - ❍ B. The participating trust buys shares in mutual funds.
    - ❍ C. The participating trust allows investors to choose the investments.
    - ❍ D. The participating trust pays a set rate of return to the investor.

Quick Answer: **314**
Detailed Answer: **316**

13. Participating trusts are frequently designed to back which of the following products?
    - ❍ A. Derivatives
    - ❍ B. Index options
    - ❍ C. Annuities
    - ❍ D. Bank certificates of deposit

Quick Answer: **314**
Detailed Answer: **316**

Choose from the following real estate investment trusts to answer the next three questions. An answer may be used once, more than once, or not at all.

- ❍ A. Real estate investment trust
- ❍ B. Equity real estate investment trust
- ❍ C. Mortgage real estate investment trust
- ❍ D. Combination real estate investment trust

14. The type of REIT that earns income from rents collected on purchased properties is known as what?

Quick Answer: **314**
Detailed Answer: **316**

15. A REIT that passes on income from purchased loans to investors is considered what?

Quick Answer: **314**
Detailed Answer: **316**

16. Beneficial owners of a trust that derives its income from construction loans and other real estate loans is known as what?

Quick Answer: **314**
Detailed Answer: **316**

Quick Check

17. A management company is a type of investment company that is structured as which of the following?

Quick Answer: 314
Detailed Answer: 316

- ❍ A. Trust
- ❍ B. Corporation
- ❍ C. Partnership
- ❍ D. Tax exempt entity

18. Which of the following statements are true of an underlying portfolio of a management company?

Quick Answer: 314
Detailed Answer: 316

I. It is managed by a board of trustees.

II. It is managed by a board of directors.

III. The portfolio investments are fixed.

IV. The portfolio investments are variable.

- ❍ A. I and III
- ❍ B. I and IV
- ❍ C. II and III
- ❍ D. II and IV

19. Which of the following statements are considered true of a management company?

Quick Answer: 314
Detailed Answer: 316

I. It follows a diversified investment strategy.

II. It follows a nondiversified investment strategy.

III. It can be open ended.

IV. It can be closed end.

- ❍ A. I and III
- ❍ B. II and III
- ❍ C. I, II, and III
- ❍ D. I, II, III, and IV

20. To qualify as diversified, a management company must have all the following except for which one?

Quick Answer: 314
Detailed Answer: 317

- ❍ A. Seventy-five percent of its assets invested in securities
- ❍ B. No more than 5% of its assets invested in the securities of one issuer
- ❍ C. No more than 5% of its assets in cash
- ❍ D. No more than 10% of the voting securities for any one issuer

Quick Check

21. Closed end management companies are capitalized in which of the following ways?

   ❍ A. Through a one-time offering of shares
   ❍ B. Through a continual offering of redeemable shares
   ❍ C. Through a secondary offering of shares
   ❍ D. Through a management fee charged

Quick Answer: 314
Detailed Answer: 317

22. Harold has decided to purchase shares in a well established closed end management company. Which best describes how he purchases the shares?

   ❍ A. He purchases the shares from the fund itself.
   ❍ B. He purchases the shares in the secondary market.
   ❍ C. He purchases the shares from an existing shareholder at the prevailing market price.
   ❍ D. He purchases the shares from an existing shareholder in the secondary market at the prevailing market price.

Quick Answer: 314
Detailed Answer: 317

23. Which of the following statements are considered true regarding management companies?

   I. Open ended management companies are considered exempt securities.

   II. Closed end management companies are considered exempt securities.

   III. Open ended management companies are required to register with the SEC.

   IV. Closed end management companies are required to register with the SEC.

   ❍ A. I only
   ❍ B. I and II
   ❍ C. II and III
   ❍ D. III and IV

Quick Answer: 314
Detailed Answer: 317

Quick Check

24. A closed end management company has an investment objective of safety and preservation of capital. The company wants to change its investment objectives. Which of the following statements is true?

   ❍ A. The investment company is not permitted to change its objectives.
   ❍ B. The investment company can change its objectives without approval.
   ❍ C. The investment company needs the approval of the SEC to change its objectives.
   ❍ D. The investment company needs majority approval of shareholders to change its investment objectives.

Quick Answer: **314**
Detailed Answer: **317**

25. The Investment Company Act of 1940 requires that an investment company with more than 100 shareholders adhere to which of the following?

   I. Register with the Securities and Exchange Commission

   II. Publicly state its investment objectives

   III. Guarantee a minimum rate of return on an investment company

   IV. Issue a prospectus to investors

   ❍ A. I and II
   ❍ B. II and III
   ❍ C. I, II, and III
   ❍ D. I, II, and IV

Quick Answer: **314**
Detailed Answer: **317**

Quick Check Answer Key

1. B

2. D

3. D

4. C

5. A

6. D

7. C

8. C

9. B

10. C

11. B

12. B

13. C

14. B

15. C

16. C

17. B

18. D

19. D

20. C

21. A

22. D

23. D

24. D

25. D

Answers and Explanations

1. **Answer B is correct.** An investment company is chosen by an investor for its professional management offered. Investors do not make the investment choices in the investment company, but rather rely on the expertise of the managers.

2. **Answer D is correct.** High share prices of investment company shares do not offer investors liquidity in the market. Investment company shares can be sold easily because of the large number of investors involved and the fact that the investment company shares are kept at a low price.

3. **Answer D is correct.** A face amount certificate does not typically invest in zero coupon bonds for an investment strategy. It typically invests in high-quality, high-grade Treasury securities such as T-notes and T-bonds and blue chip debt instruments of quality issuers.

4. **Answer C is correct.** A unit investment trust is considered an investment company that is governed by a board of trustees. Because of the trust structure, unit trusts issue shares of beneficial interest to shareholders, as opposed to normal shares of stock.

5. **Answer A is correct.** Shares of beneficial interest represent an investor's interest or ownership of the income generated by an underlying portfolio of securities. The investor does not actually own any of the underlying securities himself.

6. **Answer D is correct.** A fixed unit investment trust purchases a select portfolio of securities, which is fixed for the life of the trust. Securities cannot be changed once they are chosen because they are set for life. At maturity, a fixed UIT is considered self-liquidating because principal payments on the underlying bonds are used to pay back unit holders.

7. **Answer C is correct.** A fixed unit investment trust is considered self-liquidating. As the underlying bonds mature, principal payments are made to the trust first and then used to repay unit holders in the trust, culminating in the liquidation of the trust.

8. **Answer C is correct.** An investor with 10 units of a fixed unit investment trust can redeem his units with the issuing sponsor at all times. Sponsors continuously make a market in the units of their issued trusts.

9. **Answer B is correct.** You compute the net asset value for a unit investment trust by dividing the market value of the underlying trust portfolio by the number of outstanding units in the market.

10. **Answer C is correct.** You compute the net asset value for a unit investment trust by dividing the market value of the underlying portfolio by the number of outstanding units of the trust. In this example, you divide the market value of \$97,500,000 by the number of outstanding units of 100,000 = \$975 per unit. Matt owns 100 units, so the net asset value = \$975 × 100 = \$97,500.
11. **Answer B is correct.** You compute the net asset value for a unit investment trust by dividing the market value of the underlying portfolio by the number of outstanding units of the trust. In this example, you divide the market value of \$153,300,000 by the number of outstanding units of 150,000 = \$1,022 per unit. Susan owns 25 units, so the net asset value = \$1,022 × 25 units = \$25,550.
12. **Answer B is correct.** A participating trust differs from a fixed trust in that its pool of investments is not static. This change is achieved, however, in an indirect manner; the participating trust buys shares in mutual funds, for which investments can change constantly.
13. **Answer C is correct.** Participating trusts are typically used to back annuities, which are investment products that are sold by insurance companies.
14. **Answer B is correct.** Equity real estate investment trusts take equity positions in real estate properties. Unit holders earn income from the rents collected on these properties.
15. **Answer C is correct.** A mortgage real estate investment trust purchases mortgages and construction loans and then passes on the income from these loans to the beneficial owners of the trust.
16. **Answer C is correct.** A mortgage real estate investment trust purchases mortgages and construction loans and then passes on the income from these loans to the beneficial owners of the trust.
17. **Answer B is correct.** A management company is a corporation that issues shares of stock and whose assets consist of one or more portfolios of securities. The directors of a management company actually manage the company's portfolios, making all investment choices for the portfolio.
18. **Answer D is correct.** A management company is structured as a corporation and managed by a board of directors. The investment portfolios of the management company are variable and are determined by the managers of the fund.
19. **Answer D is correct.** A management company can either be diversified or nondiversified in its structure. It can also either be a closed end fund or an open ended fund, depending on the structure of the management company.

20. **Answer C is correct.** A diversified management company is not required to have no more than a maximum of 5% of its assets in cash. It is required to have 75% of its assets in securities, no more than 5% in securities of any one issuer, and no more than 10% of the voting securities of any one issuer.

21. **Answer A is correct.** A closed end management company is capitalized through a one-time offering of shares. The number of shares is established in the prospectus, and once the shares are sold, the company is no longer permitted to sell shares to investors.

22. **Answer D is correct.** Harold has to buy the shares in the secondary market from an existing shareholder at the prevailing market price. A closed end management company issues a fixed number of shares in a one-time offering. After the shares are sold out, investors wanting to invest in the closed end fund must buy the shares in the secondary market from an existing shareholder at the prevailing market price.

23. **Answer D is correct.** Management companies are required to register with the Securities and Exchange Commission, when they issue shares. This requirement includes both open ended and closed end funds, which are not considered exempt securities.

24. **Answer D is correct.** A closed end management company that wants to change its investment strategy is required to receive approval from the majority of shareholders in a proxy vote of the change.

25. **Answer D is correct.** The Investment Company Act of 1940 requires investment companies with more than 100 shareholders to register the offerings with the SEC. Each one must state its investment objectives in its required prospectus to all investors. It cannot guarantee any kind of return to investors.

Quick Check

Mutual Funds

1. The major difference between a closed end management company and a mutual fund is what?

   ❍ A. A closed end management company issues shares continuously and a mutual fund does not.

   ❍ B. A closed end management company issues a one-time offering of shares, and a mutual fund can continuously issue shares.

   ❍ C. A closed end fund is a no-load fund, and mutual funds are load funds.

   ❍ D. A closed end fund can advertise, and mutual funds cannot advertise.

Quick Answer: **325**
Detailed Answer: **326**

2. Which of the following statements are true regarding mutual funds purchased by an investor?

   I. Mutual funds can continuously issue new shares.

   II. Mutual funds redeem shares from investors.

   III. Mutual fund shares are redeemed in the secondary market.

   IV. Mutual funds are considered open ended management companies.

   ❍ A. I and II

   ❍ B. II and III

   ❍ C. I, II, and III

   ❍ D. I, II, and IV

Quick Answer: **325**
Detailed Answer: **326**

3. Which statement is not considered true of a money market fund?

   ❍ A. Money market funds are not considered mutual funds.

   ❍ B. Money market funds invest in money market instruments.

   ❍ C. Money market funds are for highly risk-averse investors.

   ❍ D. Money market funds have a net asset value of $1.

Quick Answer: **325**
Detailed Answer: **326**

Quick Check

4. A mutual fund that is considered a specialized fund includes which of the following?

Quick Answer: **325**
Detailed Answer: **326**

   I. A fund that invests in only transportation stocks

   II. A fund that invests in only Silicon Valley stocks

   III. A fund that invests in only foreign securities

   IV. A fund that invests in only money market instruments

   ❍ A. I and II
   ❍ B. II and III
   ❍ C. I, II, and III
   ❍ D. I, II, III, and IV

5. A tax exempt mutual fund has an investment concentration in which of the following securities?

Quick Answer: **325**
Detailed Answer: **326**

   ❍ A. Government agency debt
   ❍ B. Municipal bond debt
   ❍ C. Treasury debt
   ❍ D. Agency, municipal, and Treasury debt

6. A mutual fund family is best described as which of the following?

Quick Answer: **325**
Detailed Answer: **326**

   ❍ A. All mutual funds that invest in the same securities
   ❍ B. All mutual funds issued by the same investment company
   ❍ C. All mutual funds that continually issue new shares
   ❍ D. All mutual funds that are considered open ended

7. Which statement is not considered true of mutual fund shares that have been issued?

Quick Answer: **325**
Detailed Answer: **326**

   ❍ A. Mutual funds can only issue common stock.
   ❍ B. Mutual funds can issue preferred stock and bonds.
   ❍ C. Mutual funds may not borrow from banks in excess of three times their total assets.
   ❍ D. Mutual funds are nonexempt securities.

8. All the following are considered a violation of SEC rules that pertain to mutual funds except for which one?

Quick Answer: **325**
Detailed Answer: **326**

   ❍ A. An investor purchases a mutual fund without receiving a prospectus.
   ❍ B. A mutual fund changes its investment objective without shareholder approval.
   ❍ C. A mutual fund does not issue an annual report to shareholders.
   ❍ D. A mutual fund issues only common stock to shareholders.

Quick Check

9. Which statements are considered true of the role of an investment advisor in a mutual fund?

Quick Answer: 325
Detailed Answer: 326

I. They are appointed by the board of directors.

II. They choose the investments in the fund's portfolio.

III. They are not permitted to stray from the fund's stated investment objectives.

IV. The advisor must be approved by the fund's shareholders.

❍ A. I and II
❍ B. II and III
❍ C. I, II, and III
❍ D. I, II, III, and IV

10. The investment company that manages a mutual fund is considered which of the following?

Quick Answer: 325
Detailed Answer: 327

I. The fund sponsor

II. The fund underwriter

III. The custodian

IV. The registrar

❍ A. I and II
❍ B. II and III
❍ C. III
❍ D. IV

11. Mutual fund advertising costs have which of the following characteristics?

Quick Answer: 325
Detailed Answer: 327

I. The shareholders pay advertising costs.

II. The underwriter pays advertising costs (if not 12b-1).

III. 12b-1 funds cannot pass on advertising costs to shareholders.

IV. 12b-1 funds can pass on advertising costs to shareholders.

❍ A. I and III
❍ B. I and IV
❍ C. II and III
❍ D. II and IV

Quick Check

Choose from the following choices to answer the next four questions. An answer may be used once, more than once, or not at all.

❍ A. Custodian
❍ B. Transfer agent
❍ C. Registrar
❍ D. Auditor

12. The bank or trust company that is charged with keeping a mutual funds cash and securities is known as what?

Quick Answer: **325**
Detailed Answer: **327**

13. The area of a mutual fund that issues new shares and cancels redeemed shares is known as what?

Quick Answer: **325**
Detailed Answer: **327**

14. The area of a mutual fund that receives payments from shareholders and disburses payments such as dividends to shareholders is what?

Quick Answer: **325**
Detailed Answer: **327**

15. The area that prevents investment advisors and board of directors from exaggerating the performance of a fund's portfolio is what?

Quick Answer: **325**
Detailed Answer: **327**

16. Which statements are true of the sponsor or underwriter of a mutual fund?

I. They market funds to the public.

II. They sell shares at a markup.

III. They safeguard fund assets.

IV. They cancel redeemed shares.

❍ A. I and II
❍ B. II and III
❍ C. I, II, and III
❍ D. I, II, III, and IV

Quick Answer: **325**
Detailed Answer: **327**

17. A mutual fund that is permitted to pass advertising costs on to its shareholders is known as what type of fund?

❍ A. A no-load fund
❍ B. A 12b-1 fund
❍ C. A 1099 fund
❍ D. A 401K fund

Quick Answer: **325**
Detailed Answer: **327**

Quick Check

18. A mutual fund that markets and redeems its shares directly to investors is best described as what?

Quick Answer: **325**
Detailed Answer: **327**

- ❍ A. A load fund
- ❍ B. A no-load fund
- ❍ C. A 12b-1 fund
- ❍ D. A 401K fund

19. John agreed to purchase $1000 worth of a mutual funds shares every month, regardless of their net asset value. What type of purchase plan is this considered?

Quick Answer: **325**
Detailed Answer: **327**

- ❍ A. Dollar cost averaging plan
- ❍ B. Dollar averaging plan
- ❍ C. A net purchase plan
- ❍ D. Share cost purchase plan

20. Which of the following statements are true of a dollar cost averaging plan?

Quick Answer: **325**
Detailed Answer: **328**

I. Dollar cost averaging results in a lower per-share cost.

II. Dollar cost averaging results in a higher per-share cost.

III. Overall you purchase more shares.

IV. Overall you purchase fewer shares.

- ❍ A. I and III
- ❍ B. I and IV
- ❍ C. II and III
- ❍ D. II and IV

21. The net asset value for a mutual fund is $25.75, and the public offering price is set at $27.55. What is the sales charge on this fund?

Quick Answer: **325**
Detailed Answer: **328**

- ❍ A. 6%
- ❍ B. 6.5%
- ❍ C. 7%
- ❍ D. 7.5%

22. The net asset value for a mutual fund is $19.57, and the public offering price is set at $21.23. What is the sales charge on this fund?

Quick Answer: **325**
Detailed Answer: **328**

- ❍ A. 6%
- ❍ B. 7.5%
- ❍ C. 7.8%
- ❍ D. 8.48%

Quick Check

23. Which of the following statements is true regarding the net asset value on mutual fund shares?

Quick Answer: 325
Detailed Answer: 328

I. Net asset value is computed at the beginning of each trade day.

II. Net asset value is computed at the end of each trade day.

III. Mutual funds charge investors the forward price.

IV. Mutual funds charge investors the spot price.

- ❍ A. I and III
- ❍ B. I and IV
- ❍ C. II and III
- ❍ D. II and IV

24. The public offering price for mutual fund shares has which of the following characteristics?

Quick Answer: 325
Detailed Answer: 328

I. It is the net asset value plus the sales charge for the fund.

II. The public offering price is always higher than the net asset value.

III. The sales charge is computed by dividing the NAV by the POP.

IV. Sales charges are expressed in percentages.

- ❍ A. I and II
- ❍ B. II and III
- ❍ C. I, II, and III
- ❍ D. I, II, III, and IV

25. A mutual fund allows investors a sales charge discount for every $5000 that is invested in the fund. These incremental discounts are called what?

Quick Answer: 325
Detailed Answer: 328

- ❍ A. Fund discounts
- ❍ B. Breakpoints
- ❍ C. Letter of discount
- ❍ D. Accumulation right

Quick Check Answer Key

1. B
2. D
3. A
4. C
5. B
6. B
7. B
8. D
9. D
10. A
11. D
12. A
13. B
14. B
15. D
16. A
17. B
18. B
19. A
20. A
21. C
22. D
23. C
24. D
25. B

Answers and Explanations

1. **Answer B is correct.** The major difference between a closed end management company and a mutual fund is that a closed end management company issues shares through a one-time offering, and a mutual fund continuously issues new shares to investors.

2. **Answer D is correct.** Mutual funds are considered open ended management companies that can continuously issue and redeem shares for investors. If the investor wants to purchase or redeem her shares, she does so from the fund itself and not in the secondary market.

3. **Answer A is correct.** A money market fund is an income mutual fund for extremely risk-averse investors. The fund has a constant NAV of $1 per share, with additional shares added for dividends paid. The fund invests only in money market instruments such as T-bills, jumbo CDs, and commercial paper.

4. **Answer C is correct.** A specialized fund has at least 25% of its assets invested in specific industries such as transportation stocks or geographic regions such as Silicon Valley stocks or foreign stocks. Money market instruments are characteristic of money market funds.

5. **Answer B is correct.** Tax exempt funds invest primarily in municipal securities that generate income which is considered triple tax exempt. Investors do not pay any federal, state, or local taxes on the income generated from the fund.

6. **Answer B is correct.** A mutual fund family contain funds that are all sponsored by the same investment company. They do not have to have the same investment concentration or objectives to be considered part of the fund family.

7. **Answer B is correct.** Mutual funds are nonexempt securities that are only permitted to issue common shares of stock. They are prohibited from issuing preferred stock or bonds when selling shares to investors. They can borrow from banks at a maximum of three times their total assets.

8. **Answer D is correct.** A mutual fund that attempts to issue any kinds of securities other than common stock is in violation of SEC regulations. Preferred stock and bonds are not permitted to be issued for sale by mutual funds to investors.

9. **Answer D is correct.** An investment advisor is appointed by the board of directors and approved by the shareholders of the fund. The investment advisor selects the securities that compose the fund's portfolio. He or she cannot stray from the stated investment objective of the fund, and any changes in the investment objective of the fund must be approved by a majority of shareholders.

10. **Answer A is correct.** A mutual fund's underwriter or sponsor is the investment company that is managing the mutual fund.
11. **Answer D is correct.** A mutual fund is not permitted to pass on advertising costs to shareholders unless it is classified as a 12b-1 mutual fund. Named after the section of the Investment Company act of 1940, a 12b-1 fund is permitted to pass on advertising costs to shareholders in the sum of .75% of assets to pay for promotional and marketing expenses.
12. **Answer A is correct.** A mutual fund's custodian is typically a bank or trust company charged with keeping the fund's cash and any certificates associated with the fund's securities portfolio.
13. **Answer B is correct.** Transfer agents monitor the purchase and redemption of mutual fund shares by investors by issuing new shares and canceling redeemed shares. Transfer agents receive payments made by investors and disburse payments, such as dividends to shareholders.
14. **Answer B is correct.** In addition to monitoring the purchase and redemption of mutual fund shares, transfer agents also receive payments made by investors and disburse payments such as dividends to shareholders.
15. **Answer D is correct.** An auditor is an independent accounting firm that compiles balance sheets, income statements, and a list of all securities holdings held by the fund. Auditors prevent investment advisors and boards of directors from exaggerating the performance of the mutual funds portfolio.
16. **Answer A is correct.** A sponsor or underwriter of a mutual fund is the investment company that is managing the mutual fund. It markets funds to the public as well as sells shares at a markup to investors.
17. **Answer B is correct.** A 12b-1 mutual fund is named after the section of the Investment Company Act of 1940 that permits certain classified mutual funds to pass on advertising costs to investors, in the form of fees charged.
18. **Answer B is correct.** A no-load fund is a mutual fund that sells shares directly to the investor. No-load funds also redeem shares directly, without the use of an intermediary. As a result of their actions, no-load funds do not charge investors a sales charge when purchasing shares.
19. **Answer A is correct.** A dollar cost averaging plan is when an investor agrees to purchase the same dollar amount each period in the fund. For example, an investor might agree to purchase $100 each month in a fund, regardless of its net asset value. As the price of the mutual fund shares fluctuate, the investor purchases a varying number of shares each month but at a constant dollar amount invested.

20. **Answer A is correct**. Dollar cost averaging over time results in a lower per-share cost and consequently the purchase of more shares. The investor buys more shares when the price is low and fewer when the price is high.

21. **Answer C is correct**. To compute the sales charge on a fund with a NAV of $25.75 and a public offering price of $27.55, you determine the difference between the NAV and the POP to get $1.80. This is the total sales charge per share. You then divide the sales charge of $1.80 by the NAV of $25.75 to get a 7% sales charge.

22. **Answer D is correct**. To compute the sales charge on a fund with a NAV of $19.57 and a public offering price of $21.23, you determine the difference between the NAV and POP to get $1.66. This is the total sales charge per share. You then divide the sales charge of $1.66 by the NAV of $19.57 to get an 8.48% sales charge.

23. **Answer C is correct**. The net asset value for mutual funds is calculated at the end of a trading day. Mutual funds charge investors the forward price that is the NAV at the close of the day on which fund shares are purchased.

24. **Answer D is correct**. The public offering price is the cost to an investor of purchasing a load fund share. The POP includes the fund's NAV plus the sales charge. The POP is always higher than the NAV because the sales charge is added on. The sales charge on a mutual fund is expressed as a percentage and computed as 1 – NAV ÷ POP.

25. **Answer B is correct**. Breakpoints are given to investors as a sales charge discount for bulk purchases of the mutual fund shares. As each incremental amount is met, the sales breakpoint charge is lowered accordingly. All investors must be offered these breakpoints, or the offer is invalid.

Direct Participation Programs

Quick Check

1. Which of the following statements are true about a direct participation program?

   I. Direct participation programs are not considered taxable entities.

   II. Direct participation program income is considered nontaxable to partners.

   III. Direct participation program income is considered taxable to partners.

   IV. Investors in DPPs receive a pro-rata share of profits or losses from the program.

   ❍ A. I and III
   ❍ B. II and IV
   ❍ C. I, III, and IV
   ❍ D. III and IV

Quick Answer: **337**
Detailed Answer: **338**

2. Income produced from a direct participation program has all the following characteristics except for which one?

   ❍ A. Ninety percent of DPP income must be passed on to partners to avoid corporate taxes.
   ❍ B. DPP income is taxed at the personal level of the partners.
   ❍ C. DPPs enjoy the Pipeline Principle of taxation on income.
   ❍ D. A DPP can flow income or losses to partners.

Quick Answer: **337**
Detailed Answer: **338**

Quick Check

3. A limited partnership has which of the following characteristics?

Quick Answer: 337
Detailed Answer: 338

I. The limited partnership can have only one limited partner.

II. The limited partnership can have more than one limited partner.

III. The limited partnership can have several general partners.

IV. The limited partnership can have only one general partner.

- A. I and III
- B. I and IV
- C. II and III
- D. II and IV

4. A general partner of a limited partnership has which of the following characteristics?

Quick Answer: 337
Detailed Answer: 338

I. He has limited liability in the partnership.

II. He has unlimited liability in the partnership.

III. He is the manager of the DPP.

IV. He brings new limited partners into the DPP.

- A. I and III
- B. I and IV
- C. II, III, and IV
- D. II and III

5. Which of the following roles are general partners of direct participation programs permitted to take on?

Quick Answer: 337
Detailed Answer: 338

I. The syndicator of the DPP

II. The underwriter for the DPP

III. The partnership manager of the DPP

IV. The property manager of a DPP involved in real estate

- A. I and II
- B. II and III
- C. I, II, and III
- D. I, II, III, and IV

Quick Check

6. Which of the following statements are true of the role of a general partner in a direct participation program?

Quick Answer: 337
Detailed Answer: 338

I. A corporation can serve as a general partner.

II. Only an individual can act as a general partner.

III. Corporate general partners have limited liability.

IV. Corporate general partners have unlimited liability.

❍ A. I and III
❍ B. I and IV
❍ C. II only
❍ D. I only

7. An investor has invested 10% of her net worth in a DPP as a limited partner. The investor becomes active in the day-to-day operations of the limited partnership. How does this affect the investment that the limited partner made?

Quick Answer: 337
Detailed Answer: 338

❍ A. The investment is unaffected.
❍ B. The investor can lose a maximum of her 10% investment.
❍ C. The investor exposes herself to unlimited liability of her net worth.
❍ D. The investor is now protected from the liability of losing her 10% investment.

8. A limited partner in a direct participation program who invests in oil exploration wants to also invest in another DPP that also involves oil exploration. Which of the following statements is considered true of this action?

Quick Answer: 337
Detailed Answer: 339

❍ A. The limited partner is not permitted to invest in another DPP that competes against the original DPP.
❍ B. The limited partner loses the limited liability if she invests in a second DPP that competes against the original DPP.
❍ C. The limited partner is not restricted from investing in a competing DPP.
❍ D. The limited partner becomes a general partner if she invests in another DPP that competes against the original DPP.

Quick Check

9. A general partner in a direct participation program decides to invest in a competing partnership. Which statement is considered true of this action?

   - ❍ A. The general partner by doing so becomes a limited partner.
   - ❍ B. The general partner is not permitted to invest in a competing enterprise.
   - ❍ C. The general partner is permitted to invest in a competing enterprise.
   - ❍ D. The general partner must put up the same investment in the DPP that he was the general partner in originally.

Quick Answer: **337**
Detailed Answer: **339**

10. Which statements are considered true of a certificate of limited partnership for a DPP?

    I. All limited partners must sign the legal agreement.

    II. The general partner is not required to sign the legal agreement.

    III. It highlights how the DPP is financed.

    IV. It highlights how the DPP is managed.

    - ❍ A. I and II
    - ❍ B. I and III
    - ❍ C. I, III, and IV
    - ❍ D. I, II, III, and IV

Quick Answer: **337**
Detailed Answer: **339**

11. Which of the following actions require that a certificate of limited partnership be amended for a DPP?

    I. The addition of another limited partner

    II. The additional infusion of capital by a partner

    III. Changes in the structure of the DPP

    IV. The addition of another general partner

    - ❍ A. I and II
    - ❍ B. II and III
    - ❍ C. I, II, and III
    - ❍ D. I, II, III, and IV

Quick Answer: **337**
Detailed Answer: **339**

Quick Check

12. A limited partner wants to sell an investment stake in a DPP to a new investor. Which statement is true of this action?

❍ A. The limited partner is not permitted to sell his investment.

❍ B. The limited partner needs the approval of all the other limited partners to do so.

❍ C. The limited partner needs the approval of the general partner to do so.

❍ D. The limited partner has no restrictions on the sale of his investment in the DPP.

Quick Answer: 337
Detailed Answer: 339

13. Which of the following events dissolves a DPP limited partnership should one occur?

I. Death of a principal of the DPP

II. Withdrawal of a principal in the DPP

III. Retirement of a principal of a DPP

IV. The expulsion of a principal of a DPP

❍ A. I and II

❍ B. II and III

❍ C. I, II, and III

❍ D. I, II, III, and IV

Quick Answer: 337
Detailed Answer: 339

14. Which of the following corporate characteristics are typically not followed by limited partnerships?

I. Continuity of life or perpetuity of a corporation

II. Free transferability of investor shares

III. Limited financial liability

IV. Centralized management

❍ A. I and II

❍ B. I and III

❍ C. II and IV

❍ D. III and IV

Quick Answer: 337
Detailed Answer: 339

15. Which of the following is not a common type of direct participation program?

❍ A. Cattle breeding

❍ B. Oil and gas production

❍ C. Equipment leasing

❍ D. Gold and silver production

Quick Answer: 337
Detailed Answer: 339

Quick Check

16. All the following are advantages of a raw land direct participation program except for which one?
    - ❍ A. Raw land has a strong potential for capital appreciation.
    - ❍ B. The raw land purchased can be depreciated.
    - ❍ C. Property can be developed in adjacent areas, making the raw land increase in value.
    - ❍ D. Raw land has no management requirement.

Quick Answer: **337**
Detailed Answer: **340**

Choose from the following direct participation programs to answer the next three questions. An answer may be used once, more than once, or not at all.

- ❍ A. Cattle programs
- ❍ B. Oil and gas programs
- ❍ C. Equipment leasing programs
- ❍ D. Real estate programs

17. The type of direct participation program that invests in the purchase, development, or construction of a variety of properties is known as what?

Quick Answer: **337**
Detailed Answer: **340**

18. The type of direct participation program that uses operating and full payout lease programs is known as what?

Quick Answer: **337**
Detailed Answer: **340**

19. The type of direct participation program that purchases heavy equipment and machinery is known as what?

Quick Answer: **337**
Detailed Answer: **340**

20. Most direct participation programs are issued under which type of offering to investors?
    - ❍ A. All or none offering
    - ❍ B. Minimum/maximum offering
    - ❍ C. Best efforts offering
    - ❍ D. Firm commitment offering

Quick Answer: **337**
Detailed Answer: **340**

Quick Check

21. Which of the following statements are considered true of direct participation programs?

    I. Direct participation programs are typically done through a minimum/maximum offering.

    II. Investors must meet a suitability requirement to invest in a DPP.

    III. A DPP requires a prospectus for investors.

    IV. Most DPPs are considered tax-sensitive programs for investors.

❍ A. I and II
❍ B. II and III
❍ C. I, II, and III
❍ D. I, II, III, and IV

Quick Answer: **337**
Detailed Answer: **340**

22. A direct participation program that is known as a blind pool investment has which of the following characteristics?

    I. The general partner indicates the type of investment but not the specific investments made.

    II. The general partner indicates the specific investments that are made.

    III. The limited partners choose the investments to be made.

    IV. The Limited partners receive income from the program, whether or not the program is profitable.

❍ A. I only
❍ B. II and III
❍ C. I and IV
❍ D. III and IV

Quick Answer: **337**
Detailed Answer: **341**

Quick Check

23. Which of the following statements are considered true of a direct participation program?

Quick Answer: 337
Detailed Answer: 340

I. Investors must meet suitability requirements.

II. DPPs are considered illiquid.

III. DPPs are considered tax-sensitive securities.

IV. A DPP must issue a prospectus.

❍ A. I and II
❍ B. II and III
❍ C. I, II, and III
❍ D. I, II, III, and IV

24. A general partner in a direct participation program can earn income in which of the following ways?

Quick Answer: 337
Detailed Answer: 341

I. Sales commission as an underwriter

II. Acquisition fees for the purchase of assets

III. Financing fees for arranging bank loans

IV. Management fees for managing the DPP

❍ A. I and II
❍ B. II and III
❍ C. I, II, and III
❍ D. I, II, III, and IV

25. Any losses generated by a direct participation program and passed on to limited partners are affected in which manner?

Quick Answer: 337
Detailed Answer: 341

❍ A. Losses realized in a DPP can only offset passive income.
❍ B. Losses realized in a DPP can offset ordinary income.
❍ C. Losses realized in a DPP can only offset capital gains.
❍ D. Losses realized in a DPP can only be used in the year the loss was realized.

Quick Check Answer Key

1. C
2. A
3. C
4. C
5. D
6. A
7. C
8. C
9. B
10. C
11. D
12. C
13. D
14. A
15. D
16. B
17. D
18. C
19. C
20. B
21. D
22. A
23. D
24. D
25. A

Answers and Explanations

1. **Answer C is correct**. According to U.S. tax laws, a direct participation program set up as a partnership is not considered a taxable entity. An investor in a DPP receives a pro-rated share of any income or losses generated by the program. Income generated by a DPP partnership flows directly to partners, who are then taxed as individuals on their personal tax filings.

2. **Answer A is correct**. A direct participation program does not have to pass on any percentage of its income to avoid corporate taxation (unlike a mutual fund). Because DPPs are set up as limited partnerships, they are considered nontaxable entities. Any income or losses generated from a DPP is passed on to partners and then taxed at the personal level of the individual.

3. **Answer C is correct**. A limited partnership is a business venture that consists of at least one general partner and at least one limited partner. In practice, a limited partnership can have both more than one limited partner and more than one general partner.

4. **Answer C is correct**. A general partner of a limited partnership is considered the manager of the direct participation program. He is subject to unlimited liability in the DPP and responsible for bringing new limited partners into the investment program.

5. **Answer D is correct**. A general partner in a direct participation program can take on numerous roles, depending on her ability. She can be the syndicator or the person responsible for assembling the DPP. She can choose to be the underwriter of the DPP or the person responsible for marketing the program to potential investors. In most cases, the general partner takes on the management of the DPP program. She makes the business decisions for the DPP. With a real estate DPP, the general partner is also the individual responsible for managing any properties purchased.

6. **Answer A is correct**. A corporation can act as a general partner of a direct participation program after it meets certain requirements. As a general partner, a corporation experiences limited liability only up to the amount of its total corporate assets.

7. **Answer C is correct**. A limited partner who attempts to become involved in the day-to-day operations of a direct participation program runs the risk of losing her limited liability umbrella. When an individual limited partner takes on general partner duties, she exposes herself to unlimited liability of her net worth.

8. **Answer C is correct**. Limited partners in a direct participation program are not under any restrictions to prevent them from investing in competing programs or investments. Only general partners are prohibited from investing in a competing investment of the DPPs they are managing. This is considered a conflict of interest and under the certificate of partnership is prohibited.
9. **Answer B is correct**. A general partner has a fiduciary role in a direct participation program and is required to manage another person's funds prudently. To invest in another program with the same focus as the DPP that he manages constitutes a conflict of interest and is not permitted.
10. **Answer C is correct**. A certificate of limited partnership is a legal agreement that is required to be signed by all participants in the program. This includes the limited partners and the general partners. The certificate includes how the DPP is financed and how the DPP is managed.
11. **Answer D is correct**. A certificate of limited partnership is required to be amended if there are any significant changes to the limited partnership. This includes the addition of any new limited or general partners or a new infusion of capital by an original partner. In addition, if the partnership structure changes, the certificate must be amended.
12. **Answer C is correct**. Most limited partnerships established as a DPP require the approval of the general partner if any of the limited partners want to sell or assign their interest in the limited partnership.
13. **Answer D is correct**. A limited partnership does not have continuity of life when established. If a partner should die, retire, withdraw, or be expelled from the partnership, the limited partnership under the certificate of limited partnership is dissolved.
14. **Answer A is correct**. The IRS requires that a limited partnership have only two of the four characteristics of a corporation. The most common characteristics that a limited partnership has which differ from a corporation is continuity of life and free transferability of shares. Corporations have an unending life regardless of whether a founder or CEO dies or retires. Limited partnerships are dissolved under these conditions. Corporate stock can be freely traded by shareholders. Limited partnership stock needs the approval of the general partner to be sold or assigned by a limited partner. Limited financial liability and centralized management are typically the two characteristics that corporations and limited partnerships have in common.
15. **Answer D is correct**. Gold and silver production is not a common type of limited partnership. Limited partnerships are commonly established in such areas of business as real estate development, equipment leasing, oil and gas production, and raw land deals.

16. **Answer B is correct.** Raw land is a common type of limited partnership that invests in undeveloped land with the hope of future capital appreciation, if the land or adjacent land is developed. Land is not permitted to be depreciated by the IRS, so that is not a benefit of a raw land DPP.

17. **Answer D is correct.** A DPP that is created to purchase, develop, or construct a variety of properties is typically known as a real estate program. Those properties can include hotels, shopping centers, apartment buildings, and office buildings.

18. **Answer C is correct.** Equipment leasing DPP programs commonly focus on transportation or construction heavy equipment. These types of direct participation programs commonly use operating and full payout leases when leasing the heavy equipment.

19. **Answer C is correct.** Equipment leasing programs purchase heavy equipment and machinery and then lease them out. The program employs operating leases and full payout leases when leasing the equipment.

20. **Answer B is correct.** Most direct participation programs are sold through underwriters that arrange the offering under minimum/maximum agreements. In a minimum/maximum offering, the DPP gives the underwriter a certain amount of time to raise a pre-established minimum amount of capital. If the underwriter fails to do so, the underwriting is cancelled and the escrowed funds are returned to the qualified investors.

21. **Answer D is correct.** Direct participation programs are typically done through a minimum/maximum offering, where a minimum sales amount of the offering must be met for the program to continue. All investors purchasing a DPP must meet a suitability requirement that pertains to their financial condition to take part in the investment. The SEC requires that a DPP issue a prospectus and follow disclosure rules to potential investors. Because most DPPs are tax sensitive, they are purchased by wealthy investors looking for tax relief.

22. **Answer A is correct.** A limited partnership requires a prospectus that specifies what types of investments the program intends to make. In a blind pool investment, the general partner indicates what type of investments are made (such as oil and gas exploration) but not the specific assets to be purchased (such as land rights in Alaska).

23. **Answer D is correct.** A direct participation programs is required to issue a prospectus by the Securities and Exchange Commission. Investors purchasing a DPP must meet suitability requirements about their financial ability to handle an illiquid investment such as a DPP. Most investors in DPPs are wealthy individuals looking for tax relief, which is common to these tax-sensitive securities.

24. **Answer D is correct.** General partners can earn income from direct participation programs through a series of fees. They can include sales commissions if the general partner acts as an underwriter. They can also earn acquisition fees for the purchase of the DPP's assets, as well as financing fees for arranging bank loans. General partners also earn management fees for managing the assets and investments of the DPP.

25. **Answer A is correct.** Losses realized by a direct participation program and passed on to limited partners can only offset passive income. Passive income is that income from any program investment in which the investor does not participate in the daily management of the business venture.

Quick Check

Annuities

1. Which of the following are characteristics of annuities purchased by an investor?

Quick Answer: **351**
Detailed Answer: **352**

   I. An annuity is a contract between an insurance company and a customer.

   II. Annuities are considered tax deferred.

   III. The customer hopes to receive a greater amount than he paid into the annuity.

   IV. Annuities are primarily used for retirement accounts.

   ❍ A. I and II
   ❍ B. II and III
   ❍ C. I, II, and III
   ❍ D. I, II, III, and IV

2. All the following are characteristics of an annuity except for which one?

Quick Answer: **351**
Detailed Answer: **352**

   ❍ A. An insurance company creates a participating trust to collect payments from customers.
   ❍ B. The participating trust chooses a unit investment trust to reflect the investment objectives of the client base.
   ❍ C. Customers of the insurance company send payments to the trust created.
   ❍ D. The trust places customer payments in a separate account.

Quick Check

3. Which of the following statements are true of a separate account established for an annuity?

   I. Investor payments to an annuity are placed in a separate account.

   II. The separate account must be registered with the Securities and Exchange Commission.

   III. Annuity funds cannot be combined with other assets of the insurance company.

   IV. A trustee elected by the annuitants manages the separate account.

   ❍ A. I and II
   ❍ B. II and III
   ❍ C. I, II, and III
   ❍ D. I, II, III, and IV

Quick Answer: **351**
Detailed Answer: **352**

4. Sarah receives $1000 in dividends and interest payments for the year in an annuity that she purchased for her retirement. How are these payments taxed?

   ❍ A. They are taxed as ordinary income.
   ❍ B. They are considered tax-deferred income.
   ❍ C. They are considered tax-exempt income.
   ❍ D. They are taxed as short-term capital gains.

Quick Answer: **351**
Detailed Answer: **352**

5. The type of annuity that guarantees the investor a stated rate of return on her investment is known as what?

   ❍ A. Variable annuity
   ❍ B. Fixed annuity
   ❍ C. Life annuity
   ❍ D. Period certain annuity

Quick Answer: **351**
Detailed Answer: **352**

Quick Check

6. A fixed annuity has which of the following characteristics for an investor?

Quick Answer: 351
Detailed Answer: 352

 I. It guarantees the customer a stated return on his investment.

 II. The risk on the annuity is borne by the insurance company.

 III. The risk on the annuity is borne by the annuitant.

 IV. Fixed annuities are attractive to aggressive investors.

- ❍ A. I and II
- ❍ B. I and III
- ❍ C. I, III, and IV
- ❍ D. I, II, and IV

7. An investor purchases an annuity that has seen a rate of return over the past three years of 19%, 23%, and 34%. This is characteristic of which type of annuity?

Quick Answer: 351
Detailed Answer: 352

- ❍ A. Fixed annuity
- ❍ B. Variable annuity
- ❍ C. Separate annuity
- ❍ D. Life annuity

8. Joseph wants to purchase an annuity for his retirement that will pay him an above-average payout. He is an aggressive investor who is willing to take chances. What type of annuity should he purchase?

Quick Answer: 351
Detailed Answer: 352

- ❍ A. Variable annuity
- ❍ B. Fixed annuity
- ❍ C. Life annuity
- ❍ D. Separate annuity

9. An investor purchased a fixed annuity that guarantees an 8% rate of return to the client. The fixed annuity purchased generates a rate of return of 17% for the year. How is the return distributed?

Quick Answer: 351
Detailed Answer: 353

- ❍ A. The investor receives an 8% rate of return.
- ❍ B. The investor receives a 17% rate of return.
- ❍ C. The investor receives a 9% rate of return.
- ❍ D. The investor receives a 25% rate of return.

Quick Check

10. An investor purchased a variable annuity to fund her retirement. Which statements are true of the annuity purchased?

    I. The risk of the annuity is borne by the annuitant.

    II. The risk of the annuity is borne by the insurance company.

    III. The rate of return on the annuity is guaranteed.

    IV. The rate of return on the annuity is not guaranteed.

    ❍ A. I and III
    ❍ B. I and IV
    ❍ C. II and III
    ❍ D. II and IV

Quick Answer: **351**
Detailed Answer: **353**

11. George purchases a variable annuity for a lump sum purchase price of $10,000. What is the maximum sales charge on his purchase?

    ❍ A. $500
    ❍ B. $750
    ❍ C. $850
    ❍ D. $1000

Quick Answer: **351**
Detailed Answer: **353**

12. An assumed interest rate (AIR) on an annuity has all the following characteristics except for which one?

    ❍ A. It is a guaranteed rate of return offered on the annuity.
    ❍ B. It will be less than the actual expected return of the annuity.
    ❍ C. The AIR is found in the annuity's prospectus.
    ❍ D. It is based on the historical performance of the securities in the annuity's portfolio.

Quick Answer: **351**
Detailed Answer: **353**

13. The eventual payout of an annuity to an investor is determined by which of the following methods?

    ❍ A. By the total value of the investment paid into the annuity
    ❍ B. By the number of accumulation units the investor purchased
    ❍ C. By the net asset value of the annuity fund
    ❍ D. By the total value of the investment made, plus any dividends paid

Quick Answer: **351**
Detailed Answer: **353**

Quick Check

14. Which of the following statements are considered true of accumulation units in an annuity?

Quick Answer: 351
Detailed Answer: 353

I. Accumulation units represent a portion of the value of a variable annuity's underlying security's portfolio.

II. Accumulation units are part of the separate account of the annuity.

III. The value of the accumulation units varies.

IV. Monthly payments made by a customer add to accumulation units owned.

- ❍ A. I and II
- ❍ B. II and III
- ❍ C. I, II, and III
- ❍ D. I, II, III, and IV

15. An investor purchased 400 accumulation units of a separate account in an annuity. Which statements are true of the purchase?

Quick Answer: 351
Detailed Answer: 354

I. The value of the accumulation units remains constant.

II. The value of the accumulation units varies.

III. An investor is limited to the number of accumulation units she may purchase in an annuity.

IV. The accumulation units are used for eventual payout computation.

- ❍ A. I and III
- ❍ B. II and IV
- ❍ C. I, III, and IV
- ❍ D. II, III, and IV

16. The net asset value of an accumulation unit is computed by which of the following?

Quick Answer: 351
Detailed Answer: 354

- ❍ A. Market value of assets ÷ number of accumulation units issued
- ❍ B. Market value of assets ÷ number of accumulation units redeemed
- ❍ C. Market value of assets – liabilities ÷ number of accumulation units issued
- ❍ D. Market value of assets – liabilities ÷ number of accumulation units redeemed

Quick Check

17. When an insurance company converts accumulation units of an annuity into annuity units to determine a customer payout, this process is known as what?
   - ❍ A. Distribution
   - ❍ B. Annuitization
   - ❍ C. Securitization
   - ❍ D. Cost basis

Quick Answer: **351**
Detailed Answer: **354**

18. When an annuity matures, an insurance company uses which of the following to best determine the annuitant's payout?

   I. The life expectancy of the annuitant

   II. The number of accumulation units held

   III. Actuarial tables for the annuitant

   IV. The distribution process chosen by the annuitant

   - ❍ A. I and II
   - ❍ B. II and III
   - ❍ C. I, II, and III
   - ❍ D. I, II, III, and IV

Quick Answer: **351**
Detailed Answer: **354**

19. Under a mortality guarantee in an annuity contract, an annuitant receives payments from his annuity in which of the following?
   - ❍ A. He receives payments until all accumulation units are paid.
   - ❍ B. He receives payments until accumulation units meet the time period agreed upon.
   - ❍ C. He receives payments for as long as he lives.
   - ❍ D. He receives payments for the same amount of time he paid into the annuity.

Quick Answer: **351**
Detailed Answer: **354**

20. Kelvin purchased a variable annuity contract with a mortality guarantee. When he is 62 years old, his annuity matures, and he begins receiving $2000 monthly payments from the insurance company. How long do these payments last?
   - ❍ A. Until the accumulation units run out
   - ❍ B. Until the portfolio value is exhausted
   - ❍ C. Until the death of the annuitant
   - ❍ D. For the same number of years that he paid into the annuity

Quick Answer: **351**
Detailed Answer: **354**

Quick Check

21. An individual began receiving distribution from an annuity on a starting date when he was 57 years old. How is the distribution of the annuity payments taxed?

Quick Answer: 351
Detailed Answer: 354

- ❍ A. As ordinary income
- ❍ B. As tax-exempt income
- ❍ C. As ordinary income with a 10% early withdrawal penalty
- ❍ D. As a long-term capital gain

22. An individual invested $2000 for 20 years into a nontax qualified annuity and began receiving distribution payments at the age of 60 years old. How are the distribution payments taxed to the annuitant?

Quick Answer: 351
Detailed Answer: 355

- ❍ A. The distribution is taxed as ordinary income.
- ❍ B. The distribution is taxed as ordinary income with a 10% penalty for early withdrawal.
- ❍ C. The initial payments are tax exempt, and the remaining distribution is taxed as ordinary income.
- ❍ D. The initial payments are taxed as ordinary income, and the remaining distribution is tax exempt.

23. An investor contributed $5000 per year for 20 years into a nontax qualified annuity, and upon maturity, the annuity has accumulation units totaling $250,000. He begins receiving a distribution from his annuity at age 65. Which of the following statements are true of the annuity?

Quick Answer: 351
Detailed Answer: 355

I. The cost basis for the annuity is $100,000, and the investment basis is $150,000.

II. The cost basis for the annuity is $150,000, and the investment basis of the annuity is $100,000.

III. The investment basis is taxable, and the cost basis is tax exempt.

IV. The investment basis is tax exempt, and the cost basis is taxable.

- ❍ A. I and III
- ❍ B. I and IV
- ❍ C. II and III
- ❍ D. II and IV

Quick Check

24. An investor elected to take a lump-sum distribution from his maturing annuity. Which of the following statements are true of the distribution?

Quick Answer: 351
Detailed Answer: 355

I. The annuitant receives the full value of the separate account as payout.

II. The annuitant can purchase a fixed annuity with the lump-sum payout.

III. The annuitant can receive fixed payments from the fixed annuity.

IV. The annuitant can receive variable payments from the fixed annuity.

- ❍ A. I and II
- ❍ B. II and III
- ❍ C. I, II, and III
- ❍ D. I, II, III, and IV

25. An annuity that pays an annuitant for life but also specifies a minimum period over which payments are made is considered what?

Quick Answer: 351
Detailed Answer: 355

- ❍ A. Life annuity
- ❍ B. Life annuity with period certain
- ❍ C. Joint and last survivor annuity
- ❍ D. Unit refund life annuity

Quick Check Answer Key

1. D

2. B

3. C

4. B

5. B

6. A

7. B

8. A

9. A

10. B

11. C

12. A

13. B

14. D

15. B

16. C

17. B

18. D

19. C

20. C

21. C

22. C

23. A

24. D

25. B

Answers and Explanations

1. **Answer D is correct**. An annuity is a contract between an insurance company and a customer. The customer pays money into an annuity with the hope that he will receive a greater amount than he paid when he eventually retires. The annuity's growth is tax deferred by the IRS until retirement distribution begins.

2. **Answer B is correct**. An insurance company creates a participating trust to collect payments from its customers. The participating trust chooses a management company (not a unit trust) in which to invest that reflects the investment objectives of its client base.

3. **Answer C is correct**. A participating trust of the annuity places customer payments into a separate account, which is segregated from other assets of the insurance company. The separate account must be registered with the SEC as a security, and a board of managers elected by the annuitants oversees the separate account.

4. **Answer B is correct**. Interest and dividend income that is earned in an annuity is considered tax-deferred income for the annuitant. When the annuitant begins to receive disbursement from the maturing annuity, only then is the income earned taxed by the IRS.

5. **Answer B is correct**. A fixed annuity guarantees the customer a predetermined return on his or her investment upon the contract's maturity. The insurance company carries the bulk of the risk because it must make agreed-upon payments to the customer regardless of how well the investments perform.

6. **Answer A is correct**. Fixed annuities guarantee the customer a predetermined rate of return on his investment regardless of how well the investments perform. The risk in a fixed annuity is borne by the insurance company, and not the annuitant, due to the agreed-upon fixed rate of return regardless of investment performance. Conservative investors are most attracted to fixed annuities due to the guaranteed rate of return.

7. **Answer B is correct**. An annuity that has seen varying rates of return over the past three years is a variable annuity. It is the customer and not the insurance company that bears the risk involved in a variable annuity. The better the portfolio investments fare, the higher rate of return the investor receives. Conversely, a poorly performing portfolio is also be the investors' risk.

8. **Answer A is correct**. Joseph is best served with a variable annuity that is tied to the overall performance of the investment portfolio. As an aggressive investor, he is willing to take on the risk involved in the performance of the annuity. Only a fixed annuity guarantees the investor a stable rate of return. A variable annuity could do well or poorly, depending on the investments.

9. **Answer A is correct.** An investor who has purchased a fixed annuity receives the guaranteed stated rate of return in the annuity contract. Whether the investment earns an 8% rate of return or any other rate of return, the annuitant receives only the guaranteed fixed rate of 8%. The additional return that is earned by the investment is kept by the insurance company. If the rate of return is less than 8%, then the insurance company is responsible for making up the difference.

10. **Answer B is correct.** An investor who has purchased a variable annuity takes on the risk of the investment portfolio. There is no guarantee on the rate of return that the annuity earns. If the annuity portfolio fares well, the investor receives the entire return. If the annuity does poorly, then the investor bears this risk also.

11. **Answer C is correct.** A variable annuity is indirectly considered a security that falls under the NASD rule of a maximum of 8.5% sales charge. The separate account is actually the security, which falls under the NASD 8.5% sales charge rule. Thus, a $10,000 lump-sum payment to an annuity has a maximum sales charge of $10,000 × 8.5% = $850.

12. **Answer A is correct.** An assumed interest rate for an annuity is the projected rate of return based on current market conditions and historical performance of securities in the portfolio. The AIR is not a guaranteed rate of return and generally errs on the conservative side. That is, a company expecting an 8% return on one of its annuities would publish in the prospectus an AIR of 7%.

13. **Answer B is correct.** Accumulation units represent portions of the value of a variable annuity's underlying security's portfolio. Just as investors buy shares in companies or mutual funds, annuitants purchase shares in the separate account. These shares are called accumulation units. The eventual payout from an annuity is determined by the number of accumulation units the investor purchased.

14. **Answer D is correct.** Accumulation units represent portions of the value of a variable annuity's underlying security's portfolio. The annuitants purchase shares in the separate account. These shares are called accumulation units. Each monthly payment to an annuity adds more accumulation units to the customer's account. The value of the units in a client's account might decline, but the total number of units does not. Each accumulation unit has a value computed by the net asset value of the unit. This is determined by dividing the market value of the assets minus the liabilities by the total number of accumulation units issued.

15. **Answer B is correct.** Accumulation units increase with each monthly payment made to the annuity by the investor. The investor purchases as many accumulation units as possible with her monthly payment. The value of the units varies due to the change in price of the securities in the annuity portfolio. As the annuity matures, the payout to the annuitant is computed by the number of accumulation units held by the annuitant.

16. **Answer C is correct.** The net asset value of an accumulation units is determined by the market value of the assets minus the liabilities divided by the total accumulation units issued.

17. **Answer B is correct.** To determine how much it owes a customer upon the maturity of an annuity, the insurance company must convert the accumulation units into annuity units through a process called annuitization. Like accumulation units, annuity units are an accounting device to make bookkeeping easier for insurance companies.

18. **Answer D is correct.** Depending on the distribution process chosen by the annuitant, an insurance company employs actuary tables to determine the remaining life expectancy of the annuitant before it determines the number of annuity units the client has through a process called annuitization. The accumulation units held by the client are annuitized to determine the eventual payout she will receive.

19. **Answer C is correct.** Under a mortality guarantee, an annuitant signs a contractual agreement that he will receive disbursement payments for life. The annuitant is paid regardless of how long he lives. If the person lives longer than expected, the insurance company is required to keep making the monthly payment. If the annuitant dies one year after receiving disbursement payments, the insurance company does not have to make any additional payments and keeps the remaining funds in the annuity.

20. **Answer C is correct.** A mortality guarantee in the contractual agreement of an annuity states that the annuitant is be paid for life, regardless of how long he lives. After the annuity matures, the insurance company continues to make payments until the death of the annuitant.

21. **Answer C is correct.** If a person chooses a starting date to begin receiving annuity payments prior to the age of 59 1/2, the Internal Revenue Service charges a penalty tax of 10% on the portion of the payout. In addition, the disbursed funds are taxed as ordinary income for the annuitant.

22. **Answer C is correct.** The IRS labels most variable annuities nontax qualified, meaning that annuitants must make payments during the accumulation phase from after-tax income. The value of these payments is not taxed again, when the annuitant begins receiving payments from the insurance company. The payments made into the annuity over the accumulation phase are considered the cost basis of the annuity, and this amount is kept separate from the investment basis, or the amount that the annuity has grown over the years.

23. **Answer A is correct.** In a nontax-qualified annuity, the investor makes payments from after-tax dollars. When the annuity matures and disbursement begins, the cost basis is the amount paid into the annuity by the annuitant. In this case, $5,000 for 20 years has a total cost basis of $100,000, which is not taxed again. The value of the annuity is now $250,000. The difference of $150,000 is considered the investment basis of the annuity, which upon disbursement is taxed as ordinary income.

24. **Answer D is correct.** In a lump-sum distribution, the annuitant collects one large payment from the insurance company at the end of the annuity contract. The payment reflects the current value of the separate account and the number of annuity units belonging to the client. At this point, the annuitant may take the proceeds from the lump-sum payment and buy a fixed annuity with one of two payment options: variable installments over a designated period or designated payments over a variable period.

25. **Answer B is correct.** A life annuity with period certain has the insurance company making payments to the annuitant for life. A part of the contract states that the annuity is paid for a minimum period over which payments are made, even if the annuitant dies.

Quick Check

Retirement Accounts

1. A tax-qualified retirement plan allows an individual to do which of the following?
   - ❍ A. Receive tax-free income from the plan at retirement.
   - ❍ B. Deduct any contribution made into a plan from his yearly salary.
   - ❍ C. All contributions made into a plan are considered tax free.
   - ❍ D. Any contributions made into a plan cannot be deducted from his yearly salary.

Quick Answer: **364**
Detailed Answer: **365**

2. An individual is employed by a bank with a yearly 20% vesting pension plan. After 4 years, the individual decides to leave the bank and is told she has $18,000 in her pension plan. What amount does the employee receive?
   - ❍ A. The employee is not entitled to any payment.
   - ❍ B. The employee receives $18,000.
   - ❍ C. The employee receives $15,000.
   - ❍ D. The employee receives $14,400.

Quick Answer: **364**
Detailed Answer: **365**

3. Which of the following types of retirement accounts requires an individual to become fully vested to receive full payment?
   - ❍ A. IRA accounts
   - ❍ B. Keogh accounts
   - ❍ C. 401K programs
   - ❍ D. Roth IRAs

Quick Answer: **364**
Detailed Answer: **365**

4. The law that created Social Security and disability benefits for individuals is known as what?
   - ❍ A. SIPC
   - ❍ B. FDIC
   - ❍ C. FICA
   - ❍ D. FSLIC

Quick Answer: **364**
Detailed Answer: **365**

Quick Check

5. Which of the following types of investments are permitted to be made in an individual retirement account?

   I. Mutual funds

   II. Antiques

   III. Precious stones

   IV. Gold and silver coins

   ❍ A. I only
   ❍ B. II and III
   ❍ C. I, II, and III
   ❍ D. I and IV

Quick Answer: 364
Detailed Answer: 365

6. An individual established a self-directed IRA account at a brokerage. Which of the following statements are true?

   I. Investment decisions are made by the individual.

   II. Investment decisions are made by the broker.

   III. Speculative investments such as antiques or artwork are allowed.

   IV. Mutual fund purchases are allowed.

   ❍ A. I and III
   ❍ B. I and IV
   ❍ C. II and III
   ❍ D. II and IV

Quick Answer: 364
Detailed Answer: 365

7. All the following statements are not true of individual retirement accounts except for which one?

   ❍ A. Individuals can invest in antiques and artwork.
   ❍ B. An individual can open more than one IRA.
   ❍ C. A married couple can open a joint IRA account.
   ❍ D. An individual can roll over an IRA account twice per calendar year.

Quick Answer: 364
Detailed Answer: 365

8. An individual works part time and earns $1700 for the year. What tax deductible amount is he permitted to contribute to an IRA account?

   ❍ A. No contribution is permitted.
   ❍ B. The maximum contribution is $1700.
   ❍ C. The maximum contribution is $2000.
   ❍ D. There is no limit on the maximum contribution allowed.

Quick Answer: 364
Detailed Answer: 365

Quick Check

9. A married couple without pensions earn $50,000 in a given year. They have made a $3000 IRA contribution for the husband and a $3000 IRA contribution for the wife. What amount do they claim as taxable income?

Quick Answer: 364
Detailed Answer: 366

- ❍ A. $44,000 taxable income
- ❍ B. $48,000 taxable income
- ❍ C. $50,000 taxable income
- ❍ D. $54,000 taxable income

10. An individual at the age of 60 begins to take disbursements from her IRA account for the sum of $30,000 per year. Which of the following statements is true of the disbursements?

Quick Answer: 364
Detailed Answer: 366

- ❍ A. The disbursements are not allowed until the individual is 65 years of age.
- ❍ B. The disbursements are permitted as taxable income.
- ❍ C. The disbursements are permitted as tax-free income.
- ❍ D. The disbursements are only considered tax free at the age of 65.

11. At the age of 59, an individual withdraws $10,000 from his IRA account to pay for a daughter's wedding. Which of the following statements is true of the withdrawal?

Quick Answer: 364
Detailed Answer: 366

- ❍ A. The $10,000 is taxed as ordinary income.
- ❍ B. The $10,000 is taxed as ordinary income and pays a 10% early withdrawal penalty.
- ❍ C. The $10,000 is taxed as a short-term capital gain.
- ❍ D. The withdrawal is tax free because the individual is of the allowable minimum age for disbursements.

12. An individual at the age of 60 takes a $40,000 disbursement from her IRA account. What penalty does the IRS hit the account with, and what portion of the disbursement is taxable?

Quick Answer: 364
Detailed Answer: 366

- ❍ A. $4000 penalty; $40,000 taxed as ordinary income
- ❍ B. No penalty; $40,000 taxed as ordinary income
- ❍ C. $4000 penalty; $40,000 taxed as a short-term capital gain
- ❍ D. No penalty; $40,000 disbursement is considered tax free

Quick Check

13. An individual has $675,000 in an IRA account at the age of 65. Which of the following disbursements are allowed?

    I. A lump-sum taxable payment of $675,000

    II. Periodic payments made according to actuarial tables

    III. $50,000 per year for the remainder of his life

    IV. $4,000 per month for the remainder of his life

    ❍ A. I and II
    ❍ B. II and III
    ❍ C. I, II, and III
    ❍ D. I, II, III, and IV

Quick Answer: 364
Detailed Answer: 366

14. An individual is 59 years old and in poor health with mounting medical bills. She has an IRA worth $800,000. She takes a withdrawal of $50,000 from the IRA to pay medical bills. What is the penalty on the account?

    ❍ A. There is no penalty on the withdrawal to pay medical bills.
    ❍ B. There is a $5000 penalty on the account for the withdrawal.
    ❍ C. There is no penalty because the individual is of legal age for disbursements.
    ❍ D. The individual is not be permitted to take an early withdrawal for medical bills.

Quick Answer: 364
Detailed Answer: 366

15. A 40-year-old individual has $200,000 in his IRA account and conducts an IRA rollover for $50,000. After 90 days, the individual pays the entire $50,000 back to his IRA account. Which statement is considered true of the rollover?

    ❍ A. The rollover is not taxed because the individual replaced the money within 90 days.
    ❍ B. The rollover exceeded the maximum time limit, and the individual is hit with a 10% tax penalty.
    ❍ C. The rollover exceeded the maximum time limit, and the individual is hit with a 10% penalty, as well as having to claim the $50,000 amount on his personal taxes as ordinary income.
    ❍ D. The rollover exceeded the maximum time limit, and the $50,000 is taxed as a short-term capital gain.

Quick Answer: 364
Detailed Answer: 366

Quick Check

16. All the following statements are true of an IRA rollover except for which one?

Quick Answer: 364
Detailed Answer: 366

- ❍ A. An individual is permitted two 90-day IRA rollovers per year.
- ❍ B. An individual is permitted one 60-day IRA rollover per year.
- ❍ C. Rollovers are only permitted between qualified plans.
- ❍ D. Rollover money that is not replaced within the prescribed time frame is penalized and also taxed as ordinary income.

17. Which of the following statements are true of individual retirement accounts?

Quick Answer: 364
Detailed Answer: 367

I. IRA deposits must be made by the last day of the tax year to qualify as a contribution.

II. IRA deposits must be made by April 15 to qualify as a contribution for the previous year.

III. An individual must start taking disbursement from an IRA account by the age of 70 1/2.

IV. IRA rollovers are permitted once per year for 60 days.

- ❍ A. I and III
- ❍ B. II, III, and IV
- ❍ C. I, III, and IV
- ❍ D. II and III

18. Which of the following statements are considered true of a Roth IRA account?

Quick Answer: 364
Detailed Answer: 367

I. The maximum contribution is set at $3000 per year.

II. Contributions to the account carry no tax deduction at all.

III. Disbursements from the account are tax free.

IV. Early withdrawals from the IRA are permitted without penalty for the purchase of a first home.

- ❍ A. I and II
- ❍ B. I, II, and III
- ❍ C. II and III
- ❍ D. I, II, III, and IV

Quick Check

19. Harry opened a Roth IRA account at his local brokerage. Which of the following statements are considered true of the account?

Quick Answer: 364
Detailed Answer: 367

I. Any IRA contributions are considered tax deductible.

II. All IRA contributions are considered taxable.

III. Disbursement is permitted at the age of 59 1/2.

IV. Disbursement must begin by the age of 70 1/2.

❍ A. I and III
❍ B. II and III
❍ C. II, III, and IV
❍ D. I, III, and IV

20. Under the Employee Retirement Income Security Act, the maximum number of years a company can impose on an employee to attain full vesting in a retirement plan is what?

Quick Answer: 364
Detailed Answer: 367

❍ A. 5 years
❍ B. 7 years
❍ C. 9 years
❍ D. 10 years

21. Under the Employee Retirement Income Security Act, pension plans offered by corporations must follow which of the following rules?

Quick Answer: 364
Detailed Answer: 367

I. Each employee must be treated equally by the corporation.

II. Full vesting by employees must be attained within 7 years.

III. The corporate plan must be managed by a trustee.

IV. Investments in the plan must follow the Prudent Man rule.

❍ A. I and II
❍ B. II and III
❍ C. I, II, and III
❍ D. I, II, III, and IV

Quick Check

22. A deferred compensation plan has all the following characteristics except for which one?

   ❍ A. A corporation agrees to pay a percentage of an employee's salary after his retirement.

   ❍ B. A deferred compensation plan carries no tax benefit to the company.

   ❍ C. A deferred compensation plan carries no tax benefit to the employee.

   ❍ D. A corporation offering a deferred compensation plan to employees must offer the plan to all its employees.

Quick Answer: 364
Detailed Answer: 367

23. The type of corporate pension plan that contributes a set amount of money into the plan on a regular basis is known as a what?

   ❍ A. Deferred compensation plan

   ❍ B. Defined benefit plan

   ❍ C. Defined contribution plan

   ❍ D. Employee stock ownership plan

Quick Answer: 364
Detailed Answer: 367

24. The type of employee benefit plan that gives an employee an increasing stake in the ownership of the company is known as a what?

   ❍ A. Deferred compensation plan

   ❍ B. Employee stock ownership plan

   ❍ C. Defined benefit plan

   ❍ D. Profit sharing plan

Quick Answer: 364
Detailed Answer: 368

25. Hector works for Ace Pharmaceuticals. It offers a 401K plan with 5-year vesting to all employees. Hector earns $40,000 per year and elects to make a 10% contribution to his 401K plan each year. Ace Pharmaceuticals contributes a matching contribution up to 5% for employees. Hector leaves the company after 4 years. What amount of the contributed funds in his 401K plan can he take with him?

   ❍ A. $6400

   ❍ B. $16,000

   ❍ C. $22,400

   ❍ D. $24,000

Quick Answer: 364
Detailed Answer: 368

Quick Check Answer Key

1. B
2. D
3. C
4. C
5. D
6. B
7. B
8. B
9. A
10. B
11. B
12. B
13. D
14. A
15. C
16. A
17. B
18. D
19. B
20. B
21. D
22. D
23. C
24. B
25. C

Answers and Explanations

1. **Answer B is correct.** A tax-qualified retirement plan is one in which contributions made into the plan can be deducted from the yearly income of the contributor. The contribution made is not considered tax free, but rather tax deferred for the contributor.

2. **Answer D is correct.** An employee who has a pension plan with a 20% yearly vesting requirement needs to stay with the employer for 5 years to be fully vested. After 4 years, the employee is considered 80% vested, and if she leaves the company, she receives 80% of the value of the pension plan. The equation is $18,000 in the pension plan × 4 years at 20% = .80 = $14,400 she receives from the plan.

3. **Answer C is correct.** The only choice that requires the individual to become vested is the 401K program. A 401K typically has matching employer contributions that enable the individual to be fully vested after a maximum number of years. The maximum limit on being fully vested is 7 years. The other choices are fully vested immediately by the individual.

4. **Answer C is correct.** The Federal Insurance Contributions Act (FICA) created Social Security and disability benefits for employed individuals.

5. **Answer D is correct.** An individual retirement account is permitted to make investments in such securities as mutual funds, certificates of deposits, gold and silver coins minted by the United States, and brokerage accounts. It is not permitted to invest in such speculative investments as art work or antiques.

6. **Answer B is correct.** A self-directed individual retirement account is an account where the individual makes all investment decisions in the account. Allowable investments include mutual funds, stocks, bonds, and gold and silver coins minted by the U.S. government.

7. **Answer B is correct.** An individual is permitted to open more than one IRA account in any given year as long as his maximum deductible contribution does not exceed the $3000 maximum allowed combined. For example, an investor may open an IRA for $1000 with a broker to invest in stocks and another IRA with a bank to purchase a CD.

8. **Answer B is correct.** An individual earning $1700 in a year is permitted to open an IRA and make a tax-deductible contribution for the entire amount of his yearly earnings, as long as it does not exceed the $3000 maximum allowable deduction.

9. **Answer A is correct**. A married couple earning $50,000 in a year without employer pensions is permitted to contribute $3000 each to an IRA account. By doing so, the married couple has taxable income of $50,000 – $6000 IRA contributions = $44,000 taxable income.

10. **Answer B is correct**. A 60-year-old individual who has commenced disbursement from her IRA account is permitted to do so because she is above the 59 1/2 minimum age requirement. The $30,000 disbursement is taxed as ordinary income for the year.

11. **Answer B is correct**. An individual at the age of 59 has not yet met the minimum age requirement of 59 1/2 to take a nonpenalized disbursement from his IRA account. The $10,000 disbursement is hit with an IRS early withdrawal penalty of 10%, and it also must be claimed on the individual's yearly income as ordinary income.

12. **Answer B is correct**. A 60-year-old individual taking a $40,000 disbursement from her IRA account is above the minimum age requirement of 59 1/2. The disbursement has no penalty imposed but is taxed as ordinary income for the individual.

13. **Answer D is correct**. An IRA payout can either be made in a lump-sum payment or drawn out over time. If an investor chooses to receive periodic payments, then the number and size of the payments are based on the amount of money in the account and actuarial tables that estimate the number of years the investor might be expected to live. An account with $675,000 continues to earn interest each year, and even at a reasonably low rate of return of 6% would grow by $40,000 each year. Thus, all the choices are allowed, and the investor should have more than enough in his IRA account to finance his retirement for many years.

14. **Answer A is correct**. The Internal Revenue Service allows a non-penalized IRA disbursement prior to the minimum age of 59 1/2 for certain disabilities. Mounting medical costs fall into this category, and the $50,000 disbursement is not hit with the normal 10% tax penalty for an early withdrawal.

15. **Answer C is correct**. An IRA rollover of funds in the account is permitted once a year for a period of 60 days. If the disbursement from the old plan is not deposited in the new plan within 60 days, then the investor is liable for taxes on the disbursement for the full amount, as well as an additional 10% tax penalty for an early withdrawal.

16. **Answer A is correct**. An IRA rollover is permitted once a year in an IRA account for a period of 60 days. The rollover is only permitted between qualified IRA plans, and failure to roll the money over into a new plan within 60 days incurs a tax penalty of 10% and means that the rollover is taxed as ordinary income.

17. **Answer B is correct.** Deposits made into a qualified IRA plan must be made by April 15 (tax filing day) to qualify as a deduction for the previous year. An individual must start to take disbursements from her IRA by the age of 70 1/2 or incur taxes on the account. An IRA rollover is permitted once a year for a period of 60 days from one qualified plan to another.

18. **Answer D is correct.** A Roth IRA is somewhat different from a conventional IRA. Contributions to a Roth IRA carry no tax benefit at all, but the withdrawals from the account are tax free. The maximum contribution to a Roth IRA is also set at $3000 per year. As an added incentive for a Roth IRA, it is permitted for first time home buyers to take a disbursement from the Roth IRA without a penalty incurred.

19. **Answer B is correct.** Contributions to a Roth IRA are considered taxable to the individual. Retirement withdrawals from the Roth IRA, however, are tax free. An individual opening a Roth IRA is not permitted to take early withdrawal from the plan without a penalty up to the age of 59 1/2. The one exception to this penalty is for first-time home buyers using a disbursement from the Roth IRA without incurring the 10% penalty. Contributions to Roth IRAs need not be withdrawn at age 70 1/2, as conventional IRAs require. Remember, the disbursement is tax free because taxes were paid up front on the Roth IRA.

20. **Answer B is correct.** The Employee Retirement Income Security Act has a maximum guideline of 7 years on any vesting retirement plan offered by an employer to employees. After 7 years of service, an employee must be fully vested in the plan. Many companies require a 5-year vesting plan, but the maximum allowed is 7 years.

21. **Answer D is correct.** The Employee Retirement Income Security Act requires that all private corporation employee pension plans follow prescribed guidelines. They include that all employees be treated equally with regard to the retirement plan offered. ERISA also requires that all employees be fully vested by their seventh year in the offered plan. The plan must be managed by a trustee and must follow the fiduciary requirement of investing under the Prudent Man rule for investments made in the plan.

22. **Answer D is correct.** A deferred compensation plan does not require the employer to offer the same plan to every employee. They are generally available only to senior employees or executives in a corporation. The corporation agrees to pay a percentage of an employee's salary after his retirement or, in some cases, even after his death to his beneficiary.

23. **Answer C is correct.** A defined contribution plan is based on the idea that a set amount of money is paid into the plan on a regular basis. The contribution is usually a percentage of corporate income or employee salary. Either way, the payment made is defined in advance.

24. **Answer B is correct.** This type of plan is offered by some companies that issue stock in the market. The profits that would have gone to funding the profit sharing plan are invested instead in the corporation's stock on behalf of the employee. The corporation is allowed a tax deduction on the market value of the shares. Employee stock ownership plans typically increase worker productivity because the employee has a stake in the future of the company and its share price.

25. **Answer C is correct.** An employee earning $40,000 per year who elected to put 10% of his salary into a 401K program has made a total contribution after 4 years of $16,000 (4 × 10% of $40,000 = $16,000). The company has also matched up to 5% of the employee salary each year, and this contribution totals $40,000 × 5% = $2000 each year × 4 years = $8000. The company offers a 5-year full vesting plan, and Hector worked for the company only 4 years, so he only has 80% vesting on the amount the company contributed. That equation is $8000 × .80 = $6400. Hector can leave with his full contribution of $16,000 + 80% of what the company contributed for him ($6400), a total of $22,400.

Taxation and Securities

Quick Check

1. Passive income is most commonly generated from which type of investment?

   - ❍ A. The purchase of equity securities
   - ❍ B. The purchase of debt securities
   - ❍ C. The purchase of direct participation programs
   - ❍ D. The purchase of options

Quick Answer: **375**
Detailed Answer: **376**

2. An investor has $22,000 worth of capital gains in his portfolio and $29,000 worth of capital losses. Which of the following statements are considered true?

   I. The capital losses can be deducted dollar for dollar against the capital gains.

   II. The investor carries over $7000 in capital losses to the next year.

   III. The investor can take an additional $3000 capital loss for the year.

   IV. The investor can carry over $4000 in capital losses to the next year.

   - ❍ A. I only
   - ❍ B. I and II
   - ❍ C. I and III
   - ❍ D. I, III, and IV

Quick Answer: **375**
Detailed Answer: **376**

Quick Check

3. An investor has $17,000 in capital gains for the year and $33,000 in capital losses for the same year. What amount of capital losses does the investor carry over to the next year?

Quick Answer: 375
Detailed Answer: 376

- ❍ A. $3000 carryover to the following year
- ❍ B. $13,000 carryover to the following year
- ❍ C. $16,000 carryover to the following year
- ❍ D. The investor cannot carry over any capital losses.

4. Harry purchases 100 shares of HTH stock at $100 per share. His broker charges $750 in commission on the trade. Later in the year, he sells the 100 shares of HTH stock for $125 per share, and his broker once again charges him a sales commission of $750. What is the capital gain on the shares of HTH stock?

Quick Answer: 375
Detailed Answer: 376

- ❍ A. A capital gain of $2500
- ❍ B. A capital gain of $1750
- ❍ C. A capital gain of $1000
- ❍ D. A capital gain of $750

5. What is the cost basis for the purchase of 100 shares of TNT stock at $44 with a commission charge of $300 if the investor later sells the shares for $55 in the market?

Quick Answer: 375
Detailed Answer: 376

- ❍ A. A cost basis of $44
- ❍ B. A cost basis of $47
- ❍ C. A cost basis of $52
- ❍ D. A cost basis of $55

6. Which of the following gains is taxed at the investor's actual tax rate?

Quick Answer: 375
Detailed Answer: 376

- ❍ A. A short-term gain
- ❍ B. A medium-term gain
- ❍ C. A long-term gain
- ❍ D. All the above are taxed at an investor's actual tax rate.

7. Which of the following taxes is an example of a regressive tax rate?

Quick Answer: 375
Detailed Answer: 376

- ❍ A. Federal taxation
- ❍ B. State taxation
- ❍ C. Local taxation
- ❍ D. Social Security taxes

Quick Check

8. Acme Electronics Inc. owns 400,000 shares of GHI Corporation stock. GHI has 2,000,000 shares of common stock trading in the market. It pays a cash dividend of 50 cents on each share of stock. What amount does Acme claim as dividend income on its corporate taxes?
   - ❍ A. $200,000 in dividend income
   - ❍ B. $140,000 in dividend income
   - ❍ C. $60,000 in dividend income
   - ❍ D. $40,000 in dividend income

Quick Answer: **375**
Detailed Answer: **376**

9. LTV Corporation owns 1,000,000 shares of JTV Inc. common stock. JTV has 7,500,000 shares of common stock outstanding. JTV pays a common stock dividend of 25 cents to shareholders. What does LTV Corporation claim as dividend income on its corporate taxes?
   - ❍ A. $50,000 as dividend income
   - ❍ B. $75,000 as dividend income
   - ❍ C. $175,000 as dividend income
   - ❍ D. $200,000 as dividend income

Quick Answer: **375**
Detailed Answer: **376**

10. Corey purchases 500 shares of TNT stock at $75 per share on June 17. Two days later, he also purchases 5 TNT September 75 Puts @ 5. The TNT stock goes to $90 in the market. What is his cost basis for the 500 shares of TNT stock?
   - ❍ A. A cost basis of $70 per share
   - ❍ B. A cost basis of $75 per share
   - ❍ C. A cost basis of $85 per share
   - ❍ D. A cost basis of $90 per share

Quick Answer: **375**
Detailed Answer: **377**

11. Tim purchases an HTH convertible bond in the market at 110. Six months later, he converts the bond to 25 shares of HTH common stock. What is his cost basis for the stock?
   - ❍ A. $44 per share
   - ❍ B. $42 per share
   - ❍ C. $40 per share
   - ❍ D. $36 per share

Quick Answer: **375**
Detailed Answer: **377**

Quick Check

12. An investor purchased 1000 shares of KLM stock in the following order over the past two years for the following prices: 200 shares @ $50, 100 shares @ $52, 300 shares @ $54, 400 shares @ $58. He then sells 100 shares in the market at $67 per share. He does not designate which shares he sells. Under IRS rules, what is his cost basis on the 100 shares he sells?

- ❍ A. A cost basis of $50 per share
- ❍ B. A cost basis of $52 per share
- ❍ C. A cost basis of $54 per share
- ❍ D. A cost basis of $58 per share

Quick Answer: **375**
Detailed Answer: **377**

13. An investor purchased 10 original issue discount bonds for a price of $90. The bonds mature in 20 years. If held to maturity, how are the bonds taxed?

- ❍ A. The investor claims $50 in profits each year.
- ❍ B. The investor claims a $50 loss each year.
- ❍ C. The investor has a long-term capital gain of $1000 at maturity.
- ❍ D. The investor has a long-term capital loss of $1000 at maturity.

Quick Answer: **375**
Detailed Answer: **377**

14. Which of the following statements are true of original issue discount bonds when held to maturity?

   I. The bonds are amortized each year on the discounted amount.

   II. The bonds are accreted each year on the discounted amount.

   III. The bonds mature at the original purchase price.

   IV. The bonds mature at par value.

- ❍ A. I and III
- ❍ B. I and IV
- ❍ C. II and III
- ❍ D. II and IV

Quick Answer: **375**
Detailed Answer: **377**

15. An investor purchased a $10,000 TNT corporate bond at $90 with a 10-year maturity. After five years, the investor sells the TNT bonds at $94 in the market. What is the capital gain or loss on the bonds?

- ❍ A. A capital loss of $100 on the bonds
- ❍ B. A capital loss of $600 on the bonds
- ❍ C. A capital gain of $400 on the bonds
- ❍ D. A capital gain of $600 on the bonds

Quick Answer: **375**
Detailed Answer: **377**

Quick Check

16. David purchases a $10,000 corporate bond paying 8% Jan 1/July 1 on March 1. He purchases the bonds at $100 in the market and owes accrued interest of 62 days on the bonds totaling $137.78 to the seller. What is his adjusted cost basis on the bonds?
    - ❍ A. $10,000 adjusted cost basis
    - ❍ B. $9862.22 adjusted cost basis
    - ❍ C. $10,137.78 adjusted cost basis
    - ❍ D. $10,400 adjusted cost basis

Quick Answer: 375
Detailed Answer: 377

17. A discounted Treasury bill is taxed in which of the following ways for an investor?
    - ❍ A. As a capital gain in the year the T-bill matures
    - ❍ B. As ordinary income on the federal and state income tax returns
    - ❍ C. As ordinary income on the federal level only
    - ❍ D. As ordinary income on the state level only

Quick Answer: 375
Detailed Answer: 377

18. An investor receives $500 in mutual fund dividends that she has elected to reinvest back into the mutual fund she holds. What are the tax implications on the reinvested dividends?
    - ❍ A. Taxed as a short-term capital gain
    - ❍ B. Taxed as a long-term capital gain
    - ❍ C. Taxed as ordinary income in the year they were reinvested
    - ❍ D. Nontaxable because they were reinvested into the fund

Quick Answer: 375
Detailed Answer: 377

19. An investor purchased 10 BTO April 70 Call options @ 4. The options expire worthless in April, when BTO falls in price to $57. How is the option taxed?
    - ❍ A. It is nontaxable because the option expired worthless.
    - ❍ B. It is considered a short-term capital loss for the sum of $400.
    - ❍ C. It is considered a short-term capital loss for the sum of $4000.
    - ❍ D. It is a medium-term capital loss of $4000.

Quick Answer: 375
Detailed Answer: 377

20. Victor writes the following option contracts: 5 TNT October 40 Calls @ 5. TNT rises in value to $52. Victor is worried that the price of TNT will go even higher, so he closes out his position with a closing purchase of 5 TNT October 40 Calls @ 12 1/2. What are the tax implications on this option?
    - ❍ A. Victor has a short-term capital loss of $3750.
    - ❍ B. Victor has a short-term capital loss of $6250.
    - ❍ C. Victor has a short-term capital gain of $2500.
    - ❍ D. Victor has a short-term capital gain of $3750.

Quick Answer: 375
Detailed Answer: 377

Quick Check

21. George purchases 2 BTO April 50 Calls @ 3. BTO stock rises in value to $72 and George exercises his right to purchase the shares of BTO at $50. What is his cost basis on the 200 shares of BTO stock he receives from the exercised option?
   - ❍ A. $47 per share
   - ❍ B. $50 per share
   - ❍ C. $53 per share
   - ❍ D. $72 per share

Quick Answer: **375**
Detailed Answer: **378**

22. Kerry purchases 3 DTT May 40 Puts @ 4 in the market. DTT shares drop in value to $30 per share, and the puts are exercised by the holder. What are the tax implications on the exercised put options?
   - ❍ A. Kerry has a $1200 capital loss.
   - ❍ B. Kerry has a $1200 capital gain.
   - ❍ C. Kerry has a $1800 capital gain.
   - ❍ D. Kerry has a $1800 capital loss.

Quick Answer: **375**
Detailed Answer: **378**

23. An investor writes 5 QVC December 2001 65 Call LEAPS @ 6. After two years, the QVC LEAPS are exercised with a market price of $90. What are the tax implications to the writer?
   - ❍ A. The writer has a long-term capital loss of $1900.
   - ❍ B. The writer has a long-term capital loss of $9500.
   - ❍ C. The writer has a short-term capital loss of $9500.
   - ❍ D. The writer has a short-term capital loss of $3000.

Quick Answer: **375**
Detailed Answer: **378**

Choose from the following types of taxes to answer the next two questions. A choice may be used once, more than once, or not at all.

- ❍ A. Gift taxes
- ❍ B. Estate taxes
- ❍ C. Flat tax
- ❍ D. Progressive tax

24. A father gives his son a new car upon graduation from college. The car is valued at $40,000. What type of tax is paid on the car?

Quick Answer: **375**
Detailed Answer: **378**

25. A daughter inherits $300,000 worth of bonds from her mother and decides to hold the bonds. What type of tax is paid on the bonds?

Quick Answer: **375**
Detailed Answer: **378**

Quick Check Answer Key

1. C
2. D
3. B
4. C
5. B
6. A
7. D
8. D
9. B
10. B
11. A
12. A
13. A
14. D
15. C
16. A
17. C
18. C
19. C
20. A
21. C
22. C
23. B
24. A
25. B

Answers and Explanations

1. **Answer C is correct.** Passive income is income that a person receives without actively participating in any work or activity. Direct participation programs such as limited partnerships generate passive income for the limited partner. They are investors but cannot be involved in the managing of the DPP.

2. **Answer D is correct.** The investor can deduct dollar for dollar his $22,000 gain against his $29,000 in losses. In addition, he can deduct another $3000 in losses and carry forward the remaining $4000 to the next tax year.

3. **Answer B is correct.** The investor can write off his entire capital gain of $17,000 against his $33,000 capital loss. In addition, he may write off an additional $3000 and carry over the remaining loss of $13,000 to the next tax year.

4. **Answer C is correct.** Harry has a capital gain of $1000. He can write off the $1500 in commission fees against his gain of $2500 on the stock purchase and sale.

5. **Answer B is correct.** The cost basis of 100 shares of stock purchased at $44 with a $3 per share commission fee gives the investor a $47 cost basis on the stock.

6. **Answer A is correct.** Short-term gains are taxed at the ordinary tax bracket of the investor.

7. **Answer D is correct.** Social Security taxes are an example of a regressive tax. After a certain amount of income, the maximum amount required each year to be paid into Social Security ceases.

8. **Answer D is correct.** Acme owns 400,000 shares of the outstanding 2 million shares of GHI. This makes it a 20% shareholder. The corporate dividend exclusion allows 80% of the dividends received to be excluded from taxation. Thus, a $.50 per share dividend pays Acme $200,000, of which 80% (or $160,000) is excluded from taxation, leaving a remaining taxable amount of $40,000.

9. **Answer B is correct.** The corporate dividend exclusion allows for a company that owns less than 20% of the outstanding shares of a company to exclude 70% of the received dividend gains. LTV owns approximately 12% of JTV shares. JTV pays a $.25 per share dividend, resulting in a payment to LTV of $250,000 (1,000,000 shares × $.25). Of the $250,000 paid in dividend to LTV, 70% is excluded from taxation ($175,000), leaving a taxable dividend of $75,000 for LTV.

10. **Answer B is correct.** Corey has a cost basis on the TNT shares of the $75 at which he purchased them. A married put allows the investor to deduct the cost of a put option only if the purchase of the stock and the put are done on the same day, which they were not.
11. **Answer A is correct.** A bond purchased at $110 has a cost of $1100 for the investor. Converting the $1100 bond into 25 shares of HTH common stock gives Tim the cost basis of $1100 ÷ 25 = $44 per share.
12. **Answer A is correct.** The IRS states that if an investor does not designate the specific shares he has sold, then it is determined on a first in, first out basis. His first purchase was for $50 per share, so that is the cost basis on the sale of the 100 shares of stock.
13. **Answer A is correct.** An original issue discount purchased at issue and held to maturity has no tax implications other than the accretion of the bond over time of 20 years. The 10 bonds were purchased at $90, or $9000, and matured at $100, or $10,000. The investor accretes the $1000 over 20 years, or $50 profit each year.
14. **Answer D is correct.** An original issue discount bond is accreted each year for the amount of the discount divided by the number of years to maturity. At maturity, they mature at a par value of $100.
15. **Answer C is correct.** A bond purchased at 90 ($900) and later sold at 94 ($940) has a net gain of $40 per bond for the investor. In this case, 10 bonds result in a $400 gain.
16. **Answer A is correct.** The adjusted cost basis on a bond purchased at $10,000 with accrued interest owed is still $10,000 for the investor. The bondholder recoups his $137.78 in accrued interest on the next bond interest payment on July 1.
17. **Answer C is correct.** Treasury bills are taxed as ordinary gains for the investor on the federal tax level in the tax year received. There are no state or local tax requirements on government-issued bills, notes, or bonds.
18. **Answer C is correct.** The $500 in mutual fund dividends that have been received and reinvested into the fund are taxed as ordinary income in the year received. In a qualified account such as an IRA, they would not be taxable.
19. **Answer C is correct.** The investor has a short-term loss of $4000 on the 10 BTO April 70 Call options that expired worthless.
20. **Answer A is correct.** Victor has a short-term loss of $3750 on the sale of the 5 TNT October 40 Calls that he eventually closed out with a closing purchase of 5 TNT October 40 Calls @ 12 1/2 .

21. **Answer C is correct.** George has a cost basis on the BTO stock of the $50 strike price plus the premium of $3, which equals a $53 per share cost basis.

22. **Answer C is correct.** Kerry has a capital gain of $10 per share less the $4 premium per share on the option contracts, which equals $6. His gain is $6 per share × the 300 shares in the three contracts = $1800.

23. **Answer B is correct.** LEAPS that have been held longer than 18 months have a long-term tax basis for the investor. In this case, the QVC LEAPS went up to $90, which results in a loss of $25 per share on each contract less the $6 received on each contract. The investor has a $25 – $6 = $19 loss × 500 shares = $9500 loss on the LEAPS.

24. **Answer A is correct.** Any gift in excess of $10,000 per year is subject to a gift tax to be paid by the donor.

25. **Answer B is correct.** Inheritances are subject to both probate and estate taxes for the individual who is the beneficiary. The bonds become part of the inherited estate.

Quick Check

Macroeconomics

1. The value of all consumer goods and services produced within a country in a given year that also includes foreign companies and the goods they produce in that country is known as what?

   ❍ A. Gross national product
   ❍ B. Gross domestic product
   ❍ C. Gross net product
   ❍ D. Net national product

Quick Answer: **385**
Detailed Answer: **386**

2. An American company produces computer microchips at a factory in Italy. The total sales amount attributed to the Italian factory has what effect?

   I. It is counted toward the U.S. gross domestic product.

   II. It is counted toward the U.S. gross national product.

   III. It increases the U.S. gross national product.

   IV. It decreases the U.S. gross domestic product.

   ❍ A. I only
   ❍ B. II and III
   ❍ C. I and IV
   ❍ D. III and IV

Quick Answer: **385**
Detailed Answer: **386**

Quick Check

3. Which of the following statements are true about the expansion phase of the business cycle?

   I. Production of goods and services is increasing.

   II. Interest rates are high.

   III. Inflation is low.

   IV. Unemployment decreases.

   ❍ A. I and II
   ❍ B. II and III
   ❍ C. I, II, and III
   ❍ D. I, III, and IV

Quick Answer: 385
Detailed Answer: 386

4. The gross domestic product has gone down for two consecutive quarters, and the country has entered a recession. Which of the following is not characteristic of a recession?

   ❍ A. Unemployment has increased.
   ❍ B. Consumer demand has increased.
   ❍ C. Inflation has decreased.
   ❍ D. Business is spending less.

Quick Answer: 385
Detailed Answer: 386

Choose from the following phases of the business cycle to answer the next five questions. A choice can be used once, more than once, or not at all.

❍ A. Expansion
❍ B. Peak
❍ C. Recession
❍ D. Recovery

5. The business cycle has seen consumer demand fall as gross domestic product has dropped for two consecutive quarters. Stock prices are declining and bond prices are rising. This is an example of which stage of the business cycle?

Quick Answer: 385
Detailed Answer: 386

6. If the economy reaches a maximum growth rate, what stage of the business cycle does it fall into?

Quick Answer: 385
Detailed Answer: 386

7. New workers are hired as unemployment decreases. Interest rates are beginning to rise as corporate profits also rise. This is an example of what stage of the business cycle?

Quick Answer: 385
Detailed Answer: 386

8. Interest rates are up as companies are spending less. Inflation is on the rise and the economy has begun to falter. This is an example of what stage of the business cycle?

Quick Answer: 385
Detailed Answer: 386

Quick Check

9. The economy has bottomed out as interest rates have fallen to all-time lows. Unemployment is slowly dropping as output starts to increase. This is an example of what stage of the business cycle?

Quick Answer: **385**
Detailed Answer: **386**

10. New building permits are on the rise in the economy as new construction is a demonstrable measure of how the economy is doing. This is an example of what?
    - ❍ A. A leading indicator
    - ❍ B. A coincident indicator
    - ❍ C. A lagging indicator
    - ❍ D. A confidence measure

Quick Answer: **385**
Detailed Answer: **387**

11. Which of the following indicators is considered a lagging indicator of the economic business cycle?
    - ❍ A. The average duration of unemployment
    - ❍ B. Manufacturing and trade sales
    - ❍ C. Industrial production
    - ❍ D. New orders for consumer goods and materials

Quick Answer: **385**
Detailed Answer: **387**

12. All the following are examples of leading indicators in the economy except for which one?
    - ❍ A. New building permits issued
    - ❍ B. New orders for consumer goods and materials
    - ❍ C. M2 of the money supply
    - ❍ D. The prime interest rate offered by banks

Quick Answer: **385**
Detailed Answer: **387**

13. The standard measure of inflation in the economy is gauged by which of the following?
    - ❍ A. The consumer price index
    - ❍ B. The current phase of the business cycle
    - ❍ C. The measure of the money supply
    - ❍ D. The consumer confidence index

Quick Answer: **385**
Detailed Answer: **387**

14. Bond prices react in which manner in times of high inflationary periods?
    - ❍ A. Bond prices remain stagnant.
    - ❍ B. Bond prices rise.
    - ❍ C. Bond prices decline.
    - ❍ D. Bond prices fluctuate widely.

Quick Answer: **385**
Detailed Answer: **387**

Quick Check

15. What type of inflation occurs when business is attempting to expand production more quickly than the supply of inputs can increase?

    ❍ A. Cost push inflation
    ❍ B. Demand pull inflation
    ❍ C. Deflation
    ❍ D. Stagflation

Quick Answer: 385
Detailed Answer: 387

16. If the supply of money increases more slowly than the demand for money, the value of money rises. What type of inflation is this?

    ❍ A. Cost push inflation
    ❍ B. Demand pull inflation
    ❍ C. Stagflation
    ❍ D. Deflation

Quick Answer: 385
Detailed Answer: 387

17. The economic theory that teaches how government taxation and spending policy dictate the business cycle is known as what?

    ❍ A. Keynesian theory
    ❍ B. Monetarist theory
    ❍ C. Supply-side economics
    ❍ D. Econometrics

Quick Answer: 385
Detailed Answer: 387

18. The Federal Reserve Bank system has which of the following characteristics?

    I. The Fed controls the money supply.

    II. The Fed regulates commercial banks in the United States.

    III. The Fed acts as the bank for the U.S. Government.

    IV. The Fed sets the tax rates for the U.S. Treasury.

    ❍ A. I and II
    ❍ B. I, II, and III
    ❍ C. II, III, and IV
    ❍ D. I, II, III, and IV

Quick Answer: 385
Detailed Answer: 387

19. Which of the following measures of the money supply is considered the most liquid?

    ❍ A. M1
    ❍ B. M2
    ❍ C. M3
    ❍ D. L

Quick Answer: 385
Detailed Answer: 388

Quick Check

20. Time deposits include which of the following examples?

Quick Answer: 385
Detailed Answer: 388

I. Money held in savings accounts

II. Checking accounts

III. Bank certificates of deposit

IV. Holiday or vacation club deposits

- ❍ A. I and II
- ❍ B. II and III
- ❍ C. I, II, and III
- ❍ D. I, III, and IV

21. The Federal Reserve Bank decides to lower the reserve requirement in the Fed banking system. What effect does this action have?

Quick Answer: 385
Detailed Answer: 388

- ❍ A. It decreases the available money supply in the economy.
- ❍ B. It increases the amount that banks must hold in reserve.
- ❍ C. It enables banks to lend more in the market.
- ❍ D. It decreases the amount that banks can lend in the market.

22. An investor makes a deposit of $10,000 in a bank. Using the credit multiplier, how much in new spending is created if the Federal Reserve Bank's reserve requirement is set at 10%?

Quick Answer: 385
Detailed Answer: 388

- ❍ A. $10,000
- ❍ B. $50,000
- ❍ C. $100,000
- ❍ D. $250,000

23. Andy received an unexpected inheritance of $50,000 from a relative. He deposited the funds in his checking account at State Bank. The Federal Reserve Bank reserve requirement is set at 8%. Using the multiplier effect, how much in new spending is created by this deposit?

Quick Answer: 385
Detailed Answer: 388

- ❍ A. $50,000
- ❍ B. $100,000
- ❍ C. $450,000
- ❍ D. $625,000

Quick Check

24. Which of the following statements are considered true regarding the credit multiplier effect of money deposited at banks?

Quick Answer: 385
Detailed Answer: 388

I. The velocity of money changes from business cycle to business cycle.

II. If intermediation is greater than disintermediation, the credit multiplier effect weakens.

III. If intermediation is greater than disintermediation, the credit multiplier effect strengthens.

IV. Unfavorable bank rates increase disintermediation.

❍ A. I and II
❍ B. II and IV
❍ C. I, II, and IV
❍ D. I, III, and IV

25. Which of the following statements are true regarding the discount rate set by the Federal Reserve Bank?

Quick Answer: 385
Detailed Answer: 388

I. The discount rate is the rate at which the Fed lends to member banks.

II. The Fed encourages borrowing at the discount rate.

III. The Fed discourages borrowing at the discount rate.

IV. Borrowers at the discount rate must offer collateral for a loan at the discount window.

❍ A. I and II
❍ B. II and III
❍ C. I, II, and IV
❍ D. I, III, and IV

Quick Check Answer Key

1. B
2. B
3. D
4. B
5. C
6. B
7. D
8. B
9. D
10. A
11. A
12. D
13. A
14. C
15. A
16. D
17. A
18. B
19. A
20. D
21. C
22. C
23. D
24. D
25. D

Answers and Explanations

1. **Answer B is correct.** Gross domestic product is the measure of all goods and services produced within a country in a given year that also includes the measure of foreign companies and the goods and services they produce in the country. Gross national product does not include foreign company production in the United States as part of its measure.

2. **Answer B is correct.** An American company that produces goods in a foreign country has the sales included in the measure of the gross national product. This production increases the measure of GNP.

3. **Answer D is correct.** The expansion phase of the business cycle sees an increase in the production of goods and services while interest rates and inflation remain generally low. More workers are hired to meet the expansion, and unemployment decreases.

4. **Answer B is correct.** A recession occurs when the gross domestic product of a country has declined for two consecutive quarters. Consumer demand decreases as business production and employment also fall.

5. **Answer C is correct.** A country enters a recession when gross domestic product drops for two consecutive quarters. Consumer demand, business production, and employment all fall. Stock prices fall as funds are moved into a rising bond market.

6. **Answer B is correct.** When the economy reaches a maximum growth rate, the business cycle enters its peak. This coincides with a drop in consumer confidence, leading to higher interest rates in the market.

7. **Answer D is correct.** The economy starts to recover when unemployment decreases with the hiring of new workers. Interest rates, which have bottomed out, begin to rise again, and corporate profits are boosted, all becoming part of the recovery cycle.

8. **Answer B is correct.** The business cycle peaks when the economy sees high interest rates and increasing inflation. Consumer confidence falls off as companies spend less on capital expenditures. The economy is at a peak and has nowhere to go but downward.

9. **Answer D is correct.** The economy is in the early stages of a recovery when interest rates have bottomed out and production output starts to increase. The economy has hit bottom and begins to grow again.

10. **Answer A is correct.** The rise of new building permits is a leading indicator of the business cycle. Leading indicators tend to change before the economy as a whole changes. New building permits represent new construction. New construction brings many new workers, such as carpenters, framers, electricians, and others, back to work.
11. **Answer A is correct.** The average duration of unemployment is considered a lagging indicator. A lagging indicator changes after the economy has already moved into a new phase. Unemployment figures are typically reported after the individuals receive the benefit, so it lags behind as an indicator.
12. **Answer D is correct.** The prime interest rate is considered a lagging indicator because changes in the prime rate lag behind general economic activities as banks take time to react to changing economic conditions.
13. **Answer A is correct.** The consumer price index is a measure of consumer goods and services. It compares current costs to previous costs as it gauges inflation eroding the value of money.
14. **Answer C is correct.** Inflation represents a change in the value of money. Bonds pay investors a fixed rate of interest. As inflation rises, it begins to erode the fixed dollar amount value of bond payments. This causes bonds to drop in value in times of high inflation.
15. **Answer A is correct.** Cost push inflation occurs when businesses attempt to expand production more quickly than the supply of inputs can increase. The higher production costs are passed on to consumers in the form of higher prices.
16. **Answer D is correct.** Deflation occurs when the supply of money increases more slowly than the demand for money as the value of money rises. When this occurs, it takes fewer dollars to purchase the same goods produced, causing prices to fall.
17. **Answer A is correct.** Keynesian economic theorists believe that the government fiscal policy of taxation and spending programs has a direct impact on the business cycle. A follower of Keynesian economics advocates greater government spending during economic downturns and higher levels of government taxation during periods of economic expansion.
18. **Answer B is correct.** The Federal Reserve Bank acts as the nation's bank. Under its authority, it regulates the commercial banks in the United States and controls the money supply. The Fed does not control the tax rates of the U.S. Treasury.

19. **Answer A is correct.** The most liquid measure of the money supply is M1. M1 measures currency in circulation, demand deposits such as checking accounts, and travelers' checks. Each of these forms of money in circulation is liquid.

20. **Answer D is correct.** Time deposits are those deposits that are left for a specific period of time in return for interest payments by a bank. They include bank certificates of deposit, savings accounts, and holiday or vacation clubs.

21. **Answer C is correct.** If the Federal Reserve Bank lowers the reserve requirement, it enables banks to lend more in the market. Lower reserve requirements allow banks to lend out additional funds that are normally held in reserve.

22. **Answer C is correct.** The credit multiplier is the degree that an original bank deposit is magnified when the money is re-lent by the bank and redeposited in other banks. A $10,000 deposit at a bank with the reserve requirement set at 10% allows the bank to lend $9000 out and hold $1000 in reserve. The $9000 new loan is deposited at another bank, which has a 10% reserve requirement, making $8100 available for another loan, and so on. The multiplier can be determined by dividing 100% by the reserve requirement. In this case, it is 100% ÷ 10% reserve requirement = 10 times. Thus, a $10,000 deposit generates 10 times that amount in new spending as computed by the multiplier effect. The equation is 10,000 × 10 = $100,000.

23. **Answer D is correct.** You find the multiplier effect by dividing 100% by the current reserve requirement. In this case, the reserve requirement is 8%. The equation is 100% ÷ 8% = 12.5 times. Thus, a $50,000 deposit generates 12.5 times that amount in new spending, or $50,000 × 12.5 = $625,000 in new spending from the multiplier effect.

24. **Answer D is correct.** The credit multiplier is affected by economic conditions. As the business cycle changes, so does the velocity of money. In periods of a booming economy, money is spent faster; conversely, in a stagnant economy, the velocity of money being spent slows down. Depositing funds in banks is known as intermediation. Removing funds from a bank due to unfavorable interest rates is disintermediation. The more deposits in a bank through intermediation will strengthen the multiplier effect, not weaken it.

25. **Answer D is correct.** The Federal Reserve Bank lends at the discount rate to member banks in need of loans. This privilege is discouraged by the Fed and is only used for emergency borrowing. Banks that do borrow at the discount rate offer collateral in the form of eligible paper to secure the loan.

Quick Check

Fundamental Analysis

1. An individual who investigates a company's financial health by examining its assets, liabilities, income, and expenses is a what?

Quick Answer: **395**
Detailed Answer: **396**

- ❍ A. Technical analyst
- ❍ B. Fundamental analyst
- ❍ C. Chartist
- ❍ D. Portfolio theorist

2. Which of the following are characteristic of a growth stock in the market?

Quick Answer: **395**
Detailed Answer: **396**

   I. A small or nonexistent dividend paid

   II. Rapidly increasing market price

   III. Large dividend payment

   IV. A company that reinvests its profits

- ❍ A. I and IV
- ❍ B. II and III
- ❍ C. I, II, and III
- ❍ D. I, II, and IV

Quick Check

3. Which are characteristics of all companies required to release annual financial reports?

Quick Answer: 395
Detailed Answer: 396

I. The Securities and Exchange Commission requires full disclosure.

II. The report must be certified by an independent accounting firm.

III. Financial reports include income statements and balance sheets.

IV. Financial reports include a statement of changes to retained earnings.

- ❍ A. I and II
- ❍ B. I, II, and III
- ❍ C. II, III, and IV
- ❍ D. I, II, III, and IV

4. Each item on a balance sheet appears how often?

Quick Answer: 395
Detailed Answer: 396

- ❍ A. Once as a credit
- ❍ B. Once as a debit
- ❍ C. Twice, once as a credit and once as a debit
- ❍ D. Once or twice, depending on the item

5. A company purchased a $50,000 photo processor for production purposes. This item appears on the balance sheet in which manner?

Quick Answer: 395
Detailed Answer: 396

- ❍ A. $50,000 as a current asset and $50,000 as a short-term liability
- ❍ B. $50,000 as a current asset
- ❍ C. $50,000 as a long-term asset and $50,000 as a long-term liability
- ❍ D. $50,000 as a long-term asset

6. Choose the list of all current assets in order of liquidity with the most liquid asset first:

Quick Answer: 395
Detailed Answer: 396

- ❍ A. Cash, marketable securities, accounts receivable, inventory
- ❍ B. Cash, inventory, marketable securities, accounts receivable
- ❍ C. Cash, accounts receivable, inventory, marketable securities
- ❍ D. Cash, marketable securities, inventory, accounts receivable

Quick Check

7. Which of the following is considered true of a company's inventory using the LIFO system in a period of rising inflation?

   ❍ A. The newest inventory is the highest priced.
   ❍ B. The oldest inventory is the highest priced.
   ❍ C. The newest inventory is the lowest priced.
   ❍ D. The oldest inventory is the lowest priced.

Quick Answer: **395**
Detailed Answer: **396**

8. All the following are considered long-term assets except for which one?

   ❍ A. Inventory
   ❍ B. Notes receivable
   ❍ C. Machines and equipment
   ❍ D. Land

Quick Answer: **395**
Detailed Answer: **396**

9. All the following assets are permitted by the IRS to be depreciated except for which one?

   ❍ A. Buildings
   ❍ B. Land
   ❍ C. Machines
   ❍ D. Office equipment

Quick Answer: **395**
Detailed Answer: **396**

10. A company purchased a $300,000 building on which it takes a $10,000 per-year depreciation allowance. What type of depreciation is it taking?

    ❍ A. Accelerated depreciation
    ❍ B. Straight-line depreciation
    ❍ C. Modified accelerated cost system
    ❍ D. Term depreciation

Quick Answer: **395**
Detailed Answer: **397**

11. Which of the following are considered intangible assets of a company?

    I. Patents

    II. Copyrights

    III. Trademarks

    IV. Goodwill

    ❍ A. I and II
    ❍ B. II and III
    ❍ C. I, II, and III
    ❍ D. I, II, III, and IV

Quick Answer: **395**
Detailed Answer: **397**

Quick Check

12. Common stock is often given an arbitrary par value for bookkeeping purposes of which amount?
    - A. $1000
    - B. $100
    - C. $10
    - D. $1

Quick Answer: 395
Detailed Answer: 397

13. A company that reinvests part or all its profits rather than pay them out as dividends is characteristic of which type of security?
    - A. Preferred stock
    - B. Income stock
    - C. Aggressive stock
    - D. Growth stock

Quick Answer: 395
Detailed Answer: 397

14. Which of the following statements are true regarding a dividend paid by a company?

    I. The number of shares of stock remains the same.

    II. Shareholder equity is reduced by the amount of the dividend.

    III. Retained earnings is reduced by the amount of the dividend.

    IV. The market price is adjusted downward for the amount of the dividend.

    - A. I and II
    - B. II and IV
    - C. I, II, and III
    - D. I, II, III, and IV

Quick Answer: 395
Detailed Answer: 397

15. Which of the following is not deducted from net sales on an income statement?
    - A. Cost of goods sold
    - B. Dividends paid
    - C. Depreciation
    - D. Bond interest expense

Quick Answer: 395
Detailed Answer: 397

Quick Check

16. Which of the following items are deducted from retained earnings on the statement of changes to retained earnings for a company?

    I. Preferred dividends paid

    II. Common stock dividends paid

    III. Bond interest paid

    IV. Operating expenses

    ❍ A. I and II
    ❍ B. II and III
    ❍ C. I, II, and III
    ❍ D. I, II, III, and IV

Quick Answer: **395**
Detailed Answer: **397**

17. The acid test or quick ratio compares current assets to current liabilities but does not count which of the following items?

    ❍ A. Inventory
    ❍ B. Cash
    ❍ C. Marketable securities
    ❍ D. Accounts receivable

Quick Answer: **395**
Detailed Answer: **397**

18. A company with a balance sheet of $444,000 in current assets, $309,000 in current liabilities, $45,000 in inventory, $60,000 in accounts receivables, $52,000 in marketable securities, and $75,000 in cash has a current ratio of what?

    ❍ A. 1.43
    ❍ B. 1.29
    ❍ C. 1.24
    ❍ D. .41

Quick Answer: **395**
Detailed Answer: **397**

19. A company's long-term capital is determined by which of the following?

    ❍ A. Long-term liabilities + stockholders equity
    ❍ B. Long-term assets + stockholders equity
    ❍ C. Stockholders equity – par value of common stock
    ❍ D. Stockholders equity – bond interest payable

Quick Answer: **395**
Detailed Answer: **397**

Answer the next four questions from the following types of ratios. An answer may be used once, more than once, or not at all.

❍ A. Liquidity ratios
❍ B. Capitalization ratios
❍ C. Coverage ratios
❍ D. Profitability ratios

Quick Check

20. To determine the net profit margin for a company, an analyst uses which type of ratio?

Quick Answer: 395
Detailed Answer: 397

21. In determining whether a company has been able to meet its bond interest payments, an analyst uses which type of ratio?

Quick Answer: 395
Detailed Answer: 398

22. In determining how well a company is able to pay its bills on time, an analyst uses which type of ratio?

Quick Answer: 395
Detailed Answer: 398

23. When an analyst looks at the debt-to-equity ratio of a company, she is checking which type of ratio?

Quick Answer: 395
Detailed Answer: 398

24. All the following are ratios that measure profitability for a company except for which one?
    - ❍ A. Net profit margin
    - ❍ B. Return on assets
    - ❍ C. Return on common equity
    - ❍ D. Debt-to-equity ratio

Quick Answer: 395
Detailed Answer: 398

25. The inventory turnover ratio for a company is measured by which of the following?
    - ❍ A. Net income ÷ inventory
    - ❍ B. Cost of goods sold ÷ inventory
    - ❍ C. Net sales ÷ inventory
    - ❍ D. Operating income ÷ inventory

Quick Answer: 395
Detailed Answer: 398

Quick Check Answer Key

1. B
2. D
3. D
4. C
5. C
6. A
7. D
8. A
9. B
10. B
11. D
12. D
13. D
14. D
15. B
16. A
17. A
18. A
19. A
20. D
21. C
22. A
23. B
24. D
25. B

Answers and Explanations

1. **Answer B is correct.** A fundamental analyst investigates a company's financial health by looking at the company's assets, liabilities, income, and expenses. The analyst tries to determine how profitable the company is likely to be in the future.

2. **Answer D is correct.** A growth stock is a rapidly expanding company that tends to reinvest its earnings rather than pay a dividend to shareholders. Share prices on growth stocks tend to increase in expectation of future profits.

3. **Answer D is correct.** All publicly held companies are required by the Securities and Exchange Commission to release annual financial reports. The reports are checked by independent accounting firms to reveal whether they are accurate. The financial reports include a balance sheet, an income statement, and a statement of changes to retained earnings for investor view.

4. **Answer C is correct.** Each item on a balance sheet appears twice: once as a credit and once as a debit. For example, a company borrows $150,000 to buy new equipment. The equipment appears as a credit, and the $150,000 loan borrowed appears as a debit on the balance sheet.

5. **Answer C is correct.** A company that has purchased a $50,000 photo processor has the item appear on the balance sheet twice: once as a long-term asset and once as a long-term liability. It appears as a long-term asset because equipment has a useful life expectancy of far longer than one year.

6. **Answer A is correct.** Current assets are measured in order of liquidity. In order from most liquid to least liquid, they are cash, marketable securities, accounts receivable, and inventory. Inventory is the least liquid of current assets because it takes the longest period of time to sell current assets.

7. **Answer D is correct.** In periods of rising inflation, the LIFO accounting system of measuring inventory has the oldest inventory valued at the lowest price. These items were produced first and are still part of the inventory.

8. **Answer A is correct.** Long-term assets are goods used in the course of business that are not intended to be converted into cash. They include long-term notes, machinery and equipment, and land. Inventory is considered a current asset that can be converted into cash.

9. **Answer B is correct.** Long-term assets are goods owned by a company that are not intended to be converted into cash. All long-term assets can be depreciated over time, except for land. The IRS views land as an asset that does not wear out, so it cannot be depreciated.

10. **Answer B is correct.** Straight-line depreciation subtracts the same percentage of an asset's value each year for the entire useful life of the asset. A $10,000 yearly depreciation on a building is considered straight-line depreciation.

11. **Answer D is correct.** Intangible assets are those possessions of a company that contribute to its worth but are not physical items. They can include goodwill, patents and trademarks, and the copyrights held by a company. Intangible assets have estimated value.

12. **Answer D is correct.** Common stock normally receives an arbitrary par value of $1 by a company for tax and bookkeeping purposes.

13. **Answer D is correct.** Companies that reinvest their profits as retained earnings are characteristic of growth stocks. They pay little or no dividend to shareholders, anticipating that the market value of the stock will appreciate in value.

14. **Answer D is correct.** In the case of an announced cash dividend, the number of shares of stock and their par value remain the same. Total retained earnings and shareholder equity are reduced by the amount of the dividend. After payment of a dividend, the exchange that is listing the security adjusts the market price for the amount of the dividend downward.

15. **Answer B is correct.** Preferred and common dividends are deducted not on the income statement, but rather on the statement of changes to retained earnings. An income statement takes net sales and deducts the cost of goods sold, depreciation, and bond interest expense.

16. **Answer A is correct.** The statement of changes to retained earnings records any preferred or common dividends paid to shareholders. Interest expense is deducted on the income statement, as is operating expenses.

17. **Answer A is correct.** The acid test or quick ratio compares current assets to current liabilities with inventory being deducted from current assets. Inventory is the least liquid of current assets, and this ratio measures the company's ability to meet its current liabilities in a more stringent manner.

18. **Answer A is correct.** The current ratio for a company is current assets divided by current liabilities. This is a liquidity measure. The equation is $444,000 of current assets ÷ $309,000 in current liabilities = 1.43. This means that the company has $1.43 of current assets for every $1.00 of current liabilities.

19. **Answer A is correct.** Long-term capital is the most basic measure of capitalization for a company. You compute it by adding long-term liabilities to stockholder equity.

20. **Answer D is correct.** Net profit margin is considered a profitability ratio. This ratio compares net income after taxes to sales for the company.

21. **Answer C is correct.** Coverage ratios are used by analysts to determine whether a company can meet its bond and preferred stock obligations. The company's ability to cover its fixed charges greatly affects its ability to obtain future credit.

22. **Answer A is correct.** Liquidity ratios are used by analysts to determine how well the firm can pay its bills on time. Can it meet its current liabilities with its current assets? These ratios can include the current ratio, acid test ratio, and cash asset ratio.

23. **Answer B is correct.** Capitalization ratios look at a company's debt and equity obligations, which include bonds, preferred stock, and common stock. The debt-to-equity ratio compares long-term debt in the form of bonds and preferred stock to common equity.

24. **Answer D is correct.** The debt-to-equity ratio is a capitalization ratio that refers to a company's long-term debt and equity obligations, including bonds, preferred stock, and common stock.

25. **Answer B is correct.** The inventory turnover ratio is a profitability ratio that measures how quickly a firm is turning over its inventory. The more quickly inventory can be sold, the more profit a company can make. Inventory turnover is measured by the cost of goods sold divided by the year-end inventory.

Quick Check

Technical Analysis

1. All the following are characteristics of a technical analyst except for which one?
   - ❍ A. Technical analysts are also known as chartists.
   - ❍ B. Technical analysts analyze company financial statements.
   - ❍ C. Technical analysts use bar charts.
   - ❍ D. Technical analysts study a company's historical behavior in the market.

Quick Answer: **405**
Detailed Answer: **406**

2. When charting price movements of a security over a period of time, a technical analyst can determine which of the following?

   I. How profitable the company is going to be

   II. The best time to buy the security

   III. The best time to sell the security

   IV. When prices will begin to reverse

   - ❍ A. I, II, III
   - ❍ B. II, III, and IV
   - ❍ C. I and IV
   - ❍ D. I, II, III, and IV

Quick Answer: **405**
Detailed Answer: **406**

3. The daily range of prices for a security that is rising over time is known as what?
   - ❍ A. A reversal
   - ❍ B. An uptrend
   - ❍ C. A downtrend
   - ❍ D. A peak

Quick Answer: **405**
Detailed Answer: **406**

Quick Check

4. The reversal of an uptrend for a security signals a period when investors will do what?

Quick Answer: 405
Detailed Answer: 406

❍ A. Sell the security
❍ B. Purchase the security
❍ C. Hold the security
❍ D. Be inactive in the market

5. When a security price reverses its trend and continues to bump up against a maximum price, this is known as a what?

Quick Answer: 405
Detailed Answer: 406

❍ A. Reversal
❍ B. Resistance level
❍ C. Support level
❍ D. Saucer

6. An overbought market has which of the following characteristics?

Quick Answer: 405
Detailed Answer: 406

I. The price of the stock is higher than buyers are willing to pay.

II. Sellers outnumber buyers.

III. Buyers outnumber sellers.

IV. It is a bearish indicator.

❍ A. I and II
❍ B. I and III
❍ C. I, II, and IV
❍ D. I, III, and IV

7. All the following are considered true about a support level except for which one?

Quick Answer: 405
Detailed Answer: 406

❍ A. The market is resisting any further price decrease.
❍ B. Sellers feel the price represents a good time to sell.
❍ C. The market is considered oversold.
❍ D. Buyers outnumber sellers.

8. An overbought market has all the following characteristics except for which one?

Quick Answer: 405
Detailed Answer: 406

❍ A. Sellers outnumber buyers.
❍ B. The price of the security is higher than buyers are willing to pay.
❍ C. The price of the security will move higher.
❍ D. The security has reached a resistance level.

Quick Check

9. When a price of security has passed through a resistance or support level, the condition is known as a what?
   - ❍ A. Breakout
   - ❍ B. Trend reversal
   - ❍ C. Bottom out
   - ❍ D. Peak

Quick Answer: 405
Detailed Answer: 406

10. A breakout through a resistance level for a security leads to which of the following?
   - A. There will be more sellers than buyers.
   - ❍ B. There will be a decline in prices.
   - ❍ C. There will be an increase in prices.
   - ❍ D. A bearish sign for the security

Quick Answer: 405
Detailed Answer: 406

11. All the following investment decisions are characteristic of a breakout through a resistance level except for which one?
   - ❍ A. Entering a buy stop order above the resistance level
   - ❍ B. An investor purchasing call options
   - ❍ C. An investor selling put options
   - ❍ D. An investor selling the security short

Quick Answer: 405
Detailed Answer: 407

12. A 200-day moving average used by a technical analyst is best defined as what?
   - ❍ A. The graph of a security over a 200-day period
   - ❍ B. The graph of a security that is recalculated each day as the 200-day period moves forward
   - ❍ C. The graph of a security over any chosen 200-day period
   - ❍ D. The graph of a security over the first 200 days of trading

Quick Answer: 405
Detailed Answer: 407

13. When a technical analyst compares a 50-day moving average to a 200-day moving average for a stock and finds that the 50-day moving average rises above the 200-day moving average, he makes which of the following conclusions?
   - ❍ A. A reversal is about to occur.
   - ❍ B. An uptrend is beginning.
   - ❍ C. A downtrend is beginning.
   - ❍ D. A consolidation is occurring.

Quick Answer: 405
Detailed Answer: 407

Quick Check

14. Which of the following analytical tools are used by a technical analyst?

    I. Bar charts

    II. Moving averages

    III. Trading volumes

    IV. Advance/decline indexes

    ❍ A. I and II
    ❍ B. I, II, and III
    ❍ C. I, II, and IV
    ❍ D. I, II, III, and IV

Quick Answer: 405
Detailed Answer: 407

15. Which of the following are used by a technical analyst to confirm a major market trend?

    ❍ A. The advance decline index
    ❍ B. The short interest theory
    ❍ C. The Dow theory
    ❍ D. The odd lot theory

Quick Answer: 405
Detailed Answer: 407

Choose from the following theories to match the next five descriptions. An answer may be used once, more than once, or not at all.

❍ A. Dow theory
❍ B. Short interest theory
❍ C. Trading volume
❍ D. Odd lot theory

16. "Trading more shares of a security each day affects the market price of the stock."

Quick Answer: 405
Detailed Answer: 407

17. "A major market trend must be confirmed by the same movement in both the Dow Industrials and Dow Transportations."

Quick Answer: 405
Detailed Answer: 407

18. "Compare the number of shares sold short to the daily trading volume of a security to determine a bull or bear market."

Quick Answer: 405
Detailed Answer: 407

19. "The small, individual investor will always miss a market trend."

Quick Answer: 405
Detailed Answer: 407

20. A stock that is experiencing tremendous investor interest, causing its price to rise, is following which theory?

Quick Answer: 405
Detailed Answer: 408

Quick Check

21. Which of the following statements are true about a stock with a daily trading volume of 200,000 shares and a short interest of 300,000 shares?

I. The market is bullish on the stock.

II. The market is bearish on the stock.

III. The stock should experience a rise in price.

IV. The stock should experience a drop in price.

❍ A. I only
❍ B. II only
❍ C. I and III
❍ D. II and IV

Quick Answer: **405**
Detailed Answer: **408**

22. If the put-call ratio shows that put options outnumber call options on an index, and trading volume is heavy, a technical analyst makes all the following conclusions except for which one?

❍ A. The market is bottoming out.
❍ B. The market is oversold.
❍ C. The market is bearish.
❍ D. The market is bullish.

Quick Answer: **405**
Detailed Answer: **408**

23. The theory that a technical analyst is least likely to follow when analyzing a security is which one?

❍ A. Random walk theory
❍ B. Trading volume theory
❍ C. Dow theory
❍ D. Advance decline index

Quick Answer: **405**
Detailed Answer: **408**

24. A demonstrable increase in short interest sends which of the following signals to the market?

I. The market is bullish.

II. The market is bearish.

III. More sellers enter the market.

IV. More buyers enter the market.

❍ A. I only
❍ B. II only
❍ C. I and IV
❍ D. II and III

Quick Answer: **405**
Detailed Answer: **408**

Quick Check

Quick Answer: 405
Detailed Answer: 408

25. The theorists who believe that all public information about a company is instantly reflected in the price of its stock adhere to which of the following theories?

❍ A. Random walk theory
❍ B. Efficient market theory
❍ C. Dow theory
❍ D. Odd lot theory

Quick Check Answer Key

1. B
2. B
3. B
4. A
5. B
6. C
7. B
8. C
9. A
10. C
11. D
12. B
13. B
14. D
15. C
16. C
17. A
18. B
19. D
20. C
21. C
22. C
23. A
24. C
25. B

Answers and Explanations

1. **Answer B is correct.** A technical analyst does not analyze financial statements such as income statements and balance sheets when making a determination about the quality of an underlying security. They are used by fundamental analysts. Technical analysts use charts, graphs, and averages to identify trends.

2. **Answer B is correct.** Technical analysts believe that by analyzing patterns of past price changes, they can predict future price movements and recommend the best times to buy or sell a security. The chartists try to identify trends that signal reversals in current prices.

3. **Answer B is correct.** When the daily range of prices gradually rises over time, the path that is being followed is known as an uptrend. Prices were gradually falling indicate a downtrend.

4. **Answer A is correct.** If an uptrend were to suddenly reverse itself and begin to exhibit a drop in prices, an investor would sell his securities before they dropped too far in the market.

5. **Answer B is correct.** A resistance level is showing that the market is resisting any further price increase for the security. The price of the security keeps bumping up against the maximum price but is unable to break through that level.

6. **Answer C is correct.** The market is said to be overbought when the price of the security is higher than what buyers are willing to pay. Sellers far outnumber buyers, and because supply exceeds demand, the price must drop, indicating a bearish sign.

7. **Answer B is correct.** At a support level, most sellers feel that the price of the security has dropped too low to sell. When this occurs, the market is considered oversold. Buyers outnumber sellers, and because demand exceeds supply, the price of the security rebounds some.

8. **Answer C is correct.** In an overbought market, the price of a security moves not higher, but rather lower, because the market is showing more sellers than buyers for the stock. Due to supply and demand, the price drops.

9. **Answer A is correct.** When a security has moved through its historical resistance or support level, it is considered a breakout. Analysts believe that a breakout signals a trend that is likely to continue.

10. **Answer C is correct.** A breakout through a resistance level shows that everyone willing to sell at the resistance level has already sold. As the price moves above the resistance level, there are fewer sellers than there are buyers, forcing the price up even further.

11. **Answer D is correct.** A breakout through a resistance level is a bullish sign because there are fewer sellers than buyers. The price of the stock will continue upward. An investor selling short does not want to do so in this situation, which is counterintuitive to the strategy of selling short.

12. **Answer B is correct.** A moving average is recalculated each day as the specified period moves forward. A 200-day moving average plots the average price for the past 200 days. Each day, the previous day's price is included in the average, and the price that is 201 days old is dropped from the average.

13. **Answer B is correct.** Technical analysts study moving averages with different time frames and pay close attention to where the averages cross. If the 50-day moving average rises above the 200-day moving average, an analyst concludes that an uptrend is beginning.

14. **Answer D is correct.** The tools of a technical analyst include bar charts, moving averages, trading volumes, and advance decline indexes. In addition to studying security prices, an analyst often investigates market indexes, trading volumes, short interest, and the numbers of advances and declines.

15. **Answer C is correct.** The Dow theory states that a major market trend is only confirmed when both the Dow Jones Industrial Average and the Dow Transportation Average also follow the new high or the new low in the market. Thus, if an analyst believes that the market as a whole is experiencing an uptrend, he confirms this hypothesis by looking for peaks in both the Dow Industrials and Dow Transportations.

16. **Answer C is correct.** Analysts consider that trading volume on the number of shares or securities in a given day is an important indicator of future price movements. Volume tends to lead to price changes.

17. **Answer A is correct.** The Dow theory states that any major market trend must be confirmed by a similar reaction in both the Dow Industrials and the Dow Transportations to validate the hypothesis.

18. **Answer B is correct.** The short interest theory states that the greater the short interest, the greater number of investors who must purchase stock to cover their short positions. This is an indication that when the greater number of short sellers begins to buy, they will drive the price of the stock upward for a bullish sign in the market.

19. **Answer D is correct.** The odd lot theory assumes that the small investors, those who generally trade in odd lots, are typically wrong in their market timing when buying or selling securities. They buy at the peak price for a stock and sell at the low price. In other words, the small investor is usually wrong.

20. **Answer C is correct.** A stock that is experiencing tremendous investor interest is being purchased heavily in the market. This increases market volume on the stock and in turn sends the price of the stock upward. The theory suggests that the greater the market volume, the more likely that the stock price will move.

21. **Answer C is correct.** The short interest theory suggests that the greater the short interest number on a security, the greater the need for short sellers to eventually cover their short positions. If short interest exceeds daily trading volume by 50%, then the stock should soon see an increase in price as the short sellers move into the market to cover their short positions. When short interest exceeds daily trading volume, it is no longer a bearish indicator, but rather a bullish sign that short sellers will begin covering their positions, causing the price of the stock to move upward.

22. **Answer C is correct.** When puts outnumber calls and trading volume is heavy, a technical analyst takes it as a sign that the market is bottoming out and is actually oversold. They interprets this as a bullish sign because they feel that the stock cannot go any lower and thus must move upward.

23. **Answer A is correct.** The random walk theory states that past performance of security prices has no bearing on future price performance. The theory believes that stock prices move in a random and unpredictable manner. A technical analyst would unlikely rely on this theory for predicting stock performance.

24. **Answer C is correct.** The short interest theory looks at the number of common shares that have been sold short and have not yet been covered. Any demonstrable increase in this short interest figure sends a signal to the market that short sellers will eventually be cover their short positions and more buyers will enter the market. This is no longer a bearish sign, but rather a bullish sign.

25. **Answer B is correct.** The efficient market theory says that the market is an ideal market where all public information about a company is instantly reflected in the price of its stock. In such a situation, studying the fundamentals of a company cannot uncover any underpriced securities because perfectly informed investors have already accounted for all potential risks and rewards on the stock.

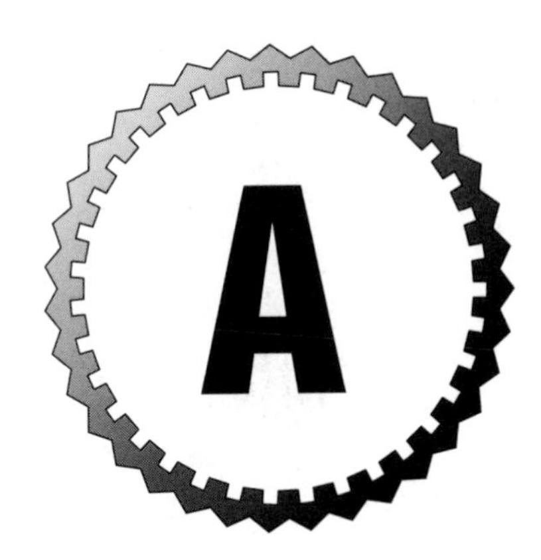

CD Contents and Installation Instructions

The CD features a state-of-the-art exam preparation engine from ExamForce. This uniquely powerful program will identify gaps in your knowledge and help you turn them into strengths. The CD also includes an electronic version of the text in Portable Document Format (PDF).

The CramMaster Engine

This innovative exam engine systematically prepares you for a successful test. Working your way through CramMaster is the fastest, surest route to successfully taking the exam. The presentation of questions is weighted according to your unique requirements. Your answer history dictates which questions you see next. It determines what you don't know and forces you to overcome those shortcomings. You won't waste time answering easy questions about things you already know.

Multiple Test Modes

The CramMaster test engine from ExamForce has three unique testing modes to systematically prepare you for a successful exam.

Pretest Mode

Pretest Mode establishes your baseline skill set. Train CramMaster by taking two or three pretests. There is no review or feedback on answers in this mode. View your topic-by-topic skill levels from the History menu on the main screen. Effective exam preparation begins by attacking your weakest topics first in Adaptive Drill Mode.

Adaptive Drill Mode

Adaptive Drill Mode allows you to focus on specific exam objectives. CramMaster learns the questions that you find difficult and drills you until you master them. As you gain proficiency in one area, it seeks out the next way to challenge you. You can master even the most complex concepts of the exam in this mode.

Simulated Exam Mode

Simulated Exam Mode approximates the real exam. By the time you reach this level, you've already mastered the exam material. This is your opportunity to exercise those skills while building your mental and physical stamina.

Installing CramMaster for the Series 7 Exam

The minimum system requirements for installation are as follows:

- Windows 95, 98, Me, NT 4, 2000, or XP
- 64MB RAM
- 18MB disk space

If you need technical support, contact ExamForce at 800-845-8569 or email support@examforce.com. You can find additional product support at http://www.examforce.com.

To install the CramMaster CD-ROM, follow these instructions:

1. Close all applications before beginning this installation.
2. Insert CD into your CD-ROM drive. If the setup starts automatically, go to step 6. If the setup does not start automatically, continue with step 3.
3. From the Start menu, select Run.
4. Click Browse to locate the CramMaster CD. In the Browse dialog box, from the Look in drop-down list, select the CD-ROM drive.
5. In the Browse dialog box, double-click on Setup.exe. In the Run dialog box, click OK to begin the installation.
6. On the Welcome screen, click Next.
7. To agree to the End User License Agreement (EULA), click Next.
8. On the Choose Destination Location screen, click Next to install the software to C:\Program Files\CramMaster.

9. On the Select Program Manager Group screen, verify that the Program Manager group is set to CramMaster, and click Next.
10. On the Start Installation screen, click Next.
11. On the Installation Complete screen, verify that the Launch CramMaster Now box is checked, and click Finish.
12. For your convenience, a shortcut to CramMaster is automatically created on your desktop.

Using CramMaster for the Series 7 Exam

An introduction slide show starts when CramMaster first launches. It will teach you how to get the most out of this uniquely powerful program. Uncheck the Show on Startup box to suppress the introduction from showing each time you launch the application. You can review it at any time from the Help menu on the main screen. Tips on using other CramMaster features appear there as well.

Customer Support

If you encounter problems installing or using CramMaster for the Series 7 exam, please contact ExamForce at 800-845-8569 or email support@examforce.com. Support hours are from 8:30 a.m. to 5:30 p.m. EST, Monday through Friday. You can find additional product support at http://www.examforce.com.

If you want to purchase additional ExamForce products, telephone 800-845-8569 or visit http://www.examforce.com.